# Writings on Revived Cornish

by

## Nicholas Williams

MA PhD DipCeltStud FLS ITIA
*Bard of the Gorsedd of Cornwall*
*Associate Professor in Celtic Languages*
*University College, Dublin*

*e*
evertype
2006

Published by / *Dyllys gans* Evertype, Cnoc Sceichín, Leac an Anfa, Cathair na Mart, Co. Mhaigh Eo, Éire / Wordhen. *www.evertype.com*.

First edition 2006. Reprinted with corrections January 2011.
*Kensa dyllans 2006. Daspryntys gans ewnansow Genver 2011.*

Editor / *Penscrefer*: Michael Everson.

Y kefyr covath rolyans rag an lyver-ma dhyworth an Lyverva Vretennek.
*A catalogue record for this book is available from dhe British Library.*

ISBN-10 1-904808-08-5
ISBN-13 978-1-904808-08-4

Typeset in Palatino by Michael Everson.
*Olsettys yn Palatino gans Michael Everson.*

Cover / *Cudhlen*: Michael Everson

Printed by / *Pryntys gans* LightningSource.

# CONTENTS

# FOREWORD

While Nicholas Williams and I were preparing for the press the third revised edition of *Cornish Today*, and of Nicholas' new book *Towards Authentic Cornish*, and were discussing those preparations with various interested people, it became clear to that some relevant articles by Nicholas, which had been published elsewhere, were unavailable or not easily available to those concerned with Cornish linguistic history and the orthography of Revived Cornish.

We first thought to include these articles as an appendix to the third edition of *Cornish Today*, but it soon became apparent from their collective length that this would be impractical. Accordingly we publish them together here as *Writings on Revived Cornish*, which we offer as a companion to the other two books.

Michael Everson
Westport, 2006

# INTRODUCTION

Most of the chapters in this book were originally published elsewhere. The last two items below, however, are new. One is a short note indicating how inconsistently George's *Gerlyver Kernewek Kemmyn* treats geographical names attested in the Cornish texts. The second shows how the recently-discovered Cornish play *Bewnans Ke* corroborates most satisfactorily my systematic criticisms of Kernowek Kemyn.

I hope that many of the articles below have significant things to say about the history of the Cornish language, its phonology, syntax, lexicon and usage. The unifying theme of all the writings below, however, is the inauthenticity of Kernowek Kemyn. As a professional Celticist, I still find it difficult to believe that such an unsatisfactory form of Cornish was ever proposed, let alone promoted. Kernowek Kemyn is, in the view of all academic observers, an artificial construct, only tangentially related to the texts upon which it claims to be based.

*Kernewek Kemmyn: Cornish for the Twenty-First Century* (1997) of Paul Dunbar and Ken George is intended as a vindication of Kernowek Kemyn. It cannot, however, be described as successful. In my most recent book, *Towards Authentic Cornish*, I have had little difficulty in dismissing George's defence of both his phonology and his orthography. It would seem that no convincing defence of Kernowek Kemyn has yet appeared, because no defence is possible.

In the following pages small revisions have been made here and there to some of the articles that have been published before. I am grateful for their assistance and support to the following: the late Professor Ellis Evans, Professor Thomas Charles-Edwards, Professor Philip Payton, Nicolas Jacobs of Jesus College, Oxford, Norma Jessop previously of Special Collections in University College Library, David Frost of St David's College, Cardiff, Daniel Prohaska, Ray Chubb, Craig Weatherhill, and Michael Everson. For all errors and inaccuracies below I am wholly responsible.

Nicholas Williams
Dublin, 2006

# ABBREVIATIONS AND REFERENCES

AB = Edward Lhuyd, *Archæologia Britannica* (London 1707 [reprinted Shannon 1971])

ACB = William Pryce, *Archæologia Cornu-Britannica* (Sherborne 1790)

ALK = *An Lef Kernewek*

*An Gannas*

*Archiv für Celtische Lexikographie*

B = Breton

Bakere 1980 = J. Bakere, *The Cornish Ordinalia*. (Cardiff: University of Wales Press 1980)

BF = O. J. Padel, *The Cornish Writings of the Boson Family* (Redruth 1975)

Bice = Christopher Bice, *The Tregear Manuscript: Homilies in Cornish*. (n.d.) [Multigraphed typescript]

Bilbao MS = Henry Jenner, 'The Cornish Manuscript in the provincial library at Bilbao, Spain', *Journal of the Royal Institution of Cornwall* 21 (192-25): 421-37

BM = Whitley Stokes (ed.), *Beunans Meriasek: the life of St Meriasek, Bishop and confessor, a Cornish drama* (London: Trübner and Co. 1872)

Borde = Andrew Borde cited from J. Loth, "Cornique moderne", *Archiv für Celtische Lexikographie* 1 (1900): 224-28

Borlase = William Borlase, *Antiquities of the County of Cornwall* (London 1754)

Broderick 1986 = George Broderick, A *Handbook of Late Spoken Manx*, vol. iii, Phonology (Tübingen 1986)

BS = *Buhé er Saent* (Vannes 1839)

Carew = F. E. Halliday (ed.), *Richard Carew of Antony: the survey of Cornwall* (London 1953)

*Carn* = *Carn: A Link between the Celtic Nations* (Dublin, ISSN 0257-7860)

*Cat.* = *Catechis Treguer: Imprimet dre urz an Aoutrou Augustin-René-Louis Le Mintier, Epscop a Dreguer,* (Marlaix 1783)

CCCG = Henry Lewis, Holger Pedersen, *A Concise Comparative Celtic Grammar* (Göttingen 1961)

CD = Émile Ernault, "Les cantiques bretons du *Doctrinal*", in *Archiv für Celtische Lexikographie,* 1 (Halle 1900) 213–23, 360–93, 556–627

CDS = W. Morris, *Cornish Dictionary Supplement, No. 3: Geryow Dyvers* (Redruth 1995)

CF = *The Charter Fragment,* text from E. Campanile, "Un frammento scenico medio-cornico", *Studi e saggi linguistici* 60-80, supplement to *L'Italia Dialettale* 26

CH = Roparz Hemon (ed.), *Christmas Hymns in the Vannes dialect of Breton* (Dublin 1956)

CLN5 = O. J. Padel, "Cornish Language Notes: 5", *Cornish Studies* 4/5 (1976-77) 15–27

CM = E. G. R. Hooper, *Kemysk Kernewek: A Cornish Miscellany* (Camborne 1963)

Commission = Commission of the European Communities (1986) *Linguistic Minorities in Countries Belonging to the European Community.* Luxembourg.

*Cornish-English Dictionary* = R. Morton Nance, *Cornish-English Dictionary* (1938) [reprinted Redruth 1990]

CPNE = O. J. Padel, *Cornish Place-name Elements* (Nottingham 1985)

CS = Caradar [A.S.D. Smith], *Cornish Simplified* (1955) [reprinted Camborne 1972]

CS2 = Caradar [A.S.D. Smith], *Cornish Simplified: Part Two,* edited by E.G.R. Hooper [Talek], (Redruth 1984)

## ABBREVIATIONS AND REFERENCES

CT = Nicholas Williams, *Cornish Today: an examination of the revived language*, first and second editions (Sutton Coldfield: Kernewek dre Lyther 1995)

CT3 = Nicholas Williams, *Cornish Today: an examination of the revived language*, third edition (Westport: Evertype 2006, ISBN 978-1-904808-07-7)

CW = Whitley Stokes (ed.), *Gwreans an Bys: the Creation of the World*, (London: Williams & Norgate 1864 [reprinted Kessinger Publishing 1987, ISBN 0-7661-8009-3])

DC = Roparz Hemon, *Doctrin an Christenien* (Dublin 1977)

Doble 1931 = G.H. Doble, *Saint Perran, Saint Keverne and Saint Kerrian* (Shiptson-on-Stour 1931)

Doble 1960 = G.H. Doble, *The Saints of Cornwall: part one: saints of the Land's End district* (Chattam 1960)

EGC = Stephen J. Williams, *Elfennau Gramadeg Cymraeg* (Cardiff 1959)

Edwards 1994 = Ray Edwards, *Kernewek Dre Lyther: Kynsa Gradh* (Sutton Coldfield 1994)

Ellis 1974 = P. Berresford Ellis. *The Cornish Language and its Literature* (London and Boston 1974)

Fowler 1961 = D. C. Fowler, "The Date of the Cornish 'Ordinalia'", in *Medieval Studies* 23, 91-125

Fudge 1982 = C. Fudge, *The Life of Cornish* (Redruth 1982)

GCSW = R. Morton Nance, *A Glossary of Cornish Sea-words*, edited by P.A.S. Pool (Marazion 1963)

GCW = Morgan Jones, *A Guide to Correct Welsh* (Landysul 1976)

George 1995 = Ken George, "Which base for Revived Cornish?", in Philip Payton (ed.), *Cornish Studies: Two* (Exeter: University of Exeter Press) 104–24

GKK = Ken George, *Gerlyver Kernewek Kemmyn* ([s.l.], Cornish Language Board 1993)

GMC1 = Wella Brown, *A Grammar of Modern Cornish* (Saltash: Cornish Language Board 1984) [Unified Cornish]

GMW = D. Simon Evans, *A Grammar of Middle Welsh* (Dublin 1964)

Gunn 1994 = Marion Gunn, *Da mihi manum* (Dublin: Everson Gunn Teoranta 1994)

HBL = *Heuryou Brezonec ha Latin* (Quimper 1806)

HCL = Henry Jenner, *A Handbook of the Cornish Language chiefly in its latest stages with some account of its history and literature* (London 1904)

HMSB = Roparz Hemon, *A Historical Morphology and Syntax of Breton* (Dublin 1984)

HPB = Kenneth Hurlstone Jackson, *A Historical Phonology of Breton* (Dublin 1967)

HTK = Graham Sandercock, Julyan Holmes, Pol Hodge and Ken George, *Henwyn Tylleryow Kernewek: Place Names in our Cornish Language* (An Gannas 1995)

*Imit.* = *Imitation hor Salver Jesus-Christ: lequeet e Brezounec* (St Brieuc 1867)

Jago 1882 = Fred W. P. Jago, *The Ancient Language and Dialect of Cornwall* (Truro 1882)

JRIC = *Journal of the Royal Institution of Cornwall*

*Kantikou* = *Kantikou Brezounek Eskopti Kemper ha Leon* (Quimper 1908)

Keats-Rohan 1992. = K. S. B. Keats-Rohan, "The Bretons and Normans of England 1066–1154: the family, the fief and the feudal monarchy", in *Nottingham Medieval Studies* 36, 4278

*Kemysk Kernewek*, edited by E. G. R. Hooper (Camborne, An Lef Kernewek 1964)

KKC21 = *Kernewek Kemmyn: Cornish for the Twenty-First Century*, Paul Dunbar and Ken George ([s.l.], Cornish Language Board 1997)

LAM = Alan Kent & Tim Saunders, *Looking at the Mermaid: A Reader in Cornish Literature 900-1900* (London, 2000)

LCB = Robert Williams, *Lexicon Cornu-Britannicum* (Llandovery 1865)

# WRITINGS ON REVIVED CORNISH

LHEB = Kenneth Hurlstone Jackson, *Language and History in Early Britain* (Edinburgh 1953)

LlCC = Henry Lewis, *Llawlyfr Cernyweg Canol* (Cardiff 1946)

Longsworth 1967 = R. Longsworth, *The Cornish Ordinalia* (Cambridge 1967)

Loth 1890 = J. Loth, "Études corniques i", in *Revue Celtique*, 18, 410-24.

Loth 1900 = J. Loth, "Cornique moderne", in *Archiv für Celtische Lexikographie* (Halle): 224-29

Loth 1902 = J. Loth, "Études corniques ii, textes inedits en cornique moderne", in *Revue Celtique*, 23, 173-200

LPMS = Mordon (R.Morton Nance), *Lyver an Pymp marthus Seleven* (St Ives 1939)

Lyon 1984 = R. Lyon, *Everyday Cornish* (Redruth 1984)

MacLennan 1988 = Gordon W. MacLennan, *Proceedings of the First North American Congress of Celtic Studies* (Ottawa 1988)

*Marvailhou* = Roparz Hemon, *Marvailhou ar Vretoned* (Brest 1930)

ME = Middle English

Mills 1999 = Jon Mills, "Reconstructive Phonology and Contrastive Lexicography: Problems with the Gerlyver Kernewek Kemmyn", in *Cornish Studies*. Second series: Seven. Exeter: University of Exeter Press. Pp. 193-218. ISBN 0-85989-644-7

Snell & Morris 1983 = J. A. N. Snell and W. A. Morris, *Cornish Dictionary Supplement: no 2* (Cornish Language Board 1983)

MW = Gareth King, *Modern Welsh: a Comprehensive Grammar* (London and New York 1993)

Nance 1949 = R. Morton Nance, *Cornish for All: A Guide to Unified Cornish* (St Ives: James Lanham 1949)

Nance 1952 = R. Morton Nance, *An English-Cornish Dictionary* (Marazion 1952) [reprinted 1978]

Nance 1955 = R. Morton Nance, *A Cornish-English Dictionary* (Marazion 1955) [reprinted 1978]

Nance 1967 = R. Morton Nance, *A Guide to Cornish Place-names* (Marazion 1967)

Norris 1859 = Edwin Norris, *The Ancient Cornish Drama* i-ii (London [reprinted New York/London: Benjamin Blom 1968])

Ó Luain 1983 = C. Ó Luain, *For a Celtic Future: A tribute to Alan Heusaff* (Dublin 1983)

OCV = "Old Cornish Vocabulary" [quoted from Norris 1859 ii: 311-435 and Campanile 1974]

OF = Old French

OM = "Origo Mundi" in Norris (1859) i: 1-219

PA = Whitley Stokes, "*Pascon agan Arluth*: 'the Passion of our Lord'", *Transactions of the Philological Society* (1860-61 Appendix 1-100)

PAA = Ray Edwards, *Passhyon Agan Arloedh* (Sutton Coldfield: Kernewek dre Lyther 1995). ISBN 0-907064-24-8

PC = "Passio Domini Nostri Jhesu Christi" in Norris 1859 i 221-479

Penglase 1994 = Charles Penglase, "Authenticity in the Revival of Cornish" in Philip Payton (ed.), *Cornish Studies: Three* (Exeter: University of Exeter Press) 96–107

PKM = Ifor Williams, *Pedeir Keinc y Mabinogi* (Cardiff 1930)

PNWP = P. A. S. Pool, *The Place-names of West Penwith*, second edition (Penzance 1985)

Pool 1995 = P. A. S. Pool, *The second death of Cornish* (Redruth 1995)

Price 1984 = Glanville Price, *The Languages of Britain* (London 1984)

Price 1992 = Glanville Price, *The Celtic Connection* (Gerrards Cross 1992)

# ABBREVIATIONS AND REFERENCES

PSRC = Ken George, *The Pronunciation and Spelling of Revived Cornish* ([s.l.]: Cornish Language Board 1986)

RC = *Revue Celtique*

RD = "Resurrexio Domini Nostri Jhesu Christi" in Norris 1859 ii 1-199

*Reg.* = *Reglamant a Vuez, vit an Dud Divar ar Meuz* (Morlaix 1868)

SA = *Sacrament an Alter* "Sacrament of the Altar" text quoted from an unpublished edition by D.H. Frost, *Sacrament an Alter: Part II* (St David's College 2003)

SDMC = Richard R. M. Gendall, *A Student's Dictionary of Modern Cornish* (Menheniot 1993)

Stokes 1860 = Whitley Stokes, "Poem of Mount Calvary: Pascon agan Arluth" in *Transactions of the Philological Society*, 1860-61, Appendix, 1-100.

TAC = Nicholas Williams, *Towards Authentic Cornish* (Westport: Evertype 2006, ISBN 978-1-904808-09-1)

*Testamant* = *Testamant Nevez hon Aotrou hag hor Zalver Jesus-Christ* (Paris 1935)

TH = John Tregear, *Homelyes xiii in Cornysche* (British Library Additional MS 46, 397) [text from a cyclostyled text published by Christopher Bice ([s.l.] 1969)]

Thurneysen 1946 = Rudolf Thurneysen, *Old Irish Grammar* (Dublin: Institute for Advanced Studies 1946)

Trans. Phil. Soc. = Transactions of the Philological Society (London)

VC = Émile Ernault, 'La vie de Sainte Catherine', *Revue Celtique*, 8 (Paris 1887) 76-95

WAD = Bruce Griffiths & Dafydd Glyn Jones, *Geiriadur yr Academi: The Welsh Academy English-Welsh Dictionary* (Cardiff 1995)

Wakelin 1975 = Martyn F. Wakelin, *Language and history in Cornwall* (Leicester: Leicester University Press 1975)

Webb 1984 = Brian Webb, *Dornlyver Ydhyn* ([s.l.]: Cowethas an Yeth Kernewek 1984)

Williams 1994 = N. J. A. Williams, "An Mhanainnis", in K. McCone, Damian McManus, Cathal Ó Hainle, Nicholas Williams, Liam Breatnach, *Stair na Gaeilge* (Maynooth 1994) 703–44

Williams 1997 = Nicholas Williams, *Clappya Kernowek: an introduction to Unified Cornish Revised* (Agan Tavas, Portreath 1997, ISBN 1-901409-01-5)

Williams 2001 = N. J. A. Williams, "Bás agus Athbheochan na Coirnise" in R. Ó hUiginn, Liam Mac Cóil (eds.), *Bliainiris 2001* (Rath Cairn, 2001, ISSN 1393-8924) 145–63

YBB = F. Kervella, *Yezhadur bras ar brezhoneg* (La Baule 1947).

# A PROBLEM IN CORNISH PHONOLOGY*

## 1. Introduction

Cornish is unique among the insular Celtic languages, in that the last native speakers died before their speech could be recorded and described by modern methods. This presents scholars and revivalists alike with a serious problem. All understanding of Cornish pronunciation has to be inferential. It is has to be deduced from the spelling of our existing literary remains and from the pronunciation of place-names and of survivals in English dialect.

Since the 1920s the Cornish revival has been using a phonology and orthography devised largely by R. Morton Nance and his collaborator A.S.D. Smith. This system, known as Unified Cornish[1], does not claim to have any theoretical basis, but it does adhere to the spelling of the Middle Cornish texts fairly closely. The quickening pace of the Cornish revival in recent years has brought about a gradual disillusionment with Morton Nance's system, or *Mordonnek*, as it is sometimes called.

In a recent work, *The Pronunciation and Spelling of Revived Cornish* (George, 1986), Ken George has suggested a new phonemic orthography for revived Cornish that, he believes, represents as closely as possible the pronunciation of Middle Cornish of the period of the play, *Beunans Meriasek*, i.e. *c.* 1505.

George's method is as follows: he systematically describes what he believes to be the phonology of Middle Cornish in the light of the Breton and Welsh cognates. He then devises a phonemic spelling based to some degree upon the Middle Cornish texts themselves, bearing in mind where the traditional orthography fails, in his view, to indicate phonemic distinctions.

Unfortunately, George's method is open to question. To attempt to set out the phonology of Middle Cornish on the basis of Welsh and Breton cognates, itself implies that Cornish is exactly comparable with the two sister languages and indeed, is midway between them. Such is not the case. Cornish is in some important ways quite unlike both Breton and Welsh. Breton is a form of South-West British taken to Gaul and adopted by speakers of Continental Celtic and/or Latin. Cornish remained uninfluenced by Gaulish. Cornish however, unlike both Welsh and Breton, has clearly been heavily influenced by Old English. Cornwall from the early tenth to the late eleventh century was part of

---

\* First published in Martin J. Ball, James Fife, Erich Poppe, & Jenny Rowland (eds.). 1990. *Celtic Linguistics: Readings in the Brythonic languages. Festschrift for T. Arwyn Watkins.* (Current Issues in Linguistic Theory; 68) Amsterdam/Philadelphia: John Benjamins.

1 See, for example, Nance (1949). Brown (1984) is a fuller description of Unified Cornish, but it contains much reconstruction and should be treated with caution.

the West Saxon kingdom and there is good evidence that English was widely spoken in Cornwall during that period. The penetration of Cornish by Old English is already clearly visible in the Old Cornish Vocabulary. Indeed all the evidence suggests that Middle Cornish has been heavily affected by Old English in its sound-system. George's analysis of Middle Cornish fails to take this influence into consideration.[2]

## 2. The Problem of British *d* and *t* in Cornish

One distinctive aspect of Middle Cornish phonology involves the development of British *t* and *d* in medial and final position. In Welsh and Breton these sounds remain stops. In Cornish they ultimately become sibilants of some kind. Indeed it seems very likely that this assibilation, which is unique to Cornish, occurred under the impact of Old English. The original opposition in British was between lenis and fortis. Such an opposition was absent from English, where the comparable opposition was one of stop versus affricate. Under the influence of English in certain environments British *t* and *d* in Cornish became first affricates and then later, continuants. The position can briefly be stated as follows:

1.1 British -*nt*, -*lt* had already become sibilants in the late Old Cornish period (*c*. 1050-1100) and were written <ns, ls>. Thus Old Cornish *dans* 'tooth' corresponds to Welsh/Breton *dant*, and Old Cornish *als* 'shore' to Welsh *allt*, Breton *aod* (Jackson, 1953: 507-08).

1.2 British *d* in final position had become a sibilant by the Middle Cornish period and was written <s>. Thus Middle Cornish *tas* 'father' corresponds to WB *tad*. In Late Cornish *tas* appears as *taz* with final *z*.

1.3 Medially before a front vowel and *w*, *d* is similarly shifted in Middle Cornish and appears as *s* or *g*/*i*. Thus Middle Cornish *wose*, *woge* 'after' corresponds to Welsh *wedi*, Breton *goude*; Middle Cornish *peswar* 'four' corresponds to Welsh *pedwar*, Old Breton *petguar* > Middle Breton *pevar*; Middle Cornish *crysy*, *crygy* 'believe' corresponds to Middle Breton *kredin*. In Late Cornish this sound is frequently written <g> or <dg>. Lhuyd (1707: 231, col 1) spells it <dzh>.

1.4 Internally *nt* had been shifted by the Middle Cornish period and was written <ns> or <ng>. Thus Middle Cornish *kerense*, *kerenge* 'love' corresponds to Middle Breton *karantez*, *karanté*; and Middle Cornish *ganso* 'with him' to Middle Breton *gantan*, *gantaff*.

---

2   Other systems of revived Cornish include Tim Saunder's "etymological" spelling and Carnoack Tithiack, favoured by Rod Lyon. See PSRC 32-4. For a compromise between Unified Cornish and Late Cornish, see Lyon (1984).

It is to be noted, however, that *nt, lt* and *d* are unaffected medially before the back vowels *a* and *o*, e.g. *caradow* 'loveable', *ledan* 'wide', and also if followed in the next syllable by *l, n* or *r*, e.g. *padel* 'pan', *fenten* 'well', *peder* 'four (fem.)'

## 3. The Loth-George Hypothesis

There is general agreement that *tas* in Middle Cornish probably meant [ta:s] or [ta:z]. Similarly Middle Cornish *dans, als* probably represent [dans] and [als] respectively. The problem is to decide what was meant by such variant Middle Cornish spellings as *wose/woge, kerense/kerenge, crysy/crygy* and Middle Cornish *peswar* but Late Cornish *padzhar*. In his solution George has followed J. Loth (1897).

Loth noticed that in *wose/woge, crysy/crygy, s* and *g* appear to be in free variation. He assumes therefore that the graphs <s>, <g> and occasionally <i/j>, represent a sound that is neither [s/z] nor [dʒ]. Had either [s/z] or [dʒ] been the sound in these words, <s> or <g> would have been written consistently. *Wose/wose, crysy/crygy* must accordingly contain a sound not easily represented by the orthography. In Late Cornish moreover we find *bohodzhak* 'poor' for Middle Cornish *bohosek* and *padzhar* 'four' for Middle Cornish *peswar*. Loth assumes therefore that the sound lying behind the Middle Cornish graphs <s> and <g> was sufficiently close to [dʒ] to develop into [dʒ] in the Late Cornish period. Loth thus takes <s>, <g> and <i/j> to represent a palatalized *d*. this sound Loth writes as <dj>. Moreover, since the *s* in Middle Cornish *ganso* 'with him' and the *s* or *g* in *kerense, kerenge* 'love' correspond to *t* in Breton *gantan, karante*, Loth assumes that the sound in these Middle Cornish words is the voiceless equivalent of *dj*, i.e. a palatalized *t*, which he writes <tj>.[3]

George adopts most of Loth's hypothesis as the basis on which to construct this part of his orthography. He thus, with Loth, takes <s>, <g> to represent a palatalized *d* in *wose/woge, bohosek, peswar, aswon* 'know', etc., and he recommends spelling these as <wodja>, <boghodjek>, <pedjwar> and <adjwon> respectively (PSRC: 81-83, 164-67). Similarly he takes *kerense* and *ganso* to contain a voiceless palatalized stop and he recommends the spellings <kerentja> and <gantjo> (PSRC: 81-83, 157-59).

## 4 Theoretical Objections to the Loth-George Hypothesis

The solution to the question *s/g* in Middle Cornish proposed by Loth and adopted by George is both elegant and consistent. Unfortunately it is based, I believe, on two quite mistaken assumptions. First, it is not true that <s> and <g> in Middle Cornish are in free variation. The distributions of the two graphs overlap considerably, but they are nonetheless different, as I hope to

---

3   Loth (op. cit., 404-06) also believed that *s* in *tas* represented [s] < [t]. This is an erroneous view, since the Old Cornish spelling <tat> 'father', was phonetically [ta:d].

demonstrate below. Secondly, Middle Cornish *bohosek, peswar, aswon*, etc. are not the immediate ancestors of Late Cornish *bohodzhak, padzhar, adzhan*, etc. The latter are dialectal variants. As I hope will become clearer later on, the evidence indicates that there were two separate Middle Cornish developments of British medial *d*: (i) [z] written <s> and (ii) [dʒ] written <g> and <i/j>.

Although it is less important to the general argument, it should also be noted here that Loth is mistaken about the final consonantal segment in *ganso* and *kerense*. The evidence indicates that <s> here in Middle Cornish represents a voiced, not a voiceless consonant.

Palatalized *d* and *t* are immediately familiar to anyone who has an acquaintance with Irish. These two sounds, to judge by George's description of them, are to be understood as a voiced alveolo-palatal plosive and its unvoiced equivalent. Loth writes them as <dj> and <tj>, while George in his phonetic notation represents them by the signs <δ> and <τ>. I will write them, as IPA does, as <dʲ> and <tʲ>.

The Gaelic languages are distinguished by having two series of consonants, palatalized and velarized. The Brythonic languages are without such an overall distinction. The consonantal inventory of Cornish, at least as far as points of articulation are concerned, seems, like that of Breton and Welsh, not to be particularly varied. Middle Cornish had both [tʃ] and [dʒ] in Middle English borrowings, for example, *chambour* 'chamber', *tuchya* 'touch' and *gentyl* 'gentle, noble,' *page* 'page'. Now, if the Loth-George hypothesis were correct, Middle Cornish would have contained the following threefold oppositions: /t /~ /tʲ/ ~ /tʃ/ and /d/ ~ dʲ/ ~ /dʒ/. These two series are in themselves highly unstable. If they had ever existed in Middle Cornish, a language lacking the overall opposition palatalized ~ velarized, they would have simplified very quickly to /t/ ~ /tʃ/ and /d/ ~ /dʒ/. This simplification did indeed take place, according to George, but not fully until *c.* 1625, i.e. not for about 500 years or so after the two series had arisen and not in the Middle Cornish period.[4]

There is a further serious theoretical objection to the suggested phonemes /tʲ/ and /dʲ/ in Middle Cornish. The change of *d* > *s* in words like *tas* 'father' and *bos* 'to be', etc., is a movement away from stopped articulation towards greater continuance. Yet according to the Loth-George hypothesis the related sound-change *d* > *s* seen, for example, in Old Cornish *bochodoc* 'poor' > Middle Cornish *bohosek*, does not involve movement towards greater continuance, but only towards a different point of articulation, from dental/dental-alveolar stop to alveolo-palatal stop. Not only would the shift of *d* > *dʲ* be quite unlike the simultaneous shift of *d* > *s* in final position, but it would also seem to be without phonetic motivation. If a final dental stop has become assibilated, by how much the more should an intervocalic dental stop experience the same change? After all, the intervocalic environment in *bochodoc* would seem to be

---

4   George dates *[ndʲ] > [ndʒ] *c.* 1575 and *[VdʲV] > [VdʒV] *c.* 1625; see PSRC 165.

more conducive to the movement obstruence → continuance than would the final position in *tad*.

## 5. Orthographical Objections

There are a number of orthographical objections to the supposed shift *d* > *dʲ* and *t* > *tʲ* in Middle Cornish. In the first place, it is curious that Middle Cornish scribes did not attempt to devise some sort of graph for /dʲ/ and /tʲ/. For /dʲ/ they could have used *dt*, *dy*, *ds*, *dg*,[5] or perhaps some other combination. If the Loth-George hypothesis were true, then /dʲ/ was by no means a marginal phoneme. It occurred widely in all positions. the failure of the scribes even to attempt separate graphs for /dʲ/ and /tʲ/ would *a priori* make one think that such phonemes never existed in the language.

In Middle English [dʒ] is usually written <i> (later <j>) before back vowels, e.g. *ioye*, *iudge*, but <g> before front vowels including *y*, e.g. *gentil*, *gyst*, *giterne*. The same rule applies in Middle Cornish with English loanwords, e.g. *iolyf* RD 2013, *ioy* OM 154 but *gentyl* OM 1566, *geyler* PC 1865. The same rule also obtains, however, in the case of the reflexes of Old Cornish *d* in Middle Cornish. Thus *crygyans*, *cregyans* 'faith' PC 1994, BM 1169, 1208, 1319, *a'n geffo* 'may have (subj.)' OM 422, *an geffa* 'id.' BM 20, but *pyiadow* 'prayer' PC 24, 224, *peyadow* (*y* for *i*) 'id.' BM 128, 1443, *peiadow* 'id.' BM 132, 3624, *peiadov* 'id.' BM 2189, 4015. Middle Cornish orthography, then, spells Middle English [dʒ] as <g> or <i> according to position. It also spells the reflex of Old Cornish *d* as either <g> or <i> according to the same criteria. It seems reasonable to assume, therefore, that Middle English [dʒ] in loanwords in Middle Cornish and native <g>/<i> < Old Cornish *d* are identical in pronunciation. <g/i>, then, in Middle Cornish cannot represent [dʲ].

The Old Cornish word for 'house' was *ti* (Norris 1859a: 425). In the Middle Cornish texts, however, the form is almost invariabley *chy*, or in its lenited form, *gy*. *Chy* seems to have arisen because the assibilation of *nt* could take place across a word boundary. It appears that Middle Cornish *\*ty* was so frequently used with the proclitic article *an*, that the whole phrase was taken as one unit and thus became *an chy*.[6] According to George, *chy* represents [tʲi:], which he recommends spelling <tji>. *Ch*, then, in the word *chy*, George believes, represents the same sound as is indicated by <s> or <g> in *kerense*/*kerenge*. If this were really so, however, one would expect *chy* (unlenited) occasionally to be written *\*sy* or *\*gy*, which it never is. Or one would perhaps more probably expect that *kerense* and *ganso* might on occasion be spelt *\*kerenche* and *\*gancho*. Middle Cornish, after all, has no aversion to the group

---

5 The graph <dg> occurs in CW, but it is based on English <dg>; see below.
6 The form *ty* survives in some place-names, e.g. *Tywardreath*, *Tywarnhayle*, *Tybesta*. Notice also *ow thy a piyadow* 'my house of prayer' PC 334, with *ty* spirantized to *thy* after *ow* 'my'.

<nch>; cf. *wrynch* 'stratagem' PC 1001. \*Kerenche, \*gancho are, however, unattested anywhere.

The absence of forms like *\*kerenche* in the texts brings us face to face with one of the most unsatisfactory aspects of the Loth-George hypothesis. According to Loth and George, <ns>, <ng> in, for example, *nyns yw, nyng yw* 'is not' represent [ndʲ], but in *kerense/kerenge* <ns>, <ng> represent [ntʲ]. Or to put it another way, we must convince ourselves that Cornish scribes frequently wrote [tʲ], a voiceless alveolo-palatal stop, as <g>.

According to George Middle Cornish /dʲ/ < British *d* became /dʒ/ *c.* 1625. If this were so, then the text of *The Creation of the World* (see Stokes, 1864) written in 1611 should still show clear evidence of unchanged /dʲ/. CW is unique in Cornish texts in using the graph <dg> before *y*. Given that the orthography of CW is late and heavily influenced by that of English, it seems reasonable to assume that <dg> in CW is based on English spellings like *bridge, judgment*, etc., and represents [dʒ]. Yet the graph <dg> in CW occurs where one would expect [dʲ] by the Loth-George hypothesis, e.g. *devidgyow* 'sheep' CW 1070, *ny bydgyaf* 'I do not pray' CW 1364, 1670, *marodgyan* 'wonders' CW 1804, 1898, *marrudgyan* 'id.' CW 2124, *grydgyan[s]* 'faith' CW 2317.

The Middle Cornish word for 'after' has various spellings in the texts, *wose, woge, wosa*. Loth and George believe that <s> alternating with <g> in these forms are variant graphs for [dʲ]. In CW, however, 'after' is only ever spelt *woʒa* (CW 1295, 1412, 1427, 1856, 1942, 2144, 2499). In CW the symbol <ʒ> is used as a graph for two quite separate sounds: [ð] initially, e.g. *ʒa* 'thy' CW 156, 233, *ʒa* 'to' CW 201, 236, *ʒom* 'to my' CW 239, *ʒawarta* 'from him' CW 266, and [z] between vowels, e.g. *y voʒa* (i.e. *y vos e*) 'his being' CW 672, *y foʒa* 'id.' CW 1249, *theʒo* 'to thee' CW 739, 1279, 2253, 2379, *a gowʒas* 'spoke' CW 2422. Quite clearly <ʒ> in *woʒa* cannot represent [ð]. It can only then stand for [z]. In CW, therefore, the word 'after' must be pronounced [wozə] or something similar, not [wodʲə].[7]

The position is similar in CW with regard to the long forms of *bos* 'to be.' In CW the spellings are as follows: 1st person sg. *esaf* CW 130, 327, 424, 1540, 1667, 1696; 3d person sg. imperf. *ega* CW 827, *esa* CW 1905, 1908, *essa* CW 2429, *eʒa* CW 2426, 2456. The third sg. imperfect clearly has two forms, [ezə] and [edʒə]. These are a continuation of the two forms in the Ordinalia, e.g. *ese* RD 514, *ege* RD 1095. Neither represents *\*edʲə].

As has been noted, George, following Loth, believes that the word for 'with him', *ganso* was pronounced in Middle Cornish [gantʲo]. This he spells <gantjo>. He also believes that [ntʲ] had become [ndʒ] by *c.* 1575. If this were so, then the spellings in CW (written 1611) should reflect the pronunciation [gandʒo]. We might then expect to find some spellings of the kind *\*<gango>, \*<ganga>, \*<gandgyo>*. Such forms do not occur. What we do find in CW are

---

7   Loth (op. cit., 416) claims that in *woʒa* in CW ʒ has the value *dj*, i.e. [dʲ]. This is special pleading and the principle of Occam's razor disposes of it.

the following: *gansa* CW 160, *ganso* CW 310, 492, 1203, *gousa* (leg. *gonsa*) CW 604, *gonʒa* CW 324, *ganʒa* CW 734, 1566. In view of the spellings with <ʒ>, it seems virtually certain that the scribe of CW pronounced the word for 'with him' as [ganzo] or [gonzə], but certainly not [gandʒo].[8]

## 6. Phonological Objections

The difference between [d] and [dʲ] is a difference in point of articulation. Before [s], a tip-alveolar fricative, one would expect the contrast between [d] and [dʲ] to be neutralized.[9] The tongue in anticipation of the following tip-alveolar consonant [s], while articulating either [d] or [dʲ] would move to the same alveolar position in readiness for the next segment. Since [s] is voiceless, both [d] and [dʲ] would be devoiced immediately before it. The 2nd person sg. preterite *redya* 'read' thus would have given *retsys* 'thou didst read' < *red* + *sys*. According to George, 'leave' in Middle Cornish, written <gasa>, is pronounced [gadʲə]. The 2nd sg. preterite with *i*-affection should then give *\*ged + sys > \*getsys, \*gytsys*. It does not, of course: *prag y'm gyssys tuch theworthy's* 'why hast thou left me any distance from thee?' PC 2957. The form *gyssys* is the regular development of *gys + sys*.[10]

As is well-known, in Late Cornish (*yth*)*esa* 'was' becomes (*th*)*era*. Similarly, *gasa* 'leave' becomes *gara*. George believes that in these two words intervocalic [dʲ] was rhotacized to [r]. He says, "the realization of /ð/ [i.e. /dʲ/] must have been close to [r]" (PSRC: 165). Presumably he means that [dʲ] was sufficiently close to [r] as to be able to change into it. Yet elsewhere [dʲ] does not, according to George, become [r] but [dʒ]. The sound [dʲ], then is apparently quite unlike [r] except in *esa* and *gasa* only.

I can think of no other instance in any European language where [dʲ] is rhotacized. The usual candidate for rhotacization is [z]. Compare, for example, English *rise* < Proto-Germanic *\*risan-*, but *rear* < Proto-Germanic *\*raizjan-*, or Latin *flōs*, *flōrem*.[11] If we assume that *esa* and *gasa* were [ezə] and [gazə] respectively, there is no difficulty. It should be noted here that Loth inconsistently took *gara* 'leave' to derive from [gazə]. He appears to have believed that [z] was the normal outcome of [dʲ] in some cases (Loth, 1897: 416).

---

8 A Late Cornish form of *ganso* [gondʒa], variously spelt, is attested. It does not occur in Middle Cornish.

9 George believes Middle Cornish *d* and *t* were alveolar, not dental; PSRC 150, 163. This makes his two hypothetical threefold series /t/ ~ /tʲ/ ~ /tʃ/ and /d/ ~ /dʲ/ ~ /dʒ/, even less credible, because the articulatory distances are so small.

10 If *esos* 'thou art' were *\*[edʲos], then the form with enclitic pronoun *-ta*, *\*edʲos + ta* > *\*edista* should give *\*etta*. The attested form is, of course, *esta* < *esosta*.

11 Nance suggested understanding *gyr tero* in *John of Chyanhor* as 2nd pl. imperative, *gortero*, 'tarry' < *\*gortoseugh*. If this were correct, it would be a further exemple of *s* [z] > *r*. See Padel (1975:23).

## 7. Further Orthographical Objections

The chief reason that Loth and George have for taking <s> and <g> or <i/j> to represent a single sound [dʲ] is that the graphs seem to be in free variation. I have already pointed out that, although they both represent the same sound— in my view [dʒ]—<g> and <i/j> are in complementary, but not free, distribution. The position with respect to <s> on the one hand and <g/i> on the other, is much more complicated. Although there is some apparently free variation, much of it can be explained by reference to the phonetic environment. Furthermore, paradigmatic pressure has regularized variation in many cases. In those instances in the surviving texts where neither phonetic environment nor paradigmatic pressure can be invoked, there is no variation or hardly any.

In BM the hero of the play, St Meriasek (Breton *Meriadec*, Latin *Meriadocus*) is mentioned no fewer than 114 times. His name is variously spelt: *meryasek* x 94, *veryasek* x 9, *meriasek* x 8, *mereasek* x 1, *varyasek* x 1, *vryasek* x 1. There are no instances with <g>. Notice further that at BM 2851-52 *meryasek* rhymes with *tasek* 'paternal'. This I take to be a full rhyme, yet *tasek* can only be for [tazek], since *g*-forms of the word *tas* 'father' are unknown.[12]

We can, I believe, be certain that the scribe of BM pronounced his hero's name as [merjazek], not [merjadʲek]. In fact, a variant [merjadʒek] was known, but it is a dialectal form, alien to BM, and indeed to classical Middle Cornish. It is certainly not a mere orthographical alternative.

The worde *gallosek* 'powerful' (Breton *galloudek*) is variously spelt in Middle Cornish: *gallosek, galosek, galosak, gollousacke* (CW 13). I have counted 40 instances of the word from PA, OM, PC, PC, RD, BM, TH, SA and CW. Only once is it spelt with a <g> as *gallogek* (RC 2376). Elsewhere in RC it is spelt with an <s> eight times.

The word *bohosek* 'poor' is much less frequent than *gallosek*. I have counted 25 examples from PA, PC, BM and TH. In all cases it is spelt with an <s>, except in one instance in BM where the plural form is written *bohogogyon* (BM 4204). I ascribe the presence of <g> = [dʒ] here to the position of the accent.

If we look at spellings with <g> rather than <s>, we find the same pattern of invariance. I have, for example, noted 32 examples of the word *crygyans, cregyans* 'faith, belief' from the texts. It is always spelt with a <g> (<dg> in CW). It is never spelt *\*crysyans*. The only example with an <s> is the curious mixed spelling *crisgians*, which occurs once in TH.

If the Loth-George hypothesis were correct, the <s> in *Meryasek, gallosek* and *bohosek* on the one hand and the <g> in *crygyans* on the other were both pronounced [dʲ]. Yet the scribal practice in all our texts makes it abundantly clear that this is not so. The surviving texts range in date from the fourteenth

---

**12** Curiously George believes that Old Cornish *tadou* 'fathers' would have developed to *\*[tadʲow]* in Middle Cornish (PRSC 81). *-adow* remained unsibilated in Middle Cornish; cf. *caradow, casadow, piyadow*, etc.

to the seventeenth century, but in this matter they all show a striking uniformity. The inescapable conclusion from the evidence of the texts is that *Meryasek, gallosek, bohosek* are to be pronounced with a [z], which *crygyans* has a [dʒ]. The forms [galodʒek] and [bohodʒogjon] do occur in the texts. One is a dialectal variant (see below), the other is phonetically determined. There is no evidence whatever for the free variation of <s> and <g> in any of these four lexical items.

John Tregear's Homilies afford us a most instructive insight into the alternation of <s> and <g>. TH spell the word for 'love' as *kerensa, gerensa* (lenited) no fewer than 28 times. Twice it is spelt *carenga*. On the other hand the adjective *\*kerensedhek* 'loving' is variously spelt *kerengyek, kerengeak*, etc., with a <g> six times. Only once does it occur as *kerensyak* with an <s>. For the most part, then, TH distinguish *kerensa* 'love' from *kerengyek* 'loving'. As is the case with *bohogogyon* mentioned above, the presence of [dʒ] in *kerengyek* is, I believe, to be explained by the position of the accent (see below). *Carenga* x 2 and *kerensyak* x 1 are analogical in origin.

## 8. Toponymic Objections to the Loth-George Hypothesis

When a people abandons its ancestral tongue, the transference of place-names from the old language to the new takes place within the community itself as part of the general language shift. The change of language typically occurs across three generations. The first is monoglot in the retreating language, the second bilingual in both, the third can speak only the advancing language only. The first generation use the retreating language for everything, including local place-names. The second generation pronounce local place-names in the "old" way even while using the "new" language. The third generation is unable to pronounce the local names in the "old" way. Members of this generation pronounce local place-names in accordance with the phonetic system of the "new" language. The transmission of place-names from one language to another, then, is entirely an oral matter. It has nothing to do with writing or orthographical systems.

According to George, Old Cornish medial *d* became [dʲ] in Middle Cornish and then fell together with [dʒ] from other sources *c.* 1625. If this were so, then place-names in Cornwall containing the reflex of Old Cornish medial *d* might be expected to show two separate developments. In those places where Cornish had been spoken in the Middle Cornish period, but had become extinct before *c.* 1625, place-names pronounced by English-speakers should show the nearest English equivalent to [dʲ]. In those places where Cornish survived beyond *c.* 1625, place-names with Old Cornish medial d should display [dʒ], spelt <dg>, <g>, <dj> or <j>.

The nearest English equivalent of [dʲ] is *d*. Palatalized *d* in Irish place-names almost invariably appears in English as *d*, e.g. *Deargail > Dargle, Spidéal > Spiddal, Cúil na gCuiridín > Killygordon*, etc. In that area of Mid-Cornwall where Cornish was spoken in the Middle Ages, but not after *c.* 1530, one might expect

Old Cornish medial *d* to appear in place-names as *d*. It does not, of course. In this area such forms with *d* do not occur. It might, then, be argued that Middle Cornish [dʲ] was so strongly palatalized that English speakers were unable to distinguish it from [dʒ]. If so, then everywhere in Mid-Cornwall Old Cornish medial *d* should appear in place-names ad [dʒ] and as [dʒ] only. This is not the case.

The reflex of Old Cornish medial *d* in place-names is not infrequently [dʒ], particularly in the west of Cornwall, e.g. *Adjaporth, Cadgwith, Kenidgack* (cf. Breton *keuneudek* 'abondant en bois à brûler'). As common a reflex of Old Cornish medial *d* in place-names, however, in West- and Mid-Cornwall is *s* or *ss*. Here are some examples: *Trelogossick* (Veryan) < *tre* + Old Cornish *\*logodec* 'place full of mice'; *Trelissick* (St Erth, Sithney) < *tre* + Old Cornish *\*guledic* 'leader'; *Rissick* (Perranarworthal) < Old Cornish *\*ridec* 'race farm'; *Tregassack* (earlier *Tregarasek*) (Ludgvan) < *tre* + Old Cornish *\*Caradec* (PN, cf. Welsh *Caradog*); *Nanphysick* (St Mewan) < *nans* + Old Cornish *fodic* 'fortunate'; *Carnsew* (Mabe) < *carn* + Old Cornish *deviov* 'gods, fairies'.[13]

If as George claims, Old Cornish medial *d* gave first [dʲ] and then [dʒ], these place-names and others like them are quite inexplicable. It is impossible to explain the medial sibilant from Old Cornish *d* in these names by the Loth-George hypothesis. The above place-names are in my view quite sufficient to refute the suppose shift [d] > [dʲ] in Cornish, even if no other evidence were forthcoming.

## 9. A Suggested Solution: Schema
In the preceding pages I have attempted to show why the supposed development of Old Cornish *d, t* > Middle Cornish *dʲ, tʲ* is illusory. It would perhaps be right for me at this point to set out exactly how I believe British and Old Cornish medial and final *d, t* developed in Middle Cornish. This I will now do.

2.1  In medial and final position the second segment in *lt, nt* was affricated to *ts* already in the Old Cornish period, i.e. before *c.* 1100. Thus Primitive Cornish *\*[alt], \*[nant], \*[kerenteθ] became *\*[alts], \*[nants], \*[kerentseθ].

2.2  Probably at the same period *t* in *ti* 'house' became *\*[tsi] after the article, thus *\*[an tsi] 'the house'.

2.3  Intervocalic *t < d + h* was affricated to *ts* in some words, e.g. *\*[pɪsketa] > [pɪsketsa] 'to fish'.

2.4  Probably slightly later, i.e. *c.* 1100, *d* was affricated to *dz* finally,and medially before certain vowels and *w*: *\*[taːdz] 'father', *\*[marxadz] 'market', *\*[boxodzek] 'poor', *\*[pedswar] 'four', *\*[adzwon] 'know'.

2.5  Similarly before a stressed front vowel or yod followed by a stressed vowel initial *d* was affricated to *dz* in some common words, when

---

13 The place-names in this section and their etymologies are from Padel (1985).

immediately preceded by a proclitic with final $n$: *[an dzɪːð] 'the day', *[an dzevan] (< Lat. *daemonem*) 'the demon', *[an dzjawl] 'the devil', *[an dzeves] 'he has', *[an dzevɪθ] 'he will have'.

2.6 Medially after $l$ and $n$ ts was voiced to $dz$: *[kerentseθ] > [kerendze], *[gweltsek] 'grassy' > *[gweldzek].

2.7 In certain conditions, notably before stressed front vowels and yod + vowel, [dz] was palatalized to [dʒ]: *[an dzɪːð] > [an dʒɪːð], *[kridzjans] > [kridʒjans], *[an dzeves] > [an dʒeves].[14] Similarly *[an tsi:] became [an tʃiː].

2.8 Some varieties of Cornish applied the rule of palatalization more consistently than others. This gave rise to forms like [pɪdʒɪ] 'to pray' as against *[pɪdzɪ], [krɪdʒɪ] 'to believe' as against *[krɪdzɪ], [kerendʒe] as against *[kerendze], [logodʒen] 'mouse' as against [logodzen].

2.9 These varieties of Cornish had a tendency to palatalize $dz$ where there was no following high front vowel to motivate such palatalization. Thus *[guidz] 'blood' became [guːdʒ], *[adzwon] became [adʒwon] and *[pedzwar] became [pedʒwar].

2.10 The palatalizing varieties of Cornish also palatalized [ts] > [tʃ]: *[pɪsketsa] > [pɪsketʃa].

2.11 [dz] was simplified to [z] and fell together with [z] from intervocalic -s-, e.g. [gwezjyon] 'servants', written <gwesyon> and with [z] in English loanwords, e.g. [prajzjə] 'praise', written <praysya>.

2.12 [ts] was simplified to [s] and fell together with [s] in initial position and [s] from earlier -ss-, e.g. [nesa] 'next', written <nessa>.

2.13 In some dialects intervocalic [z] < [dz] was rhotacized sporadically to [r]: *era* 'was', *gara* 'leave'.

## 10. Discussion of Above Schema

All stages except 2.13 were complete before the Middle Cornish period. 2.13 was never general. It appears to have occurred early in the sixteenth century.

If the above schema is in outline correct—as I believe it is—then Cornish never possessed either [tʲ] or [dʲ]. In fact the dental/alveolar inventory of Middle Cornish is both simple and and stable: (voiceless) /t/ ~ /θ/ ~ /s/ ~ /tʃ/ ~ /ʃ/ and (voiced) /d/ ~ /ð/ ~ /z/ ~ /dʒ/ ~ (/ʒ/). This persisted, albeit with the sporadic change [z] > [r] (and possibly also [dʒ] > [ʒ] in some words; see note 19 below) until the death of Cornish in the eighteenth/nineteenth centuries.

2.4 That [d] became [dz] before simplifying to [z] seems guaranteed by the Cornish name for *Market Jew*. This place-name, which means 'Thursday Market', was originally Old Cornish [marxad jow], spelt *Marchadyou*, *Marcadyou*. It then became [marxadz jow]; compare the spelling *Marghasdiow*

---

14 Lewis & Pedersen (1961: 155) believe that "palatalization" > [dʒ] occurs before front vowels, but they accept Loth's view that [dʲ] is the starting point; see also LHEB 397.

(1359). The final [dz] in [marxadz] was then palatalized before the yod in [jow] to give [marxadʒ jow / ow]. This latter is the form given by Lhuyd as (lenited) *Varha Dzhu*.[15] Spellings like *Marghas yow* (PC 2668), *Markasiou* (AD 1261) and *Margasiou* (AD 1277), etc., are etymological.[16]

2.6 The voicing of *nts > ndz* seems to be guaranteed by the common spelling *kerenge* 'love' and the absolutely universal spelling of *bolungeth* 'wish', later *blonogath*, with <g>. Loth was led astray here by Breton. The MB equivalents of *kerense / kerenge* and *bolungeth* both contain *nt*: *caranté, carantez* and *bolunté, boluntez*. If *nts* had not already become *\*ndz* in these words in Cornish, it could not have palatalized to [dʒ], spelt <g>. George follows Loth here and takes *kerenge, bolungeth* to stand for *\*[kerentʲe]* and *\*[boluntʲeθ]*. One might coneivably take the spelling <kerense> to mean the finall consonant was voiceless, but not *kerenge*. As *bolungeth, blonogath* are never spelt with an <s>, we can, I believe, be certain that the group <ng> was voiced in this word and others like it.

2.8 This whole question of palatalization before *i* is discussed below. Palatalization before *e* is less common than before *i*. The difference between, for example, *gallosek* and *gallogek* may have something to do with the unrounding of the vowel in the final syllable. Where *ö* in *\*gallodzök* unrounded to *e* early, *dz* palatalized to [dʒ]. Where *\*gallodzök* persisted, [dz] had already simplified to [z] before the *e* could palatalize it.

2.9 Lhuyd writes *gûdzh* 'blood' and *lûdzh* 'grey', but elsewhere in Late Cornish the word for 'grey' is *looez*. Note also the spelling *oydge* 'age' CW 2101. In Middle Cornish the words for 'blood', 'grey' and 'age' are not infrequently written with the vowel *oi* or *oy*. This reflects the Old Cornish forms *guit* (Norris 1859a: 379), *\*luit* and *\*uit*, with yod before the final consonant. It is this yod that has triggered palatalization in these words in some dialects.

2.11 I say that [dz] simplified to [z]. In fact *d*, *\*dz* and *z* are all probably partially-voiced lenes. English speakers would have heard the half-voiced lenis *z* as either [s] or [z]. This would account for the occurrence of *s(s)* in place-names. Notice also, incidentally, that the stage *dz* is written *ts* in the thirteenth-century place-name *Retsic* (AD 1233; Pool 1973-66), modern *Rissick*.

## 11. Dialect Variation in Late Cornish

Late Cornish no longer uses the spelling-system of the Middle Cornish literary language, but rather follows the orthographical conventions of English. Moreover, Edward Lhuyd uses his own "universal alphabet", i.e. an early system of phonetic transcription. If the above schema from 2.1 to 2.12 is correct, then we would expect to see in Late Cornish a series of words in which

---

15 AB 253, § 7. Cf. also the place-names *Bogee, Bojea* both from *bod + yuf*; see Padel (1985: 140).

16 These and the other early instances of the name *Market Jew* are quoted in Fowler (1961).

[z] alternates dialectally with [dʒ]. This is precisely what we do find. Note the following doublets from Late Cornish (I give the forms with [dʒ] after the diagonal stroke)[17]: *pazuera* 'fourth' Lhuyd, *peswarra* Pryce, *bozvevah* (leg. *bosverah*) Gwavas MS, *bizwau·dhu* (Newlyn 1875; see *Trans. Phil. Soc.* (1876), 539)/ *padgurra* 'fourth' J. Boson, *padzhuera* Pryce, *pagwera* T. Boson; *karensa* 'love' Pryce, *grensa* T. Boson/ *karendzha* Lhuyd, Pryce, *crenga* N. Boson, *crenjah* Kerew; *uoze* 'after' Lhuyd, *guozna* 'after that' Lhuyd, *guozma* 'after this' Lhuyd/ *udzhe* 'after' Lhuyd, *ugge* N. Boson, *vge* T. Boson, *udzhna* 'after that' Lhuyd, *udzhma* 'after this' Lhuyd; *azuan* 'know' Lhuyd'/ *adzhuan* 'know' Lhuyd; *nawnzack* 'nineteen' Pryce/ *nowndzhak*[18] 'nineteen'; *genzyns* 'with them' Lhuyd' *gyndzhanz, gynzhans* 'with them' Lhuyd.

Notice also the Late Cornish alternation in the long forms of the verb *bos*: *idzha* 'is' Lhuyd (AB: 242a, for example)/ *eravi, eram* 'am' (e.g. AB: 250b), *thera* 'was' (e.g. BF: 9), etc. *Eram* are from *\*eza + m, \*eza*, with [z], while *idzha, igge* is from Middle Cornish *ugy* [ydʒɪ], with reduced final vowel before the enclitic pronoun.

Alongside the above [z/d] alternation in Late Cornish one can also set the similar alternations in place-names, for example (forms with [dʒ] appear after the diagonal stroke): Old Cornish *\*melin-di* > *Mellinsey/ Mellingey*; Old Cornish *\*hendi* > *Hensy-wassa/ Hengy-vghall*; Old Cornish *\*adwy* 'gap' > *Assa-wine/ Adja-porth*; Old Cornish *\*cadwith* > *Tre-gaswith/ Tre-gadgwith*; Old Cornish *\*gueltec* 'grassy' > *Car-walsick/ Illis-wilgig*.

A similar and quite remarkable alternation between [s]/[z] and [dʒ] survives in the English dialect of Cornwall. People who washed in St Meriasek's well in Camborne were known as *Merrasicks* (Jago, 1882: 216) or *Merrasickers* (BM, introduction p. xii) by the local inhabitants. They were also known as *Moragicks, Mearagaks* (Jago, ibid.). Moreover, *Merry-geeks* or *Merajacks* (Ellis, 1974: 40) was a general nickname for Camborne people themselves. These various survivals clearly continue two separate reflexes of the name of St Meriasek, [merjazek] and [merjadʒek].[19]

The question remains how to explain the distribution of forms in [z] and [dʒ]. As for the reflexes of Old Cornish *d* before unstressed *i* and *y*, it would seem form place-name evidence that, curiously enough, palatalization could occur or fail to occur anywhere in the Cornish-speaking area. I discuss some of the evidence from the texts for this kind of palatalization below. As far as less motivated palatalization is concerned, i.e. before *w, e*, etc. (in *caswyth, gallosek,*

---

**17** Unless otherwise stated these examples are taken from AB, Pryce (1790), Loth (1900) and Padel (1975).

**18** Quoted by Jackson (1967: 793). Note further that Middle Cornish *bohosek* 'poor' and Middle Cornish *ollgallosek* 'omnipotent' are recorded in Late Cornish as *bohodzhak* (Lhuyd) and *agallasack* (Norris 1859b: 466), i.e. with [dʒ] and [s]/[z] respectively.

**19** Lhuyd (AB 224) gives the name as *Meriazhek*. This is apparently a weakened form of *Meriadzhek*. The weakening of [dʒ] > [ʒ] is noticeable in CW, where enclitic *ge* 'thee' is devoiced after *s* to *sche* (not *\*che*); e.g. CW 316, 268.

etc.), it seems from place-names that Cornish-speaking Cornwall falls into two separate regions. Before examining them, however, something will have to be said about the extent of the Cornish-speaking area itself and the origins of the standard language.

## 12 Celtophone Cornwall in the Middle Ages

Old Cornish *rid* 'ford' and *bod* 'dwelling-plce' became *res* and *bos* in Middle Cornish. According to Jackson, the change *-d* to *-s* was already beginning *c.* 1100.[20] In the area of east Cornwall between the Tamar to the east and the Camel and Fowey rivers to the west, place-names exhibit forms of these two etyma with *d* rather than s. It has been suggested, therefore, that Cornish was extinct in this area before *-d* > *-s*, i.e. before *c.* 1100.

This argument is based on a false assumption. Certainly English settlement before the Norman Conquest had been more widespread in this far eastern part of Cornwall than further to the west. It is also very likely that English was spoken by many in this area before the advent of the Normans. The appearance of place-names in English with original *d* rather than shifted *s* does not, however, mean that Cornish was extinct in this part of Cornwall by *c.* 1100. It means only that the English had been familiar with names of settlements in the area since before the change *-d* > *-s* began.

Let us look at an Irish parallel. There are many place-names in Ireland that contain the element *áth* 'ford', *Athy, Athlone, Athboy, Athenry*, for example. The <th> in these names in English is pronounced as [θ], even though [θ] in Irish had become [h] by the end of the twelfth century (Thurneysen, 1946: 76). Yet Irish continued to be spoken in the area of Athy and Athlone until the nine-teenth century. In the district around Athenry in County Galway it continued well into the twentieth.

The place-name *Redruth* in western Cornwall contains the pre-1100 form of *rid* 'ford', yet Cornish continued to be spoken in the surrounding district well into the seventeenth century.

There is direct evidence that Cornish was spoken east of the Camel-Fowey line until the middle of the fourteenth century at the very least. In 1349 the prior of Minster near Boscastle and many of his community and tenants died of the Black Death. A chaplain could not be found for the parish, since none of the surviving friars spoke Cornish (Wakelin, 1975: 88-9). Obviously in Minster *c.* 1350 many of the laity were monoglot Cornish-speakers. this could hardly have been the only district east of the Camel-Fowey line that Cornish. We can, I think, be fairly confident that Cornish was widely spoken in this most easterly region of Cornwall into the fourteenth century and beyond.

There is certainly good evidence that Cornish was spoken in Bodmin and the Bodmin district in the fourteenth century. In 1354/5 Brother John, a

---

**20** LHEB 396-98. This dating may be slightly too late, given that the phonetic processes occur sooner than they appear in orthography.

member of the Franciscan house in Bodmin, was appointed penitentiary to hear the confessions of both those who knew Cornish and those who knew English (Wakelin: 89). Moreover wer read in the same fourteenth-century source of a certain priest, Ralph de Tremur, form Lanivet just west of Bodmin, who spoke Cornish and English fluently.[21]

The Norman invasion was obviously of the utmost significance for Cornish. The use of a new language, French, in administration and law could only mean the weakening of English in Cornwall—at least initially. Moreover, many Bretons were given land in Cornwall and presumably brought with them Celtic-speaking servants and retainers.[22] The renewed links with Brittany clearly affected Cornish literature greatly. It is significant that all surviving Middle Cornish literature (except for TH) owes more to Breton and French models than to Middle English.[23]

It is very likely that the survival of Cornish in Minster and presumably elsewhere in the far east of Cornwall, was a direct result of the Norman invasion. The presence of Breton-speakers and the weakening of English probably produced something of a revival in the fortunes of Cornish in those districts where, judging by the place-names, it had been in decline. I would even suggest that the town of Bodmin, as a result of the Norman Conquest, became strongly Cornish in speech, whereas before the coming of the Normans it had probably been largely Anglophone.[24]

---

21  Ellis (1974: 33). De Tremur also knew French and Latin. He was instituted to the rectory of Warleggan. John de Grandisson, Bishop of Exeter (1327-69), to whom we owe the reference to de Tremur, presumably mentions that de Tremur could speak Cornish because it was of use to him in his parish. He was excommunicated for heresy, however. At all events, it is likely that Cornish was spoken at Warleggan in the mid-fourteenth century.

22  Some observers refer to the Norman Conquest as the Armorican Return, so important do they regard the presence of Bretons in Cornwall and the renewed contacts with Brittany. Cf. the observation of Tim Saunders: "Linguistically, Cornwall remained fairly stable from the Armorican Return until the rise of the centralizing Tudor state, approximately four hundred years. Cornu-Breton formed the medium of daily intercourse over the most of the territory, except in the East which it shared with Western English", Ó Luain (1983: 253).

23  For the relationship of the *Ordinalia* to French and Breton models, see Longsworth (1967: 1-2) and Bakere (1981: 1). Note that PA and OM contain traditions uncommon in England, but common in France; Bakere (1980: 105). BM deals with a Breton saint and is largely set in Brittany.

24  George believes that Cornish was spoken widely in east Cornwall after the Norman Conquest. He says "After the Norman invasion, Cornish was less under threat from English, for English itself was threatened by French. Cornish was spoken by the vast majority of the populace except in the far north-east which had been settled by English-speakers", Commission (1986: 194).

## 13. The Origin of Standard Middle Cornish

The Middle Cornish texts are remarkable for the uniformity of their spelling and grammar. Apart from CW, all our surviving literary remains exhibit essentiallly the same orthography and accidence. We are obviously dealing with a highly cultivated and standardized form of language.

The orthography of the Old Cornish *Vocabularium Cornicum* is clearly that inherited by Cornish from the Common British period (see LHEB 67-75). The *Vocabularium*, however, shows some admixture of Old English spelling habits.[25] The orthography of Middle Cornish continues this spelling system but with a number of Anglo-Norman features, e.g. <gh> for [x] and <th> for [θ]. Clearly Middle Cornish spelling has been influenced by the presence of the Normans in Cornwall. Middle Cornish orthography also exhibits the assibilation of Old Cornish *d, t* (the subject of this article), that started sometime in the late 11th century. I would suggest that standard literary Middle Cornish arose in the hundred or so years after the Norman Conquest, probably in the period 1150-1175.

Standard languages do not emerge in a vacuum. They are usually the speech of high prestige group in a place where power is exercized. Now it is clear from the Domesday Survey and other sources that the centre of power in Cornwall at this period was Bodmin.[26] I assume, therefore, that literary Middle Cornish was developed from the earlier Old Cornish standard by educated clerics and others in and around Bodmin in the latter half of the twelfth century.

## 14 The Eastern and Western Dialects of Cornish

There is evidence that Cornish was widely speoken in or near Padstow *c.* 1540.[27] It was spoken by the older generation in St Ewe near St Austell in 1595.[28] Two generations previously, i.e. *c.* 1535, it was presumably spoken by everyone in the district. It seems probable, therefore that the Cornish was the everyday language in the early sixteenth century at least as far east as Padstow and St Austell—if not further east. Indeed there is excellent toponymic

---

25 Old Cornish uses three Anglo-Saxon letters, þ, ð and p that are virtually unknown in Welsh and completely so in Breton; LHEB 67-75.

26 See Wakelin (1975: 69-70). Notice also that the gospel-book containing the records of manumitted slaves was written in Bodmin in the period 940-1040.

27 John Leland visiting Cornwall at some time during the years 1535-43 noted that Padstow was called *Lodenek* in Cornish. This implies, I think, that Cornish was widely spoken in the Padstow area at the time. See Ellis (1974: 58).

28 In a deposition of the Bishop's Consistory Court a girl at St Ewe in 1595 said she heard two of the witnesses talking together in Cornish and English; Wakelin (1975: 89). This can only mean that a girl heard two people older than herself talking Cornish with a large admixture of English words and phrases. Even when a language is dying, truly bilingual conversations are not normal.

evidence that Cornish was spoken in pockets as far as the Tamar until the second half of the sixteenth century.

As has been suggested above, Cornwall as far east as the Camel-Fowey line appears to fall into two separate dialect regions. in the eastern part of this are, to jusge from place-name evidence, the reflex of Old Cornish medial and final *d* is always *s* (except before *i* or yod). In the western area Old Cornish medial and final *d* sometimes appears as [dʒ].

To exemplify the dialectal variation between [s/z] and [dʒ], I list below the place-names containing reflexes of five different Old Cornish etyma: (i) *\*adwy* 'gap'; (ii) *\*cadwith* 'thicket'; (iii) *logoden* 'mouse', *\*logodec* 'place of mice'; (iv) *\*gueltec* 'grassy'; (v) *Cadoc* PN, cf. *Madoc*. The forms containing [dʒ] are given after the diagonal stroke:

(i) *Assa Govrankowe* (Gwennap 1580); *Assawine* (?Illogan 1582)/ *Adga Bullocke* (Lelant); *Adgewella* (Camborne); *Adgyan Franck* (Constantine 1649); *Adgaporth* (Madron 1614); *Adgawinkack* (Ruan Major); *Agahave* (Ruan Major); *Aja-Bullocke* (Perranuthnoe); *Aga-Gai* (Sennen); *Agareeth* (St Hilary 1665); *Nangidnall* (< *Goone Agga Idnall* 1670) (Madron).

(ii) *Tregaswith* (St Columb Major); *Rosecassa* (St Just in Roseland)/ *Cadgwith* (Grade); *Trecadgwith* (St Buryan).

(iii) *Trelogossick* (Veryan); *Legossick* (St Issey)/ *Parken Legagen* (St Keverne 1710).

(iv) *Carwalsack* (St Stephen in Brannel)/ *Illiswilgig* (Scilly)

(v) *Ventongassick* (St Just in Roseland); *roscarrack* (< *\*Ros Casek*) (Budock); cf. *Polmassick* (< *pons* + *\*Madoc*) (St Ewe)/ *Porth-cadjack Cove* (Illogan).[29]

Several things must be noted about the above list. First, I have had access only to O. J. Padel's work on place-name elements while compiling it. I am, therefore, unaware for the most part of earlier forms for any of the names given.[30] It is more than likely that further information would mean revising and/or expanding the list.[31]

---

29 Notice also that Tregassack in Ludgvan was called *Tregaragek* in 1326; Pool (1973: 71). This name is obviously from *tre* + *\*Carasek*, the Cornish equivalent of Welsh *Caradog*. In Penwith the form in *-agek* would be the expected one.

30 Early forms of some place-names in West Penwith often show *s* as well as *g*, e.g. *Lanscoisek* 1302, *Lanscoegek* 1327, modern *Lescudjack*; see Pool (1073: 57). The *s*-forms reflect standard spelling; see also note 29 above. I do not agree, however, with Padel's etymology of *Bosoljack* (Gulval) < *bod* + *\*houliek* 'sunny'. The earlier forms given by Pool are *Bossulsek* 1334, *Bossolsak* 1478, *Bossulsack* 1575. I would understand the second element as *\*solsek* < *sols* 'shilling, money', with the transferred sense 'wealth, cattle'; cf. Breton *saout* 'livestock'.

31 I suspect that if they had survived, the names *Assawine* and *Assa Govrankowe* might conceivably have shown <dg> as well as <ss>. This would mean the loss of one item from our list, but it would not invalidate the general argument, since the two names in *Assa-* are at the far western limit of the *s*-area.

The second point to notice is the remarkable consistency of the distribution. This is particularly apparent from the accompanying map.

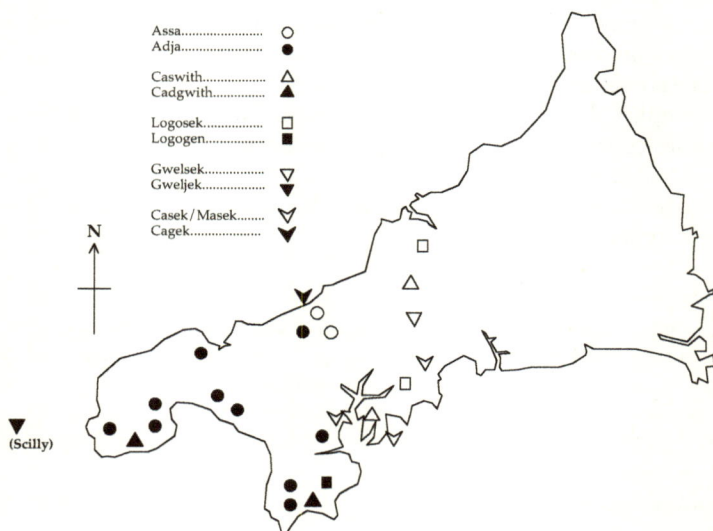

**Map 1.** The alternation <s> ~ <g>/<j> in place-names.

Thirdly it is to be observed that the two dialects seem to overlap in the Camborne-Illogan area. This is exactly what one would expect, given the two forms *Meriasek* and *\*Meriagek* associated with Camborne.

The fourth point to notice is the following. The distribution of forms shown in the above list and map could no doubt be refined by examining the distribution of *Boj*-forms in place-names as against the cas of *Bos*-. Unfortunately, the picture is complicated in the case of *Boj*- by the presence of eastern forms with initial *yod* in the second element, e.g. *Bogee* (St Ervan), *Bojea* (St Austell) < *bod* + *\*yuf* 'lord' (Padel, 1975: 140). This and other difficulties mean that the question of *Bos*-/*Boj*- will have to be left for the moment.

The final note to be made about the list and map is that they involve only one isogloss. The alternation of [n] ~ [ᵈn] in place-names, I believe, is also a function of region, east versus west, not of period. If this alternation in place-names were mapped, it would present a picture similar to that of [s]/[z] ~ [dʒ].[32]

---

[32] For the distribution of *-dn* in place-names, see Wakelin (1975: 79). The explanation given there for them is incorrect, I believe. Since *-dn* occurs in BM, it is probably older than the early sixteenth century. I would place it at least as early as the mid-

Of course attempts have been made to expalin the variation of [s]/[z] with [dʒ] in place-names of the kind listed above in terms of chronology. By this view [s]/[z] is older than [dʒ], into which it developed in those areas where Cornish survived.[33] This view is incorrect for two reasons. First, because Cornish did not survive significantly longer in the [dʒ] area than in the [s]/[z]. Indeed *Illiswilgig* with [dʒ] in Scilly must have developed before Cornish died in the islands and much earlier than the death of the language in West Cornwall itself. Secondly, [dʒ] is not, and cannot be, a phonetic reflex of [z]. The two sounds in the place-names we have discussed are distinct and mutually exclusive developments of *[dz] < [d]. If Middle Cornish [z] had developed into Late Cornish [dʒ], then [z] from whatever source should appear in Late Cornish as [dʒ]. We should find in Late Cornish forms like *edzhella 'lowest' (not *ezella*), *preedzhyo 'praise!' (not *preezyo*) and *Sawdzhon 'Englishmen' (not *Sawson*).

I have explained briefly above why I believe that standard Middle Cornish emerged in Bodmin. Bodmin is at the eastern end of our area in which the 'unmotivated' palatalization of [dz] > [dʒ] was unknown. This was the reason, I would suggest, that standard Middle Cornish consistently writes <peswar>, <bohosek>, <gallosek>, etc. Only rarely in the Middle Cornish texts does one encounter forms with [dʒ], *gallogek*, for example. Such forms reflect the scribe's more westerly dialect. Even though literary Middle Cornish could tolerate *gallogek*, forms like [guːdʒ] 'blood' and [oːdʒ] 'age' appear to have been quite inadmissible and are not attested until CW.

Literary Middle Cornish was obviously cultivated at a number of centres. The *Ordinalia* are associated with Glasney, near Penrhyn.[34] BM was alsmost certainly written in Camborne.[35] We have a dramatic fragment that may have been written in St Stephen in Brannel (see Fudge, 1982). A life of St Columba in Cornish, now lost, was in all probability written in St Columb Major (see Ellis, 1974: 69). CW was written in Helston, while TH were probably written in Newlyn East. Clearly the influence of literary Middle Cornish was widespread and of considerable importance at least until the dissolution of the

---

fifteenth century. It appeared late in spelling because it was considered substandard. Note, however, that it attested in Scilly.

**33** See Wakelin (1975: 75-6) and cf. the rather naïve statement of Rod Lyon: "Del ve leverys kens, yth esa trelyans a'n son 'd' dhe'n son 's' ha wosa dhe 'j'. Mes… yth esa trelyans a ogas dhe bup lytheren 's' dhe 'j' kens oll pan esa an 's' ynter deu vogalen." [As has been mentioned there was a mutation of the sound 'd' to 's' and afterwards to 'j'. But… there was a mutation of almost every letter [sic] 's' to 'j', in particular when the 's' was between vowel.] in Ó Luain (1983: 236). Nance also believed that s gave j in place-names; see, for example, Nance (1967: 4).

**34** See Fowler (1961) and Fudge (1982) for references.

**35** Fudge (1982: 22-4). Note that at the end of part one of BM the Duke invokes the blessing of Christ, Meriasek, patron of Camborne and of Mary of Camborne upon the audience: *wy agis beth gor ha gruek/banneth crist ha meryasek/banneth maria cambron* BM 2508-10.

monasteries. Even CW, written some 80 or 90 years after the Reformation, though modern in spelling in some ways, is very much in the Middle Cornish literary standard and tradition.

When we come to Late Cornish we find that the literary standard has almost been forgotten, The language is now confined to the western extremities of Cornwall; here forms in [dʒ] are normal in speech. The only spelling known to the Bosons, to Gwavas, Kerew, etc., was that of English. The only dialect of Cornish known to them was the moribund speech of the west. Edward Lhuyd, though he uses his own phonetic alphabet, again has only the dialect of the far west as evidence for the pronunciation of Cornish. Indeed he tell us that most of his oral material was gathered in St Just in Penwith.[36] It is not astonishing, then, that Late Cornish should aboun in forms containing [dʒ], where s only had been the rule in the Middle Cornish period.[37]

If western Cornish dialects were so given to forms in [dʒ], it may be legitimately asked why forms like *pezwara*, *kerenza*, etc., survive in Late, and therefore written, Cornish. There are two reasons. As has been noted above, 'unmotivated' palatalization was not universal and invariable in western dialects. For example CW, written in Helston in 1611, always writes <woʒa> [woʒə], never [wodʒə]. Similarly the place-name *Trelissick* in Sithney and St Erth (< *tre* + Old Cornish *guledic* 'leader') shows s not [dʒ]. Even in the far west, then, dialects may have been mixed. The second reason is that even where the dialect was prone to palatalization, in former times at any rate, speakers would have been in regular maritime and other contact with dialects further east. Such dialects would have been of higher social standing than that of the westerners. Even if the western dialects had not been spontaneously mixed, constant contact with speakers from further east would have tended to make them so.

### 15. Palatalization in the Texts

Having discussed the origin and significance of the alternation *s* ~ *g*, I should like to finish this article by examining in some depth the alternation as it is to be observed in our surviving Middle Cornish texts.

The palatalization in 2.7 is clearly the most universal. *An geyth* 'the day' and forms of *a'm bus* after *y'n*, *a'n* are invariably spelt with <g>/<i> in the texts. Similarly, words containing Old Cornish *d* followed by yod + vowel are always

---

36 "An for' a 'rykemeraz vi dho dheska an nebaz skianz-ma a'n Tavazeth Kernûak o enradn dre skrefyanz dhort genauo an bobl en Gorleuen Kernou enuedzhek en pleu *Yst*." [The method I adopted to learn this little knowledge of the Cornish dialect was in part through writing down from the mouths of the people in the west of Cornwall, in particular in St Just in Penwith], AB: 222.

37 Richard Angwyn of St Just in Penwith, who died *c*. 1671-75, was a scholar of Cornish who could read and write the language. All his papers were destroyed after his death. See Ellis (1974: 88). It is likely that Angwyn, when speaking Cornish, said [bohodʒek], [adʒwon] and [gu:dʒ], but he probably wrote them with an *s*, at least some of the time.

palatalized, e.g. *brygyon* 'boil', *esgygyow* 'shoes', *cregyans/cregyans* 'faith' (see below). The position is similar in place-names. Note, for example, *Rees, Rice* < Old Cornish *rid*, but *Ridgeo* < pl. *\*ridiou* (Padel 1985: 198 A).

Palatalization before a high front but unstressed vowel is much less consistent. this is obvious from place-names, where one finds doublets of the kind *Melinsey/Mellingey* (Padel, 1985: 161), *St Issey/St Jidgey* (ibid., 204, 304; cf. also *Mevagissey*), etc. If we compare the spelling of the three forms *crysaf* (*cresaf*) 'I believe', *crysy/crygy* 'to believe' and *crygyans* 'belief, faith' in the Middle Cornish texts, we obtain the following picture (the g-forms are given after the diagonal stroke):

|      | *crysaf* | *crysy/crygy* | *crygyans* |
|------|----------|---------------|------------|
| PA   | -/-      | -/-           | 0/1        |
| OM   | 2/0      | 6/0           | 0/1        |
| PC   | -/-      | 0/3           | 0/4        |
| RD   | 3/0      | 2/24          | 0/7        |
| BM   | 7/0      | 4/0           | 0/6        |
| TH   | -/-      | 17/1          | 0/10       |
| SA   | -/-      | 0/2           | 0/1        |
| CW   | -/-      | 0/4           | 0/2        |

**Table 1**

The first point to notice here is that *crysaf* always has *s*, *crygyans* always *g* (the spelling *crisgians* in TH has not been included). This is compelling evidence that <s> and <g> are not in free variation. The second point to notice is that the hesitation *St Issey/St Jidgey* is reflected in *crysy/crygy*. We appear to have two separate groups among the texts. OM, BM and TH prefer *crysy*, while PC, RD, SA and CW prefer *crygy*. The position is similar, though not identical, in the case of *pysaf* 'I pray', *pysy* 'to pray'. I tabulate the instances with those of *pysadow/peiadow* 'prayer' in Table 2. Again forms in *g/i* are given after the diagonal stroke.

|      | *pysaf* | *pysy/pygy* | *pysadow/peiadow* |
|------|---------|-------------|-------------------|
| PA   | -/-     | 7/0         | 1/0               |
| OM   | 2/0     | 5/0         | 1/0               |
| PC   | 2/0     | 1/6         | 0/3               |
| RD   | 4/0     | 0/6         | -/-               |
| BM   | 10/0    | 31/0        | 0/7               |
| TH   | -/-     | 1/0         | 2/0               |
| SA   | -/-     | 0/1         | 1/1               |
| CW   | 0/2     | 0/1         | -/-               |

**Table 2**

Here *pysaf* is spelt universally with an *s* except in CW. Presumably the 1st person sg. in CW, *pydgyaf* (CW 1364, 1670) has been reshaped on the basis of the verbal noun. It can hardly be from a dialectal 3rd sg. *[pi:dʒ] (cf. *oydge* 'age' CW 2101), since the 3rd sg. in CW ends in [z]: *my ath pyese* CW 617, *ath pys* CW 172.[38] As far as the verbal noun in Table 2 is concerned, it is obvious that the texts hesitate in their spelling in precisely the same way as with *crysy*. PA clearly falls into the *s*-group (there was no evidence for *crys* in PA), as do OM, BM and TH. On the other hand, PC, RD, SA and CW prefer *g*. The sample is small, but is agreement with the pattern vis-à-vis *crysy* gives it the appearance of verisimilitude. Notice incidentally that both *pysy* and *pygy* survive in Late Cornish. Lhuyd gives both *pizi* and *pidzhi* (AB: 250b, AB: 223).

As far as both *crysy* and *pysy* are concerned, BM is the text least likely to palatalize. This does not mean, however, that BM never palatalizes before a high front vowel. Note, for example, the quite remarkable alternation: *dewosa*, *dewose* 'bleed' BM 1575, 1584, 1619, but *dewogys* 'bled' BM 1556.

A further isogloss cuts across the *pysy/pygy* division. PC and BM regularly have [dʒ] in the word for 'prayer', while *pysadow* occurs elsewhere (though there are no examples from either RD or CW), and SA has one example of each. The basic form *[pidzadow] is analogical anyway, since *d* would not assibilate before *a*. The reason that *dz* in *[pidzadow] was palatalized in some dialects is probably to be sought in the position of the accent. It would appear that *dz* had a tendency to become [dʒ] before back vowels, if such back vowels bore the accent. This would explain such forms as *bohogogneth* 'poverty' BM 2010, *bohogogyon* 'poor people' BM 4204. For the alternation of *kerensa* with *kerengeak* [kerendzeðek] in TH, see 2.7 above.

If we look at the reflexes of Old Cornish *ni(n)d* 'not' before forms of the verb *bos* 'to be', we obtain the following interesting picture (again *g*-forms are given after the diagonal stroke):

|      | *nyns yw* | *nyns ues* | *nyns usy* | *nyns o* | *nyns esa* |
|------|-----------|------------|------------|----------|------------|
| PA   | 0/3       | 0/4        | 0/1        | 0/8      | 0/3        |
| OM   | 3/0       | 17/0       | 1/0        | -/-      | -/-        |
| PC   | 7/0       | 4/0        | -/-        | -/-      | -/-        |
| RD   | 12/0      | 2/0        | 1/0        | -/-      | 1/1        |
| BM   | 16/0      | 14/0       | 1/0        | 2/0      | 1/0        |
| TH   | 19/3      | 15/5       | 8/3        | 10/2     | 4/1        |
| SA   | 0/9       | 0/2        | 0/2        | 0/4      | 0/2        |
| CW   | 1/6       | 0/11       | -/-        | -/-      | 0/2        |

**Table 3**

---

38 Notice, however, Pryce under "Mottoes and Sentences" cites *me a pidge thu Deew* 'I pray to God'.

It is apparent from this table that all Middle Cornish texts favour either the *s*-forms (OM, PC, RD, BM) or the *g*-forms (PA, SA, CW). There is no variation except in TH. Clearly the writer's dialect was a mixed one. At all events, there is a little support in the above table for the contention that <s> are in free variation. The origin of *nyng* rather than *nyns* is not difficult to explain. *Nyng* < *[nɪnd] arose spontaneously in some dialects before a hight front vowel in *yw* 'is'. This was then generalized. *Nyns* on the other hand represents the normal development of *nind* before *ues* [œːs] and *usy*/*ugy* [yzɪ, ydʒɪ].

I have already alluded to the different treatment of Old Cornish -*d*- in *esof*, *esa*, etc., on the one hand, and *usy*, *ugy* on the other. The following table gives the spelling of the three forms of *esof* 'I am', *esa*/*ega* 'was' and *usy*/*ugy* 'is'.

Here again the picture is as one would expect. With *esof* there is no variation; <s> is universal. With *esa* <s> is much commoner than <g>. On the other hand, *ugy* is slightly commoner overall than *usy*. *Ege* in RD and *ega* in TH are presumably the result of palatalization before the original -*e* of the ending: *[edze] > [edʒe] > [edʒə].

In Table 4 below, *ege* has yielded to paradigmatic pressure from *esof*, *esos*, etc., and *esa* is the usual form. Only with the high front ending in *usy*, *ugy* is palatalization at all common. Notice incidentally that SA not only exhibits five examples of *esa* and none of *ega*, but also has a number of instances of *era* < *[eza].

|      | *esof* | *esa* | *usy* |
|------|--------|-------|-------|
| PA   | -/-    | 44/0  | 0/2   |
| OM   | -/-    | 1/0   | 1/3   |
| PC   | 1/0    | -/-   | 0/1   |
| RD   | -/-    | 3/1   | 1/3   |
| BM   | 3/0    | 3/0   | 4/0   |
| TH   | 2/0    | 44/1  | 37/36 |
| SA   | -/-    | 5/0   | 0/13  |
| CW   | 6/0    | -/-   | 6/1   |

**Table 4**

## 16. Wosa 'after'

I have already discussed the word 'after' in CW. The distribution of *s*- and *g*-forms in the texts as a whole is as follows (*g*-forms are given after the diagonal stroke): PA -/-; OM 0/2; PC 1/5; RD 0/3; BM 7/0; Th 31/0; SA -/-; CW 7/0. Clearly [wozə] is the only form in BM, TH and CW. There is no "free variation". The three plays of the *Ordinalia* prefer [wodʒə]. Reflexes of both [wozə] and [wodʒə] occur in Late Cornish, as has been noted before.

One of the two instances in OM is not *woge* but *wege* (OM 2828). This is probably not a mistake, but a historic variant. The British form was *wodiɣ*; with *i*-affection this gave Old Welsh *guetig*, Welsh *wedi*, Middle Cornish *wege*.

An unaffected *wodiy persisted side-by-side with *wediy, however, giving Breton *goude* and Middle Cornish *wose, wosa* (Lewis and Pedersen, 1961: 109). It is possible that Middle Cornish *woge* is a conflation of *wediy > wege and *wodiy > wose.

### 17. Tressa, tryge 'third'

The Proto-British word for 'third' was *tritiyo-, giving Welsh *trydydd*, Breton *trede*. The regular Middle Cornish development would have been *tryge, trege* if [d] > [dz] > [dʒ], and *tryse* if [dz] became [z]. *Tryge, trege* occurs five times in RD (339, 452, 681, 691, 2605), but nowhere else in Middle Cornish. Elsewhere the form is *tresse, tressa, tryssa, trissa*. This form in PA, OM, BM, TH and CW occurs in all 32 times. *Tryse* is nowhere attested. Loth (1897: 416) takes *tryssa, tressa* as an orthographic variant of *trege*, with <ss> as yet another graph for [dʲ]. He cannot be right. First, because [dʲ] does not exist, and secondly, because <ss> is used regularly in Middle Cornish as a graph for [s] between vowels from a variety of sources, e.g. *brassa* 'greater', *ressys* 'thou gavest', *grassa* 'to thank', *Massen* < Lat. *Maximus*.

In *tryssa, tressa* the medial consonant is by analogy with *nessa* 'next'. The series: *kensa* 'first', *nessa* 'next', *tryse* 'third' has quite understandably become *kensa, nessa, tryssa*. Although *tryssa* is the customary form in standard Middle Cornish, the (?western) dialect of RD prefers *tryge*. So also does Late Cornish, for John Boson writes *tridgea, tridgia* (Padel, 1975: 52, 55).

### 18 Back-spellings, etc.

The alternation of [z] and [dʒ] in speech obviously led to a certain amount of confusion in spelling. If, as seems probable, [z] was considered preferable to [dʒ] in some words, one mught expect scribes to substitute <s> for <g>, even where <g> was the correct spelling. This indeed has happened in a few cases. Note, for example, *ow hobersen* 'my habergeon' for *ow hobergen* at RD 2536 and *nynsevith* (TH 40), *nynsevas* (TH 49) for *nyngevith* and *nyngevas* respectively.

More important than such purely graphemic slips are the cases of back-formation in speech itself. BM is the text least likely to write <g> where it is possible to write <s>. I take this to mean that the scribe was particularly careful to adhere to standard norms. Camborne was in all probability, however, in an area where *s*-forms and *g*-forms were somewhat confused. This factor appears to have led the scribe of BM to adopt spellings in which *g* is unetymological, e.g. *martegen* 'perhaps' (Breton *marteze*) at BM 61. *Martegen* was probably the form in the Camborne dialect.

One could also perhaps explain *falge* (< English *false*) at BM 777, 987, 1161, etc., and *calge* (Breton *cals*) at BM 2046 in this way. It may be, however, that these two forms are analogical in origin. Compare also Late Cornish *algia* [aldʒə] instead of the expected *alsa* (Welsh (g)allasai). *Falge, calge* and *algia* have in all probability been influenced by the frequency of forms in *-lg-* from Old Cornish *-lt-*, e.g. *\*gwelgek* 'grassy' (*Illiswilgig*), *\*algyow* 'shores', etc.

A similar analogical formation is probably the explanation for certain place-names. The word *lesyow* 'herbs' (Welsh *llysiau*) occurs in the place-names *Lidgiow, Bithen Ligdeo* and possibly *Ponslego* and *Carn Lodgia* (Padel, 1985: 142 (s.v. *les* 'plant')). Here *lesyow* has becaome *\*legyow* under the influence of forms like *\*regyow* 'fords' (< Old Cornish *\*ridiou*) and Late Cornish *lidzhiw* (< *\*ludeu*) 'ashes'.

Before leaving the topic of how the texts spell the reflexes of Old Cornish *d*, the following point should be made. Judging by the distribution of *s-* and *g-* forms, it is apparent that the dialect of OM differs considerably from that of PC and RD. Whatever the original authorship of the three plays, it seems likely that the scribal exemplar of the *Ordinalia* in the Bodleian manuscript was written by two different hands. Moreover, the original scribe of OM was probably form further east in Cornwall than the scribe of PC and RD.

## 19. Conclusions

Neither /$t^j$/ nor /$d^j$/ ever existed in Cornish. Where Old Cornish *t, d* were assibilated, they became in standard Middle Cornish either [tʃ], e.g. *chy*, [s], e.g. *pyskessa*, [z], e.g. *bohosek*, or [dʒ], e.g. *bolungeth, an geyth, crygyans*. Some more western dialects, where standard Cornish had [z], written <s>, frequently preferred [dʒ]. [dʒ] for standard [z] is not common in the Middle Cornish texts, but is abundant in our fragmentary remains of Late Cornish, which are exclusively western in provenance.

Since neither /$t^j$/ nor /$d^j$/ ever existed in Cornish, there is no reason to introduce them into the revived language. Indeed there is every reason to resist their introduction. A historically accurate orthography can perfectly well indicate the phonemic reflexes of Old Cornish *t, d* in Middle Cornish with <t>, <d>, <ss>, <s>, <ch> and <j>, i.e. as is the case already in Unified Cornish. Whatever orthography is recommended for revived Cornish, it ought not contain the unnecessary and unhistorical graphs <tj> and <dj>. My advice to the linguistic planners of the Cornish revival would be that of John Chyanhor's master to him after three years' labour (Padel, 1985: 17): *Bethez gueskez duath, ken gueskel eneth, rag edda eu an guella point a skeeans oll*: 'Do nothing without second thoughts, for that is the best advice of all.'

# WHICH CORNISH?*

I am very happy to be here in Cornwall after an absence of a mere 29 years. It is encouraging to hear so much Cornish spoken, even if it is distressing to know that the revival is very split—and completely unnecessarily as well.

You will, I am sure, want to know who I think I am, coming over here and telling you how you should revive your language. I can almost hear you asking yourselves "Who exactly is this interloper?" I was born and brought up on the Essex side of London. While at school I taught myself Cornish from Caradar's *Cornish Simplified* (1959). I won a prize for Cornish verse in the Gorsedd competition of 1961 and still in my teens became a language bard in 1962 in Newquay, where I took the bardic name *Golvan* "Sparrow". This wasn't because I saw myself as a Cockney sparrow; it was more because I thought of the sparrow like myself as small and chirpy.

I read Classics and English language in Oxford and then, because I had an interest in Cornish, I did a postgraduate course in Celtic there and learnt Irish. I went to live Ireland in 1967 and have been in Ireland virtually continuously ever since. I now make a comfortable living in University College, Dublin teaching Irish to the Irish through the medium of Irish. I have, of course, never lost my interest in Cornish, though I was a quiescent member of the revival for years. It was only the adoption of Kernowek Kemyn that jolted me out of my semi-retirement from Cornish. I believe that Kernowek Kemyn is not Cornish and am very unhappy that it was ever proposed or promoted.

In 1995 *Kernewek dre Lyther* published a book of mine, *Cornish Today*, in which I examine the three kinds of Cornish at present being used. I conclude in my book that Unified is by far the least unsatisfactory form of the language and Kernowek Kemyn is so mistaken that it should be abandoned. Dr Charles Thomas of the Institute of Cornish Studies called it "an unjustifiably wrong turn". I believe he was absolutely right. I have not the slightest doubt that Kernowek Kemyn will be abandoned. The only question is how soon.

I do not here wish to say much about so-called "Modern Cornish", better called "Revived Late Cornish". It seems unwise to me to base the revival on the Late Cornish of the decline rather than on the rich and idiomatic language of the Middle Cornish period. The attempt to revive Cornish in the Anglicized spelling of the seventeenth century, I believe, has little to recommend it.

---

\* A lecture given in Lostwithiel in September 1996, chaired by Dr Philip Payton, Director of the Institute of Cornish Studies.

# WHICH CORNISH?

Revived Late Cornish and Kernowek Kemyn alike make a fundamental error. They both assume that Middle Cornish and Late Cornish are very different and that we must therefore choose either the one or the other. This is not so. Middle Cornish and Late Cornish are effectively one and the same. This is not just my view; it was also the opinion of Henry Jenner, the first revivalist and the finest linguist Cornwall has ever had. The two forms of Cornish differ only in the matter of their spelling. Kernowek Kemyn repudiates Late Cornish in favour of Middle Cornish. Yet Kernowek Kemyn uses <k> in *krev* 'strong', *kov* 'remembrance', <hw> in *hweg* 'sweet', *hwegh* 'six' and <v> in *ov* 'I am', *gwelav* 'I see' where Unified Cornish uses <c>, <wh> and <f> respectively. These spellings in Kernowek Kemyn are Late, not Middle Cornish.

As well as *Cornish Today* I have written a *Supplement to Cornish Today* and have two further articles[1] against Kernowek Kemyn in the press. I have by the way some copies of the *Supplement* with me (a snip at £2 each and a ripping good read). If anyone wants a copy, he or she should speak to me afterwards. I intend to continue writing against Kernowek Kemyn until the desired outcome is achieved, that is, that Kernowek Kemyn is abandoned.

I am not doing so out of any personal vindictiveness. God forbid. It gives me no pleasure to find fault with other people's efforts. I criticize Kernowek Kemyn because I believe it is my duty to do so. As a professional Celticist and someone who has known Cornish for more than 30 years, I know that Kernowek Kemyn is not Cornish and I can explain why it isn't. While Kernowek Kemyn continues to be taught and promoted, it is doing the revival enormous damage. I accept of course that Kernowek Kemyn was devised and adopted in good faith by people who had the interests of Cornish at heart. One does not doubt their motives. Their judgment, however, is seriously open to question.

The supporters of Kernowek Kemyn who have read my book and the *Supplement* fall into three discrete categories, A, B and C.

A. This group is comprised of those who believe that my criticisms are valid and have already begun to distance themselves from Kernowek Kemyn. I know of several such people. Since I live outside Cornwall, I don't know of them all, but I suspect that there are others.

B. The second group are those who believe my criticisms are valid but think that it is too late to change Kernowek Kemyn now. The editor of the *KDL Newsletter* is one of these. On 15 February 1996 he wrote to a correspondent on the Continent and sent me a copy of the letter. He said:

> I wonder whether you will have read the Nicholas Williams book yet. The small amount of research I have done myself suggests to me that most of

---

1 See "'Linguistically sound principles': The case against Kernowek Kemyn", pp. 38–64 below, and "Pre-occlusion in Cornish", pp. 65–92 below.

what he says about Cornish phonology is right and that Ken George will have difficulty in countering it.

The editor of the *KDL Newsletter* nonetheless thinks that Kernowek Kemyn cannot now be replaced. The same view was expressed by the author of a letter which appeared in *An Gannas* in March 1996. The writer says:

> Nyns eus edhomm dhyn ni a yeth yw pella diberthys yn hanow skolhygieth. Kernewek Kemmyn, martesen gans gwennogennow—yw gwrians da, hag yn sur [yth] yw gwell es chanj moy
>
> [We do not need a language that is further divided in the name of scholarship. Kernowek Kemyn, perhaps with warts, is a good creation and it is certainly better than a further change].

Since Unified Cornish was the only form of the revived language for 60 years and since the Cornish Language Board did not think twice about replacing it with something inferior, this argument seems to me to have little force. Kernowek Kemyn was introduced because it was wrongly believed to be more authentic than Unified Cornish. If it can be shown that Kernowek Kemyn is far less authentic than Unified, as it can, then Kernowek Kemyn loses any *raison d'être* it may have had.

C. The third group of supporters of Kernowek Kemyn are those who believe (or at least, wish to believe) that my criticisms of Kernowek Kemyn are insubstantial and of no importance. The editor of *An Gannas* appears to fall into this category of inveterate optimists.

If anybody really does believe that my criticisms are entirely invalid, I would ask him to remember the matter of <tj> and <dj>. Let me explain. In August 1987 the Cornish Language Board adopted Kernowek Kemyn on the mistaken grounds that it was more authentic than Unified Cornish. At the same time I in Dublin acquired a copy of George's book *The Pronunciation and Spelling of Revived Cornish*. I read it and was astonished. The sounds /tʲ/ and /dʲ/ were being recommended for revived Cornish and they were to be spelt <tj> and <dj>. I could understand writing <tj> and <dj> in Dutch, Norwegian, or Croatian—but in Cornish? I wrote an article setting out why it seemed to me that /tʲ/ and /dʲ/ were mistaken. The article was finally published in 1990. Already by 1988 a typescript copy was being read here in Cornwall. In the periodical *Carn*, number 68 (Winter 1989/90), under the title *Kernowek Kemyn Up-Date* we read the following by Ken George, the deviser of Kernowek Kemyn:

> Nicholas Williams in a brilliantly argued paper to be published later this year, has put forward strong arguments to show that the phonemes /τ/ and /δ/

never existed. Close examination of his evidence confirms this.... To everyone's relief, this will mean the disappearance of the corresponding graphemes <tj> and <dj> (*Carn* 68: 16).

I dispute two aspects of that passage. In the first place, my article was in no sense brilliantly argued. I said nothing that was, in my view, not obvious to any scholar who had examined the question in detail. In the second place I take issue with the expression "his evidence". I lived and indeed live in Dublin. I had no evidence that was not available to George. All I had were the texts of Middle Cornish and Late Cornish: the *Passion Poem*, the Ordinalia, *Beunans Meriasek*, John Tregear, the Creation, the writing of the Bosons, Wella Kerew, Edward Lhuyd, Pryce and also Padel's book on place-names. None of this is *my* evidence; it was readily available to George when he suggested his <tj> and <dj>.

At all events I was instrumental in relieving Kernowek Kemyn of <tj> and <dj>. Had it had not been for my article, Kernowek Kemyn would still write **Y'n termyn eus passys yth edja trygys yn Synt Leven den ha benyn yn tyller kriys Tji an Hordh** (I am quoting from George's book *The Pronunciation and Spelling of Revived Cornish*). But for me, Kernowek Kemyn speakers would still be saying **wodja** 'after', **adjwon** 'know', **kerentja** 'love', **gantjo** 'with him', **boghodjek** 'poor', **gallodjek** 'powerful', **pedjwar** 'four', **krydji** 'believe', **pydji** 'pray', **nyndj udji** 'is not', etc. If I was correct about <tj> and <dj> (as George has admitted), is there not a *prima facie* probability that there is at least some substance to my further criticisms of Kernowek Kemyn? Kernowek Kemyn shorn of <tj> and <dj> is the still the same old Kernowek Kemyn. It is all the same vintage. Those who tell you that my criticisms are as nothing, deceive only themselves.

In my article about <tj>, <dj> I praised other aspects of Kernowek Kemyn. This I bitterly regret, since I was not telling the truth. I lauded George's efforts because I wished to encourage this new, apparently more scientific approach to Cornish. I hoped that by being polite, I would be able to get rid of the absurd <tj> and <dj>. I was aware that Kernowek Kemyn was mistaken, though I did not then realize just how mistaken it was. At the same time as I was praising George, I was writing to the publisher Len Truran advising him not to have anything to do with the new system. Foolishly, I thought that Kernowek Kemyn would not be accepted without considerable revision. How naïve I was! My greatest regret is not that I praised Kernowek Kemyn insincerely, but rather that I did not write *Cornish Today* until 1995. Had my book been published in 1988, Kernowek Kemyn would never have got as far as regrettably it has.

Ken George was the inventor of Kernowek Kemyn. I say "inventor" advisedly, since most of the sound system and the spelling of Kernowek Kemyn is fiction rather than fact. Now that I have written in detail and at length against Kernowek Kemyn, George finds himself in something of a quandary. And he certainly has my sympathy. At one moment he claims that my criticisms are worthless. The next moment he appears to admit that perhaps I may have a point here and there. In *An Gannas* December 1995 he described my critique of Kernowek Kemyn as a *chi kartennow*, 'a house of cards' and asserted that the more he looked at my arguments, the weaker they became.

In his interim response to my criticisms in the magazine *Kernow*, however, he appears to be admitting that Kernowek Kemyn is not as perfect as he had once hoped. Let me give you some passages to compare and contrast. In his 1986 book *The Pronunciation and Spelling of Revived Cornish*, George wrote:

> I can therefore state with confidence that Revived Cornish, as exemplified by the phonological base described in this chapter [i.e. Kernowek Kemyn], is closer to the Cornish of 1500 than were either OldC or LateC. What is more, it is closer to the Cornish of 1500 than is, say, the "Geordie" dialect to standard English (PSRC: 91).

Note the self-assured tone when describing Kernowek Kemyn: "I can therefore state with confidence…". That was in 1986. Since the appearance of my book in 1995, however, George is apparently not quite as convinced as he was of the excellence of Kernowek Kemyn. In *Kernow* (January 1996) he wrote:

> There is a measure of uncertainty ("experimental error") associated with the reconstruction of Cornish. Some is due to the variation within the traditional language…. Once a reconstruction approaches traditional Cornish so closely as to be within the zone of uncertainty, it is possible for two reconstructions to be within the zone of uncertainty and yet to differ (*Kernow* 14: 9-10).

A tone of certainty has been replaced by a "zone of uncertainty". Yet what George says is quite simply untrue. There is room for some uncertainty in revived Cornish and indeed I can tell you, if you wish, exactly where the uncertainties are. There is no room for the huge differences in spelling and sounds between Kernowek Kemyn and Unified Cornish. It is no use invoking "experimental error" here, since there is no "experiment". We are talking about historical linguistics, not natural science. We can't put Kernowek Kemyn and Unified Cornish in test-tubes and leave them overnight; nor can we examine them under the microscope. We can do nothing but read the remains of traditional Cornish as closely as possible and draw our conclusions. It is not a question of "experimental error" but of *error* pure and simple. Kernowek Kemyn is mistaken.

George wrongly believes that Middle Cornish had two long /o/ vowels. Since he believes that there were two such vowels in Middle Cornish, one open and one closed, George is compelled to spell one of them: **koes** 'wood', **goes** 'blood', **hwoer** 'sister', etc. Indeed he criticizes Nance for not making the distinction. In *The Pronunciation and Spelling of Revived Cornish* George says of Nance:

> There are so many such pairs [i.e. words distinguished—according to George—by a closed versus an open long *o*], that is is difficult to believe that Nance was unaware of this difference; and one suspects that he deliberately over-simplified the language to make it easier to learn (PSRC: 126).

Nance was absolutely meticulous in all things. If he had believed there was a difference, he certainly would not have suppressed it. The problem here is not about Middle Cornish so much as Late Cornish, since in Late Cornish some words with Middle Cornish long /oː/ have long /uː/. George does not seem to realize that Nance was perfectly well aware of the problem and attempts to solve it in the introduction to his 1938 dictionary. (Note, however, in the short passage that I have just quoted George says: "one suspects [Nance] deliberately over-simplified the language to make it easier to learn." That was in 1986.)

In 1996 after the appearance of my book George wrote as follows:

> The orthography of Kernewek Kemmyn has got its priorities right: it balances the need for historical authenticity with the need for a phonemic system, giving priority to the latter (*Kernow* 14: 10).

By "phonemic" George means that the spelling should be regular and involve one symbol or set of symbols per sound. Kernowek Kemyn replaced Unified Cornish for one reason only: that it was believed to be more authentic. Now apparently, as a result of my criticism of Kernowek Kemyn, George is saying that authenticity isn't all it's cracked up to be. Authenticity is all very well but a regular spelling takes precedence. *George believes that it is more important for revived Cornish to be regular than to be authentic.* If I may be allowed to paraphrase, George seems to be saying that Kernowek Kemyn simplifies Cornish in order to make it easier to learn. Yet in 1986, before my book had appeared, George actually rebuked Nance for doing just that. He wrote: *'one suspects that [Nance] deliberately over-simplified the language to make it easier to learn.'* Ironically by insisting on two long *o* vowels, when Middle Cornish had only one, George is making Cornish harder to learn as well as less genuine.

Let me digress here for a moment to say something about the difficulty or otherwise of revived Cornish. It is the job of those reconstructing Cornish to render the reconstruction as authentic as possible. Authenticity is the overriding criterion—indeed it ought to be the *sole* criterion. When learners come to the reconstruction, however, they will learn it at their own pace and to their own degree of competence. They may favour "easy" constructions and forms over "hard" ones. That is at the level of the learner only. The underlying reconstruction must be as authentic as possible, irrespective of complexity or simplicity.

To those who espouse Kernowek Kemyn I would say this: we are reviving a language as we believe it to have been. If we know our reconstruction is mistaken, then we must change it, whatever the cost. Otherwise we are not reviving Cornish. Kernowek Kemyn was devised among other things to give revived Cornish academic respectability. You will not be astonished to hear that Celticists outside Cornwall are very sceptical indeed of Kernowek Kemyn's claims to be authentic. Now that Kernowek Kemyn itself is no longer claiming to be authentic, who shall blame them?

Why and how is Kernowek Kemyn mistaken? In the first place, one must question the wisdom of the Cornish Language Board in adopting Kernowek Kemyn so quickly. From 1928-1987 there was only one kind of revived Cornish in existence, Unified Cornish. Moreover Unified Cornish contained within itself a considerable amount of variation and scope for revision. Correction of a few points is probably necessary. But the Cornish Language Board did not set up a committee to examine Unified Cornish and recommend improvements. That would have been sensible. Instead they adopted Kernowek Kemyn, a totally new and unhistorical form of Cornish—a radical rewriting of the language that does not resemble in sounds or spelling the traditional Celtic speech of Cornwall at *any* period in her history. Kernowek Kemyn is the work of one man, not a professional linguist, let alone a professional Celticist. Before adopting Kernowek Kemyn in its entirety, the Cornish Language Board did not submit the new system to a panel of Celtic scholars outside Cornwall. Nor did they canvass users of Cornish to ask them what they thought of the new form of the language. The Cornish Language Board adopted and began vigorously to promote Kernowek Kemyn without any independent assessment and with a minimum of consultation. To say that the Board acted imprudently is an understatement.

Now that I have shown, and continue to show, that Kernowek Kemyn is very mistaken indeed, various members of the Cornish Language Board are expressing anger towards me. A classic case of shooting the messenger.

The errors in Kernowek Kemyn are threefold: theoretical, orthographical and phonological. I'll deal very briefly with these in turn.

### Theoretical errors of Kernowek Kemyn

Kernowek Kemyn is constructed on the assumption that Middle Cornish is very close to Breton and Welsh. If the Welsh and Breton evidence and the evidence of the Middle Cornish texts are at variance, Kernowek Kemyn gives more heed to Welsh and Breton than to the texts. Yet it is quite clear that Middle Cornish is very different from Welsh and Breton. The Welsh for 'father' is **tad** and for 'after' is **wedi**. The Breton for 'father' is **tad** and the word for 'after' is **goude**. In Middle Cornish, however, 'father' is **tas** with an *s* and 'after' is **wose** with an *s* or **woge** with a *g*. This change of *d* to *s* or *g* occurred in

Cornish at some time between Old Cornish and our earliest Middle Cornish texts, *c.* 1150–1250. The assibilitation of **d** is unique to Cornish and does not occur in either of its sister languages. Such an important change indicates that something very far-reaching has occurred between Old and Middle Cornish. If Cornish is unlike Welsh and Breton in this important respect, the experienced historical linguist would expect it to differ from them significantly in a host of other ways. Yet it apparently never once occurred to George that Middle Cornish might be very different from both Welsh and Breton.

The real difference between Cornish on the one hand and Welsh and Breton on the other is the influence of English. Until the early nineteenth century there was little English in Wales and there was, of course, no English in Brittany. In Cornwall, to judge by the Bodmin Manumissions, Old English (Anglo-Saxon) had made inroads already in the Old Cornish period. It seems that between Old and Middle Cornish the language was strongly affected by Middle English and had become in some ways more like English and less like Welsh and Breton. Nowhere was this so important as in the vowels. This whole development I call the Prosodic Shift and I can show exactly how it has influenced Middle Cornish phonology and why therefore Kernowek Kemyn is seriously at odds with the evidence.

Cornish has been heavily influenced by an early form of English, but that does not make Cornish any less Cornish or any less Celtic. Cornish became extinct in the late 18th century and revived Cornish is the language of an earlier period. As a result there are ways in which revived Cornish is more Celtic than, for example, modern Welsh.

### Orthographical errors in Kernowek Kemyn

Even if Middle Cornish were not radically different from Old Cornish, Kernowek Kemyn can be faulted in another way. Unified Cornish seeks to regularize the spelling of the medieval texts. It widens the use of <j> to places where the scribes write <g> for example **yn y jy** for Middle Cornish **yn y gy** 'in his house'. Moreover Unified Cornish borrows <dh> from Lhuyd to represent the sound of voiced **th**. Some people criticize on the grounds that it is never used in traditional Cornish. The *Passion Poem*, however, uses the letter yogh <ʒ> to represent the sound of voiced **th**. I like to understand <dh> as just a convenient and modern way of representing the symbol <ʒ> on contemporary keyboards. After all Edward Lhuyd used for the yogh of the *Passion Poem* as early as 1707.

Generally speaking therefore there is little or nothing in Unified Cornish that is not in the Middle Cornish texts. Kernowek Kemyn on the other hand rewrites the spelling of Middle Cornish entirely and produces a bizarre and exotic spelling. **Kammbronn** is only the most notorious example. The late Peter Pool rightly observed:

Kernewek Kemmyn is something quite different, an entirely artificial creation which does not resemble Cornish as used by Cornish people at any time in history. To those accustomed to Unified ... Kemyn has an alien and somehow sinister appearance, as if the language had somehow been taken over by robots and reduced to the status of a code.

Except that Kernowek Kemyn is not a code, since a code is generally expected to be consistent.

Had the sound system of Kernowek Kemyn been even partially correct, this distortion of the orthography might—and I say *might*—have been justified. Since the phonology of Kernowek Kemyn is very mistaken, the distortion is as inauthentic as it is unnecessary. Kernowek Kemyn looks wrong because it is wrong.

## Phonological errors in Kernowek Kemyn

The spelling of Kernowek Kemyn with its novel use of <i> and <y>, its <oe> and its curious doubling of letters is based on certain mistaken assumptions about the the sound-system of Middle Cornish. These assumptions can be summarized as follows:

1.  Kernowek Kemyn is unaware of the alternation of vowels in monosyllables and disyllables: **byw** but **bewnans**, **bedheugh** but **bydh**, etc. In fact Kernowek Kemyn is inconsistent since it writes **blydhen** 'year' not **bledhen**, **gwydhenn** 'tree' not **gwedhenn**, **hwyja** 'vomit' not **hweja** but it does write **Kernewek** rather than *Kernywek and **kewsel** rather than *kywsel. I have discussed this whole question elsewhere and do not intend to say anything more about it here except this: Kernowek Kemyn is badly mistaken on this point because the deviser does not seem to know about the vocalic alternation in Welsh which also occurs in Cornish. The alternation has been largely lost in Breton and this may in part explain why the deviser of Kernowek Kemyn is ignorant of this essential feature of Middle Cornish.
2.  The second assumption wrongly made by Kernowek Kemyn is even more serious. Kernowek Kemyn assumes that Cornish, like Welsh and Breton had three lengths of vowel, short, half-long and long. Kernowek Kemyn also assumes that this system of three lengths disapppeared in the early 17th century (*c.* 1600) since it is clear that Late Cornish had only two lengths, short and long as in English. Kernowek Kemyn is badly astray on this point.

The reshaping of vowel length could not possibly have happened *c.* 1600 for several reasons. The loss of half-length was a major change in the language. If it had occurred *c.* 1600, one would expect to find vast differences in the sound system of John Tregear (*c.* 1555) and *The Creation of the World* (1612). Such differences are wholly absent—indeed *The Creation of the World* is more archaic

34

in ways than *Beunans Meriasek* (1504). Secondly we know from Lhuyd that vowels in monosyllables had lengthened before *c.* 1690. They can hardly have shortened *c.* 1600 only to lengthen again within 80 or so years. The change from three lengths to two lengths (the Prosodic Shift) is part of the same movement seen in the assibilation of **tad** to **tas**. It occurred at the end of the Old Cornish period under the impact of Middle English. It is overwhelmingly apparent from the Middle Cornish texts themselves that there was no half-length in Middle Cornish.

This question is absolutely crucial for understanding why Kernowek Kemyn is mistaken but it is rather technical. Welsh and Breton have three possible lengths of vowel: long, half-long and short. This means that vowels can either be of a single length (short), of a double length (half-long) or of a triple length (long). Take the Welsh word **tad** 'father'. That has a long vowel. You can almost here the three *a*'s in it: **taaad**. The plural **tadau** 'fathers' has a half-long vowel: **taadau**. It is of only two lengths. The word **mam** 'mother' and the plural **mamau** 'mothers' have a short vowel of one length only. I have taken my examples from Welsh but Breton is similar.

Notice two things. In the first instance native speakers feel that half-long and long are really aspects of the same thing since neither is short. Vowels to the native-speaker are either short or not-short. Modern Breton grammars actually go one further and treat half-long as the same as long. The second thing to notice is that a unit of length is known as a *mora*, the Latin word for 'delay'. **Tad** therefore has a trimoric vowel, whereas **tadau** is bimoric and **mam** is unimoric.

Old Cornish had this threefold system. Under the impact of Middle English it appears that Middle Cornish lost the threefold distinction and acquired a simple twofold one, long and short. In fact what happened was this: stressed syllables where possible were all shortened but were correspondingly more vigorously pronounced. This meant that three morae became two morae and two morae became one mora. This process I refer to as the Prosodic Shift. Take a word like **myres**, **myras** 'to look' and the monosyllabic **myr**! 'look!' or **ef a vyr** 'he looks'. Before the shift the monosyllable **myr**! look! had three morae: **miiir**. The dissyllable **myres**, **myras** had two morae: **miires**. After the shift **miiir** with three morae reduced to two: **miir**, whereas **miires** reduced to one **mires**. **Miir** is still not-short. It is still longish, because it still has two morae, the length of the original half-long.

The stressed vowel in **mires** <myres> on the other hand is now short. The vowel was half-long and is now short. A short vowel is relatively more lax and less tense than its long counterpart. This means that short *i* is open, i.e. the tongue and organs of speech are slacker than for long *i*. Compare English **sheep** with English **ship**. The open slack vowel in **mires** is so much lower in the mouth than the vowel in **miir** that it is near to *e*. Short *y* and short *e* are not always kept separate in Middle Cornish.

If what I am saying is correct, we should expect in the Middle Cornish texts to find **myr**! 'look!' and **ef a vyr** 'he looks' always spelt with <y>, but the dissyllabic forms **meras**, **veras** to be spelt on occasion with <e>. This is precisely what we do find. Notice the following examples of the disyllable with *e*: **meras** PA 215d, TH 49a, 50a; **veras** PA 168b, OM 2325, BM 4074, TH 2, 3, 7, 9; **veres** BM 4351; **verys** PC 1257 and the following examples of the monosyllable with *y*: **myr** BM 935, 1805, 3194, 3229, 3270, 3656; cf. also the monosyllabic form in **my a vyr** 'I will look' OM 1251. There are instances of **myras** with <y>, but none of *mer with <e>. This indicates that *e* and *y* in such items are not in free variation. **Meras** clearly has a short vowel. If so, Kernowek Kemyn is mistaken in believing that it has a half-long one and therefore in spelling it with the same vowel /i/ as the monosyllable **mir**. Kernowek Kemyn **mires** is, therefore, wrong.

But there are very many other words which Kernowek Kemyn spells with <i> when it is quite clear that the vowel is not /i/ but /ɪ/ <y> or /e/ <e>. Examples include **whelas** 'to seek', **y gela** 'the other', **screfa** 'to write' but **scryf**! 'write!'. The word **trega** 'dwell' is interesting. George is perplexed by the way in which this word frequently has *e/y* rather than /i/ and he admits he doesn't understand why. At all events he spells it with <y> rather than <i>. In fact of course **trega** has *e* in disyllables only. In monosyllables the vowel is always *y*. Note the following from John Tregear: *may hallan ny bewa ha* **trega** *in charite, ha nena ny a* **dryg** *in du ha gans du, ha du a* **dryg** *innan ny* 'that we may dwell in charity and then we will dwell in God and with God and God will dwell in us' (TH 30). The monosyllable **dryg** < **tryg** has two morae: **triig**, whereas the dissyllable has one mora in the stressed vowel: **trega** < **tryga**. That one sentence is enough to show that in TH there was no half-length. Similar examples could be taken from BM and the rest of the texts. If Middle Cornish had no half-length—and it didn't—then the arbitrary rewriting of the spelling system in Kernowek Kemyn is not only unnecessary, it is mistaken.

There are many further errors in Kernowek Kemyn that are a direct result of the same fundamental error, namely the assumption that Middle Cornish had half-length. I have set them out in detail in *Cornish Today* and elsewhere. One mistake in particular I have already mentioned. That is the belief that Middle Cornish had two different long *o* sounds spelt <o> and <oe> in Kernowek Kemyn respectively. Perhaps in the discussion after this talk there will be an opportunity to explain how Kernowek Kemyn has misread the evidence and why therefore such spellings as **koes** 'wood', **loes** 'grey', **hwoer** 'sister, **ev a woer** ' he knows', **oen** 'lamb', etc. are inauthentic. The editor of the *KDL Newsletter* by the way agrees with me (and Nance and Jenner and Caradar) on this point. In January of this year he wrote to George and sent me a copy of the letter. He wrote:

Mes gans hemma oll kales yw krysi nag yw an gwir gans N[icholas] W[illiams].... Mars yw gwir nag eus marnas unn son o, ni a yll defendya yn mes an lytherennans "oe" yw nebes hager dell yw res avowa ha ny vydh res perthi kov mars yw res skrifa po ha leverel koedh po kodh. Ytho nowodhow da vydh

[All the same it is difficult to believe that Nicholas Williams is not right.... If it is true that there is only one sound o, we can remove the spelling "oe" which, it must be admitted, is rather unsightly and it will not be necessary to remember whether to write <o> or <oe> and to say "koedh" or "kodh". It will therefore be a change for the better.]

Unified Cornish is greatly superior to Kernowek Kemyn and should never have been abandoned by the Cornish Language Board. I have recommended a number of minor emendations to the spelling of Unified Cornish. These have been accepted by Agan Tavas. I also suggest simplifying the construction of sentences in Unified Cornish in line with the language of John Tregear and the other Tudor texts. I am currently, with the approval of Agan Tavas, working on a handbook of revised Unified Cornish or *Kernowek Unys Amendys*.[2] I hope the book will be finished before the end of this year and will be available early in 1997. Emending Unified Cornish is sensible. Rewriting Cornish is not.

Before I finish let me make a plea to you all. If you use Kernowek Kemyn, please give it up as soon as you can. If you are thinking of learning it, don't. If you hesitate between Kernowek Kemyn and Unified Cornish, stick with Unified. The revival cannot afford three systems, particularly when the most widely used form of the language is so mistaken. Cornwall needs her own language but that language is not Kernowek Kemyn.

The time has come to begin the retreat from Kernowek Kemyn. The revival will achieve neither authenticity, academic respectability nor unity until Kernowek Kemyn is rejected. Only when Kernowek Kemyn is abandoned, will Cornish speakers find peace of mind.

---

2   This appeared as *Clappya Kernowek* (Williams 1997).

# "LINGUISTICALLY SOUND PRINCIPLES": THE CASE AGAINST KERNOWEK KEMYN*

I recently published a book (CT) in which I provided a critique of the forms of Neo-Cornish currently in use. Among other things I listed 25 ways in which I believe the sound-system and spelling of Kernowek Kemyn to be mistaken. I further suggested that in the interests of the Cornish revival Kernowek Kemyn should be replaced. Many of my arguments were of a somewhat technical nature. I should like, therefore, to discuss some of them here in a more general way and thereafter to make some brief comments about the future of the revival.

Kernowek Kemyn is the creation of Ken George of the Department of Marine Science, University of Plymouth. George's new pronunciation and orthography were first published in PSRC in 1986. The Cornish Language Board accepted his proposals in July 1987 on the grounds that the new system was more authentic than Unified Cornish. This assessment of Kernowek Kemyn was unduly optimistic at the time, since the proponents of Kernowek Kemyn themselves have subsequently admitted that the system, as it was first proposed, contained a serious flaw. The error in question involved the spelling and pronunciation of words like *chy* 'house', *kerensa* 'love' and *wosa* 'after'.

## The "phonemes" *tj* and *dj*

Cornish differs from Welsh and Breton in its treatment of inherited internal and final *d* and internal *nt*. The Welsh and Breton for 'father' is *tad* whereas the Cornish is *tas*. The Welsh for 'after' is *wedi* and the Breton is *goude*. In Middle Cornish 'after' is written *wose* or *woge*. The Breton for 'love' is *karantez* whereas the Middle Cornish is either *kerense* or *kerenge*. George interpreted this alternation of *s* and *g* in the Middle Cornish texts as reflecting a sound that was difficult to represent. He assumed that the underlying sound in *wose*/*woge* was similar to the combination *d* + *y* in the English phrase *could you*, for example. He argued that this collocation of sounds was difficult to represent properly and that therefore the scribes sometimes wrote *s* and sometimes *g*. George's interpretation of *s ~ g* was not his own, since he was taking up a suggestion first made by Joseph Loth in 1897 (RC 18: 410-24). George recommended spelling the sound in question as *dj*. Similarly he recommended spelling the *s*/*g* of *kerense*/*kerenge* as *tj*. He also proposed spelling *chy* 'house' as *tji*.

In an article which was eventually published in 1990 (Williams 1990) I adduced a whole range of arguments, theoretical, orthographical and

---

*   First published in *Cornish Studies*. Second series: Four. 1996. Exeter: University of Exeter Press. Pp. 64–87. ISBN 0-85989-523-8

toponymic, to show that the "phonemes" *dj* and *tj* had never existed and should not therefore be introduced into the revived language. George read my article in unpublished form and agreed with my arguments. As a result *dj* and *tj* were removed from Kernowek Kemyn and were replaced by *s*, *j* or *ch*, exactly as I had proposed. The graphs *s*, *j* and *ch* were those used in Unified Cornish and by the Middle Cornish scribes themselves, though the texts used *g* rather than *j* in certain cases.

Several things should be noticed about this episode. In the first place, Kernowek Kemyn before 1989-90 might have contained sentences like *Nyndj edjov vy ow krydji yth edja Kerentja gantjo yn y dji* 'I do not believe that Kerensa was with him in his house' where Unified would have written *Nyns esof vy ow cryjy yth esa Kerensa ganso yn y jy*. The spelling of Unified Cornish is very much closer to the spelling of the Middle Cornish texts than Kernowek Kemyn is to them. The Unified forms *nyns, esof, Kerensa, ganso* are all attested in the Middle Cornish texts; *cryjy* and *jy* are more usually *crygy* and *gy* respectively. None of the Kemmyn forms *nyndj, edjov, krydji, kerentja, gantjo, dji* is attested in Cornish at any period. Unified Cornish attempts to systematize the spelling of Middle Cornish while Kernowek Kemyn rewrites it.

In the second place, the two graphs *dj* and *tj* were so bizarre that many Cornish-speakers could not bring themselves to use them. When I demonstrated that they had never existed, some supporters of Kernowek Kemyn were delighted. If *dj* and *tj* were abolished, then the major obstacle to the general acceptance of Kernowek Kemyn would be removed. *Dj* and *tj* were indeed replaced by *s* and *j* and the proponents of Kernowek Kemyn continued as though nothing had happened. One wonders whether this was really prudent.

When one major feature of their system had been proved to be seriously mistaken, it might have been wise of them to pause and take stock. They had, after all, claimed that *dj* and *tj* were an integral part of Cornish that had gone unnoticed hitherto. W. Brown put it as follows:

> Some of these genuine Cornish sounds have not before been recognised though they occur in other Celtic languages. Such a pair are the "tj" and "dj" of the new system where the "j" acts like the glide vowels "i" and "e" of Gaelic in palatalising the preceding sound (*Carn* 60: 18).

Brown's comparison of Gaelic here is baffling. The Gaelic languages have a fully-developed opposition between palatalized and velarized consonants. The Brythonic languages lack such a double series of consonants and the comparision is therefore invalid. The reason that *dj* and *tj* had not hitherto been recognized was obvious: they never existed.

I explained the alternation of *s* and *g/j* as follows. Everywhere Old Cornish *d* became *dz* and this latter in final position simplified to [z], written *s*. In some cases, however, the consonant [dz] was palatalized to [dʒ] where [ʒ] is the sound of *s* in the English word *leisure, pleasure*. The whole complex [dʒ] was effectively the same as the English *j*-sounds in *jam* and *gentle* and was in consequence written *j* or *g* in Middle Cornish. The variation seen, for example, in *wose* ~ *woge* was to some extent one of dialect. Western Cornish tended to favour *j/g*, whereas more easterly dialects preferred *s*.

At first George accepted this explanation and he publicly expounded it at the "Cornish Weekend" in St Erth in April 1989 (*Carn* 66: 11). Thereafter he changed his mind and offered a different explanation. He now suggests that Old Cornish *d* in some words became some kind of *s* in the Middle Cornish period and that this idiosyncratic *s* became *j/g* in about 1675. He put forward his new hypothesis in an article written in Kernowek Kemyn and published in France (George 1992). This latter explanation of George's raises some interesting questions.

In the first place, if the result of Old Cornish *d* was indeed a special kind of *s*, then George really owes it to the speakers of Kernowek Kemyn to describe this particular *s* in precise terms in order that they may use the "correct" pronunciation in their speech. George claims that the nature of this *s* < *d* is *testenn rag paper arall* "the subject of a further article" (1992: 66) but no such article has yet appeared.

The second point to notice is this: George arrived at his new opinion as a result of an analysis of place-names throughout Cornwall. Unfortunately in his article he does not actually cite any place-names. Indeed his discussion is distinguished by an absence of evidence.

There is a third point to notice. In his article of 1992 George asserted that Old Cornish *d* became a particular variety of *s* in Middle Cornish and that in the Late Cornish period, i.e. *c*. 1675, this distinctive *s* became *j/g*. In his first discussion of the alternation *s* ~ *j/g*, however, George demonstrated that *s* and *j/g* were contemporaneous with each other in Middle Cornish. Indeed he cited the ratio of s-forms to *j/g*-forms in the Middle Cornish texts (1986: 112-13). George's researches demonstrate that *s* and *j/g* occur together in Middle Cornish. Yet he is now urging that in some cases *j/g* is a Late Cornish development of Middle Cornish *s*. George would thus appear to be making two mutually contradictory statements, one of which he has shown to be untrue.

At all events George no longer claims that *dj* and *tj* were part of the sound-system of Middle Cornish and as a result he has removed them from his own orthography. As I have hinted, this itself involves an important question of method. When these sounds, *dj* and *tj*, which had "not before been recognised" were shown to be fictions, the Language Board might well have rethought their whole position. If one part of the phonology of Kemmyn was mistaken, then it was not unlikely that there were further aspects of the system that were less than perfect. Possibly a moratorium on the promotion of Kernowek Kemyn would have been in order until such blemishes had been identified and eliminated.

In fact Kernowek Kemyn contains two further errors in its phonology which, though less obvious than *tj*, *dj*, are much more serious. I have space here to deal with them only very briefly.

**Vocalic alternation**
The sound-systems of Welsh and Cornish differ from that of Breton in a significant way. In Welsh and Cornish certain vowels alternate with each other according to whether they occur in monosyllables on the one hand or disyllables or polysyllables on the other. This vocalic alternation arose because in the very earliest Welsh, Cornish and Breton the accent in disyllables was on the final and not the penultimate syllable. In the case of Breton, however, the alternation has subsequently been lost. In Welsh the word for 'carry!' is *dwg*, where the vowel *w* is the approximate equivalent of English *oo* in *food*. 'I carry', on the other hand, is *dygaf*, where the *y* in the disyllable is pronounced rather like the vowel in the English words *worm*, *heard* or *firm*. In Cornish 'carry!' is *dog*, while 'I carry' is *degaf*. When in Welsh *y* occurs in monosyllables it is pronounced like a long *i* as in English *seen* or a long centralized *i*, the latter being a distinctively North Welsh pronunciation. In Welsh, therefore, the 2nd singular imperative *bydd* 'be!' (*dd* = the *th* of English *smooth*) is pronounced with a long *i* (of either kind), whereas the 2nd plural imperative *byddwch* 'be!' has the vowel of English *worm*, etc. The pronunciation of the two vowels is different in Welsh, although both are written *y*. The same alternation also occurs in Cornish where the alternation appears as *y ~ e*. Thus the singular imperative is *byth* 'be!' but the plural is *betheugh* 'be!' (*bedheugh* in Unified Cornish).

Kernowek Kemyn is aware of the vocalic alternation *o ~ e* and *y ~ e* in Cornish, since it writes *dog* 'carry!' (singular) but *degav* 'I carry' (Brown 1993: 138-39) and *bydh*! 'be!' (singular) but *bedhewgh* 'be!' (plural) (ibid.: 130). Further examples of *o ~ e* alternation are not common in Middle Cornish and there are good reasons why this should be so. The alternation *y ~ e* is very frequent indeed in the Middle Cornish texts, however. Kernowek Kemyn prefers to ignore it in the overwhelming majority of cases and to write and pronounce the historic *e* as *y*. Here are some examples of historic *e* written *y* in Kernowek Kemyn. For the sake of comparison I include the Unified Cornish spellings and at least one example from the traditional Cornish texts:

| Kemyn | Unified | Traditional |
|---|---|---|
| *blydhen* 'year' | *bledhen* | *blethen* BM 565 |
| *gwydhenn* 'tree' | *gwedhen* | *gvethen* OM 186 |
| *hwyja* 'vomit' | *wheja* | *huedzha* AB: 177b |
| *hwytha* 'blow' | *whetha* | *wethugh*! 'blow!' BM 4563 |
| *ynys* 'island' | *enys* | *enys* OM 2592 |
| *Ynys* 'Shrovetide' | *Enes* | *Enez* AB: 46b. |

It should be noticed, however, that Kernowek Kemyn is inconsistent in its spelling of such words. We have already noted *bydh* but *bedhewgh*. Other items with *e* and not *y* include *eva* 'drink', *krena* 'tremble', *ledan* 'wide' and *tevi* 'grow'. It is perhaps significant that George himself is perplexed by some of these words, for he believes the root vowel should be *y* and not *e*. He says of *tevi* "N.B. This word is found only 7 times in trad. Cor., with the commonest spelling *tevy* (4 times); the cognates suggest that *tyvi* might be more correct" (GKK: 309). Of *ledan* he says "N.B. Regular development would give *\*lydan*, but the limited textual evidence favours <e>" (GKK: 197). *Ledan* is in fact the expected form.

The *y* ~ *e* alternation is particularly striking in the case of the diphthong *yw*. In Welsh *yw* is pronounced differently, for example, in the monosyllable *byw* 'alive' and the disyllable *bywyd* 'life'. In the monosyllable the vowel is *i* (or centralized *i*) + *w*, whereas in the disyllable the vowel is the neutral vowel + *w*. The equivalents in the earliest stratum of Middle Cornish are *byw* or *byu* 'alive' but *bewnans* or *beunans* 'life'. A variant *\*bywnans* with *yw* in the stressed syllable is unknown in the Middle Cornish texts. *Bywnans*, however, is the form in Kernowek Kemyn. The *y* in this word and others like it is entirely due to a false analogy with Welsh.

In September 1987 I wrote to George with my misgivings about *inter alia* his spelling the name of the play *Bywnans Meryadjek* 'The Life of St Meriasek' with *yw* rather than *ew*. His answer was *Ny welav travith kamm gans* byw; *yndelma yth yw skrifys yn Kembrek; … ytho y skrifav* Bywnans Meryadjek 'I see nothing wrong with *byw*; it is written thus in Welsh; … therefore I write *Bywnans Meryadjek*'. George, then, spells *bywnans* with a *yw* because *byw* 'alive' has *yw* in Welsh. He ignores the difference between the vowel of the Welsh monosyllable *byw* 'alive' and the Welsh disyllable *bywyd* 'life'. He apparently forgets that the Cornish equivalent of Welsh *yw* in dissyllables is *ew* and that *bewnans* 'life' would better be spelt with *ew*, exactly as is the case in Unified Cornish.

Kernowek Kemyn is not consistent in the matter of *yw/ew* for it writes *Kernewek* and not *\*Kernywek* (Welsh *Cernyweg*) and *kewsel* rather than *\*kywsel*. There is no consistency in the treatment of the *yw/ew* in disyllables/polysyllables because the proponents of Kernowek Kemyn are apparently unsure about this important aspect of Cornish phonology.

## The Prosodic Shift

The absence of vocalic alternation is a serious enough fault in Kernowek Kemyn. There is, however, a further error in the sound-system of Kernowek Kemyn which is graver still, for it involves almost all the vowels and many of the consonants.

Breton and Welsh have three possible lengths of stressed vowel: short, half-long and long. Short vowels are pronounced with one duration of length, half-long vowels have two and fully long vowels have three. The technical name for a duration of length is *mora*, the Latin word for 'delay'. One can say therefore that in Breton and Welsh stressed vowels can have one, two or three morae. In Welsh the stressed vowel of *tad* 'father' has three morae, the stressed vowel of *tadau* 'fathers' has two morae, whereas the root vowel of *mam* 'mother' and *mamau* 'mothers' has one mora only. Native speakers of Welsh and Breton consider long and half long to be varieties of the same thing, since in neither case is the vowel short. The unconscious opposition in the minds of speakers is between short and not-short. Indeed in Breton grammars it is customary to treat long and half-long as long—and to deal with short by itself.

There can be no doubt that at one stage Cornish shared the Welsh and Breton system of threefold length. There is no doubt either that before the period of our earliest Middle Cornish texts the threefold distinction had given way to a double distinction of short and long. I assume that the shift from long: half-long: short to long: short occurred in early Middle Cornish under the impact of English.

When we say that short, half-long and long became short and long, we are really saying the following: short remained, half-long became short and long became half-long. Vowels with one mora retained it, whereas vowels with two or three morae lost one. Schematically this can be represented as follows: $1 > 1$, $2 > 1$, $3 > 2$. It is apparent that old half-long vowels and old short vowels after the shift are identical in length. This whole process I refer to as the Prosodic Shift. After the Prosodic Shift the stressed vowel in *tas* 'father' had two morae, in *tasow* 'fathers' the stressed vowel had one mora while the stressed vowels in *mam* 'mother' and *mamow* 'mothers' each had one mora.

I mentioned that the Prosodic Shift occurred under the influence of English. English has a distinction of short and long only. Moreover stressed vowels in English are pronounced with relatively greater vigour than in Welsh or Breton. This feature was brought over into Middle Cornish. In Middle Cornish syllables lost in length but gained in intensity. Not only did long and half-long vowels shorten as a result of the Prosodic Shift, but unstressed vowels lost much of their intensity and were reduced to the neutral vowel or schwa (of which more in a moment).

The immediate cause of this Anglicization of the sound-system of Cornish was, I believe, the Norman Conquest of England. Before the conquest Cornwall had been in the West Saxon sphere of influence and the West Saxon kings were also kings of England. At the conquest English lost much of its status, Bretons settled in considerable numbers in Cornwall and links with Brittany were re-established. Many Cornish people who had become English-speaking under the West Saxons started to relearn Cornish. Within a generation or two many erstwhile English-speakers were now Celtophone, but they brought into their Cornish English features, particularly in the matter of the length and vigour of vowels.

My reasons for believing that the Prosodic Shift was already in place before our earliest Middle Cornish texts is this: the Middle Cornish texts exhibit in their spelling a whole range of features that can be explained only by assuming that in the language of the Middle Cornish scribes half-long had become short and long had become half-long. At CT § 12.1 I list 17 separate features that can be explained only by reference to the Prosodic Shift.

No one disputes that the Prosodic Shift is a fact of Cornish phonology. George agrees that the shift occurred, but he dates it later than I do. He says:

> *Circa* 1600, the Cornish quantity system changed, so as to conform mor[e] to the English system. The half-long vowels were eliminated, usually becoming short (PSRC: 68).

If half-long became short "*circa* 1600" (cf. George 1995: 114), then the shift must have occurred between the writing of TH (*c.* 1555) and the writing of CW (August 1611). The Prosodic Shift was a major event in the history of the language and would have had far-reaching effects on the entire sound-system. Were the date *c.* 1600 correct, one would expect to find huge differences in phonology between TH on the one hand and CW on the other. This is not the case. Indeed in some ways the phonology of CW (1611) is more archaic than that of BM (1504).

There is a further argument against the later dating of the Prosodic Shift. We know from spellings like *plêu* 'parish' in AB (*c.* 1700) that in Late Cornish stressed monosyllables had actually lengthened. *Plêu* seems by the Late Cornish period to have acquired three morae. This lengthening was presumably well established by Lhuyd's day. Yet, according to George's dating, syllables were shortening *c.* 1600. They can hardly have shortened *c.* 1600 only to lengthen again before 1700. We must assume, therefore, that the shortening had taken place much earlier. I date the Prosodic Shift to *c.* 1300 at the latest.

I mentioned above that there are no fewer than 17 features of Middle Cornish phonology which indicate that the Prosodic Shift was already a *fait accompli* before our earliest Middle Cornish texts. I intend now to examine a few of them very briefly.

### *Myr* 'look!' and *meras* 'to look'

We know from comparision with Breton *mirout* 'to look' that the Cornish word *myres*, *myras*, 'to look' originally had a half-long vowel. Similarly we know that the monosyllabic imperative *myr*! 'look!' had a long vowel. Indeed we could write the pre-Prosodic Shift forms of these two words as follows: [miires], and [miiir] where each [i] represents one mora. As a result of the Prosodic Shift, however, [miiir] 'look!' would have lost a mora to become [miir], while [miires] 'to look' would have lost a mora to become [mires]. The disyllabic [mires] thereafter would have had one mora only in its stressed vowel. Or to put it another way, after the Prosodic Shift the stressed vowel would have been short.

It is a universal rule of phonetics that short vowels are less tense than their long/half-long equivalents. That means that any short vowel is pronounced with less vigour than its long/half-long counterpart and in consequence is pronounced with the tongue lower in the mouth. We can see the same kind of opposition between high/tense/long and lower/lax/short in the English pair *seat* but *sit*. After the Prosodic Shift Cornish *myras* [mires] 'to look' would have had an relatively lax vowel. This would be so much lower in the mouth than [ii] that it would be an open *i* or even a closed *e*. Were the Prosodic Shift a reality in Middle Cornish, we might expect to see the word *myras* 'to look' written *meras*, whereas the monosyllabic *myr* should always appear as *myr*. This is precisely what we do find. Notice the following examples of the disyllable with *e*: *meras* PA 215d, TH 49a, 50a; *veras* PA 168b, OM 2325, BM 4074, TH 2, 3, 7, 9; *veres* BM 4351; *verys* PC 1257 and the following examples of the monosyllable with *y*: *myr* BM 935, 1805, 3194, 3229, 3270, 3656; cf. also the monosyllabic form in *my a vyr* 'I will look' OM 1251.

The same alternation between *e* in disyllabic forms and *y* in monosyllabic forms occurs with the verbs *scryfa*, *screfa* 'to write', *whylas*, *whelas* 'to seek' and *tryga*, *trega* 'to dwell'. The reason is the same. The operation of the Prosodic Shift means that the half-long vowel of the disyllable is now short and is less tense than previously. It has therefore become *e*.

Kernowek Kemyn is unaware that the Prosodic Shift has already occurred in Middle Cornish. Kernowek Kemyn therefore spells both monosyllabic and disyllabic forms of *myres*, *scryfa* and *whylas* with *i*, that is to say with a "half-long" closed *i*: *mires*, *skrifa*, *hwilas*. With the verb 'to dwell', however, the devisers of Kernowek Kemyn have encountered something of a problem. Of the four verbs in question *tryga*, *trega* is the commonest in the texts and is very frequently spelt with *e* in the root syllable. This has perplexed George. Under *tryg* 'position' his dictionary says:

> One would expect /trig/, but the word and its compounds behaved as if they contained /I/ [open *i* which alternates with *e*] instead of /i/ [closed *i*] (GKK: 320-21).

In fact, of course, *tryg* 'position' has a long closed *i* [triig] < [triiig]. It is the disyllabic forms that have an open *i* or *e* [triga]/[trega] < [triiga]. /ɪ/ [i.e. open *i*] in *tryga*, *trega* is not unexpected. After the operation of the Prosodic Shift on Middle Cornish anything else would be remarkable.

The corollary of course is the following. If *trega* has an open *i* or *e*, then *scryfa*, *whylas* and *myras* have the same open *i* or *e* in their stressed syllable. In which case *mires*, *skrifa* and *hwilas* in Kernowek Kemyn are mistaken. And the same is true of many other words as well.

## The diphthongization of final long *i/y*

It is a commonplace of Cornish phonology that long final *i* or *y*, when it is not followed by a consonant, tends to diphthongize to *ei* or *oi* in the later language. It is for this reason that Lhuyd writes *ky* 'dog' as *kei* and *ny* 'we' as *nei* (AB: 46a, 100a). George believes that the shift of long *i* to a diphthong *ei, oi* occurred in the period *c.* 1525 – *c.* 1625 and was a result of the Great Vowel Shift (PSRC: 110; George 1995: 112-13). The Great Vowel Shift was a major reshaping of the vocalic system of English that began in the latter part of the fifteenth century. As a consequence of the Shift the long *i* of Middle English *ride* (with approximately the vowel of Modern English *read* or *reed*) became a diphthong *oi* or *ai* as it is in Modern English.

There are problems with ascribing a phonetic change in one language to a similar change in another. Cornish was, it is true, heavily influenced by English and lived and died under the shadow of English. It was, nonetheless, a different language. If one vowel in Cornish underwent the English shift, we should expect other vowels to do so. If Cornish *ky* became *kei* because of the Great Vowel Shift, then we would expect Cornish *gun* 'down' to become *\*gown*, just as Middle English *hous* (pronounced *hoose*) became Modern English *house*. If the shift long *i/y* > *ei* were based on English, one would expect it to operate in the same kind of environment as the English change. The shift of English long *i* to a diphthong occurs everywhere. The change long *i/y* in Cornish, on the other hand, is confined to absolute final position.

The diphthongization of Cornish long final *i/y* has nothing whatever to do with the English Great Vowel Shift. It is much earlier and is entirely to do with the Cornish Prosodic Shift. We know that the diphthongization of Cornish *i/y* is early in Cornish because it is already present in the rhymes of PA. Since PA was composed *c.* 1400 the diphthongization is probably earlier still. PA § 21 rhymes *otry* 'outrage' (which is stressed on the second syllable) and *dry* 'to bring' with *pray* 'prey' and *joy* 'joy'. Similar rhymes occur throughout the *Ordinalia* and the rest of the Middle Cornish texts (CT § 3.5).

The reason for the diphthongization is as follows. In final position when unprotected by any consonant final long *y/i* in Cornish before the Prosodic Shift had three morae. It could therefore be represented as [iii], for example in [driii] 'bring' or [kiii] 'dog'. Since the final segment is at the end of an unprotected syllable, it would tend to become semi-vocalic. I therefore analyse the sequence [iii] in final position as [ii] followed by [j], where [j] is approximately equivalent to *y* in English *yes*. I therefore write [iij] rather than [iii]. After the operation of the Shift [iij] was reduced to [ij]. In this reduced vowel, however, the first element is now short. In consequence the short first element decreased in tension *i* to give [ɪj], where [ɪ] is the *i* in English *sit*. The two elements of the vowel continue to differentiate themselves and the end result is [əj] where [ə] is the neutal vowel. It is this new diphthong in *dry* and *otry* that rhymes with *prey* [prej] and *joy* [dʒoj] at PA § 21.

## The alleged two long *o*-vowels (<o> and <oe>) in Kernowek Kemyn

George, mistakenly in my view, believes that Middle Cornish had two long *o*-vowel phonemes. One was open [ɔː] and was the result of lengthening of *o* before single consonants. It occurred, for example, in such words as *bos* 'to be', *mos* 'to go' and *ros* 'he gave'. These are written in Kernowek Kemyn as <bos>, <mos> and <ros> respectively. The second long *o*, according to George, derived from Old Cornish [ui] (itself from both earlier [ui] and [oi]), which first lowered to [oi] then monophthongized to [oː]. This latter vowel occurred, according to George, in such words as *los* 'grey', *mos* 'table' and *ros* 'net', which in Kernowek Kemyn he writes as <loes>, <moes> and <roes>. George also believes that long closed [oː] was raised to [uː] *c.* 1625 (PSRC: 129). This, he believes, explains Late Cornish [uː], where Middle Cornish has [oː], e.g. in such words as *looez* 'grey', *cooze* 'wood' and *booze* 'food'.

George's hypothesis concerning two varieties of long *o* is not, I believe, correct. In the first place by George's reckoning Old Cornish [ui] became first [oː] and was then raised to [uː] *c.* 1625. Yet, as George himself admits, in the Middle Cornish texts we find that the reflex of Old Cornish [ui] is already [uː] in some words, for example *scouth* 'shoulder' PC 658, 2623, *duscouth* 'shoulders' RD 2500 (rhyming with *ruth* 'red'), *gouth* 'falls' PC 2626, *glous* 'pang' PC 1147, *lous* 'grey PC 19, *trous* 'foot' PC 860, 1223 and *bous* 'food' RD 541 (rhyming with *cafus* 'to get').

It would appear therefore that George's explanation for the raising of *[oː] > [uː] is unlikely to be accurate. For it to be so, we would have to assume not only that [ui] lowered to [oi], monophthongized to [oː] and was raised again to [uː] (which are in themselves an improbable series of sound-changes), but also that the whole process took place between the Old Cornish period and the writing of the *Ordinalia*, i.e. between *c.* 1100 and *c.* 1375. One wonders whether there would really have been enough time.

There are moreover a number of place-names beginning with *Cus-* 'wood', where the vowel has shortened from [uː] to [u] inside English, e.g. *Cusgarne* (Gwennap), *Cusvey* (Gwennap), *Cusveorth* (Kea) and *Cuskayne Farm* near Probus. Many other toponyms with *Cos-* 'wood' as their first element show <o> rather than <u>, e.g. *Coswinsawsin, Cosskeyle, Cosawes, Cossabnack*, etc. These have clearly shortened before George's hypothetical raising of [oː] > [uː]. Moreover we know that *Coosebean* in Carrick was *Cusbyan c.* 1400 (Weatherhill 2005: 33). It is likely, therefore, that *Cusgarne* and *Coswinsawsin* were adopted into English at the same period. Since names with the first element 'wood' exhibit both *Cos-* [kos] < [koːs] and *Cus-* [kus] < [kuːs], it would seem that the Middle Cornish variants *cos* 'wood' [koːs] and *cous* 'wood' [kuːs] were contemporaneous. One was not a development of the other. In other words Late Cornish *kûz* 'wood' is not a development of earlier Middle Cornish *cos* (<koes> in Kernowek Kemyn); it is rather a dialectal variant. Notice, moreover, that further evidence from place-names disproves George's belief that there were two separate long *o*'s in Middle Cornish (see now TAC: chapter 7).

There are further problems with George's view that there were two separate long *o*'s in Middle Cornish—even if we revise his chronology of their development. The Middle Cornish words containing the reflex of Old Cornish [ui] or [oi] include *huir* 'sister', *coir* 'wax' and *oin* 'lamb'. Yet in Late Cornish we find *hor* 'sister' (AB: 152b), *kor* 'wax' (AB: 47b), and *oan* 'lamb' (AB: 2a). Where is George's putative shift of [oː] > [uː]? Moreover Old Cornish *\*bluid* 'years of age' appears in Late Cornish as both *blouth* (Bodinar) and *bloath* (N. Boson, BF: 27), i.e. with both [uː] and [oː]. If George's alleged shift [oː] > [uː] really occurred, it must have operated in some words only. In *\*bluid* George's shift of [oː] > [uː], if it occurred, must have taken place in some dialects but not in others.

The spellings of the Middle Cornish texts themselves are further evidence against George's understanding of this question. The Middle Cornish scribes write <oy> for [oi] in native words, e.g. *oy* 'egg' BM 3302, *oye* 'egg' CW 1379; *moy* 'more' PA 72d, 104d, 116d, OM 829; *roy* 'give' OM 444, 680, PC 1706. They also write <oy> for [oi] in borrowings from English, e.g. *ioy* 'joy' PA 21d, 30a, OM 517, 558, PC 9, 30, 80, CW 2055; *voys* 'voice' OM 577, 1436, PC 2026 and *oyl* 'oil' OM 694, 703, *oyle* 'oil' CW 939, 2075. They often write George's [oː] (<oe> in Kernowek Kemyn) as <oy> or <oi>, e.g. *boys* 'food' PA 10d, 42a, PC 720; *\*moys* 'table' PA 45a; *troys* 'foot' PA 46d; *poys* 'heavy' PA 10b, 237b; *coys* 'wood' OM 2589, BM 2088. They also, however, frequently write George's [ɔː] (<o> in Kernowek Kemyn) as <oy> or <oi>, i.e. as a diphthong, although this vowel had never actually been a diphthong. Here are some examples from the Middle Cornish texts: *boys* 'to be' PA 49b, 110b, 122a, BM 494, 522, 878, 1026; *bois* 'to be' TH 3, 15a, 17a, 26a; *doys* 'to come' BM 557, 609, 4222; *moys* 'to go' PA 117d, BM 689; *mois* 'to go' TH 1, 6, 13a, 17a, 25a; *nois* 'night' TH 52; *coyth* 'old' OM 855, TH 38a; *coith* 'old' TH 27, 28a, 52a.

The scribes regularly write Old Cornish long *o* (George's *\*[ɔː]) as <o>, as can be seen from the following examples: *bos* 'to be' OM 19, 74, 186, PC 62, 96, 284; *mos* 'to go' OM 184, 451, 681, PC 50, 87, 235; *ros* 'he gave' PA 81b, OM 2136, 2225, PC 1228; *nos* 'night' OM 458, 1516, 2769, PC 671, 890, 914. The scribes also, however, not infrequently write George's *\*<oe> (i.e. long closed [oː] < earlier [oi] < [ui]) in the same way as <o>, e.g., *bos* 'food' OM 366, 378, 1810, PC 618, 623, RD 1685, TH 41; *cos* 'wood' OM 364; *y uos* 'his table' (< *mos*) RD 860; *ros* 'net' TH 34; *tros* 'foot' OM 1762; *los* 'grey' RD 965; *pos* 'heavy' RD 2274; *gos* 'blood' RD 1119, *y wos* 'his blood' RD 2431, *a wos* 'of blood' PA 149b. That is to say, they often write George's <oe> as though it were his <o> [ɔː].

The simplest explanation for all this is surely as follows: Middle Cornish originally had [oi] from earlier [ui]. This was written <oy>, but by the late fourteenth century had monophthongized to [oː]. It was thus identical in pronunciation with original [oː] in words like *bos* 'to be', *mos* 'to go' and *ros* 'he gave'. By the time of the manuscripts of PA and the *Ordinalia* (i.e. the beginning of fifteenth century) the graph <oy> could therefore have two values i.e. [oi] as in *voys* 'voice', *joy* 'joy' and *moy* or [oː] as in both *boys* 'to be' and *boys* 'food' and in both *moys* 'to go' and *moys* 'table'. Moreover the pairs, 'table' ~ 'to go' and 'food' ~ 'to be' were often also written <mos> and <bos> – as well as <moys> and <boys>.

If George's hypothesis were correct, we would have to believe that <oy> had three separate values, i.e. [oi] in *joy, roy, voys* and *oyl*, [oː] in *moys* 'table', *boys* 'food' and *roys* 'net', and [ɔː] in *moys* 'to go', *boys* 'to be' and *doys* 'to come'. According to George these are three different vocalic sequences, that always remained separate, even though they were frequently written identically. Moreover the last two are completely confused with such variants as *boys, bos* and *moys, mos* representing both his <bos> and *<boes> and <mos> and *<moes>.

It seems to me difficult to believe that Middle Cornish ever had anything other than one long *o* [oː]. This vowel had two origins. In the first place *bos* 'to be', *mos* 'to go' and *ros* 'he gave' had [oː], which was the result of earlier lengthening. On the other hand, I assume that Old Cornish *ui* (< *ui* and *oi*) first lowered to *oi*, a trimoric sequence [ooi]. Then as a result of the Prosodic Shift, this lost one mora internally to become [oo], written <o>. Because this had originally been a diphthong, it continued to be written as <oy> or <oi> in the Middle Cornish texts. It is quite apparent, however, that by the time of BM, if not before, the reflex of earlier *oy* and original long *o* were pronounced the same and were in consequence regularly rhymed together. Look for example at the following rhymes from BM: **mos** 'go' – *y* **woys** 'his blood' BM 130-31; *the* **voth** 'thy will' – *ny* **goth** 'behoves not' BM 584-85; *age* **gos** 'their blood' – *y hyl* **boys** 'can be' BM 1599-1603; *age* **goys** 'their blood' – *mar mynogh* **bos** 'if you will be' BM 1642-43; *mar kyl* **boys** 'if it can be' – *yowynk ha* **loys** 'young and grey' BM 2168-71.

In syllable final, however, original *ui* did not simplify to [oː], but maintained the final semivocalic segment and lost one mora internally. This is why, I believe, that in absolute auslaut, the reflex of Old Cornish *ui* gives <oy>, e.g. *moy* 'more', *oy* 'egg', while it gives *o* internally, e.g. *ros* 'net', *bos* 'food', *cos* 'wood', etc. George's hypothesis is quite unable to explain this different treatment of his putative long [oː] <oe>. There is no reason, by George's reckoning, for Old Cornish [ui] to have given *moy* 'more', *oy* 'egg' on the one hand, but *<loes>, *<koes>, Late Cornish *looz* 'grey', *booze* 'food', *kûz* 'wood' on the other.

I, following Nance, assume that in some western dialects before *s* and *s* < *d*, and in certain other environments, Old Cornish [ui] did not lower before monophthongizing. Instead Old Cornish *cuit* 'wood' and *buit* 'food' in western Cornish monophthongized with [ui] unlowered and became *cous* and *bous* respectively. These appear in Late Cornish, which is exclusively western, with *u* or *oo* for [uː] (*kûz, booze*), where standard Middle Cornish has [oː] (*cos* or *coys, bos* or *boys*). It should be noted that the spellings with <ou> in Middle Cornish, are confined to the two texts PC and RD. For other reasons, I believe that the two plays PC and RD were western in origin. The dialectal variants *cos* and *cous* also explain the difference between, *Coswinsawsin, Cosskeyle* (< *Cos-*), for example, on the one hand, and *Cusveorth* and *Cuskayne* (< *Cous-*) on the other.

In a word George's hypothesis of the two long *o*'s in Middle Cornish cannot be sustained. His spellings, e.g. *<moes>* 'table', *<boes>* 'food' but <mos> 'to go' and <bos> 'to be' introduce into revived Cornish distinctions which did not exist in the traditional language.

## Consonant doubling in Kernowek Kemyn

The Prosodic Shift, then, is an integral part of Middle Cornish phonology. Middle Cornish has no half-long vowels, only long and short. Kernowek Kemyn on the other hand insists on three lengths. Since Kernowek Kemyn wants its spelling to represent the pronunciation as clearly as possible, the system attempts to distinguish short vowels from "half-long" ones by doubling the following consonant. The vowels in *cam* 'bent' and *bron* 'hill' are both short and since Kernowek Kemyn mistakenly believes that Cornish also had half-long vowels, *cam* must be spelt as *kamm* and *bron* as *bronn*. Thus the name *Camborne*, which is everywhere spelt in Middle Cornish as *Cambron*, in Kernowek Kemyn becomes *Kammbronn*. Such a spelling would have some justification if Cornish had three vocalic lengths. Because Cornish has only two, *Kammbronn* is without justification. The initial *k* is another problem and this I discuss briefly below.

Before I leave the question of vocalic length I should like to make some apology for my previous negligence in this matter. When I wrote my article (Williams 1990) against *dj* and *tj* in Kernowek Kemyn, I posited such forms as [wo·ze] 'after' and [e·ze] 'was' with half length in accordance with George's assumptions. Subsequent investigation has convinced me that such forms were fictions. My praise for George's new orthography in the first section of the article was also unwise. It was prompted by a desire to encourage Cornish revivalists but was based on an inadequate examination of Kernowek Kemyn. Quite apart from *dj* and *tj* I already had reservations about the new system and indeed had communicated some of them to George himself.

## ew > ow

We have seen above that Kernowek Kemyn insists on spelling disyllables with *yw* when the vowel ought to be *ew*. This is not all, however. As a result of the Prosodic Shift the whole system of Cornish diphthongs was reshaped. Diphthongs before the shift could have either a half-long or a short first element. Thereafter the first element of all diphthongs was short. This had far-reaching effects. Among other things *yw* in monosyllables became *ew* and *ew* in disyllables became *ow*. Thus, for example, earlier *byw* 'alive' and *clewes* 'to hear' became *bew* 'alive' but *clowes* 'to hear'. Disyllabic forms of the verbs *kewsel* 'to speak', *tewlel* 'to throw' and *clewes* 'to hear' almost always have *ow* in their root syllable in BM, TH and CW. Here are some examples of the verb 'to hear' from these three texts: *ny clowys* BM 191, *re glowes* BM 527, 802, *pan glowe* BM 1030, *del glowas* BM 1160, *clowugh* BM 1890, *clowys* BM 2224, *ny glowys* BM 2238, *a glowes* BM 2394, *a glowas* TH 4a, 30, *clowas* TH 4a, 5, 41, *the glowes* TH 38a, *clowes* TH 41a, *a glowas* CW 140, *tha glowas* CW 637, *a glowses* CW 770, *pan glowa* CW 1136, 1205, *a glowaf* CW 1166; cf. *Klouaz, dho glouaz* 'to hear' AB: 44a. It will be readily seen, therefore, that *\*klyw, \*klywes*, etc. of Kernowek Kemyn are completely at variance with the traditional texts.

## Unstressed vowels

Nowhere are the effects of the Prosodic Shift more clearly seen than in the unstressed vowels. When stressed syllables were shortened but reinforced as a result of the Prosodic Shift, unstressed syllables were correspondingly weakened. This meant that the quality of unstressed vowels was very largely lost and that most unstressed vowels fell together as the neutral vowel schwa. This is the *uh*-like vowel heard in the unstressed syllable of such English words as *mother, gammon, Christmas*, etc. or like an unstressed variety of the first vowel in Welsh *bywyd* to which reference has already been made.

The reduction of unstressed vowels can be clearly seen in the Middle Cornish texts by the way in which such vowels are indifferently spelt. The word for 'one', for example, is variously spelt *onan, onen, onon* or *onyn*. Similarly 'to wait' is *gortes, gortos, gurtas* or *gortays*, while 'people' is either *pobal, pobel* or *pobyl* (see CT § 7.7 for references). In these words and in others like them Kernowek Kemyn seeks to maintain the quality of the unstressed vowel. In the word for 'one' the unstressed vowel is *a* in Kernowek Kemyn and this is, in theory at least, to be pronounced *a*.

Such an unjustifiable spelling and pronunciation has presented editors with a problem. In the introduction to his Kernowek Kemyn edition of PA Ray Edwards discusses the spelling of the words *onan* 'one' and *honan* 'self' and says:

> This is the *G.M.* [i.e. GKK] spelling though in only one case in our Poem do we find *honan* rhyming with a word ending in *-an*. Ken George has come to the conclusion that these words were written with *-yn, -an* or *-on* endings depending of the words with which they were set to rhyme. In almost every case the rhyming words in the Poem end in *-on* so that *onon / honon* do likewise in the MS. implying, I would think, that these final rhyming syllables are just neutral vowels. Out of the three, the ending *-an* was chosen [i.e. by Kernowek Kemyn] in imitation of Welsh and Breton forms with the unfortunate result for this Poem that these syllables will appear not to rhyme and the reader will have to treat them as neutral vowels for them to do so (PAA: 20).

Edwards here with his customary acuity has come upon a major flaw in Kernowek Kemyn. It is not therefore astonishing that Edwards, though a user of Kernowek Kemyn, has consistently expressed doubts about aspects of it.

Edwards's observation concerning the nature of unstressed vowels in PA leads inevitably to a further conclusion. Kernowek Kemyn has been made to conform to Welsh and Breton in the matter of unstressed vowels. Yet it is quite clear from the rhymes in the PA that Cornish by the late fourteenth century was already radically different from the other two languages in having reduced unstressed vowels to schwa. This cannot be an isolated phenomenon. If unstressed vowels are reduced in Cornish it must be that stressed vowels are correspondingly more vigorous. It is *a priori* likely, therefore, from Edwards's conclusion, that the Prosodic Shift was a fact by the time of PA. His one pertinent observation implies first, that the phonology of Cornish was radically different from Welsh and Breton in a variety of ways and secondly, therefore, that Kernowek Kemyn is mistaken.

## The origins of the errors in Kernowek Kemyn

If we understand how Kernowek Kemyn came to be so mistaken, we can ensure that never again need revived Cornish be disfigured by similar errors. The first and most immediate reason for the defects of Kernowek Kemyn is that the handbooks of Celtic linguistics which deal with Cornish are themselves inadequate. The best book ever written about Cornish is Henry Jenner's HCL of 1904 and it is a great pity that it has never been reprinted. The work was written by a revivalist for the incipient revival and yet it contains much of interest to the academic Celticist. It does not explicitly deal with the question of vocalic alternation. As far as vocalic length is concerned, it assumes that Cornish has short and long only. The other two readily available works that deal with Cornish are CCCG of Holger Pedersen and Henry Lewis, which was first published in 1937 (and reprinted with a supplement in 1961), and Henry Lewis's LlCC, published in 1923 and revised in 1946. Henry Lewis was a Welshman and a Celtic scholar. His knowledge of Cornish was not particularly profound and he had, of course, no interest in speaking the language. In his section on morphology in LlCC Lewis does not even trouble to write his own paradigms. Rather he appears to have based his verbs and prepositional pronouns on Norris (1859 i-ii). Although Norris was editing the *Ordinalia,* he appends to his work a very useful "Sketch of Cornish Grammar" (ii 123-308) which forms the basis of Lewis's descriptions. Lewis's work on Cornish appears to have been extensively used by George for GKK and presumably elsewhere.

Lewis's section on Cornish phonology in LlCC is as unsatisfactory as it is brief. Nowhere does he explicitly discuss the question of vocalic alternation. Instead he makes a few inaccurate and misleading remarks, for example:

Yr oedd y deuseiniaid *ew ow* ac *yw* yn ymgymysgu. Er enghraifft ceir *dev* 'Duw' yn odli â *lyfryow* 'llyfrau' ac â *gu* 'gwayw', ffurf amrywiol ar *gv* yw *guv* sy'n odli â *tu* = Cym. *tu*, *ihesu* a *tru* = Cym. *tru*, a cheir hefyd y furf *gev*. Yn ymyl *dev* ceir y ffurf *dv* yn odli â *ihesv*, a digwydd y ffurfiau lluosog *dvow* a *duwow*. Eto ceir *dev* a *jhesu* yn odli â *vertu* 'virtue' Ffr. *vertu*, *dev* yn odli â *plu* 'plwyf', a *virtu* yn odli ag *yw* 'yw'[,] *lyw* 'lliw' a *gyw* 'gwiw'. Dyma *ev ow yw uv* ac *u* felly i gyd yn dynodi'r un sain!

[The diphthongs *ew ow* and *yw* are not kept distinct. One finds, for example, *dev* 'God' rhyming with *lyfryow* 'books' and *gv* 'spear', *guv* is a variant of *gv* which rhymes with *tu* = Welsh *tu*, *ihesu* and *tru* = Welsh *tru*, and the variant *gev* is also attested. Alongside *dev* one finds the form *du* rhyming with *ihesv*, and the plurals *dvow* and *duwow* occur. Moreover, *dev* and *jhesu* are found rhyming with *vertu* 'virtue', French *vertu*, *dev* rhymes with *plu* 'parish' and *virtu* rhymes with *yw* 'is', *lyw* 'colour' and *gyw* 'worthy'. This means that *ev ow yw uv* and *u* all denote the same sound!] (LlCC: 7).

Moreover, at no point does Lewis discuss the question of vocalic length in Middle Cornish and the way in which the inherited system has given way to an English-based one. If, then, the treatment of Cornish phonology in the academic handbooks is mistaken and confused in places and wanting in others, the treatment of both topics in Kernowek Kemyn becomes intelligible.

There are more basic reasons for the errors of Kernowek Kemyn. It is almost always true that if an academic enterprise is unsuccessful, it is so because the underlying theory is defective. Kernowek Kemyn is constructed on such an inadequate theoretical basis. We know that George had read Loth's article of 1897, for it was from there that he derived his ideas about *tj* and *dj*. In the same article Loth makes the following observations:

> Les regrets que peut nous causer l'extinction du cornique sont, en partie, atténués par le fait que les deux langues brittoniques vivantes en sont très voisines, le breton surtout qui forme avec le cornique un groupe si intime qu'on peut les considérer comme deux dialectes voisins d'une même langue. Le cornique moyen était incontestablement moins éloigné du breton-armoricain pris dans son ensemble que le breton de Quiberon ne l'est actuellement de celui de Saint-Pol-de-Léon

> [Our regrets at the death of Cornish are to some degree alleviated by the fact that the two living Brythonic languages are very close to it, Breton in particular forming with Cornish such a close linguistic group that we can consider them as two related dialects of the same language. Middle Cornish was without doubt closer to Breton as a whole than the modern Breton dialect of Quiberon is to that of St-Pol-de-Léon] (RC 18: 401-02).

This statement of Loth's is untrue. The unique treatment of *d* and *nt* in Cornish is sufficient evidence that Cornish was in significant ways quite unlike Breton. Cornish was a language in its own right with its own history and its own individual phonology. To claim otherwise is to misread the evidence. It is quite clear, however, that Loth's view has been an important influence on George's thinking and therefore on Kernowek Kemyn.

If Cornish and Breton were dialects of the same language (as George following Loth appears to believe) then the phonology of Cornish can be deduced from comparison with Breton. There is no need to read the Middle Cornish texts closely to see what the speakers of the language actually wrote.

Worse still, if the comparison with Breton gives one result and a reading of the texts gives another, then it must be the Middle Cornish texts that are mistaken.

Caradar liked to spell as far as possible as the texts did and consequently on occasion found himself in disagreement with Nance. Compare Caradar's remarks about *annowy* 'kindle':

> Tregear a scryf "annowy". Mes chanjya annowy dhe "enawy" a wra Mordon. Prag? Awos bos "enaoui" yn Bretonek! Mes annowy a yl yn ta bos nes dhe'n Keltek Cotha ha Kernewek yu
>
> [Tregear writes "annowy". But Nance changes annowy to "enawy". Why? Because 'enaoui' is the Breton form! But annowy may well be closer to the earliest Celtic and it is Cornish] (CM: 43).

George, possibly following Nance's example, says of Caradar's desire to imitate the spelling of the Middle Cornish texts: "This is a weak principle, because it again takes no account of the pronunciation" (PSRC: 27). George implies that the Middle Cornish scribes could not write their own language properly. If what they wrote does not agree with the phonology of Middle Cornish as understood by a comparison with Breton, then the scribes are wrong. This is indeed a curious approach to the study of Middle Cornish.

Although on occasion he allowed himself to be swayed by Breton, Nance based Unified Cornish on the texts. Unified Cornish is mistaken, I believe, in a few relatively trivial ways, but because it adheres closely to the sources, it is recognisably Cornish. The same cannot be said for Kernowek Kemyn. *Agan Tavas*, the society for the promotion of Unified Cornish, recently declared:

> Sadly, students of revived Cornish must now choose between several differing forms of the language. Agan Tavas recognises the validity of any form based on the language as used by Cornish people at any time, but favours the continued use … of Unified Cornish, the form settled by Nance over sixty years ago and used by everyone until recently. Agan Tavas opposes the use of invented forms of the language which lack any historical authenticity (Morris 1995: back cover).

Similarly P.A.S. Pool has tellingly observed:

> Kemyn is something quite different, an entirely artificial creation which does not resemble Cornish as used by Cornish people at any time in history. To those accustomed to Unified (...) Kemyn has an alien and somewhat sinister appearance, as if the language had somehow been taken over by robots and reduced to the status of a code (Pool 1995: 6).

## A "phonemic" orthography

Kernowek Kemyn is sometimes known as "Phonemic Cornish" because its orthography claims to adhere closely to phonemic principles. Put simply, "phonemic" means that any sound in the language will always be represented in writing by the same letter or combination of letters. Moreover any letter or combination of letters will have only one phonetic value. As an attempt at a phonemic orthography Kernowek Kemyn can be criticized on four grounds. In the first place, it uses the same combination of letters to represent different sounds. In the second place, it uses different letters to represent the same sound. In the third place, since the phonology of Kernowek Kemyn is mistaken, the spelling makes false distinctions. In the fourth place, by squeezing a fifteenth-century language into the strait-jacket of an arbitrary twentieth-century spelling Kernowek Kemyn violates the orthographical traditions of Cornish. I will examine each of these four problems in turn.

In Kernowek Kemyn the graph *oe* is most frequently used to represent closed *o*, for example in *moes* 'table', *koes* 'wood', *kavoes* 'to get'. A separate closed *o* never existed in classical Middle Cornish, but I will accept it here for the sake of argument. In *aloes* 'aloes' and *Kembroes* 'Welshwoman', however, the same combination of letters represents *o* followed by open *e*. It should be noticed incidentally that *\*Kembroes* 'Welshwoman' is George's invention and is, in my view, mistaken. The word should be *Kembres*, and this is Nance's form (CT § 13.11).

In Kernowek Kemyn the combination *sh* normally represents the *sh* sound of English *ship*, *shoe*. Examples in Kernowek Kemyn include *sham* 'shame', *okkashyon* 'occasion', *bushel* 'bushel'. Not infrequently, however, *sh* represents *s* + *h*, where the two sounds are in adjacent syllables, for example in *eshe* 'facilitate', *kaleshe* 'harden', *leshanow* 'nickname', *leshenwel* 'to nickname', *leshwoer* 'stepsister', *neshe* 'approach' and *neshevin* 'kinsman'. In some instances GKK explains where *sh* = *s* + *h*. Elsewhere the reader is left to fend for himself.

At the beginning of GKK there is a section (20-22) called "Recommended pronunciation", where the spelling and pronunciation are described. We are told unstressed *i* resembles "*i* in English *bit*". We are also told that unstressed *y* is like "*i* in English *bit*". We are further told that unstressed *u* is pronounced like "*i* in English *bit*". Three symbols, therefore, *i*, *y* and *u*, are pronounced identically. This is a repudiation of the phonemic principle of one sound per symbol.

Kernowek Kemyn ordains that final *k* in words like *medhyk* 'doctor', *marghek* 'knight' and *dewdhek* 'twelve' is pronounced *g* before vowels and *k* before consonants. On the other hand in words like *rag* 'for', *hweg* 'sweet' the consonant is written *g* but is pronounced *g* before vowels and *k* before consonants. This is a further departure from the phonemic principle. It is, I believe, mistaken as well, since in Middle Cornish words like *wheg* 'sweet' always had a final *g* and words like *methek* 'doctor' always had a final *k* (see CT § 8.8-14).

In Kernowek Kemyn consonants are frequently doubled in order to distinguish the preceding short vowel from the equivalent "half-long" vowel. The opposition between short and "half-long" could occur only in stressed syllables. Any syllable that does not bear the stress is automatically short. This does not prevent such syllables being spelt in Kernowek Kemyn with a redundant double consonant, for example *gwedrenn* 'glass', *glasenn* 'green-sward', *kribenn* 'comb'. Some words in unstressed *-en* have a single rather than a double *n*, for example *reken* 'bill', *blydhen* 'year'. Thus the element *-en* or *-enn*, which is always pronounced the same way, has two different spellings. This is yet a further departure from the phonemic principle.

Because the underlying phonology of Kernowek Kemyn is defective, the imposed orthography is also flawed. Kernowek Kemyn believes that Middle Cornish has three diphthongs *iw*, *yw* and *ew*, when in fact Middle Cornish had only two of them, i.e. *yw* and *ew*; and in monosyllables they were not always kept separate. Moreover in disyllables *ew* became *ow* as a result of the Prosodic Shift. Kernowek Kemyn therefore writes 'two hands' as *diwleuv*, i.e. with a high closed vowel in the stressed syllable, even though the item in question is spelt *dule*, *dula* in BM, *dewla*, *dewleff* in TH, *dowla* in SA and was obviously pronounced *dewla*, *dowla*. There are many other distinctions maintained in Kernowek Kemyn which have no basis in Middle Cornish (for an itemized list see CT § 13.39).

Because the orthography of Kernowek Kemyn was intended to be "phonemic" the traditional orthography of Cornish is perforce ignored. Middle Cornish, like English, writes the sound *k* as *k* before front vowels, e.g. *kyk* 'flesh', *kellys* 'lost'; as *c* before back vowels, e.g. *cane*, *cana* 'to sing', *coth* 'old'; and as *qu* before the sound *w*, *u*, e.g. *quyk* 'quick', *queth* 'garment'. In order to render the orthography of Kernowek Kemyn "phonemic", in all positions the sound *k* had to be written *k*. In consequence we find in Kernowek Kemyn such unhistorical spellings as *kath* 'cat', *koth* 'old', *koedha* 'to fall', *kwykk* 'quick' and, of course, *Kammbronn* 'Camborne'. It is quite true that the texts do on occasion use *k* before a back vowel. The word *cuntell* 'collect', for example, is spelt *kuntell* in BM at lines 1508, 1515, 1544 but the word for 'quick' is *quik* at BM 1552. Generally speaking the traditional texts use *c* and not *k* before back vowels and the revived language should do so. The combination *kw* has no foundation in traditional Cornish.

The spelling of Kernowek Kemyn has been recast according to a faulty phonology. Because the phonology is mistaken, the spelling is also inadmissible. But even if the phonology had been largely correct, the spelling of the texts should not have been arbitrarily altered. Traditional Cornish is extinct. The language revival is attempting to resuscitate a dead language. It cannot legitimately recast that language and simultaneously claim that it is reviving a traditional form of speech.

We have possibly two parallels for the case of Cornish. Hebrew has been successfully revived, although it had ceased to be a vernacular for almost two millennia. Yet Israeli Hebrew, although it has lost much of its Semitic character, uses the traditional orthography of the biblical and rabbinical language. A parallel closer to home is that of Manx. Manx died as a traditional language in the early 1970s. The revived language uses the traditional orthography of Manx, even though it is notoriously difficult for learners. The Cornish revival should do the same. It should use the traditional orthography for the language rather than a 1980s orthography that is itself based on a whole series of misconceptions—and is inconsistent as well.

Before leaving the question of the spelling of Kernowek Kemyn, a final observation ought to be made. Kernowek Kemyn has deliberately recast the traditional orthography of Cornish in order to make it correspond with the phonology of the language. Since the deviser of Kernowek Kemyn has, in my view, failed to understand the phonology of Middle Cornish adequately, we cannot expect Kernowek Kemyn to reflect the sounds of traditional Cornish very closely. Yet the spelling of Kernowek Kemyn is not even successful on its own terms. It was the intention of the devisers of the system that the pronunciation of each word would be immediately apparent from the spelling. In which case it is odd that GKK should give the phonetic representation of so many headwords alongside the Kernowek Kemyn spelling. If the orthography were truly phonetic, these phonetic representations would be redundant, since the pronunciation of each word would be obvious. Could it be that the deviser of Kernowek Kemyn has less than total faith in his own orthography?

### Defending the *status quo*

In July 1987 the Cornish Language Board accepted Kernowek Kemyn in its entirety because, as they announced themselves,

> The Cornish Language Board feels that the work that has been done by Dr. Ken George in his book 'The Pronunciation and Spelling of Revived Cornish' is a great improvement for the language.
>
> Therefore for the sake of the authenticity of the language and for the sake of those who come after us, the Language Board accepts the proposals (Edwards 1994 [iii]).

It is apparent, then, that the advocates of Kernowek Kemyn proposed and promoted their system because they thought it to be more authentic than any other form of revived Cornish. If it can be shown that Kernowek Kemyn is less authentic than other varieties of Cornish, Kernowek Kemyn loses whatever *raison d'être* it may have had.

It is unlikely that those who support Kernowek Kemyn will be prepared to abandon their system immediately in spite of all its manifest faults. Already they are using various arguments against further change. At least five different, and in some cases mutually exclusive, reasons are being put forward in favour of the *status quo*. Let us look at them.

# WRITINGS ON REVIVED CORNISH

1) *To replace Kernowek Kemyn with a revised variety of Unified would be to add to the varieties of Neo-Cornish. There are already enough forms of Revived Cornish without increasing their number.*

Until 1987 there was only one variety of Neo-Cornish, namely Unified Cornish. The proponents of Kernowek Kemyn introduced their system (and in so doing split the language movement) on the grounds that Kernowek Kemyn was authentic in a way that Unified was not. To the proponents of Kernowek Kemyn, then, authenticity is the sole criterion of legitimacy. The most authentic form of Neo-Cornish is the only one to which revivalists can give their loyalty. If Kernowek Kemyn is the most authentic form of Neo-Cornish, then Kernowek Kemyn is the system to follow. If Kernowek Kemyn is not authentic, as I am now suggesting, then Kernowek Kemyn has no legitimacy. The number of varieties of Neo-Cornish is irrelevant.

2) *There is no need to replace Kernowek Kemyn because it is only a spelling. Unified Cornish and Kernowek Kemyn are varieties of the same thing.*

This view is widely held even by those who do not support Kernowek Kemyn. In a recent review of a Celtic phrasebook (Gunn 1994), for example, the reviewer says of the Cornish in it: "Strictly Unified and Common [Cornish] differ only in spelling" (*Carn* 91: 20). This view is without foundation. It is apparent from PSRC that the deviser of Kernowek Kemyn intended that his new system should be pronounced very differently from Unified Cornish. Kernowek Kemyn was, for example, to have three vowel-lengths, to distinguish between open and closed *i*, and open and closed *o*, and to pronounce *s/j* as *dy*. If Unified and Kernowek Kemyn differ only in spelling, then the introduction of Kernowek Kemyn was unnecessary. If Kernowek Kemyn is the same thing as Unified but in a different garb, then the introduction of Kemmyn and the ensuing split were frivolous. If Kemmyn and Unified really do not differ significantly, the proponents of Kernowek Kemyn can hardly justify the continuing use of their system, particularly since Unified Cornish is the more authentic of the two.

3) *Kernowek Kemyn spells phonetically and is therefore easier to learn than any other form of Cornish.*

This was the view expressed by the reviewer of CT in *An Gannas* (number 226, October 1995, 10) who wrote,

> Skila veur dhe asa KU war agan lergh o bos res dhe lytherennans arnowydh sywya an sonyow, a-ban vydh ogas pub dallether sowsneger dre nas, nyns o hemma an kas y'n Oesow Kres pan wodhya an dus leverel an geryow yn ewn ha ny vern yn tien fatell vedhens skrifys!

[An important reason for leaving Unified Cornish behind was that there was a need for a modern orthography to follow the sounds, since almost every beginner is a native speaker of English; this was not the case in the Middle Ages when people knew how to pronounce the words properly and it did not matter completely how they were spelt].

Notice first of all the *non sequitur* in the first part of this passage. Kernowek Kemyn had to be introduced because the overwhelming majority of Cornish learners were native-speakers of English and the orthography of Unified Cornish was apparently less than ideal for them. It is indeed a novel principle in linguistic planning that a minority language must adapt its spelling to suit the native language of its learners. Could one imagine Welsh, Irish, or even Manx doing so?

The real point to notice in the passage is this: the reviewer claims that the orthography of Kernowek Kemyn is close to the phonology of Cornish. His claim, however, is far from being true. The orthography of Unified, though not aspiring to be either "modern" or "phonemic", is far closer to the pronunciation of Middle Cornish than Kernowek Kemyn is. If the spelling of Kernowek Kemyn were really accurate, if it in fact reflected the pronunciation of Middle Cornish, there might possibly be some justification for it. The spelling of Kernowek Kemyn is not even phonetic by its own criteria, as we have seen above. Moreover, the orthography of Kernowek Kemyn reflects the pronunciation of Middle Cornish inadequately.

It should also be observed that the reviewer does not claim the spelling of Kernowek Kemyn reflects a different phonology but merely that it is more closely related to the sounds than is Unified Cornish. Nowhere does he suggest that the underlying sound system is different. If the sound system of Unified and of Kernowek Kemyn are effectively the same, why was Kernowek Kemyn ever introduced? Can it be that since the problems with *dj* and *tj*, the proponents of Kernowek Kemyn are no longer sure that they alone pronounce Cornish properly?

4) *Any form of Cornish is as good as any other.*

A correspondent of mine, who is a firm supporter of Kernowek Kemyn, wrote to me recently to defend the continued use of the system. He suggested that any orthography for Cornish was as good as any other since all forms of the language were varieties of Cornish. He asserted moreover that the spoken, and not the written language was the crucial thing. In addition he confessed that he liked talking to speakers of Unified Cornish because he found them easy to understand.

If the proponents of Kemmyn really do believe that one system is as good as any other, it is difficult to understand why they insisted on replacing Unified Cornish. The divisions that occurred after 1987 have certainly not advanced the language. Indeed many learners of Cornish have abandoned their studies as a result of the divisions among revivalists. Others have similarly been deterred from learning Cornish. None of this would really have mattered if Kernowek Kemyn were demonstrably superior to Unified Cornish which it replaced.

My correspondent also claims that the written form of Neo-Cornish is irrelevant, since the spoken language is what really matters. He likes Unified speakers because their Cornish is readily intelligible to him. This argument is a curious one for a proponent of Kernowek Kemyn. If the written form is much less important than the spoken form, then the proponents of Kernowek Kemyn have split the movement and hindered the revival and all for a mere orthography.

5) *It is too late to replace Kernowek Kemyn with another system. Kernowek Kemyn is too well established to be emended or replaced.*

The argument from expediency is perhaps the most frequent reason put forward by speakers of Kernowek Kemyn in favour of the *status quo*. It is also the weakest. Unrevised Unified Cornish was a perfectly serviceable system, but the Cornish Language Board replaced it with Kernowek Kemyn on the grounds that Kemyn was more authentic. If Kemyn can be shown to be far less authentic than Unifed, the supporters of Kemyn can hardly argue that it is too late now to replace their system. Unified Cornish was in place from 1928 to 1987 but the supporters of Kernowek Kemyn substituted their own system after a minimum of consultation.

## Kernowek Kemyn: conclusion

None of the arguments in favour of maintaining Kernowek Kemyn carries any weight. Many people have understood for the last eight years that Kernowek Kemyn is mistaken both in conception and in execution. I trust that since the publication of CT this sad truth will become more widely known. Kemyn was introduced because its proponents believed it was the best possible system. As W. Brown put it in 1987:

> [T]he need to set a standard for Cornish pronunciation which is as accurate as possible and appropriate to the form of the language which we have adopted has induced the Kesva to support the system put forward by Ken George as being the best we are likely to get (*Carn* 60: 18).

Far from being the new dawn the Language Board believed it to be, Kernowek Kemyn has proved to be something of a blind alley: "an unjustifiably wrong turn" as Dr Charles Thomas put it (quoted in Penglase 1994: 101). For the good of the revival and for the sake of unity the Cornish Language Board should now replace Kernowek Kemyn with a more authentic Cornish, based on the "linguistically sound principles" which George himself advocates (PSRC: 41).

We are not dealing here with a matter of convenience, of not "rocking the boat", of administrative difficulties. The question is a moral one. Kernowek Kemyn bears little resemblance in sounds or spelling to the traditional language of Cornwall at any period in her history. It is therefore fair neither to the present generation nor to future generations to persist with Kernowek Kemyn. Since Kernowek Kemyn is flawed and since it cannot be satisfactorily revised, it should be abandoned.

## The way forward

In *Cornish Today* I suggested ways in which Unified Cornish might be improved. My recommendations included reforms to the sound-system that would render Unified more authentic and modifications to the accidence and syntax that would simplify the grammar in line with the later texts. Before I say a little about my recommendations I should like to make a few general observations about the Cornish revival and the methods by which we arrive at our Neo-Cornish systems.

Let us start from first principles. We wish to revive Cornish but are uncertain which form of the language to use. It is clear, however, that the Middle Cornish of the texts and the Late Cornish of the seventeenth and eighteenth centuries are phonetically one and the same language (see CT §14.2-3). As far as inflection and syntax are concerned Middle and Late Cornish are very close indeed. This is not just my opinion, it was Jenner's as well:

> As for grammatical forms, it will be seen that the writer is of [the] opinion that the difference between Middle and Modern Cornish was more apparent than real, and that except in the very latest period of all, when the language survived only in the mouths of the least educated persons, the so-called "corruptions" were to a great extent due to differences of spelling, to a want of appreciation of almost inaudible final consonants, and to an intensification of phonetic tendencies existing in germ at a much earlier period (HCL: x-xi).

It is, I believe, imprudent to base revived Cornish on the late language for two main reasons. In the first place, Late Cornish is relatively limited in scope when compared with the mediaeval and Tudor texts. In the second place, Late Cornish uses a spelling based on English. This orthography did not arise through choice but was forced upon the later writers because they knew no other. Someone who can read Late Cornish only will find reading any other form of the language virtually impossible. If we wish to revive the traditional language of Cornwall, then we should revive it with its traditional orthography.

Unified Cornish was based on the mediaeval language and in particular upon the *Ordinalia* and PA. I am not convinced that this was completely sensible. It would surely have been more prudent to base the revived language on the latest possible period at which the language was still a full vernacular and still written in the traditional orthography.

We have five extensive Middle Cornish texts, PA, the *Ordinalia*, BM, CW and TH. The last three form a unity as far as date is concerned. BM was written in 1504. Tregear wrote his homilies *c.* 1550. Although William Jordan wrote CW in August 1611, the original text was almost certainly composed before the Reformation, i.e. *c.* 1530-40. Together these texts form a linguistic unity. Their spelling is traditional yet they exhibit grammatical features that become common in the later language.

In CT I recommend using BM, TH and CW, the "Tudor texts", as the basis for a revised version of Unified Cornish. This revision I call Unified Cornish Revised or UCR. Since Late Cornish is identical with Tudor Cornish from the phonetic point of view, we can legitimately base the phonology of UCR on Lhuyd's description in AB. This is an important point, because Lhuyd's description of Cornish, though imperfect, is the only phonetic description of the language that we have.

As a result of a detailed analysis of Lhuyd and of the Cornish texts themselves I recommend revising the phonology of Unified Cornish slightly in five ways:

1) Unified Cornish does not distinguish the long *y* (pronounced *ee*) of *mys* 'month' from the vowel of *gwyth* 'trees' or *byth* 'will be'. These latter should probably be pronounced *gwedh* and *bedh* respectively. There is much uncertainty here, however, since it is clear that *bys* 'world' and *ys* 'corn' were pronounced with a long *i* (*ee*) in some varieties of Late Cornish, rather than with the long *e* that one would posit by comparison with other words. UCR writes *gwedh* 'trees', *bedh* 'will be' and allows both *bes* and *bys* 'world'. [The hesitation between *y* and *e* in some etyma may have something to do with the analogy of *y ~ e* in *scryf* but *screfa*].

2) Unified Cornish does not properly distinguish between the *œ*-vowel of *dues* 'come' and the *ü*-vowel of *y dus* 'his people'. That the two sounds were distinct in Middle Cornish is guaranteed by the way in which one unrounds to *e* in Late Cornish and the other to *i/y* (*ee*). Even so, the failure of Unified Cornish to distinguish the two vowels is not entirely unjustified, since we know, for example, that on occasion *ues* 'is' becomes *ees* in Late Cornish rather than *ês*.

3) Unified Cornish spells 'to hear' as *clewes* and 'Cornish' as *Kernewek*. It is quite clear, however, that from the period of PA onwards original *ew* in disyllables and polysyllables is becoming *ow*. UCR therefore writes *clowes* 'to hear', *cowsel* 'to speak', *towlel* 'to throw', *Kernowek* 'Cornish' and is thus faithful to practice of the Tudor scribes.

4) Unified Cornish is uncertain about the value of *g/k* in words like *wheg* 'sweet', *medhek* 'doctor'. After an exhaustive analysis of the evidence I conclude that final consonants were heavily affected by the Prosodic Shift (CT §§ 8.8-19). Stressed syllables have *g* whereas unstressed syllables have *k*: *wheg* 'sweet' but *anwhek* 'bitter', *rag* 'for' but *marrek* 'knight'. The same alternation is also operative in UCR for *b/p*: *mab* 'son', *neb* 'who' but *morrep* 'seashore', *modryp* 'aunt'. Similarly after a stressed

vowel *f* is pronounced *v* in words like *nef* 'heaven', *of* 'I am', etc. Final *th/dh* is a problem, but I believe it is correct to write *ladh* 'kill!', *bedh* 'be!' on the one hand, and *meneth* 'mountain', *gwrageth* 'wives' on the other.

5) Unified Cornish writes *gh* both finally and medially. The commoner practice of the Cornish scribes, however, is to write *myrgh* 'daughter' but *myrhes* 'daughters', *yagh* 'healthy' but *yehes* 'health'. I follow the scribes here and alternate medial *h* (pronounced *h*) with final *gh* (pronounced as *ch* in Scottish *loch*). This alternation was also observed by Jenner who says: "Note that when a syllable is added to a word ending in *gh*, the *g* is omitted" (HCL: 86 fn.).

In CT I also make detailed recommendations for the simplification of the inflection and syntax of Neo-Cornish. A full discussion of my recommendations would be out of place here and I simply refer the interested reader to CT §§ 18.1- 21.18. It is nonetheless perhaps worth mentioning three points.

Firstly, I recommend using *fatel, tel, del* to introduce indirect statement. This means that UCR will say *Yth esof vy ow crejy tel wrug ow mab y wul solabrys* 'I believe my son has already done it' where Unified would use the more cumbersome *My a grys ow map dh'y wul solabrys* or *My a grys y'n gwruk ow map solabrys*. This syntax is well established in Middle Cornish. Edwards lists several examples of *del* and one of *fatel* introducing indirect statement in PA (PAA: 15-6). There are instances of *fatel* + indirect statement in RD and BM. In TH and SA the use of *fatel* to introduce indirect statement is very common indeed (for references see CT § 21.17). The view that *(fa)tel, del* + indirect statement is confined to Late Cornish (George 1995: 108) is very wide of the mark.[1]

Secondly, I recommend using *mynnes* 'to wish' as an auxiliary to express the future, for example *Me a vyn screfa lyther avorow* 'I shall write a letter tomorrow'. This syntax is to be found in all the Middle Cornish texts with personal subjects (CT §21.19). It is also attested on occasion with impersonal subjects, for example *mar myn ov descans servya* 'if my learning will be adequate' BM 524. The opinion that *mynnes* expressing the future occurs in Late Cornish only (George 1995: 108) is groundless.

Thirdly, it should be noticed that many of the reforms of syntax and inflection are already in use by some speakers of Unified Cornish (see, for example, Lyon 1984).

CT has met with a very warm welcome from revivalists. All those who have read the book appear to believe that there is now a strong case against Kernowek Kemyn. Ray Edwards is typical when he writes:

> Dr Williams' book (...) should be studied by all serious students of the language and in particular members of the Cornish Language Board. Our ultimate aim

---

1    See "Indirect statement in Cornish and Breton", pp. 111–119 below.

should be to make our revived Cornish as authentic as possible even if further changes are seen to be necessary (*K.D.L. Annual* July 1995).

I am particularly pleased to see that my proposals for UCR are now (November 1995) being studied in depth by *Agan Tavas* to determine how far the society should adopt them. The Cornish revival cannot afford conflicting systems. More than anything the revival needs unity of purpose and action, but unity will not be achieved until Cornish-speakers agree upon one generally acceptable variety of Cornish. Such agreement cannot be reached, however, until spurious forms of the language are rejected.

# PRE-OCCLUSION IN CORNISH*

## Introduction

**0.0** "Pre-occlusion" means the distinctive pronunciation in later Cornish of *n* as [$^d$n] and of *m* as [$^b$m]. In Late Cornish *pen* 'head', for example, appears as *pedn* and *tam* 'bit, piece' is *tabm*. Probably the first scholar to notice the phenomenon of pre-occlusion in Cornish was Edward Lhuyd. He prefaces his Cornish Grammar in AB with an address to the people of Cornwall written in his idiosyncratic and highly Cymricized Cornish. Here Lhuyd refers to four "corruptions" which he has noticed in the spoken Cornish of his own day (*c.* 1700). He describes the first two "corruptions" as follows:

> An Legriaz kensa yu gorra an litheren *b*, arâg an litheren m, gen leverel ha skrefa *Tybm, tabm, kabm, gybman, krobman* ha *kylobman,* &c. enlê Tym, tam, kam gymman, kromman ha kylomman. An eil yu gorra an letheren *d*, arág an letheren n; ha kouz endella enlêh *pen, pan, pren; guyn, guan, bron, brynan*; pedn, padn, predn, guydn, guadn, brodn, brydnan

> [The first corruption is to put the letter b before the letter m and to pronounce and to write *tybm, tabm, kabm, gybman, krobman* and *kylobman,* etc., instead of *tym, tam, kam, gymman, kromman* and *kylomman*. The second is to put the letter *d* before the letter *n* and thus instead of *pen, pan, pren, guyn, guan, bron, brynan* to pronounce *pedn, padn, predn, guydn, guadn, brodn, brydnan*] (AB: 223)

Pre-occlusion is not, as far as I am aware, attested in Cornish until the sixteenth century. The earliest examples known to me are the three instances of the word *bedneth* 'blessing' for earlier *benneth* at BM 198, 225 and 226. The bulk of BM was written in 1504 but the first few hundred lines in which these forms occur are possibly of a slightly later date. Examples of pre-occlusion are not common in place-names until the late sixteenth and seventeenth centuries (see 2.1). It is likely, however, that the origin of pre-occlusion in Cornish is much older than the sixteenth and seventeenth centuries.

## The Cornish Prosodic Shift

**1.0** Pre-occlusion in Cornish is, I believe, related to another phenomenon in Cornish phonology, namely the overall shortening of long and half-long vowels. It is probable that at one time in its history Cornish resembled both Welsh and Breton in having three vocalic lengths, long, half-long and short. It is also clear that by the time of our earliest Middle Cornish texts, i.e. the fourteenth and early fifteenth centuries, Cornish has lost half length and has

---

* First published in *Studia Celtica* XXXII (1998), 129–154.

long and short only. This radical reshaping of syllabic length is suggested by a whole range of developments in the Middle Cornish texts. The shortening, which I refer to as the Prosodic Shift, is so important for our understanding of Cornish phonology that we must examine it here in some depth.

The length of vowels in Old Cornish was probably similar to that of Welsh and Breton. In stressed monosyllables the vowel was long in final position or before a short consonant. If the final consonant was long, the vowel of the monosyllable was short. In polysyllables a stressed vowel was half-long before a historically short consonant and short before a historically long one. In Old Cornish, therefore, *tat* 'father' (< *tatos*) would have had a long vowel, whereas *mam* 'mother' (< *mamma*) would have had a short one. The plural *tatou* 'fathers' (< *tatowes*) would have had a half-long stressed vowel, whereas the stressed vowel of the plural *mamou* 'mothers' (< *mammowes*) would have been short. In Old Cornish the vowel of *da* 'good' (< *dagos*) would have been long, whereas the vowel of *dater* 'goodness' would have been half-long. The threefold opposition between long, half-long and short can be understood as one of a single mora, of two morae and three morae respectively. The vowel of *tat* and *da* have three morae, the stressed vowel of *tatou* and *dater* have two morae each, whereas the vowel of *mam* and the stressed vowel of *mamou* are both of one mora only.

The evidence suggests that half-length disappeared between Old Cornish and the period of our earliest Middle Cornish texts. This can hardly mean that half-length disappeared while long and short remained as they were. It must rather imply a general shortening throughout the vocalic system. Short vowels remained, whereas half-long vowels and long vowels alike lost one mora each. In Old Cornish *tat* had three morae, *tatou* had two and the (stressed) vowel of *mam and mamou* alike had one. By the Middle Cornish period *tas* 'father' probably had two morae and the (stressed) vowels of *tasou* 'fathers', *mam* 'mother' and *mamou* 'mothers' probably all had one mora only.

I have been speaking confidently of the general shortening of vowels in the transition from Old to Middle Cornish without citing any corroborative evidence. The effects of the Prosodic Shift are so pervasive in Middle Cornish, however, that there is certainly no lack of evidence. Historically short vowels occurred in originally closed syllables, that is to say, before a geminate or fortis consonant. In consequence consonants were sometimes doubled in Cornish to show that the preceding vowel was short. I suggested above that *da* 'good' in Old Cornish probably had three morae whereas the vowel of *dater* 'goodness' had two. If the shortening of vowels in Middle Cornish were a reality, *dader*, the Middle Cornish equivalent of Old Cornish *dater*, ought to have had a short vowel rather than a half-long one. In which case we might perhaps expect *dader* 'goodness' to be written in the Middle Cornish texts with a double medial <d>. This is exactly what we do find. Here are a selection of examples: *dadder* BM 485, 499, 2229, 3173, 4463, 4515, TH 11, 30a; *daddar* TH 11a, 12; *ʒadder* PA 3c, BM 189, 228; *thadder* OM 973, PC 3097, RD 1224, BM 528, 2240, 2274,

4271, 4490, 4494; *thaddar* TH 14. If the stressed vowel in *dader* and similar words was half-long, these spellings are inexplicable. If on the other hand the vowel was short, they make perfect sense.

**1.1** Further evidence for the Prosodic Shift can be seen in the treatment of long vowels in absolute final position. Historical long /iː/ written <y> often appears in Late Cornish as a diphthong. Lhuyd, for example, writes *kei* 'dog' (AB: 46c), *nei* 'we' (BF: 17), *hei* 'she' (BF: 17) and *krei* 'cry' (BF: 17). Similarly Nicholas Boson writes *chei* 'house' (BF: 15) and *trei* 'three' (BF: 15). There are definite examples of a diphthongal spelling of historical /iː/ from as early as the sixteenth century. Tregear writes *whay* for *why* 'you (plural)' at § 33a and Borde writes *tray kans* for 'three hundred' (Loth: 226). There are forms from the *Ordinalia* (fourteenth-fifteenth century) that could possibly be interpreted as representing a diphthongized long vowel, for example *avey* 'enmity' OM 314, *rey* 'to give' PC 537, *agey* 'within' PC 627 and *may fey* 'that thou be' RD 2023. There are in addition many rhymes in the medieval texts that indicate diphthongization was already in place from the fourteenth century at the latest. PA is possibly the earliest complete text in Middle Cornish and may have been composed in the first half of the fourteenth century, though the earliest manuscript is later than that. At § 21 of PA the four rhyming words are *otry* 'outrage' (stressed on the final syllable), *dry* 'to bring', *pray* 'prey' and *ioy* 'joy'. In order for these rhymes to work the vowel in both *otry* and *dry* must be pronounced with a diphthong, which I assume was [əj].

There further instances in the other medieval texts of historic /iː/ rhyming with diphthongs. Here are some examples from the *Ordinalia* and BM: *ny* 'we' ~ *joy* joy' OM 555-8, *ty* 'thou' ~ *moy* 'more' OM 946-8, *deffry* 'indeed' ~ *ioy* 'joy' OM 1374-8, *bynary* 'ever' ~ *fay* 'faith' PC 907-10, *dry* 'to bring' ~ *fey* 'faith' PC 1993-6, *vercy* 'mercy' ~ *ioy* 'joy' RD 76-7, *th'y* 'thither' ~ *ioy* 'joy' RD 185-6, *ny* 'we' ~ *moy* 'more' RD 560-1, *ny* 'we' ~ *ioy* 'joy' RD 1201-2, *why* 'you' ~ *ioy* 'joy' RD 1285-6, *deffry* 'indeed' ~ *ioy* 'joy' RD 1432-3, *pry* 'clay' ~ *ioy* 'joy' RD 1561-3, *gy* 'thee' ~ *moy* 'more' RD 2036-7, *d'y* 'thither' ~ *ioy* 'joy' RD 2515-6, *company* 'company' ~ *ioy* 'joy' RD 2639-41, *vy* 'I' ~ *vay* 'kiss' BM 507-8, *ny* 'we' ~ *moy* 'more' BM 1874-7, *thefy* 'defy' ~ *fay* 'faith' BM 2475-6 and *eredy* 'indeed' ~ *fay* 'faith' BM 3552-3.

The diphthongization of final /iː/ was, I assume, a result of the Prosodic Shift. Before the shift /iː/ in absolute auslaut would have had three morae and could have been understood as [iˑj], that is to say a half-long nucleus followed by a semivocalic coda. The semivocalic nature of the second element would have been an inevitable consequence of the vowel's standing in auslaut, in particular before a following vowel. After the shift [iˑj] would have lost one mora to become [ij]. But [i] was now short and would necessarily have been less tense than when half-long. The whole complex would therefore have been [ij] where the nucleus and coda were at slightly different heights in the mouth. Once the vowel had split in this way, the two elements would have continued to move apart and the end result would have been [əj] or the like. It is this that gives an adequate rhyme with /oj/, /ej/, and /aj/ in the texts.

**1.2** Another striking feature of the Middle Cornish texts is the way they spell the word for 'God'. Not infrequently the word is *dev*, for example at OM 73, 115 or *dew*, e.g. at OM 2136 and PC 49. In OCV the word is *duy* and it would seem that *dew* is a metathesised form of the Old Cornish. The same metathesis has occurred in Welsh *Duw* but not in Breton *Doue*. The commonest Middle Cornish spelling of the word 'God' is *du*. I have noticed the following examples from PA alone: *du* 4d, 6d, 8b twice, 12d, 14d, 24a, 30b, 42d, 43b, 45d, 51d, 55b, 57a, 57c, 58c, 62a, 75a, 86d, 93a, 93b, 95d, 100d, 122a, 129c, 135c, 143b, 163d, 192b, 195d, 197d, 208d, 210d, 252d, 259a; *Du* 3a, 44a; *thu* 1d, 15a 90c, 246b; *3u* 27c, 17b. It should be noted further that *du* at PA 129c rhymes with *yw* 'is' and is clearly to be pronounced /dɪw/ or similarly. *Du* as a spelling is at first sight perplexing and indeed Henry Lewis was apparently baffled by it (LlCC: 7).

The Middle Cornish word for 'black' is usually written <du>, <dv>, for example at OM 1778 *shyndys of gans cronek dv* 'I have been harmed by a black toad'. Yet under 'Ater *Black, Dark*' Lhuyd gives Cornish *Diu* (AB: 44). It would seem that as early as the fourteenth century the Cornish word *du* 'black' was pronounced [dɪw] or [dew] and was close in pronunciation to the word *dew* 'God'. In consequence scribes frequently wrote *dew* 'God' as <du>. The diphthongization of *du* 'black' to *\*dyw* is, I believe, further evidence for the Prosodic Shift. Before the Prosodic Shift the word for 'black' would have been /dy:/ where the vowel was trimoric. We could analyse this vowel as consisting of a half-long [yˑ] followed by a semivocalic coda [ɥ], i.e. a fronted [w]. Such an analysis would be in keeping the Old Cornish form *duw* in OCV where <w> (represented in the manuscript by the Old English letter *wynn*) probably meant [ɥ]. After the Prosodic Shift the half-long nucleus was shortened and in consequence untensed. It was therefore slightly lower than the high front coda. In this way the long vowel had become a diphthong. It would seem that the two elements differentiated themselves further and the nucleus unrounded while the coda unfronted: [dyˑɥ] > [dyɥ] > [døɥ] > [dew]. Thus the final result was [dɪw] or [dew], and it is this that is the origin both of the spelling <du> 'God' and Lhuyd's *diu* 'black'. The shift *du > dyw, dew is* parallel with *try > trey* and indeed is part of the same process in Cornish.[1]

---

1  George, who dates the Prosodic Shift to the seventeenth century, has noted the diphthongization of /iː/ but believes that the vowel became [ɪj] *c.* 1525 and [əj] *c.* 1625. Moreover, he suggests that the immediate origin of the 'breaking' of /iː/ was the English Great Vowel Shift (PSRC: 110). This view is difficult to sustain. The rhymes in PA and the *Ordinalia* indicate that /iː/ had already become [əj] by the late fourteenth or early fifteenth centuries at the latest. The shift is due to circumstances inside Cornish itself. It has nothing to do with the English Great Vowel Shift of the late fifteenth century. Indeed we should be very wary of ascribing phenomena in one language to the sound-changes of another. Cornish lived and indeed died in the

The word for 'spear' in Middle Cornish (cf. Welsh *gwayw*) is comparable with that for 'God'. It is not infrequently written in the texts with a diphthong, for example, *gew PA* 218c, *CW* 992; *gyw PA* 219b, 221a, *giu PC* 3010 and *guv* P, C 2922, RD 432, 1015. On occasion, however, it is spelt with <u>, for example *gu* RD 491, 1117, 2586, BM 2604. The word was pronounced /giw/ in Middle Cornish. As is the case with *du* 'God' <u> in *gu* represents /ɪw/.[2]

In CT (§ 3.9) I suggested that the Cornish word *plu* 'parish' was originally /plu:/ (cf. Breton *plou-* in toponyms) and that as a result of the Prosodic Shift this went through the following states: [plu·w] > [plʊ·w] > [plǫw] > [plew] to give <plew> in some of the sources. There are two serious problems with this explanation of mine. In the first place, if the word really did go through a stage *[plǫw] where the vowel was a centralized *o*, it is difficult to see why *plu* did not become *\*plow*. In the second place and more seriously, the Breton simplex was *ploue* not *plou*. *Plou* is the form in toponyms. With *ploue* compare Welsh *plwyf* 'parish'. The three Brythonic etyma derive from Latin *pleb(em)* in which the root vowel is long.

I should like here to offer what I hope is a more convincing explanation for Middle Cornish *plu, plew* 'parish'. OCV gives the word as *plui* in the phrase *hebrenchiat plui* 'presbyter' [leader of a parish 'priest']. *Plui* would appear to be similar phonologically to *duy* 'God' in OCV. If Old Cornish *duy* underwent metathesis to become *dev, dew*, it seems probable that *plui* underwent a similar development to become *plew*. It is this that was variously written <plew> (TH 25a; cf the toponyms *Plewe-Golen, Plewgolom* CPNE: 259) and <plu> (RD 247, 2584)—exactly as 'God' was spelt either <dew> or <du> and 'spear' was <gew> or <gu>.[3]

---

shadow of English but it was always a different language. Its phonology at all periods is distinct from that of English and is governed by its own laws. The sound-changes of English are irrelevant for Cornish except insofar as English borrowings in Cornish are concerned. It should also be noted that the shift of Cornish /i:/ to [əj] is parallel to the shift of Cornish /y:/ to [ɪw]. Of this latter sound-change George says: "In final position and before /x/, [y:] > [ɪu:] as in English, possibly *c.* 1625" (PSRC:136). It is clear from the spelling <du> in PA for <dew> that the shift [y:] > [ɪw] had already occurred by the fifteenth century. It had nothing to do with English except insofar as the Prosodic Shift itself was indirectly the result of English in Cornwall. The two changes i.e. diphthongization of /i:/ and /y:/, are comparable with each other. One would therefore expect them to occur at the same time.

2    Because he dates [y:] > [ɪw] to the seventeenth century George is perplexed by the word for 'spear' and is uncertain how it should be spelt in Neo-Cornish. His solution is to assume that there were two forms in Middle Cornish: 1) *guv* which has been "influenced by B[reton] *goaf*", and 2) *gyw* (GKK: 121, 132).

3    George says of *plu* 'parish': "N.B. The development of this word was irregular" GKK: 255. If, as seems likely, the development was *pleb(em) > pluy(f) > plyw* written <plu>, <plew>, it was completely regular.

**1.3** There are numerous other ways in which the Prosodic Shift has affected the long vowels of Cornish (see CT §§ 3.117). It had far-reaching effects on the short vowels as well. It is likely, for example, that the vowel in words like *scryfa* 'to write' (Breton *skrivañ*), *myres* 'to look' (Breton *mirout*), *tryga* 'to dwell' (Welsh *trigo*) and *whylas* 'to seek' (cf. Welsh *chwilio*) in Cornish was originally a half-long high front /iˑ/. In the texts, however, these disyllabic items are not infrequently spelt with <e>. Here are some examples:

'to write': *screfys* PA 188d twice, BM 2766; *screfis* BM 394

'to look': *veras* PA 168b, OM 2325, BM 4074; *verys* PC 1257; *veres* BM 4351, *verays* BM 733; 4433, *merovgh* BM 95; *merugh* BM 1577, 2086

'to dwell': *trege* PA 37b, 214c, OM 566, 1711 BM 947, 1344, 2948; *trega* OM 2665, BM 4348; *tregys* PA 7b, BM 816; *tregis* PA 85d, 93c, 255d; *tregough* OM 1893, *tregugh* BM 4566; *dregas* PA 213d; *drege* PC 3002

'to seek': *whela* PA 21c, 198d; *welas* OM 378; *whelas* PA 145d, 156b, 257d, OM 1139; *wheleugh* PA 68b, 168d, RD 781; *weleugh* PA 69b; *weles* BM 2758.

Forms with <e> are attested in Late Cornish also: *skrepha* AB: 146c, *screfa* BF: 46, *screffez* RC 23: 187, 188, 195; *meraz* BF: 58, *meraz* ACB, *mero* BF: 53, RC 23: 189; *trega* AB: 64c; *whelaz* BF: 15 twice, RC 23: 198 and *whelas* ACB: Ff2 four times. It should be noted, however, that in the Middle Cornish texts monosyllabic forms of these verbs are invariably spelt with <y>: *scryf* PC 421; *myr* BM 1450, 2542, 3194; *tryg* OM 1104, *dryk* PA 212d, *dryg* OM 556, 2112, *dryc* OM 925; cf. Late Cornish *meer* 'look!' (BF: 15).[4]

This alternation *e ~ y* is another effect of the Prosodic Shift. Before the shift the vowel of /skriˑfe/ 'to write' would have had two morae but the monosyllable /skriːf/ would have had a trimoric vowel. After the shift the disyllable would have lost one mora to become /skrife/ whereas the monosyllable would also have lost one mora to become /skriˑf/. After the shift the disyllabic form would have had a short vowel which would have been less tense than its half-long counterpart. /skrife/ would thus have been realized as [skrɪfə] or [skrefə] and it is this which is frequently written <screfa> in the texts. The monosyllabic /skriˑf/ on the other hand would still have had a vowel of more than one mora and would not have become lax. It is for this reason that the monosyllabic forms are always written with <y> and not <e>. The alternation seen, then, in *meras ~ myr* is further evidence that in Middle

---

4   George ignores the alternation of <y> in monosyllables with <e> in disyllables since he believes the vowel in the disyllabic forms is half-long [iˑ]. He is unable in consequence to explain the almost universal spelling of *trege, trega* 'to dwell' with <e> rather than <y>. He says of *tryg* 'position': "the word and its compounds behaved as if they contained /ɪ/ instead of /i/" (GKK: 320–21).

Cornish vowels were either short (one mora) or long (two morae) and that an intermediate half-length was no longer part of the language.

**1.4** Another remarkable feature of Middle Cornish is the way in which unstressed vowels are indifferently spelt with any vowel. The word for 'prophet', for example, has an etymological <u> in the unstressed syllable, *profus*, and it so spelt on occasion, e.g. at PC 970, 989, 2672 and 2884. It is also spelt *profos* PC 2367, RD 66, 1686, *profes* PC 562 and *profis* PC 1923. This variation in spelling would seem to indicate that the final vowel had been reduced to schwa before the period of out texts. *Profus* is by no means an isolated example. Here are some further etyma with the variant spellings as they occur in the texts:

'one' (original /a/): *onan* OM 3, 12, 99, 1192, PA 42c, 43b, 71b, 81a, 145b, 154c, 199a; *onen* OM 57, 2099, 2308; *onon* PC 772, PA 25b, 89c, 124d twice, 137b, 138a, 163b, 242c; *onyn* TH 7a, 7a

'self' (original /a/): *honan* OM 16, 94, 2248, 2650, PA; *honon* PA 25d, 37d, 81c, 89d, 101b, 160d, 169a, 187b, 256d; *honyn* BM 3641, TH 1, la, 4, 7a

'heart' (original /o/): *colan* OM 357, TH 20a; *colen* OM 365, 428, PA 115c, BM 2049, 2408; *colon* OM 527, 1264, 1376; *colyn* BM 628, 1804

'certain' (original /a/): *certan* OM 14, 93, 494, 1313, TH 3; *certen* OM 918, BM 2034, 2067, 2073; *certyn* BM 1744, 2515, 447 1; *certyn* BM 3006

'to wait' (original /o/): *gortes* OM 1718, BM 3655; *gortos* PA 164d, 250d; *gurtas* TH 13a; *gortays* BM 2472

'children' (original /e/): *flehas* OM 975, 1159, 103 1, BM 1782, 3153; *flehes* OM 1036, BM 2014, TH *fleghys, flehys* OM 1588, 1611, 1623, PA 149d, 168c, 246c; *flehis* TH 23a

'hard' (original /e/): *cales* OM 1525, RD 244, 1987; *calas* OM 1482, RD 1086, 2024, 2260; *calys* PA 196d, 209d

'ship' (original /e/): *gorhal* OM 1050; *gorhel* OM 950, 1146, 1158, BM 467; *gorhyl* OM 1040, 1047, 1124

'people' (original /e/): *pobal* OM 1843; *pobel* OM 1543, 1557, 1564, 1574; *pobyl, pobyll* OM 1803, 1832, PA 6b, 89d, 97c, BM 2022, 23243 TH 4.

I understand this weakening of unstressed syllables as a further aspect of the Prosodic Shift. I assume that as a result of the shift stressed syllables lost in length but gained in intensity. As stressed syllables were given a more vigorous articulation unstressed syllables lost vigour and in consequence unstressed vowels tended to be reduced to the neutral vowel schwa.

**1.5** If our analysis is correct, it would seem that as a result of the Prosodic Shift the articulation of Cornish changed radically. Before the shift Cornish would have had relatively long stressed syllables which contrasted with unstressed syllables by length as much as by articulatory vigour. After the shift, however, stressed syllables lost length but increased considerably in vigour. Unstressed syllables meanwhile became noticeably weaker. As result of the Prosodic Shift Cornish ceased to resemble Welsh and Breton from an articulatory point of view but instead became more like Middle English. Indeed there is little doubt that the presence of Middle English in Cornwall was the ultimate cause of the Prosodic Shift.

**1.6** The idea of a continuous retreat of Cornish is quite misleading and does not correspond with the evidence we have. From the Norman Conquest to the Reformation there was no steady decline in Cornish. Quite the opposite. I believe that in the first century or so after the Conquest English was in decline in Cornwall and Cornish was in the ascendant. I have several reasons for this view.

We know from the Bodmin Manumissions that in the tenth and eleventh centuries the class of landowners in and around Bodmin were Saxons speaking Old English. Moreover Cornwall from the tenth century onwards was ecclesiastically part of Wessex. Cornwall's bishop and many of his clergy were English-speaking. By the thirteenth century, however, Cornwall was producing mystery plays on a large scale for a largely monoglot Cornish audience. Those who wrote, transcribed and staged these plays must have been clerics and must have been Cornish-speakers.

If we look at our surviving Cornish literature we can see that it is based on French and Breton models and owes little to Middle English, I assume that in the generation or so after the Conquest, Saxon landowners and Saxon clerics were largely replaced by French-speakers and, more importantly, by Bretons. There is good evidence for a large influx of Bretons into Cornwall after the Conquest. Indeed some speak not of the "Norman Invasion" but of the "Armorican Return". Certain aspects of the Breton contingent in England immediately after the Norman Conquest have been examined by K. S. B. Keats-Rohan. A number of things are clear from this study. In the first place it is apparent that the Bretons who acquired land in the Conqueror's English domains were very conscious of their Breton origins and fiercely loyal to their homeland. In the second place it seems that although they were not many in absolute terms, Breton landowners were proportionally more numerous in Cornwall than in any other county. According to the Domesday Book (1086) Breton landowners represented no less than 37 per cent of the total in

Cornwall. This compares with 22 per cent in Devon and 18 per cent in Norfolk (Keats-Rohan 1992: 75 fn 117).

It is true that those of the Breton nobility who received land in Cornwall took their titles from places in eastern Brittany that are no longer Celtophone. It must be remembered, however, that in the mid-ninth century Breton was spoken by at least a proportion of the population as far east as a line running approximately from Mont St Michel in the north, south to near Combour, Montfort, Baulon, Derval and Pontchâteau to end at the estuary of the Loire slightly to the cast of St Nazaire. By 1200 the Breton-speaking area had retreated to ten or so miles of the present linguistic frontier (see HPB: 2127). It seems none the less reasonable to assume that at the time of the Norman Conquest there were considerable pockets of Breton even in the far east of Brittany.

It is, of course, unlikely that the Breton nobles who followed William I were themselves Celtophone. Many of their followers would have been Breton-speakers, in particular those from central and western Brittany. The mere presence of a significant proportion of Bretons in Cornwall would have been enough to encourage close maritime links between Cornwall and Brittany. It is also significant that the Middle Cornish names *Marya* 'Mary', *Jhesus* 'Jesus', *Jowan* 'John' and *Loundres* 'London' are French or Breton. Indeed the Breton forms of 'Mary' and 'Jesus' in Middle Cornish suggest that Breton clerics were of particular importance in medieval Cornwall. There is, moreover, good evidence for the presence in Cornwall of large numbers of Bretons until the Reformation (RC 32: 2905).

The influx of Bretons after the Conquest must have had a detrimental effect on English in Cornwall. As I result, I believe, many English-speakers in Cornwall began to speak Cornish again. At first re-Celticized Cornishmen would have been bilingual. Within a generation or two many must have been monoglot Celtic speakers.

As well as being spoken in Cornwall, Wales and Brittany, Brythonic was also spoken in Cumbria. This territory stretched from the present county of that name to southern Scotland. The original capital of the Britons of the northwest was Dumbarton, 'fort of the Britons'. The Norman Conquest did not assist the Britons of Cumbria to maintain their language. The Cumbrians unlike the Cornish did not experience the reestablishment of links with British-speaking cousins over the sea. Cut off from their Welsh kinsmen to the southwest, they were condemned to cultural assimilation with the Anglo-Norse around them. As a result Cumbrian retreated very quickly and was extinct by the thirteenth century. The difference in fortunes between Cumbrian on the one hand and Cornish on the other is impossible to explain without reference to the strengthening of relations between Cornwall and Brittany after the Norman Conquest.

**1.7** OCV is probably evidence of a Celtic resurgence in Cornwall. OCV is in a language transitional between Old and Middle Cornish and was probably written in the first half of the twelfth century. It is based upon the Old English-Latin vocabulary of Ælfric of Cerne and contains almost a thousand Latin words and their Cornish equivalents. OCV, then, was written about two generations after the Norman Conquest. It is based upon an Anglo-Saxon work and attempts to provide a basic vocabulary of Cornish. It was clearly written by someone familiar with Old English and Cornish who wished to assist others in learning the Celtic tongue.

The new prosodic system brought Cornish closer to English in its phonology than it had been previously. It is difficult not to see the influence of English on Cornish in the question of quantity. Modern English is essentially a language in which stressed syllables are of short duration but of high intensity. The sound-changes of Middle English would lead one to believe that Middle English was similar to Modern English in this respect. It is unlikely that the influence of English on Cornish was simply the result of an increasing number of English-speakers in Cornwall. It is more likely, I think, that the English-speakers had themselves become Cornish-speaking and brought into their new vernacular their English speech-habits. One such Anglicized feature was intensification and shortening of syllables that I refer to as the Prosodic Shift.

## Pre-occlusion in Cornish

**2.0** Before the Prosodic Shift it is likely that Cornish had a fortis /nː/, the reflex of British *-nd-* and *-nn-*, and a lenis /n/. The difference between the two was probably a matter of the relative obstruction of the airflow. When pronouncing /nː/ the tongue was probably in greater contact with the alveolar or palatal area of the mouth than would have been the case with /n/. Comparison with some of the more conservative Modern Breton dialects also suggests that /nː/ in Cornish was probably not only more vigorous than /n/, but was longer in duration as well. I assume that the reflex of British */wiːnon/ 'wine' (< Lat. *uinum*) would in Cornish before the shift have had a final lenis, /gwiːn/. On the other hand the reflex of British */penno/ 'head' would have had a fortis, /penː/, that was both noticeably more vigorous and longer than its lenis counterpart.

The Prosodic Shift involved shortening syllables on the one hand and simultaneously reinforcing them on the other. This would have meant the loss of the opposition /nː/ ~ /n/. The long fortis /nː/ would have retained its vigour but would have lost length. Similarly the lenis /n/ would have maintained its brevity but would have increased in vigour. In a word /nː/ and /n/ would have fallen together as a short fortis. Yet the opposition lenis/fortis was crucial to maintaining an adequate number of distinctions in the system. I assume therefore that in the case of /nː/ and /n/ the opposition fortis ~ lenis was replaced by a different contrast. The historic fortis lost length but was now preceded by a furtive unexploded stop, /peᵈn/, in order to distinguish it from the newly reinforced /n/. Acoustically the difference between /pen:/ before the shift and /pe$^d$n/ after it may not have been so great as to warrant a new spelling. Certainly the scribes continued to write 'head' as <pen> without indicating in spelling that pre-occlusion had taken place.

The same phenomenon is attested where /n:/ occurred medially rather than finally. The word *benneth* 'blessing' (< Vulgar Latin *ben'dictio)*, for example, before the shift would have contained a geminate fortis: /'ben:eθ/. After the shift, however, the medial consonant would have been shortened and pre-occluded to /$^d$n/ and the whole word would have had the shape /'be$^d$nəθ/, where incidentally the reinforcement of the stressed syllable has weakened the unstressed vowel to /ə/. This would have been written <benneth> both before the shift and after it. It was only in the sixteenth century that the unexploded stop in /$^d$n/ acquired separate status and came to be shown in writing.

**2.1** By the Late Cornish period it is clear that short monosyllables had lengthened again. Lhuyd, for example, has the following spellings: *blêu* 'hair' (AB: 46a), *plêu* 'parish' (AB: 11 3b), *têu* 'fat' (AB: 120c), where the graph <êu> implies a trimoric diphthong [e·w]. Compare Rowe's *deaw* 'two' (RC 23: 199). Similarly Nicholas Boson spells Middle Cornish *ple* 'where?' as *po leea* (BF: 16) which seems to imply [pə'le:ə)] and his spelling *mouy* 'more' (BF: 29) is probably for [mu·j]

Although the lengthening is attested in writing in final stressed diphthongs only, this is probably a result of the inadequacies of the orthographical systems in use in the Late Cornish period. If stressed diphthongs in auslaut lengthened, it is likely that stressed syllables everywhere had a tendency to lengthen. In which case the stressed syllables of *pen* and *benneth* would also be expected to lengthen. The result of the increase in length was that the unstopped consonant in [pe$^d$n] gained in length to become a full consonant: [pedn]. At the same time as [pe$^d$n] lengthened to [pedn] the first syllable of ['be$^d$nəθ] lengthened to ['bednəθ] with [d] and [n] as more clearly defined consonants, though in the same syllable. It was this, I assume, that was written <bedneth> in BM (see 0.0 above). The first recorded instance of <dn>, then, was in the first few hundred lines of BM. Padel cites *Pednanpill* in Feock from 1597 (CPNE: 290). Pool, for example, cites the following forms from Penwith: *Nansquidnyow* 1591, *Boskednan* 1623, *Busweddon* 1641, *Rosevidny* 1657, *Codnagoath* 1658, *Towidnacke* 1659 (PNWP: 40-69). CW, which was written (though not composed) in 1611 has over 50 examples of pre-occluded /n:/, such as *pedn* 182, 1090, 2318, *bydnarre* 1161, *tedna* 1466, *badna* 1474, *gwadn* 1679, *avadn* 1809, etc.

**2.2** Pre-occlusion will not occur when the *n* is immediately followed by a voiceless plosive. Thus Lhuyd writes *vedn* (BF: 16, 17) but *menta* (BF: 16 twice, 17). It also appears that /n/ when followed by /j/ became /n:j/ early enough to allow pre-occlusion. As examples one might cite *vargidniaz* < *\*bargynya* 'to bargain' (BF: 17), *fortidniez* < *\*fortunya* 'to make fortunate' (BF: 31) and *aprodnioe* 'tabliers, aprons' (RC 23: 177, RC 24: 157) < *\*apronyow*.

Pre-occlusion does not occur when the preceding vowel is unstressed. The definite article *an* is from Common Celtic *\*sindo-*, *\*sinda-* but is never pre-occluded since it is always an unaccented proclitic. Curiously, however, *un* the numeral 'one' and the indefinite article is pre-occluded. I have noticed the following examples from CW: *idn dewges* 'one deity' 6, *vdn dew* 'one God' 11, *vdn spyes* 'a space' 1969, *vdn rew* 'in a row' 2145, *vdn venyn* 'a woman' 2213, *udn mabe* 'one son' 2539. One would not expect *un* to be pre-occluded since it contains etymological /n/: < *\*oino-*. We must assume that in the Old Cornish period the long vowel in *un* was shortened when the word was weakly accented and the final /n/ was reinterpreted after the short vowel as /nː/. This weakly accented /ynː/ must have been generalized to places where it bore the full accent and in consequence the final consonant was pre-occluded.

**2.3** There were apparently some dialects of Cornish that did not undergo pre-occlusion of /nː/. This, I assume, was because they had already before the Prosodic Shift lost the distinction between fortis and lenis. In these dialects of Cornish it appears that the reduction of /nː/ to /n/ in some etyma resulted in a compensatory lowering of the preceding vowel. Before the loss of half-length the two words 'woman' and 'blessing', for example, would have been doubly distinct in their first syllables. They would have had both differing vowel lengths, half-long ~ short, and different medial consonants lenis ~ fortis: /ˈbeˑnen/ and /ˈbenːeθ/, where the fortis was both longer and more vigorous than the lenis. In those dialects, however, that had lost the opposition lenis ~ fortis the two items would have been distinct only in vocalic length. In such dialects the stressed vowel of *benneth* was already less tense than the vowel *of benen*, since it was short while the vowel in *benen* was half-long. Allophonically in these dialects *benneth* would have been [ˈbæneθ]. When half-length disappeared with the operation of the Prosodic Shift the lowered allophone in *benneth* became fully phonemic: /ˈbanəθ/, written *banneth*. In those dialects that maintained the distinction /n/ ~ /nː/, /nː/ was pre-occluded to /ˈbednaθ/. We will see below that *benneth/bedneth* and *banneth* are in complementary distribution in the texts.

**2.4** In theory the opposition lenis ~ fortis cannot exist in Cornish with *m* since the lenis variety of *m* had become /v/ by lenition in the late British period, and therefore *m*, wherever it occurred, was *ipso facto* a fortis. Comparison with Breton, however, indicates that in Cornish a new opposition of fortis [m] ~ long fortis [mː] arose spontaneously in the language. [mː] was usually the reflex of British medial *-mm-* and *-mb-* and occurred in Cornish only after a stressed vowel. Thus, for example, *cam* 'bent' (< British *\*kambo-*) and *kemer* 'take!' (< British *\*kombere*) before the Prosodic Shift were probably [kamː] and ['kemːer] respectively. *Kemeres* 'to take' (< British *\*kombereto-*), however, would have been [ke'meˑres], since the *m* < *mb* was before, not after, the accent.

The opposition [mː] ~ [m] was entirely determined by position. It is possible that English or French loanwords may have been borrowed into Cornish that contained a stressed vowel followed by [m]. Whether such items could have survived intact seems doubtful. If they existed, they would have tended to conform to the native pattern and substitute stressed short vowel + [mː] for stressed short vowel + [m]. This substitution would have prevented the emergence of /mː/ as a separate phoneme. At all events, I assume that before the Prosodic Shift there were in Cornish two oppositions: 1) the phonemic /n/ ~ /nː/ on the one hand and 2) the allophonic [m] ~ [mː] on the other.

With the operation of the Prosodic Shift the opposition [mː] ~ [m] was transformed, being replaced by [ᵇm] and [m]: [kaᵇm], ['keᵇmər] but [ke'merəz]. As was the case with pre-occluded *n,* pre-occluded *m* was not shown in writing until the sixteenth and seventeenth centuries. When /ᵈn/ and /ᵇm/ became /dn/ and /bm/ respectively /bm/ would of necessity have ceased to be an allophone of /m/. The first example of pre-occluded *m* is probably to be found in SA (*c.* ?1570) which has <mamb> for <mam> 'mother' at § 59. This I take to represent [maᵇm] . Pre-occluded *m is* common in CW: *lebmyn* 70, 80, 2091, 2240, 2487; *gybmar* 692; *vabm* 1203; *kybmys*, *kebmys* 1284, 2146; *cabm* 1603; *hebma* 2499 and *obma* 2523. Just as there were dialects that had lost the opposition /nː/ ~ /n/, so there were dialects that had lost the opposition [mː] ~ [m].[5] In these dialects the pre-occlusion of *m* could not occur.

That the opposition [mː] ~ [m], where it occurred, was allophonic and not phonemic is seen clearly from the divergent development, of the two items 'thence' and 'hence'. The word for 'thence' was in origin *a le na* 'from that place' for *\*a'n le na*. I assume that already before the shift this had developed into a single accentual unit: *alena* [a'leˑna] in which the long vowel of *le* has been reduced to half-long. When the shift occurred the half-long vowel was shortened to give [ə'lenə]. This appears in the texts as <alena>, for example at CW 508, 934, 1725 and 1823. It is written <alenna> by Rowe in the late seventeenth century (*Ha moaze a lenna* 'et en allant de là' RC 23: 191), but the geminate <nn> is merely a graph to show that the vowel is short. There is no pre-occlusion of the *n.* The case of 'hence' is different. The original form would have been *\*a'n le ma,* which would have given *\*a le ma* [a'leˑma] before the Prosodic Shift. With the operation of the shift the half-long vowel of *le* in [a'leˑma] was reduced to short. In consequence /m/ now stood immediately after a short stressed vowel. It was therefore realized as its long allophone [mː] which itself was undergoing the transition to [ᵇm]. The word thus became [ə'leᵇmə] and later [ə'lebmə]. The first appears as <alemma> in the texts, e.g. at

---

5   It is more likely that those dialects which did not display the opposition [mː] ~ [m] had lost it rather than failed to develop it. The dialects that retained the opposition were the western ones and these were the more conservative.

RD 135, 151, 362, 393, 805, 1237, 1610 and 1960. The second is represented by <alebma> at CW 1208 and 2080.

**2.5** I believe that the more easterly parts of Celtophone Cornwall lost the opposition /n/ ~ /n:/ before the Prosodic Shift and as a result pre-occlusion of *n* could not occur in them. In the same way these more easterly areas abandoned the opposition [m:] ~ [m] or had never developed it. Pre-occlusion seems very largely to be a western phenomenon. It is well attested in Late Cornish which is by its very nature western in provenance. Moreover if we examine the place-name evidence closely we see that pre-occlusion is confined to the western part of Cornwall. Having collected all the certain examples of pre-occlusion from the index of CPNE, I have supplied them all with an etymology where possible and have put them in alphabetical order of the parish or town in which they occur. The result is as follows:

>  *Chytodden* < *chy war an ton* (Breage)
>  *Pengwedna* < *pen ?Gwenna* (Breage)
>  *Chytodden* < *chy war an ton* (Camborne)
>  *Pencobben* < *pen *comm* (Camborne)
>  *Chegwidden* < *chy gwyn* (Constantine)
>  *Crack-an-Godna* < *crak an godna* (Constantine)
>  *Park-an-Gubman* < *park an *goumman* (Constantine)
>  *Park-an-Toddan* < *park an ton* (Constantine)
>  *Park-Cabben* < *park cam* (Constantine)
>  *Park Tobma* < *park tom* (Constantine)
>  *Pedn Billy* < *pen byly* (Constantine)
>  *Penbothidnow* < *pen + budinnow* (Constantine)
>  *Polgwidden Cove* < *poll gwyn* (Constantine)
>  *The Ladden* < *?glan* (Crowan)
>  *Pednanpill Point* < *pen an *pyll* (Feock)
>  *Porthgwidden* < *porth gwyn* (Feock)
>  *Pednvadan* < *pen tal van* (Gerrans)
>  *Ingewidden* < *hensy wyn* (Grade)
>  *Polgwidden* < *poll gwyn* (Grade)
>  *Carnaquidden* < *kernyk gwyn* (Gulval)
>  *Cascadden* < *casek gan* (Gwennap)
>  *Menergwidden* < *meneth gwyn* (Gwennap)
>  *Tolvaddon* < *tal van* (Illogan)
>  *Landewednack* < *lann to-Winnok* (Landewednack)
>  *Kilcobben Cove* < *kyl *comm* (Landewednack)
>  *Peddenporperre* < *pen + ?* (Landewednack)
>  *The Gabmas* < *camas* (Lelant)
>  *Pedndrea* < *pen an dre* (Lelant)
>  *Porth Kidney Sands* < *pol cumyas* (Lelant)
>  *Menwidden* < *men wyn* (Ludgvan)
>  *Nangidnall* < *gun aswy enyall* (Madron)
>  *Pednpons* < *pen pons* (Madron)

# PRE-OCCLUSION IN CORNISH

*Pedn Venton < pen-fenten* (Madron)
*Todne Rosemoddress < ton* + PN (Madron)
*Trewidden < tre wyn* (Madron)
*Lo Cabm < loch cam* (Mullion)
*Pedn Crifton < pen ?\*crygh* (Mullion)
*Crockagodna < crak an gonna* (Mylor)
*Park Tuban < park tom* (Paul)
*Pedn Bejuffin < pen + mydzhovan* (Paul)
*Pedn Tenjack < pen denjack* (Paul)
*Pedny coanse < pen an \*cawns* (Paul)
*Todden Coath < ton coth* (Paul)
*Street an Dudden < stret an don* (Penzance)
*Blankednick < blyn + ?* (Perrananaworthal)
*Codnidne < conna yn* (Perranzabuloc)
*Pedn-an-drea < pen an dre* (Redruth)
*Pednanvounder < pen an vounder* (Ruan Major)
*Chirgwidden < chy gour gwyn* (Sancreed)
*Codnagooth < conna goth* (Sancreed)
*Cudedno < cudynnow* (Scilly)
*Enys Dodnan < enys don* (Sennen)
*Pedden an wollas < pen an wlas* (Sennen)
*Croc-an-codna < crak an gonna* (Sithney)
*Cudno < conna* (Sithney)
*Pednavounder < pen an vounder* (Sithney)
*Prospidnack < \*prys \*pynnek* (Sithney)
*Taban Denty < tam denty* (Sithney)
*Ventonvedna < fenten \*fenna* (Sithney)
*Chytodden < chy ton* (St Agnes)
*Codna-coos < conna cos* (St Agnes)
*Godna < conna* (St Anthony in Meneage)
*Codna Willy < conna whilen* (St Buryan)
*Pridden < \*pen-ryn* (St Buryan)
*Parke an Clibmier < park an colomyer* (St Erth)
*Park Todden < park ton* (St Ewc)
*Brevadnack < bre vannek* (St Hilary)
*Tolvadden < tal van* (St Hilary)
*Pedn Olva < pen guilva* (St Ives)
*Porth Gwidden < porth gwyn* (St Ives)
*Balleswidden < bal + ?* (St Just in Penwith)
*Cargodna < crak an gonna* (St Just in Penwith)
*Cudna Reeth < conna ruth* (St Just in Penwith)
*Leswidden < lys gwyn* (St just in Penwith)
*Marcradden < men crom* (St just in Roseland)
*Chywednack < chy wynnek* (St Keverne)
*Frogabbin < forth gam* (St Keverne)
*Gull Gwidden < gwel gwyn* (St Keverne)
*Laddenvean < \*lann vyghan* (St Keverne)
*Pednavounder < pen an vounder* (St Keverne)
*Pedn-myin < pen men* (St Keverne)

*Pedn Tiere* < *pen-tyr* (St Keverne)
*Polpidnick* < *pol \*pennek* (St Keverne)
*Pednvounder* < *pen an vounder* (St Levan)
*Carlidna* < *kelennow* (St Mawgan in Meneage)
*Carnwidden* < *carn gwyn* (Stithians)
*Amalwhidden* < *amal gwyn* (Towednack)
*Beagletodn* < *begel tom* (Towednack)
*Chytodden* < *chy ton* (Towednack)
*Park Gwidden* < *park gwyn* (Towednack)
*Skillywadden* < *? + gwan* (Towednack)
*Towednack* < *to-Winnok* (Towednack)
*Street Eden* < *stret yn* (Truro)
*Carn Pednathan* < *carn pen ethen* (Veryan)
*Calvadnack* < *kal vannek* (Wendron)
*Crackagodna* < *crak an gonna* (Wendron)
*Garlidna* < *grelynyow* (Wendron)
*Roselidden* < *ros \*lyn* (Wendron)
*Boswednack* < *bos wynnek* (Zennor)
*Pedenleda* < *pen lether* (Zennor)
*Pedn Kei* < *pen ky* (Zennor).

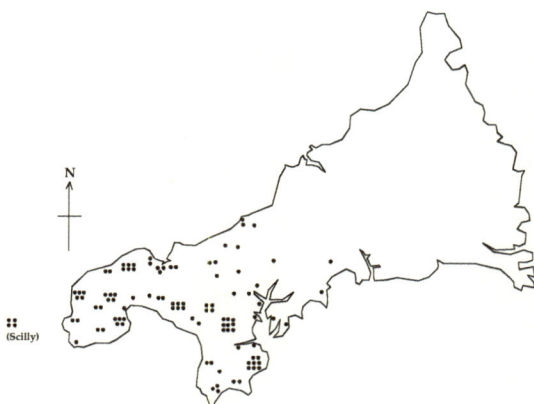

Figure 1: Pre-occlusion in Cornish place-names.

**2.6** Apart from one stray each in Veryan, St Ewe and Perranzabuloe, none is farther east than Truro.[6] Moreover it is clear that the names with pre-occlusion are particularly numerous in the far west. This cannot simply be because Cornish survived longer in the west than further east, since pre-occlusion is also recorded in Scilly, where the language died early. I cite one place-name from Scilly in the list of toponyms above. I have noticed three further place-

---

6  There are no doubt further strays east of Truro which I have not noticed because I do not have the evidence here in Dublin.

names in Scilly that are not listed by Padel but which appear to exhibit pre-occlusion: *Codnors Rocks, Pednbrose* and *Pednathise Head.* See also the accompanying map.

There is good evidence that Cornish was spoken in the far cast of Cornwall until the fifteenth century at least (CT §§ 11.1–5).[7] Moreover, the toponym *Polpidnick* in St Keverne < *pol pennek* shows pre-occlusion but not *ack* < *ek*. Since *ack* does not normally occur in toponyms before the sixteenth century, we must assume that pre-occlusion is as old. In which case its absence from central and eastern Cornwall cannot be explained chronologically. It is much more likely that the presence or absence of pre-occlusion is a dialect feature. Pre-occlusion could occur only in dialects that maintained the oppositions /n/ ~ /n:/ and [m] ~ [m:]. judging by the distribution of pre-occlusion in toponyms, these conservative dialects were the western ones.[8]

---

7   This view has been dismissed by some observers through what appears to be mere prejudice. That Cornish was spoken as far as the Tamar until the fifteenth century at least was suggested first by Jenner (HCL: 11). There is good evidence of monoglots in Minster near Boscastle in 1347 and of bilinguals in Bodmin in 1354 (Wakelin: 889). It is likely also that Cornish was used in the parish of Menheniot until the reign of Henry VIII (HCL: 123; *Cornish Banner* 3/1980: 22). The real evidence for the survival of Cornish in the far cast of Cornwall until the fifteenth century is to be found in the place-names. Penultimate stress and the preservation of unstressed syllables in many eastern toponyms indicate that such names were not borrowed into English until the late fourteenth and early fifteenth centuries. Toponyms like *Hendra* (Davidstow), *Pathada* (Linkinhorne), *Trevozah* (South Petherwin) and others like them must have been Cornish until the close of the medieval period. Notice also the eastern place-names *Lantallack Cross* (near Landrake), *Lithiack* (near St Germans), *Tresallack* (near Treburley) and *Trewethack* (St Endellion); *ack* < *ek is* not known in toponyms elsewhere in Cornwall much before the sixteenth century. The name *Tresawson* 'settlement of the Englishmen (i.e. Anglophones)' in Lanreath could not on phonological grounds have been borrowed into English before the late Middle English period yet the name implies that English-speakers were the exception rather than the rule in the area until then.

8   There were other ways in which western Cornish was more conservative than the dialects of further cast. The Old Cornish for 'blood', for example, was *guit* (OCV 65 7a). The Late Cornish form recorded by Lhuyd from the far west of Cornwall was *gûdzh* (AB: 144a). I assume that the development was as follows: /gu·id/ <guit> > */gu·idz/ > /gu:dʒ/ <gûdzh>. The standard Middle Cornish fonn was *goys, gos* which rhymes with *mois* /mo:z/ (BM 1301) and with *boys* 'to be' /bo·z/ (BM 1599-1603, 1642-3). The development of the standard form was probably /gu·id/ > */go·idz/ > /go·iz/ > /go:z/. The stage /go·iz/ is probably the origin of the spelling <goys>. In PA, for example, historic /o·i/ in rhymes is spelt <oy>, e.g. *oys* 'age', *poys* 'heavy', *woys* 'blood' and *boys* 'food' at § 10, whereas historic /o·/ is usually spelt <o> in rhymes, e.g. *ov tos* 'coming' and *nos* 'night' at § 63. In the texts, nonetheless, the graph <oy> is on occasion used for words that had never contained /ui/, e.g. *droys* 'brought' PA 119a, *doys* 'come' BM 4476, *moys* 'go' BM 4364, *boys* 'be' PA 49b, 122a, BM 522 and *goyff* 'smith' PA 155a.

**2.7** CW was written in Helston by William Jordan in 1611. He was clearly copying from an earlier exemplar but much of the spelling may well be Jordan's own. CW has about 75 examples of pre-occlusion in approximately 2,500 lines. BM written in 1504 has three examples of pre-occlusion. John Tregear's homilies were written *c.* 1555–60, that is to say, roughly in the same period as BM and CW They are the longest single Cornish text we have and contain approximately 30,000 words. Yet not once does Tregear exhibit any example of pre-occlusion. It is likely therefore that Tregear came from the Cornish-speaking area where pre-occlusion did not occur, i.e. well to the east of Truro. It has been suggested that Tregear may have come from Newlyn East (Ellis: 65). His dialect certainly supports this view.[9] SA is relatively short yet it has one apparent instance of pre-occlusion, as we have seen. If it is indeed an example of pre-occlusion, it is likely that the author of SA, unlike his contemporary John Tregear, was of westerly provenance.

I have suggested above that the spellings <bedneth> and <banneth> may represent the forms of the word in the area of pre-occlusion on the one hand and in the area of no pre-occlusion on the other. <bedneth> occurs in BM but before pre-occlusion began to be shown in writing, the form would have been written <benneth>. I have also suggested on other grounds that the dialect of PC and RD may have been western, whereas the dialect of OM may have been rather more eastern (see above p. 24). We might therefore expect the more easterly text OM to exhibit the spelling <banneth> and the westerly texts to show <benneth>. This is precisely what we do find:

OM: *banneth* 471, 472, 911, 1579, 1723, 1827, 1917, 1969, 2168, 2585; *banat* 726; *bannath* 2433; *benneth* 2265

PC: *benneth* 265, 560, 706, 928, 947, 2549, 2567; *bennath* 308, 704, 1803

RD: *benneth* 818, 823, 1556; *bennath* 1579, 1605, 1873, 2237, 2238; *vennath* 2643.

There is one example only of *benneth* in OM and no example at all of *banneth, banneth* in PC or RD. I think we can be sure that we have uncovered here a significant dialect isogloss.

The text of BM appears to be the work of two hands. The first scribe was apparently responsible for the text up to line 250 or thereabouts. For 'blessing' this scribe writes *beneth* at line 31, *benneth* at 50, 53, 54, 201, 202 and *bennath* at

---

9   Nance was struck by the lack of pre-occlusion in Tregear, for he says of the homilies: "It would be interesting to know where this Cornish was written, for though it is much like that of the Creation Play which Jordan must have copied in 1611 from a manuscript of near Tregear's time, yet he uses nowhere the *b* and *d* which all late writers are apt to insert between a short stressed vowel and *m* and *n*, as *tabm, pedn* for *tam, pedn*." (*Old Cornwall* 5 i: 26)

63. Three times he writes *bedneth* with pre-occlusion (BM 198, 224, 225). The second scribe seems to have been responsible for some lines between 210 and 220 and for the rest of the play. Here *banneth is* the rule, for example at 211, 217, 506, 507, 533, 581, 1011, 2677, 3093, 3179, 3705, 3706, 4306, 4307, 4365, 4557, 4559. I assume that the dialect of the first scribe was more western than that of the second scribe and that the second scribe's dialect did not exhibit pre-occlusion. That the second scribe of BM came from the area of no pre-occlusion is probably also to be understood by the way he rhymes *tena* 'draw' < *tenna* (Late Cornish *tedna*) with *then rena* 'to those' at 1509–10. Absence of pre-occlusion is also consonant his common spelling of *omma* 'here' (Late Cornish *ubma, ubba*) as *oma*, for example at 657, 783, 1444, 1449, 1644, 1652, 1702, 1708, 1919, 2009, 2969, 2979, 3660, 3830, etc.

**2.8** We have already mentioned that William Jordan, the scribe of CW, was probably copying from an older exemplar. It is interesting to observe, therefore, that Jordan writes *bannath* 'blessing' CW 105 and *banneth* CW 1871 but *bedna* CW 1541. It is probable that *bannath, banneth* represent the dialect of his exemplar and that *bedna* was his own spoken form. In which case it is likely that Jordan's early sixteenth-century original was probably composed by someone from farther cast than Truro.

It is also noteworthy that two forms of *mynnaf* 'I will' are attested in CW: A, with <i> in the stressed syllable and pre-occlusion, and B, with <a> in the stressed syllable but without pre-occlusion:

A *vidnaf* 36; *vidna* 1154; *vydnaf* 1457

B *vannaf* 134, 507, 578, 648, 682, 1088, 1380, 1697, 2360; *manaf* 313, 471, 503; *mannaf* 314, 1362, 2231; *mannaff* 1697.

*Madna* 'I will' with pre-occlusion is attested in Late Cornish, for example *ybma na vadna vi ostia* 'here I will not lodge' (BF: 18). In CW, however, the form with *a* in the root syllable is never pre-occluded. It is possible, therefore, that *mannaf* is analogous with *bannath* and is a feature of Jordan's more easterly exemplar. Indeed the spelling <mannaff> with final <ff> at CW 1697 is suggestive of a sixteenth-century source.

Pryce gives *bednath* 'blessing', *bedneth* 'blessing' (ACB: page opposite Ff). Since Pryce's work (1790) plagiarized the efforts of Gwavas and Tonkin of fifty years earlier, much of it dates from the first half of the eighteenth century. By this period Cornish was confined to the western extremities of the peninsula. *Bednath, bedneth* rather than *banneth is* therefore only to be expected.

**2.9** The word *benneth/banneth* does not seem to occur in PA anywhere. I have suggested tentatively (CT § 12.7), however, that PA may have been written to the east of Truro. This view is corroborated by the spellings *hena* 'that man' for *henna* at PA 43b and *caman* 'step' for *cammen* at PA 204a, 205a. *Henna* before the Prosodic Shift had /n:/ and *cammen* had [m:]. Since the scribe of PA writes both with a single rather than a geminate consonant, we can assume that in his dialect there was no distinction between medial /n:/ and /n/ on the one hand or between [m:] and [m] on the other. In which case his dialect would have been without pre-occlusion and is unlikely to be western. This conclusion is not certain, however. Forms without pre-occlusion occur alongside those with pre-occlusion in Late and therefore western Cornish. I have suggested at 2.3 above that dialects without pre-occlusion lowered /e/ > /a/ before /n/ < /n:/. We have an excellent example of the complementary distribution of [e$^d$n] and [an] in Lhuyd's *hana, hedda* (< *hedna)* 'that man, he' (AB: 73b). It would be interesting to know the origin of Lhuyd's form *hana.*

Before we leave the etymon *banneth* the following point should be emphasized here: the spelling <banneth> is widespread in the Middle Cornish texts. <banneth> presupposes that [æ], the lowered allophone of /e/ before /n:/, has in some forms of Cornish acquired phonemic status. In which case it is safe to assume that /n:/ itself is no longer distinct from /n/. That in turn implies that the Prosodic Shift has operated in the language. The spelling <banneth> is therefore an indication that consonantal and vocalic length have been radically reshaped in Middle Cornish and that half-length as a separate entity has disappeared.

**2.10** In certain late texts pre-occluded consonants underwent further development. The monosyllabic [radn], [pedn] lengthened still further to become [radən], [pedən] which are represented by such spellings as Nicholas Boson's <radden>, <pedden> (BF: 25, 27). At the same time pre-occlusion in disyllables also went a stage further. In *hedna* for earlier *henna,* for example, the *d* which had arisen through pre-occlusion had so acquired full consonantal status that it absorbed the following nasal: ['hen:a] > ['he$^d$nə] > ['hednə] > ['hedə]. It is ['hedə] that is meant by Lhuyd's <hedda> cited at § 2.6 above. This assimilation of the original sonant by the preceding product of pre-occlusion is particularly common with *m.* I have noticed the following examples from Nicholas Boson: *lebben* < *lemmyn* 'now' (BF: 25, 27 x 2), *ubba* < *umma* 'here' (BF: 25, 29 x 2).

The masculine demonstrative pronoun *hemma is* pre-occluded in CW which writes <hebma> at line 2499. In Nicholas Boson, however, the word is never pre-occluded. Boson always has <hemma> (BF: 25, 27 twice, 29 twice). This is perplexing until we remember that Middle Cornish has two forms of the pronoun, for example, *hemma* at OM 1427 and *helma* at BM 135. *Hemma* /hem:a/ < *\*hen+ma* is regularly pre-occluded to [he$^b$mə] and this is *hebma* in CW. *Helma* is probably for *\*hen (yn) le ma* 'that in this place' and is not pre-occluded because the medial consonant cluster is /lm/, not /m:/. I assume that after the operation of the Prosodic Shift the medial cluster in *helma* was regressively assimilated from [lm] to [m] giving [hemə]—too late for pre-occlusion to occur. It is this latter form [hemə] which presumably lies behind *hemma* without pre-occlusion in Nicholas Boson's writing.

**2.11** The Gaelic languages originally had a full set of fortis-lenis oppositions in the sonants: /n:/ ~ /n/, /m:/ [m] ~ /m/ [v, w], /l:/ ~ /l/ and /r:/ ~ /r/ and the four sets also had palatalized equivalents. As with the Brythonic languages lenis *m* became *v* or *w* (often with nasal colouring). In modern Irish and Scottish Gaelic the oppositions /n:/ ~ /n/ and /l:/ ~ /l/ are relatively well preserved. In those dialects that have lost the opposition the preceding vowel has been lengthened in compensation or has been diphthongized. In Manx on the other hand the distinction between fortis and lenis in the sonants has been lost without either lengthening or diphthongization. In Manx [n:] and [n], for example, are allophones of /n/ (Broderick: 14). Manx, unlike the other Gaelic languages, exhibits pre-occlusion. The phenomenon is similar to that in Cornish but is more widespread, since /l/ and /ŋ/ can be pre-occluded as well as /m/ and /n/. Moreover, in Manx pre-occlusion can occur after long stressed vowels as well as after a short one, though a pre-occluded long vowel often shortens as a result. As examples of Manx pre-occlusion one might cite [tro:ᵇm] *trome* 'heavy' (Old Irish *tromm*); [kaᵇm] *cam* 'crooked' (Old Irish *camm*); [be:ᵈn], [beᵈn] *bane* 'white' (Old Irish *bán*); [kʲoᵈn], [kʲo:ᵈn] *kione* 'head' (Old Irish *cenn*); [kiᵈn] *keayn* 'sea' (Old Irish *cuan*), [luɣŋ] *lhong* 'ship' (Old Irish *long)* and [kʲiᵈl] *keeyll* 'church' (Old Irish *cell*) (Broderick: 29–30).

It is quite remarkable that the Cornish for 'bent' is historically *cam* but in the later language was pronounced [kaᵇm] while the Manx for 'bent' is *cam* and in the spoken language was [kaᵇm]. I have elsewhere put forward the view that Manx may be the modern descendant of the pidgin-Gaelic acquired by the Norsemen when they settled in the Gaelic world in the ninth and tenth centuries (Williams 1994: 73841). I suggest above that many of the distinctive features of Middle Cornish are results of the Prosodic Shift and that the shift itself occurred when English-speakers learnt (or, rather, re-learnt) Cornish. Both Cornish and Manx, then, may be Celtic languages in the mouths of Germanic-speakers. The presence of pre-occlusion in both is probably no coincidence.

## Pre-occlusion in Neo-Cornish
**3.0** The publication of HCL in 1904 marked the beginning of the Cornish revival. Since that date there has been a consistent and increasingly successful attempt to resuscitate Cornish as a spoken language. The legitimacy of the enterprise has been criticized by Price (1984, 1992) but his criticisms are difficult to sustain.[10] It is important that Neo-Cornish should be as close as possible to the traditional language but the absence of native-speakers means that the pronunciation and spelling of Neo-Cornish are in themselves

---

10  An answer to some of Price's criticisms will be found in CT §§ 0.1–0.8.

controversial. Three systems have been widely used since the inception of the revival and they differ from one another in many ways including their approach to pre-occlusion.

**3.1** In some ways the most scholarly system of Neo-Cornish was that proposed by Jenner in HCL. Because Jenner deliberately chose the later stages of Cornish as the starting-point for his system, pre-occlusion is an important feature of it. Nonetheless, Jenner disapproved of pronunciations like *ubba, pedden* and *hedda* which he referred to as "vulgarisms" (HCL: 63).

Jenner's Neo-Cornish was replaced in the late 1920s by a system devised by R. Morton Nance. This latter was the only variety of the revived language in use until the late 1980s and is known as Unified Cornish. Unified Cornish unlike Jenner's is based on the medieval language and in particular the Middle Cornish of the *Ordinalia* and PA. Nance disapproved of pre-occlusion because he regarded it as a late "corruption". He says:

> **m, n** in late pronunciation when following a stressed short vowel developed a **b** and **d** before them, as **pedn, tabm**; this is not adopted in Unified Cornish (Nance 1949: 1).

It is true that the standard literary language did not write pre-occlusion and that Tregear's dialect was without it. Nevertheless, Nance's rejection of pre-occlusion is perhaps not completely justified. Unified Cornish uses, among others, both BM and CW as foundation texts and both BM and CW exhibit pre-occlusion. Unified Cornish also bases much of its phonology (and indeed part of its spelling) on Lhuyd's description of Cornish, yet Lhuyd not only records pre-occlusion but actually refers to pre-occlusion of *n* and m as distinctive if "corrupt" features of contemporary Cornish (see 0.0). Nance himself examined exhaustively both the place-names and the English of western Cornwall for the light they could shed on the pronunciation of Cornish. Yet it was in the far west of Cornwall that pre-occlusion is most marked in place-names.

**3.2** Since 1987 the Cornish Language Board, the umbrella body concerned with the promotion of the language, has been using a further variety of Neo-Cornish known as Kernowek Kemyn or 'Common Cornish'. This system was devised by Dr Ken George of the Department of Marine Science, University of Plymouth. It was created in answer to the perceived inadequacies of Unified Cornish and claims to be based on a thorough and scholarly analysis of the phonology of Middle Cornish. I drew attention some years ago (Williams 1990; see pp. 1–25 above) to a serious flaw in Kernowek Kemyn as it was first proposed and the error in question has now been removed. I have since attempted a more detailed analysis of the rest of Kernowek Kemyn (CT §§ 13.139).

There are, in my view, many defects in Kernowek Kemyn and it would be out of place to list them all here. One basic error and the immediate cause of a number of the other errors, is the deviser's dating of the Prosodic Shift. This occurred, according to George, *c.* 1600.[11] Since, however, Kernowek Kemyn claims to be based on Cornish *c.* 1500, the system takes no notice of the shift—even though its effects are pervasive in the language of BM. Indeed the effects of the shift are already much in evidence in the language of the earlier texts, the *Ordinalia* and PA.

If the Prosodic Shift had a far-reaching effect upon the phonology of Middle Cornish and Kernowek Kemyn ignores it completely, we cannot expect the sound-system of Kernowek Kemyn to resemble the phonology of Middle Cornish very faithfully. In fact I have suggested that there are at least 25 ways in which the phonology of Kernowek Kemyn is inauthentic (CT § 13.39). There are numerous further errors, however, that I have not yet discussed in detail anywhere. Some of these concern the question of pre-occlusion and I will examine them briefly here.

**3.3** I have suggested above that the pre-occlusion of [pen:] > [pe$^d$n] and of [tam:] > [ta$^b$m] were the direct result of the Prosodic Shift. Kernowek Kemyn ignores the effects of the Prosodic Shift on Middle Cornish. Inconsistently, however, it allows pre-occlusion in pronunciation, if not in writing. George gives the "recommended pronunciation" of Cornish /n:/ as follows:

> When following a stressed vowel, [nn], which is to be interpreted as similar to a prolonged [n], but stronger. The realization [dn], although not widely recorded until c. 1575, and therefore somewhat later than the date of the phonological base, is acceptable since it increases the difference between /n/ and /nn/. (PSRC: 194)

In central Cornwall, the area in which the standard language probably arose, as we have seen the distinction between /n:/ and /n/ had already been lost before the Prosodic Shift. Thus /gwi:n/ 'wine' and /gwin/ 'white' before the shift became /gwi·n/ and /gwin/ after it. John Tregear, I believe, is our last recorded writer of this non-pre-occluding dialect.[12] In the more westerly area the distinction between /n:/ and /n/ survived until the shift. Thereafter the opposition /n:/ ~ /n/ was reshaped as /$^d$n/ and /n/: /gwi:n/ ~ /gwi$^d$n/. Since pre-occlusion involves the shortening and reinforcing of /n:/ > /$^d$n/, pre-occlusion was impossible before the operation of the shift.

---

**11** "*Circa* 1600, the Cornish quantity system changed, so as to conform mor[el] to the English system. The half-long vowels were eliminated, usually becoming short." (PSRC: 68). George has now changed his mind and dates the loss of half-lenth to *c.* 1625.

**12** It would now seem that the scribe of the recently-discovered play *Bewnans Ke* is a later (*c.* 1575–85) writer, whose dialect lacks pre-occlusion(see pp. 190–91 below).

Kernowek Kemyn, therefore, is guilty of three errors here. In the first place, it denies that the Prosodic Shift has occurred before the appearance of the earliest Middle Cornish texts. In the second place, it is unaware that the opposition /n:/ ~ /n/ had been lost in much of the Cornish-speaking area before the operation of the shift. In the third place it welcomes a pre-occluded pronunciation of original /n:/ even though such a pronunciation would have been impossible without the Prosodic Shift and the rest of Kernowek Kemyn phonology presupposes that the shift was still to come.

**3.4** As far as the pre-occlusion of *m* is concerned, Kernowek Kemyn is also unsatisfactory. Kernowek Kemyn posits /m:/ and /m/ yet it also encourages pronouncing the "phoneme" /m:/ as [bm]:

> The pronunciation [bm], although not recorded until c. 1575, and therefore somewhat anachronistic, is acceptable since it increases the difference between /m/ and /mm/ [i.e. /m:/1 (PSRC: 191).

It should be noticed first that George treats /m/ and /m:/ as though they were separate phonemes. Since, however, /m/ was always a fortis and [m:] could occur only after a stressed vowel (which before /m/ was short of necessity), it is doubtful whether [m:] ever had phonemic status. Moreover, it is likely that much of the Cornish-speaking area lacked the pronunciation [m:] of /m/ even before the Prosodic Shift. Secondly, it should be observed that when George calls the pronunciation [bm] "anachronistic" he is only too accurate. [m:] was the pronunciation of /m/ after a stressed vowel before the operation of the Prosodic Shift. As a consequence of the shift [m:] became [$^b$m]. [$^b$m] could not coexist with half-length in Cornish.

In those dialects which had the allophone [m:], it was to be found only immediately following the stress. Elsewhere /m/ was pronounced [m]. George says:

> The word *kemer* 'take!' was so spelled by Nance under the influence of the verbal noun *kemeres* 'to take', in which the phonemically [sic!] geminate /mm/ has been reduced to [m] [sic! *read* /m/], since it is preceded by an unstressed vowel. As LateC *kebmer* shows, the spelling *kemmer is* the correct one (PSRC: 193).

This criticism of Nance is groundless. The dialects that pre-occluded /m/ did so when the allophone was [m:]. These dialects were western. Standard Middle Cornish probably arose in central Cornwall where the allophonic alternation [m] ~ [m:] had never developed. In the standard language, therefore, /m/ everywhere was [m]. Since, moreover, the opposition [m:] ~ [m] was allophonic only and not phonemic, even in those dialects which originally had the distinction, it was not necessary to show it in writing. After the operation of the Prosodic Shift those dialects which had had the allophonic alternation [m:] ~ [m] replaced it by [ᵇm] ~ [m]. This alternation was still allophonic only and did not therefore need to be written. The chief reason for writing consonants double in Middle Cornish was to show that the preceding vowel was short. Of necessity the vowel preceding the fortis /m/, whether [bm] < [m:], or [m], was short. The consonant preceding /m/ was therefore frequently doubled, though not consistently so. Here are some examples of *kemer* 'take!' and *kemer* 'takes' from the texts:

A (with <mm>)
*kemmer* OM 331, BM 30779; *kymmer* OM 367, 387, 403, 849, 1332, 1454, 2615, 2722, 2787; *gymmer* BM 1112, 1452, PC 156 1, RD 88, 1083; *kemmyr* OM 1021

B (with <m>)
*kemer* OM 70, 179, 1841, PC 2132, 2987, 3129, PA 6c, BM 1899, 2168, 2633, 2879, 3797, 4365; *kemar* PA 225c; *kymer* OM 145 7, RD 1545, 2015, 2081; *gemer* BM 1914.

It can be readily seen that both <mm> and <m> occur in all texts. George asserts that Nance constructed the spelling <kemer> by analogy with <kemeres>. It is more probable that Nance got <kemer> where he found most of his spellings, in the medieval texts. Indeed the traditional Cornish texts are the only legitimate source for the orthography of Neo-Cornish

George's recommended "phonemic" spelling for the verb 'to take' is <mm> in all positions. Kernowek Kemyn therefore writes <kemmer> 'take! takes' and <kemmeres> 'to take'. Yet George tells us that before the accent /mm/ i.e. /m:/ is "reduced to [m]", so that <kemmeres> has [m] rather than [m:]. The distinction in Kernowek Kemyn between [m:] and [m] is entirely determined by position, i.e. [m:] after a stressed vowel and [m] elsewhere. In which case the two are allophones of the same phoneme. Since Kernowek Kemyn claims to be phonemic, the two items ought to be written identically.[13]

It is probable that the scribe of PC and RD pronounced *kemer* as ['keᵇmər] yet he is content to spell the word both as <kymmer> on the one hand and <kemer>, <kymer> on the other. This would suggest that for him the opposition [ᵇm] ~ [m] was purely allophonic. In short, the two items /m:/ and /m/ of Kernowek Kemyn were not separate phonemes. They were, of course,

---

13 From the sixteenth century onwards the Cornish for 'Cornish' has /ow/ in its stressed syllable (CT §§ 15.8, 16. 1) and indeed the first attested example of the word is *Cornowok* from 1572 (Wakelin: 89). Nance's form *Kernewek* is his own invention. This was adopted by Kernowek Kemyn even though Kernowek Kemyn usually spells the reflex of British *-ow-* + *i*-affection with <yw> by false analogy with Welsh. The word for 'common' appears as <kemyn> with a single *m* at BM 3215. *Kemyn* is also Nance's form. Since the medial consonant of *kemyn* was a long fortis only by its position, i.e. after a stressed vowel, and since the orthography of Kernowek Kemyn claims to be phonemic, *kemmyn* might better be spelt in Kernowek Kemyn as <kemyn>. If, then, "Kernewek Kemmyn" were consistent on the one hand and phonemic on the other, it would call itself *Kernywek Kemyn*. See following note.

phonemically distinct when [ᵇm] became [bm]. Kernowek Kemyn encourages [bm], which was the pronunciation in the traditional language from the sixteenth century onwards, even though the phonological basis of Kernowek Kemyn is to a large extent Old Cornish, if it is anything.

**3.5** Nance spelt the Cornish word for 'to tremble' as <crenna>, which, according to George, is a misspelling (PSRC: 194). Kernowek Kemyn writes the word with a single <n> because of the Welsh and Breton cognates *crynu* and *krenañ*. In Welsh and Breton the word has a single <n> and the preceding vowel in Welsh and Breton is accordingly half-long.

Since George believes that Middle Cornish has half-length he is compelled to spell 'to tremble' with a single <n>. In so doing, however, he is at variance with the Middle Cornish scribes themselves. I have collected the following examples of the etymon from the texts: *crenne* PA 53d, *crenne* OM 1453, *krenne* PC 2995, *crennas* RD 1772. I have no instance of 'to tremble' from the texts with a single medial <n>. If Nance "misspelt" the word, then the Middle Cornish scribes misspelt it as well! In fact the scribes knew what they were doing when they wrote <crenne>, etc. They wrote a geminate <nn> in this word (and Nance imitated them) because the stressed vowel was short.

The word for 'to buy' is parallel with the word for 'to tremble'. The Welsh and Breton cognates are *prynu* and *prenañ* respectively. This Kernowek Kemyn spells <prena> as did Nance.[14] In the texts 'to buy' is occasionally spelt with a single <n> and metathesis, *perna* PA 4d 5c, BM 1463; *pernas* PA 5d, 51b, 105b, for example. A common spelling, however, is with <nn>. Notice the following examples: *brenne* PC 922; *prennas* RD 62, 147, 830, 1204, 2431, 2562, BM 2521; *prenne* PA 196d, RD 165, 1543, 2622; *prenna* BM 868, 2746; *prennys* PA 9b, 252c; *brennas* RD 242; *prynnes* RD 686; *prynnys* RD 1162 and *prynnas* RD 1184.

In the texts, then, *crenna* is always spelt <nn> and *prena* is frequently so. In neither etymon does pre-occlusion occur in the later language. Lhuyd, for example, gives *dho kema* 'tremo' (AB: 166a) and *dho perna* 'emo' (AB: 56c), where both items have undergone metathesis. He also cites *krenna* 'to tremble' (AB: 245a) and *prenna* 'to buy' (AB: 231a). In no instance does either etymon exhibit pre-occlusion. The <nn> in these items in Middle and Late Cornish is simply a way of indicating that the preceding vowel, though formerly half-long, is now short. George when discussing *n* in Late Cornish says:

> The grapheme <nn> which was often used medially (e.g. LateC *bennen* 'woman') indicates merely that the preceding vowel had become short instead of half-long (SPRC: 194).

---

**14** Kernowek Kemyn spells 'to tremble' as <krena> and 'to buy' as <prena>. Yet it spells Cornish *enys* 'island' and *Enes* 'Shrovetide' with <y>, <ynys> and <Ynys> by false analogy with Welsh. If Kernowek Kemyn were consistent it would spell 'to tremble' as <kryna> and 'to buy' as <pryna>.

In the view of this statement it is astonishing that George does not draw the obvious conclusion from the spellings <crenna> and <prenna> in the medieval texts. <crenna> and <prenna> are, in my view, quite sufficient in themselves to indicate that there was no separate half-length in Middle Cornish. Since half-length was unknown in Middle Cornish, it should not be introduced into the revived language.

**3.6** The Cornish word for 'ramsons, garlic' is recorded by Lhuyd as *kinin* (AB 1: 15). In view of Old Welsh *cennin* and Old Irish *cainnenn* one would expect this word to have medial /dn/ < /n:/ in Late Cornish. If Lhuyd's *kinin is* indeed Late Cornish, it is unexpected. Lhuyd may have derived it, as he derived much of his Cornish vocabulary, from OCV which gives *kenin euynoc* 'algium' [clawed garlic 'garlic'] with a single <n>.[15]

Pool cites the Penwith toponym *Boskednan* in the following forms: *Boskennen* 13 10, *Boskennan* 1313, 1570, *Boskednan* 1623 (PNWP: 40) and he suggests that the second element may be either *kenen* 'reeds' or *conyn* 'rabbit'. Neither is likely, since neither has medial /dn/ < /n:/. I prefer to understand the second element as *kennyn* 'ramsons'. If this suggestion is correct, we have an instance of *kennyn* to set against Lhuyd's apparently anomalous *kinin*. George says of the word *kenin* 'garlic, ramsons':

> N.B. Although W[elsh] has <nn>, the C[ornish] could not have contained /nn/, or the word would have had [dn] in the LateC; but Lhuyd wrote *kinin* (GKK: 1601).

In the light of *Boskednan* this note should perhaps be revised.

We have already seen that the Cornish word for 'thence' is *alena* in the mediaeval texts and *alenna* in the seventeenth century. The <nn> in the late spelling is graphemic only and indicates that the preceding vowel is short. George says of *alena*:

> N.B. spelled *alenna* by Nance; the etymology indicates <n> [recte /n/], and if it had contained /nn/, it would have become *aledna in LateC. (GKK: 28).

The criticism of Nance is misplaced. Nance spelt the word with <nn> because Jenner did ('*alenna, en mes alenna*, thence' HCL: 152). The geminate <nn>, though not attested in the medieval language, is found in the seventeenth century. George believes that <nn> in Middle Cornish means /n:/, which in turn implies pre-occlusion in Late Cornish. This is not so, however, as is clear

---

15 OCV is oddly inconsistent in its treatment of <n> and <nn>. Notice also *benen* 'sponsa' [woman 'wife'], *benen rid* 'femina' [unattached woman 'woman'] but *bennen val* 'matrona' [goodwife 'matron']. It is possible that *kenin* for expected *\*kennin* in OCV and *bennen* for *benen* indicate the loss of the opposition /n/ ~ /n:/ and the beginning of the Prosodic Shift.

from the Middle Cornish spellings <prenna> 'to buy' and <crenna> 'to tremble' (see above).

## Summary

**4.0** Before the period of the Middle Cornish texts Cornish underwent a radical reshaping of its sound-system which is referred to above as the Prosodic Shift. Syllables shortened but gained in intensity In consequence half-length as a separate entity disappeared from the language. The Prosodic Shift had pervasive effects upon the phonology of Cornish. Pre-occlusion, the distinctive Cornish development *pedn* 'head' < *pen* and *tabm* 'bit' < *tam* was also a direct result of the Prosodic Shift but did not appear in writing until syllables began to lengthen again probably in the sixteenth century.

Pre-occlusion was largely confined to the far west of Cornwall. In the more easterly part, in which the standard literary language probably arose, pre-occlusion was unknown, presumably because /n:/ had fallen together with /n/ and the allophone [m:] of /m/ was unknown.

The variety of Neo-Cornish known as Kernowek Kemyn is very unsatisfactory. Perhaps its most serious fault is its most basic one: Kernowek Kemyn posits three vocalic lengths when Middle Cornish had only two. From this one error many others derive. I have listed many of these secondary errors elsewhere (CT § 13.39). We can now add to their number the following:

1) Although it ignores the Prosodic Shift, Kernowek Kemyn allows pre-occlusion in pronunciation which is itself a direct consequence of the shift.

2) The allophone [m:] of /m/ was entirely determined by position. Spellings like <kemmer> and <kemmyn> in Kernowek Kemyn are therefore unnecessary. Kernowek Kemyn, however, believes that /m/ and */m:/ were phonemically distinct in Middle Cornish. In which case to spell them identically, e.g. in <kemmeres> and <kemmer>, is a repudiation of the phonemic principle which Kernowek Kemyn claims to espouse.

3) The proponents of Kernowek Kemyn because they are unaware that the Prosodic Shift is early, misunderstand the function of <nn> in words like *crenna* 'to tremble', *pre(n)na* 'to buy', and *ale(n)na* 'thence'. In consequence discussion of these items in the handbooks of Kernowek Kemyn is mistaken and misleading.

# *NEBBAZ GERRIAU DRO THO CARNOACK:*
# A FEW WORDS ABOUT CORNISH*

## Introduction

I intend to say a few words today about the Cornish language in general. My title *Nebbaz gerriau dro tho Carnoack* 'a few words about Cornish' is the name of a short essay on the Cornish language written *c.* 1690 by Nicholas Boson of Newlyn.[1] At the beginning of his essay Boson says *Gun tavaz Carnoack eu mar pur gwadnhez uz na ellen skant quatiez tho e wellaz crefhe arta* 'Our Cornish language is so very weakened that we can scarcely expect to see it strengthen again'. Boson's fears were justified. Within a hundred years Cornish had become extinct. Who exactly was the last native speaker is doubtful. The honour is usually given to Dolly Pentreath of Mousehole who died in 1777. Her neighbour, William Bodinar, writing in 1776, however, claimed that four or five people in the village knew Cornish.[2] We must assume that Dolly was one of them.[3] All the speakers were over eighty years of age and it would seem that Cornish had ceased to be spoken by the year 1800.[4]

Cornish died out before the rise of modern linguistic science. The nearest we have to a scientific description of Cornish is the account of the language given by Edward Lhuyd in his *Archaeologia Britannica* of 1707. Lhuyd spent only a few months in Cornwall and preferred to consult learned antiquarians rather than illiterate native speakers. He also used manuscript sources in preference to spoken ones[5] and never really understood some aspects of Cornish syntax. Although he must be treated with care, Lhuyd is of incalculable value in the study of Cornish.

We have no modern speakers to act as controls for any conclusion we may draw about Cornish. There is therefore an unavoidable circularity to anything we say about the language. The study of Cornish is consequently both fascinating and frustrating. One can read Middle Cornish and be struck at

---

* O'Donnell Lecture given at the Taylor Institution, University of Oxford, 22 May 1998.

1 See O. Padel, *The Cornish Writings of the Boson Family* (Redruth 1975) 24-37, referred to hereafter as BF.

2 See J. Loth, "Cornique Moderne", *Archiv für Celtische Lexikographie* i (Halle 1900) 224-29.

3 Bodinar, who had some traditional knowledge of Cornish, died in 1798.

4 For the question of the last years of Cornish see P. A. S. Pool, *The Death of Cornish* (Cornish Language Board 1982).

5 In the introduction to his Cornish grammar in *Archaeologia Britannica* (AB) Lhuyd acknowledges his debt among others to Nicholas Boson but he says that he got most of his knowledge of Cornish from manuscripts lent to him by Jonathan Trelawny, bishop of Exeter, John Anstis M.P., and the antiquarian John Keigwin (AB: 222).

times by the beauty of the diction. What one cannot do with any certainty is to pronounce the poetry as a native speaker of traditional Cornish would have done.

Boson calls Cornish *Carnoack*. Other attested spellings include *Curnooack*, *Kernuak*, *Kernooak*, *Kornooack* and *Kernuack*. The earliest known form is *Cornowok* from 1572.[6] It is very likely that the Cornish originally called their language *Brethonek* < *Brittonika* (*cf. Brezhoneg* 'Breton' < *Brittonika*). The name *Kernuack, Cornowok* < *Kornowika* (< *Kernow* 'Cornwall') is, I think, unlikely to have been widely used until the Norman Conquest, when many Bretons settled in Cornwall and it became necessary to distinguish the now distinct forms of South-West Brythonic from each other.

**The remains of Cornish**

Cornish is usually divided into three periods. Old Cornish is the language until the early twelfth century. The longest Old Cornish document is actually transitional between the Old and Middle forms of the language and is known as the *Old Cornish Vocabulary* (OCV).[7] It is a Cornish-Latin glossary, containing approximately 1,000 items, which has been dated to *c.* 1100. I suspect it is slightly later than that.

Apart from a single fragment we have five Middle Cornish texts. The first is *Pascon agan Arluth* (PA)[8], 'the Passion of Our Lord', a poem of 259 stanzas of eight lines on the passion, crucifixion, and resurrection of Christ. PA is archaic in language and may date from the late thirteenth century. In the third stanza, for example, we read *pan gemert kyg a werhas* 'when he took flesh of a virgin'. This is the only surviving *t*-preterite in Cornish. Elsewhere 'he took' is invariably *kemeras*, the regular *s*-preterite.

The next text is a cycle of three mystery plays known as the *Ordinalia*.[9] The three plays are *Origo Mundi* (OM), 'the Origin of the World'; *Passio Christi* (PC), 'the Passion of Christ'; and *Resurrexio Domini* (RD), 'the Resurrection of the Lord'. The *Ordinalia* may date from the fourteenth century. They certainly originated in the collegiate church of secular canons in Glasney near Penryn in West Cornwall. Glasney was the major scriptorium of medieval Cornwall and it is clear that the canons did much to cultivate Cornish religious literature and to promote a measure of literacy in the language and a consistent spelling-system.

---

6  In depositions of the bishop's court in Exeter in 1572 William Hawysh deposed that upon *dew whallon gwa metton in eglos de Lalant* ['upon All Saints' day in the morning in the church of Lelant'] that Agnes Davy was called "whore and whore bitch" in English "and not in Cornowok" (quoted by M. F. Wakelin, *Language and History in Cornwall* (Leicester 1975) 89).

7  See E. Norris, *Ancient Cornish Drama* (London 1859 [reprinted New York 1968]) ii 311-435; E. Campanile, *Profilo etimologico del cornico antico* (Pisa 1974).

8  W. Stokes, "Pascon agan Arluth: the Passion of our Lord", *Transactions of the Philological Society* (1860-61) Appendix 1-100.

9  The only complete edition is Norris (1859); see note 7.

The next text is the play *Beunans Meriasek* (BM)[10], 'the Life of St Meriasek'. Meriasek or Meriadec was a Breton and much of the play is set in Brittany. Meriasek was also patron saint of Camborne in Cornwall and part of the action takes place there. The colophon of BM tells us it was written by Dominus Rad[ulphus] Ton in 1504. He is likely to have been the author as well as the scribe. BM contains more than 4,500 lines and was acted, like all Cornish plays, in the open air and over a period of days.

The next text was not discovered until 1947 and is a Cornish translation by John Tregear of twelve homilies by Edmund Bonner, the Catholic bishop of London under Mary Tudor. Bonner's homilies were published in 1555 and Tregear's Cornish version (TH)[11] is not much later. Tregear lards his Cornish version with English words in the same way that Breton priests adorned their sermons with French borrowings. Here is a short passage to illustrate what I mean:

> rag pub ober a wryoneth ew **contaynys** in **charite** hag inweth an **decay** a **cherite** ew an **destruction** a'n bys ha'n **banyshment** a **virtu** ha'n **cawse** a oll **vicis** in mar ver ogasty mayth usy pub den ow **framya** thotha y honyn **charite** warlerth y **vynd** ha'y **appetyd** y honyn. Kyn fo y vewnans vith mar **detestabyll** the Thu ha the then, whath eff a ra **supposia** inna y honyn y bosa gonsa **charite**. Rag henna me a ra desquethis thewgh lell ha **pleyn descripcion** a **charite**, **not** an **ymaginacion** a then mas an **very** gyrryow ha **exampill** agan **Saviour** Jhesu Crist

> [for all works of truth are contained in charity and also the decay of charity is the destruction of the world and the banishment of virtue and the cause of all vices, inasmuch almost as everybody frames charity to himself according to his own mind and appetite. Be his life never so detestable to God and to man, still he supposes in himself that he has charity. Therefore I will show you the true and plain description of charity, not the imagination of man but the very words and example of our Saviour Jesus Christ.][12]

Tregear's vocabulary may be full of English but his inflection and syntax are perfect. I regard his homilies as of the utmost importance for two reasons. In the first place, they are as long as the three plays of the *Ordinalia* put together. In the second, they are the only Middle Cornish text we have in prose rather than verse. They have, incidentally, never been properly edited.

The fifth and final text of Middle Cornish is *Gwreans an Bys* (CW)[13], 'the Creation of the World'. This play was written by William Jordan in Helston in 1611 and deals *inter alia* with the fall of Lucifer, the creation, the fall of Adam, the death of Cain and Noah's flood. References to Limbo in the play suggest a

---

10  W. Stokes, *Beunans Meriasek: The Life of Saint Meriasek* (London 1872).

11  John Tregear, *Homelyes xiii in Cornysche* (British Library Add. MS 46, 397). The only text available is a cyclostyled version published by Christopher Bice ([*s.l.*] 1969).

12  TH 21.

13  W. Stokes, "Gwreans an Bys: the Creation of the World" *Transactions of the Philological Society* (1864 part iv).

pre-Reformation origin and there is an allusion in CW to a second play, now lost, dealing with the redemption of mankind. CW is similar in ways to OM, though we do not know whether Jordan was the author of CW or merely the scribe. An interesting point about CW is that it was written some 80 years after the dissolution of the monasteries, Glasney among them. Jordan's spelling, though clearly derived from the medieval orthography, has many features alien to the traditional spelling.

Late Cornish, the term used for anything written after the Civil War, is entirely spelt in *ad hoc* orthographies based on contemporary English spelling. Such spelling-systems (if that is the right word) are inconsistent and owe little to the orthography of the Middle Cornish texts. There is, moreover, very little Late Cornish. The most important texts are *Nebbaz gerriau dro tho Carnoack* to which I have referred, a folk-tale recorded by Lhuyd[14], a few translations of parts of the Bible[15] and some letters, inscriptions, occasional verses, and other fragments.

The total remains of Cornish are slight. The position is not the same as with Manx, which is a complete language. In 1549 the Cornish rebelled against the first English Prayer Book of Edward VI. One of their objections to the 1549 book was that many of them understood no English.[16] No translation into Cornish followed, however. Neither is there a translation of the Bible.

### The assibilation of Old Cornish /d/

If one compares OCV with the Middle Cornish texts, one sees that the language has undergone a major change between the two periods. This is partially a matter of vocabulary. OCV cites Celtic words which have been replaced by French or English borrowings in Middle Cornish. As examples one might cite OCV *auon* 'river' but Middle Cornish *ryver*; Old Cornish *blodon* 'flower' but Middle Cornish *flowr*; Old Cornish *steuel* 'dining room, room' but Middle Cornish *rom* and Old Cornish *kinethel* 'generation, nation' but Middle Cornish *nacyon*. This list could be extended considerably.

The real difference between Old and Middle Cornish is phonetic. One important Middle Cornish change is the assibilation of Old Cornish *-d-* > Middle Cornish *-s-*. Thus, for example, Old Cornish *tat* 'father' /taːd/ is Middle Cornish *tas* and Old Cornish *bochodoc* 'poor' is Middle Cornish *bohosek*. Actually this process of assibilation has already begun in OCV, where 'tooth' is *dans* (*cf.* Welsh *dant*) and 'shore' is *als* (*cf.* Welsh *allt*).

---

14  This is the story of *John of Chyanhor*, a version of the international tale of the three counsels. It may well have been the work of Nicholas Boson. See BF: 14-23

15  The most important biblical translations are probably Rowe's version of 3 Genesis, 2 and 4 Matthew, edited and published by J. Loth in *Revue Celtique* 23: 173-200. A version of 1 Genesis by John Boson is to be found in BF: 51-3.

16  A brief account of the rebellion against the Prayer Book will be found in P. Berresford Ellis, *The Cornish Language and its Literature* (London 1974) 60-3.

The assibilation of final /d/ is fairly straightforward since the end result is almost always spelt <s> in Middle Cornish, *e.g. tas* 'father', *gwlas* 'country', *los* 'grey', *bos* 'food', *gos* 'blood', *os* 'age', etc. Internally, however, in Middle Cornish the reflex of Old Cornish /d/ is sometimes written <s> and sometimes <g> or <j>. Thus in Middle Cornish one finds both *ege* and *ese* 'was', *gallosek* and *gallogek* 'powerful', *kerense* and *kerenge* 'love' and *nyns ew* and *nynj ew* 'is not'. Forms with internal <g> or <j> predominate in Late Cornish and this led some commentators to conclude that /dʒ/ was a late reflex of earlier /s/ or /z/. There are a number of difficulties with this view, however. Phonetically it is actually quite difficult to get from /z/, a voiced continuant, to /dʒ/, an affricate. Besides, if Middle Cornish /z/ > Late Cornish /dʒ/, it is difficult to see why *tas* and *gwlas* do not become *\*taj* and *\*gwlaj*. Or for that matter, why did *Sawzon* /'saʊzɒn/ 'Englishmen' not become Late Cornish *\*Sawjon* /'saʊdʒɒn/ and why is *preezyo* /'preːzɪɒ/ 'praise!' not *\*preedzhyo* /'preːdʒɪɒ/?

My own explanation is that /z/ and /dʒ/ are variants that existed side by side. Old Cornish first assibilated /d/ to /dz/. In the standard language in most contexts I assume that /dz/ simplified to /z/, which was written <s>. In some cases, before high front vowels, for example, the second element in /dz/ palatalized to /ʒ/ and the whole complex became /dʒ/, written <g> or <j> in the medieval texts. There is evidence from placenames, moreover, that the more westerly forms of Cornish had a tendency to prefer /dʒ/ where more central areas had <s>. This explains why /dʒ/ is common in Late Cornish. The later language was by definition confined to the west of Cornwall since the language had become extinct further east.

Two other points are worth noting. The two plays of the *Ordinalia* PC and RD have a slight tendency to prefer <g> over <s> in some words, in particular *cregy* 'to believe', *pegy* 'to pray' and *woge* 'after'. This suggests that PC and RD were written by a scribe from further west in Cornwall than OM or PA, for example. The second point is that forms in <g> or <j> are always less common than forms with <s>. Even though the main centre for the cultivation of Cornish was in Glasney, it seems probable that standard Middle Cornish arose in the major towns of Mid-Cornwall, in Bodmin and Lostwithiel, rather than further west. It appears that the dialects of Mid-Cornwall preferred <s> to <g>.[17]

I have already mentioned St Meriasek, patron saint of Camborne, and the main character in BM. People who washed in St Meriasek's well in Camborne were known in English dialect as *Merrasicks*[18] or *Merrasickers*[19] by the local inhabitants. Moreover *Merry-geeks* or *Mera-jacks* were nicknames for Camborne

---

**17** See N. J. A. Williams, "A problem in Cornish phonology" in M. J. Ball, et alii, *Celtic Linguistics: Ieithyddiaeth Geltaidd* (Amsterdam and Philadelphia 1990) 241-74; see pp. 1–25 above

**18** F. Jago, *The Ancient Language and Dialect of Cornwall* (Truro 1882) 216.

**19** BM introduction xii.

people themselves.[20] Behind *Merrasicks* and *Merajacks* lie two separate variants of the saint's name: *Meryasek* and *Meryajek*. Toponymic evidence suggests that the isogloss line between /z/ and /dʒ/ may have run through the Illogan-Camborne area. *Merrasick* is a form from one side of the line and *Merajack* from the other.

People bathed in St Meriasek's well, by the way, as a cure for for mental illness. In BM the saint says:

| | |
|---|---|
| Inweth an dour ou fenten | [Also the water of my well |
| rag den varijs in certen | for a deranged man indeed |
| peseff may fo eff ely | I pray that it may be a salve |
| thy threy arta thy skyans | to bring him again to his senses. |
| ihesu arluth a selwans | Jesus, lord of salvation, |
| gront helma der ʒe vercy | grant this by thy mercy].[21] |

## The Cornish Prosodic Shift

Welsh and Breton preserve three separate vowel lengths. In certain monosyllables the vowel is long, *e.g.* Welsh *tad* 'father', Breton *tad*. In related disyllables the vowel is half-long, *e.g.* Welsh *tadau* 'fathers', Breton *tadoù*. In other monosyllables the vowel is short, *e.g.* Welsh *mam* 'mother', Breton *mamm*. In related disyllables the vowel remains short, since it cannot be shortened any further, *e.g.* Welsh *mamau* 'mothers', Breton *mammoù*. Long and half-long are regarded by native speakers of the languages as varieties of long—since neither is short. Indeed, modern Breton grammars always treat half-long as long. One can speak schematically of this common Brythonic system of length by saying that vowels are long if they have three units of length or morae, half-long if they have two morae and short if they have one only.

It is likely that Old Cornish had the same system of length which Welsh and Breton still have. There is, however, overwhelming evidence that Middle Cornish was moving from a threefold opposition of long, half-long, and short to a new system of long and short. This can hardly mean merely that vowels of two morae lost one mora and became short. There must rather have been a general shortening throughout the system. Long vowels lost one mora and became half-long whereas half-long vowels lost one mora and were thereafter identical with original short vowels. What seems to have happened in Middle Cornish was that stressed syllables were both shortened on the one hand and pronounced with greater intensity on the other. As a corollary unstressed syllables lost intensity and reduced to the neutral vowel /ə/.

This shift from threefold length and a relatively weak distinction between stressed and unstressed syllables to twofold length and more marked opposition between stressed and unstressed syllables I call the Prosodic Shift. It is, I believe, of the utmost importance for understanding the unique

20  Ellis, *op. cit.* 40.
21  BM 1005-10. Note that in the passages cited the letter <ʒ> *yogh* is used for /ð/
98

developments in Cornish phonology. The Prosodic Shift is, by the way, impli-
cated in the assibilation of Old Cornish /d/. It has many further ramifications.

## Gemination of consonants in Middle Cornish

One of the first reasons for believing that half-long vowels were shortening in
Middle Cornish is the way in which such vowels are frequently followed in the
Middle Cornish texts by a double consonant. Gemination of consonants is a
sign that the preceding vowel is short, since vowels are historically short when
they were originally followed by double consonants. Welsh *mam* is short
because the word was originally *\*mamma*; in Modern Breton *mamm* is actually
written with a double <mm>. The Cornish word for 'good' is *da*, and
'goodness' is *dader*. Historically this latter had a half-long stressed vowel. Yet
frequently in the Middle Cornish texts the word is written <dadder>[22] or
<daddar>.[23] Tregear has so many examples that when I tried to count them I
had to give up. There are many other words which historically have a single
consonant and yet are written with a double one, *e.g. marrow* 'dead'[24], *ennoc*
'Enoch'[25], *gwelles* 'to see'[26], *prenna* 'to buy'[27], etc. Given the conservatism of our
scribes it is remarkable that these forms should be written at all.

## The development of final /iː/

Historical long /iː/ written <y> often appears in Late Cornish as a diphthong.
Lhuyd, for example, writes *kei* 'dog'[28] (Welsh *ci*), *nei* 'we'[29] (Welsh *ni*), *hei*
'she'[30] (Welsh *hi*) and *krei* 'cry'[31] (Breton *kri*). Similarly Nicholas Boson writes
*chei* 'house' [32] (Breton *ti*) and *trei* 'three'[33] (Welsh and Breton *tri*). There are
examples of a diphthongal spelling of historical /iː/ from as early as the
sixteenth century. Tregear writes *whay* for *why* 'you (plural)' once[34] and in
another sixteenth-century source we find *tray kans* for 'three hundred'.[35] In the
texts we find many rhymes which suggest that <y> has already diphthongized
by the Middle Cornish period, *e.g. ny* 'we' – *joy* 'joy'[36]; *ty* 'thou' – *moy* 'more'[37];

---

22 *E.g.* PA 3c, PC 3097, RD 1224, BM 189, 485, 499, 528, 2229, 3173, 4271, TH 11, 30a.
23 *E.g.* TH 11a, 12, 14.
24 OM 2702, BM 3524.
25 RD 197.
26 TH 6, 8a, 32a. *Cf. gweller* 'is seen' BM 1571.
27 PA 7a, 9b, 196d, PC 767, 922, RD 62, 147, 165, BM 868, 885.
28 BF: 46a.
29 BF: 17.
30 BF: 17.
31 BF: 17.
32 BF: 15.
33 BF: 15.
34 TH 33a.
35 This is to be found in Borde's Cornish dialogues; see Loth, "Cornique moderne" 226.
36 OM 555-58.
37 OM 946-48.

*deffry* 'indeed' – *ioy* 'joy'[38]; *dry* 'to bring' – *fey* 'faith'[39]; *th'y* 'thither' – *ioy* 'joy'[40]; *ny* 'we' – *moy* 'more'[41]; *pry* 'clay' – *ioy* 'joy'[42]; *gy* 'thee' – *moy* 'more'[43] and there are many others.

Why has /i:/ become a diphthong? Let us assume that trimoric /i:/ was in fact [iii]. Because the final element was unprotected by any consonant, it was before vowels consonantal in quality. We can therefore analyse /i:/ as [iij] or perhaps better as [i·j], that is to say a dimoric nucleus [i·] followed by a quasi-consonantal coda. As a result of the Prosodic Shift the dimoric [i·] was shortened to [i]. The newly shortened vowel is more lax than when it was half-long and it lowered to [ɪ]. The original trimoric long vowel /i:/ is now [ɪj]. Once the vowel has broken into two parts at different heights, the two parts continue to diverge and the final result is a diphthong /əj/ or /ej/. This is considered an adequate rhyme for words in /oj/ and /ej/ and is written <ei> in Late Cornish.

### Final /y:/

Something very similar occurred with /y:/ in absolute final. The Cornish for 'black' is *du* but Lhuyd spells it <diu>.[44] 'God' is spelt <deu>[45], <dew>[46], or rarely, <dyw>.[47] In some texts, however, in particular PA and TH, 'God' is invariably <du>. The Cornish word for 'black' and for 'God' are thus pronounced and spelt identically. Let us assume that 'black' was originally /dy:/ with a trimoric vowel. This we can perhaps analyse as a dimoric [y·] followed by a quasi-consonantal coda [ɥ], that is to say [y·ɥ]. As a result of the Prosodic Shift [y·ɥ] lost one mora to become [yɥ]. But the newly shortened vowel [y] was more lax than previously and thus lowered to [ø]. In the new diphthong, [øɥ], the two elements are now at different heights in the mouth and continued to move apart. The nucleus, as well as lowering, unrounded while the coda remained high and round but lost its front quality. The result was /ɪw/. The word for 'black' continued to be written <du> but was homophonous with the word for 'God' and the two are indifferently written <du>.

The pronunciation of *du* 'black' as /dɪw/ is particularly noticeable at one point in *Resurrexio Domini*. Pontius Pilate's body is so accursed that the grave rejects it and it springs into the air. One of the two men attempting to bury Pilate says:

---

38 OM 1374-78.
39 PC 1993-96.
40 RD 185-86.
41 RD 560-61.
42 RD 1561-63.
43 RD 2036-37.
44 BF: 44a.
45 *E.g.* OM 1188, 1190, 1193, 1196.
46 *E.g.* PC 49, CW 490, 630.
47 *E.g.* *thyw* with lenited initial at RD 1018.

Pur harth dun thotho whare—
gorryn ef y'n beth arte:
    du yw y lyw

[Very boldly let us go to him soon—
let us put him in the grave again:
    black is his hue].[48]

Here a double internal rhyme is clearly being used for comic effect.

### The development of short /i/

Further evidence for the Prosodic Shift can be seen in the development of historic half-long /iˑ/ in words like *scryfa* 'to write' (Breton *skrivañ*), *tryga* 'to dwell' (Welsh *trigo*), *whylas* 'to search' (Welsh *chwilio*) and *myras* 'to watch' (Breton *mirout*). In disyllabic forms in Cornish the original half-long /iˑ/ lost one mora to become short /i/. But short /i/ is more lax than when half-long and lowers to [ɪ] or [e]. It is for this reason that in all these etyma the vowel in disyllables is frequently written <e>. There are so many instances of this phenomenon that it would be tedious to cite them all. Here are a mere handful (ignoring initial mutation here): <screffa>[49], <screfa>[50], <screfys>[51], <screfis>[52]; <trege>[53], <trega>[54], <tregys>[55], <tregis>[56]; <whela>[57], <whelaf>[58], <whelaff>[59], <whelas>[60], <wheles>[61]; <merough>[62], <merowgh>[63], <meras>[64] and <meres>[65].

Monosyllabic forms, however, have a dimoric (*i.e.* long) vowel and are always written with <y>: <tryk>[66], <tryg>[67], <myr>[68] and <scryf>.[69] Notice in

48  RD 2109-11.
49  TH 19, 27a, 33.
50  TH 48.
51  PA 188d x 2, BM 2766.
52  BM 394.
53  PA 37b, 214c, OM 566, 1711, BM, 947, 1344.
54  OM 2190, 2665, BM 4348, CW 981, 1722, TH 2, 39a.
55  BM 687, 816, 1963, CW 246, TH 39a.
56  PA 46c, 84a, 85d, 89d, 93c, 255d.
57  PA 21c, CW 483.
58  CW 1695.
59  TH 22a.
60  PA 90a, 145d, 156b, 257b, 257d, OM 1139, CW 1691, TH 8a, 18a, 30a, 36a.
61  TH 27a.
62  PA 125c, CW 1550.
63  TH 49a, CW 736 x 2.
64  PA 168b, 215d, OM 2325, BM 4074, TH 49a, 50a.
65  BM 4351.
66  PA 212d.
67  OM 1104, 2112, 39a.
68  BM 935, 1805, 3194, 3229, 3270, 3656.
69  PC 421.

particular the striking alternation between the unimoric /e/ and the dimoric /y/ in the following from Tregear: *may hallan ny bewa ha **trega** in charite, ha nena ny a **dryg** in du ha gans du, ha du a **dryg** innan ny* 'that we may live and dwell in charity and then we will dwell in God and with God and God will dwell in us'.[70]

The alternation *e ~ y* in *trega ~ tryg, screfa ~ scryf, meras ~ myr* became such a feature of Cornish morphophonology, that it established itself analogically elsewhere. The two verbs *pesy/pegy* 'to pray' (*cf.* Breton *pediñ*) and *cresy/cregy* 'to believe' (*cf.* Welsh *credu*) have etymological /e/ in the root, yet in Cornish the monosyllabic forms are often written <pys> and <crys> with <y>.

## The development of Old Cornish /ui/

Old Cornish /ui/ corresponds both to Welsh *wy*, e.g. Old Cornish *luit* 'grey', Welsh *llwyd*; Old Cornish *buit* 'food', Welsh *bwyd*; and to Welsh *oe*, e.g. Old Cornish *huis* 'age', Welsh *oes*; Old Cornish *cuit* 'wood', Welsh *coed*. In the course of the thirteenth and fourteenth centuries Old Cornish /ui/ appears to have lowered first to /oi/ and then monophthongized to /o:/. Again we are almost certainly seeing an effect of the Prosodic Shift. I assume that in the word *cuit* 'wood', for example, the diphthong was originally trimoric: /u·i/. It shortened and lowered, passing through a stage [o·i]. This is well attested in medieval versions of place-names, *e.g. Coyspenhilek, Coyse Laydock, Coys Penryn*[71] and in the texts.[72] Eventually the vowel became indistinguishable from long /o:/ derived from other sources. In PA and the *Ordinalia* the reflex of Old Cornish /ui/ and long /o:/ do not rhyme, because both texts date from a period when they were still different. By the time of BM, however, earlier /ui/ and /o:/ are identical in pronunciation. They are both indifferently written <o> or <oy> and rhyme indiscriminately. Here are some examples (the words that had /ui/ in Old Cornish are marked in bold):

*me a vyn mois* 'I will go' – *y **woys*** 'his blood'[73]
*age **goys*** 'their blood' – *y hyl boys* 'can be'[74]
*age **goys*** 'their blood' – *mar mynnogh bos* 'if you wish to be'[75]
*mar kyl boys* 'if it can be' – *yowynk ha **loys*** 'young and grey'[76]
*kyn moys* 'before going' – *han **boys*** 'and the food'[77]
*creseff y voys* 'I believe it to be' – *yonk na **loys*** 'young or grey'[78]
*ov toys* 'coming' – *yonk ha **loys*** 'young and grey'[79]

---

70  TH 30.
71  See O. Padel, *Cornish Place-name Elements* (Nottingham 1985): 67.
72  *E.g. ha coys penryn in tyen* 'and Penryn wood entirely' OM 2589 and *carou guyls a coys* 'a wild hart from a wood' BM 1618.
73  BM 130-31.
74  BM 1599-1603.
75  BM 1642-43.
76  BM 2168-71.
77  BM 3926-29.
78  BM 4415-18.
79  BM 4476-78.

Old Cornish /ui/ became Middle Cornish /oː/ only if followed by a consonant. If /ui/ was in absolute final position it lost a mora internally, not finally, and appears in Middle Cornish as <oy>, for example *moy* 'more' (Welsh *mwy*) and *oy* 'egg' (Welsh *wy*). The different development can be seen in the Cornish equivalents of Welsh *mwy* 'more' on the one hand *mwyhau* 'increase' on the other, for in Cornish these are *moy* but *moghhe*.[80]

In some western dialects of Cornish it seems that /ui/ did not invariably lower to /oi/ before becoming a monophthong. In these dialects the reflex of Old Cornish /ui/ is /uː/. In Late Cornish, which is by definition western, we find *kûz* 'wood', *lûz* 'grey' and *bûz* 'food'. The failure to lower /ui/ is largely confined to words ending in Old Cornish /d/ which later assibilated to /z/. There are also sporadic instances before /ð/ and /θ/. Before /n/ and /r/ Old Cornish /ui/ appears in Late Cornish as <ô>, for example *kôr* 'wax' (Welsh *cwyr*); *gôr* 'knows' (Welsh *gwyr*); *kôn* 'dinner' (Welsh *cwyn*); *dôn* 'carry' (Welsh *dwyn*) and *ôn* 'lamb' (Welsh *oen*).

Because of its preference for <g> to <s> in *pegy*, *cregy*, etc. I believe that PC and RD were probably western in origin. In PC we find *scouth* 'shoulder' with /uː/, not *scoth* (Welsh *ysgwydd*), and it rhymes with *gouth* 'behoves' also with /uː/ rather than /oː/.[81] There are further examples of /uː/ for /oː/ in PC and in RD, notably *bous* 'food'[82] and *trous* 'foot'[83] (Welsh *troed*). We thus have corroborative evidence of /uː/ for /oː/ in western Middle Cornish.

Place-names also support this view. The western toponyms *Cusgarne* (Gwennap), *Cusvey* (Gwennap) and *Cusveorth* (Kea) all have the first element *Cus-*. This can only be a shortening that has taken place inside English of the Cornish element *cous* 'wood'; *cf.* English *husband* < *housebonde*.

Perhaps most significant evidence for a western /uː/ as against more easterly /oː/ are those many toponyms in Mid- and West Cornwall in *-goose* and *-coose* (< *cos* 'wood' < Old Cornish *cuit*). There has clearly been some standardization of these place-names. It is clear, nonetheless, that *-goose*, *-coose* must have two different origins. In Mid-Cornwall *-goose* and *-coose* reflect the Middle Cornish form *cos* /koːs/, adopted into English before the middle of the fifteenth century. The long *o* in these names has undergone the English Great Vowel Shift. Cornish. *Cos* /koːs/ has thus become /kuːs/ in exactly the same way that Middle English *gos* has become Modern English *goose* /guːs/. The vowel /uː/ in Mid-Cornwall is therefore the regular reflex of Middle English /oː/.

In West Cornwall on the other hand names in *-cos*, *-gos* would for the most part have been adopted into English after the Great Vowel Shift—since Cornish was still the language of the bulk of the population in the region until well after the Reformation. Had *cos* in this area been borrowed after the change

---

80  I have given some examples of *moy* 'more' above. Note *mohghaho* OM 297, *moghheen* BM 1265 and *moghheys* BM 2402.

81  PC 658, 2623-26.

82  PC 688, RD 541.

83  PC 1223.

of *gos* to *goose*, it would appear in toponyms as *-cose*, *-gose*. The forms *-coose*, *-goose* in West Cornwall can only reflect Cornish /kuːs/, *i.e.* the same form that gave rise to *Cusgarne*, *Cusvey* and *Cusveorth*.

The presence of dialect in Cornish should not astonish us. Cornish is a Brythonic language and like Breton and Welsh it is certain to have had dialects. Given that Cornwall is much smaller in size than either Wales or Brittany the sum (though not the proportion) of dialectal variation is likely to have been less in Cornwall than in the other two countries. Cornwall is long from east to west but narrow from north to south. Dialect features are more likely to have divided Cornwall vertically rather than horizontally. Cornwall has a very extensive coastline and the Cornish were always great sailors. This fact might well have tended to render dialect isogloss lines less than completely clear-cut, since movement by sea could have taken eastern features westward and western features eastward.

By using the Cornish texts and toponyms I have isolated three dialect features in Cornish, namely: (a) <g>/<j> as against <s>/<z>; (b) /uː/ against /oː/ as a reflex of Old Cornish /ui/ and (c) pre-occlusion. Pre-occlusion refers to the pronunciation of, for example, *gwyn* 'white' as *gwydn* [gwɪdn] and *tam* 'bit' as *tabm* [tæbm]. Although all three features divide a western area from a more easterly one, the isogloss line (as far as it can be ascertained) must in each case be drawn in a different place.

## Unstressed syllables

It is abundantly clear in Middle Cornish that the vowels of unstressed syllables have fallen together. Here, for example, are the variant spellings from the texts of a number of different lexical items. For simplicity's sake I ignore initial mutation and quote the form with its unmutated initial.

'one' (original /a/): <onan>[84], <onen>[85], <onon>[86],<onyn>[87]
'heart' (original /o/): <colon>[88],<colan>[89], <colen>[90], <colyn>[91]
'to wait' (original /o/): <gortos>[92], <gortes>[93], <gurtas>[94], <gortays>[95]

---

[84] OM 3, 12, 99, 1192, PA 42c, 43b, 71b, 81a, 145b, 154c, 199a.
[85] OM 57, 2099, 2308.
[86] PC 772, PA 25b, 89c, 124d x 2, 137b, 138a,163b, 242c.
[87] TH 7a x 2.
[88] OM 527, 1264, 1376.
[89] OM 357, TH 20a.
[90] PA 115c, OM 365, 428, BM 2049, 2408.
[91] BM 628, 1804.
[92] PA 164d, 250d.
[93] OM 1718, BM 3655.
[94] TH 13a.
[95] BM 2472.

'children' (original /e/): <flehes>[96], <flehas>[97], <fleghys>[98], <flehys>[99], <flehis>[100]

We can be quite sure that in all cases the vowel in question is the neutral vowel /ə/. The reduction in unstressed syllables again is part of the Prosodic Shift: the language is moving away from lightly stressed and sonorous vowels and a relatively weak opposition between stressed and unstressed syllables. It is moving towards heavily stressed vowels on the one hand and very reduced unstressed vowels on the other. What we are really talking about here is a shift from a system like that of Welsh to a system like that of English. The Prosodic Shift is really the difference in prosody between Welsh *Caradog* /ka'radog/ and English *Craddock* /'kradək/—or perhaps one should say the difference between Old Cornish *bochodoc* /bo'xodök/ and Late Cornish *boadjack* /bo'adʒək/.[101]

## Vocalic alternation

Although Welsh is written phonetically, <y> has two values, for example in *Cymry* 'Welshmen'. The first <y> is pronounced with a neutral vowel, a stressed /ə/, and the second has a clear sound. This alternation has its origins in an earlier period of the Brythonic languages when the syllable containing the neutral vowel was unstressed. The variation in *y*-sounds is of systematic importance in Welsh because one finds it, for example, in such pairs as *bydd* 'he will be' but *byddaf* 'I will be' or *chwys* 'sweat' but *chwysu* 'to sweat'.

The same vocalic alternation is very noticeable in Cornish where the Welsh neutral vowel appears as <e> and the clear vowel is <y>. We thus in Cornish get such pairs as *byth* 'he will be' and *bethaf* 'I will be'[102], *dyth* 'day' and *dethyow* 'days'[103], *gwyth* 'trees' (collective) and *gwethen* 'tree'[104], *pryf* 'reptile' and *prevyon* 'reptiles'[105], *prys* 'time, meal' and *preggyow* 'meals'[106], *tyf* 'he grows' and *tevy* 'to grow'[107], *yyf* 'drink!' and *eva* 'to drink'[108], *whys* 'sweat' and *whesa* 'to sweat'.[109]

---

**96** OM 1036, BM 2014, TH 7a.
**97** OM 975, 1031, 1159, BM 1782, 3153.
**98** OM 1588, 1611.
**99** PA 149d, 168d, OM 1623.
**100** TH 23a x 2.
**101** This is the form in Bodinar's letter quoted at the end of this lecture.
**102** *E.g. byth* PA 17d, 44c, 125c but *bezens* 'let be' PA 55b, 57d, 113c (I ignore initial mutation).
**103** *E.g. dyth* PA 93c, CW 92 but *deȝyow* PA 169b, *dethyow* CW 1850.
**104** *E.g. gwyth* TH 9 but *gwethan* TH 3a.
**105** *E.g. prif* CW 1055 but *prevyon* OM 1160.
**106** *E.g. prys* OM 674, 1213 but *preggyou* BM 1972.
**107** *E.g. ny dyf* 'grows not' OM 712 but *ou tevy* 'growing' OM 1985.
**108** *E.g. yyf* 'drink!' OM 1916 but *eve* 'to drink' OM 2435.
**109** *E.g. whys* 'sweat' OM 273 but *wese* 'he was sweating' PA 58c.

In each case I have pronounced the long <y> as /iː/ but perhaps I should not have done so. The vowel in *byth, dyth, gwyth, pryf*, etc. was in Old Cornish not /iː/, but a long open /ɪː/. The operation of the Prosodic Shift ought really to have lowered this vowel to /eː/, perhaps via the stages [ɪˑɪ] > [eˑɪ] > [eː]. In fact variants with <e> are attested in the texts. We find, for example, *beth* 'he will be'[110], *deth* 'day'[111], *gweth* 'trees'[112], *pref* 'reptile'[113], etc. *Bêdh* is Lhuyd's form, for example. Yet the shift is incomplete and halfhearted. In many etyma forms with <y> remain common and it is quite clear from CW and Late Cornish that the vowel in question is the high front one /iː/.

Why should this be so? You will remember how the operation of the Prosodic Shift introduced a new vocalic alternation in Cornish in such words as *scryf ~ screfa, tryg ~ trega, myr ~ meras*. This was extended to give *crys ~ cresy* and *pys ~ pesy*. It seems that this new alternation also affected the earlier one of *byth ~ bethaf, dyth ~ dethyow, gwyth ~ gwethen* and partially aborted the natural development to *beth, deth, gweth* etc. In Cornish therefore one finds *beth/byth ~ bethaf, deth/dyth ~ dethyow, pref/pryf ~ prevyon* and *teffe*[114]*/tyf ~ tevy*. The Prosodic Shift was working itself out during the early Middle Cornish period. This means that the phonology of the language is in transition and as a result is often difficult to interpret. The case of half-hearted alternation, to which I have just referred, is typical.

### The origin of the Prosodic Shift

If we look at our surviving Cornish literature we can see that it is based on French and Breton models and owes little to Middle English. The names 'Jesus' in Middle Cornish is *Jhesus* /'dʒezys/, 'Mary' is *Marya* and 'London' is *Londres*.[115] These are all borrowed from Middle Breton. We can assume that in the generation or so after the Norman Conquest, Saxon landowners and Saxon clerics were replaced by French-speakers and more importantly by Bretons. There is good evidence for a large influx of Bretons into Cornwall after the Conquest. Indeed some speak not of the "Norman Invasion" but of the "Armorican return". William the Conqueror made the Breton, Robert earl of Mortain, ruler of Cornwall. Although not many in absolute terms, proportionally Bretons were more numerous in Cornwall than in any other county.[116]

The Prosodic Shift brought Cornish closer to English in its phonology than it had been previously. It is difficult not to see the influence of English on Cornish in the question of quantity. Modern English is essentially a language

---

110 I have counted over 50 instances of *beth* 'will be, be!' in BM, for example.

111 *E.g. deth* PC 722, 724, 1496, 1669.

112 *E.g. gweth* PA 16b.

113 *E.g. hager bref* 'ugly reptile' PA 169b and *tebel preff* 'evil reptile' BM 4133.

114 *E.g. eff a deffe* 'he grows' TH 7.

115 *E.g.* Borde's *Pes myllder eus alemma de Londres?* 'How many miles is it from here to London?' (Loth, "Cornique Moderne" 227).

116 See K. S. B. Keats-Rohan "The Bretons and Normans of England 1066-1154: the family, the fief and the feudal monarchy", *Nottingham Medieval Studies* 36 (1992): 42-78.

in which syllables are of short duration but of high intensity. The sound-changes of Middle English would lead one to believe that Middle English was similar to Modern English in this respect.

As a result of the Norman Conquest close relations were re-established between Cornwall and Celtophone Brittany. English ceased to be the language of administration, being replaced by French. Cornishmen and women who had become Anglophone while under West Saxon rule were now at pains to learn Celtic again. I would suggest that as Cornish re-established itself in Cornwall, English speech-habits were introduced into the newly Celticized speech of the previously Anglophone Cornishmen and Cornishwomen of Mid- and East Cornwall. In Cornwall the absolute number of original Celtic speakers was probably not large enough to swamp the Anglicized Cornish of the post-Norman period. As a result Anglicized phonological features persisted in the language. This I would suggest is the immediate cause of the Prosodic Shift.

If there is anything in this view of mine, it does involve a paradox. It means that increased Breton influence in the generations after the Norman Conquest led to the Anglicization of the Cornish language. Had the Norman Conquest not occurred, however, Cornish would almost certainly have died out entirely. Extinction, after all, was the fate of Cumbric.

## Revived Cornish

Although Cornish became extinct at the end of the eighteenth century, there has been a movement since the early years of the twentieth to resuscitate the language, and by the 1970s it was achieving some success.

From 1928 until the 1980s the only form of the revived language was **Unified Cornish**.[117] This was devised by R. M. Nance (1873-1959) and his collaborator, A. S. D. Smith (1883-1950). Unified Cornish based itself on the medieval texts, in particular the *Ordinalia* and PA. Nance systematized the spelling and adopted <dh> from Lhuyd to represent /ð/ and used <j> everywhere for /dʒ/. The phonology of Unified Cornish was problematic in some points of detail. Because Nance stayed very close to the spelling of the medieval texts, however, Unified Cornish was undoubtedly Cornish.

The most serious defect of Unified Cornish is its fondness for the quaint, archaic and medieval. Tregear's homilies did not come to light until 1947 and Nance did not have an opportunity to study them until he was in his late seventies. By that time Unified Cornish was already well established. I have recently suggested a number of ways in which Unified Cornish might be emended and modernized on the basis of Tregear's inflection and syntax. My revision of Unified Cornish I call **Unified Cornish Revised** and a full account will be found in my recent book *Clappya Kernowek*.[118]

---

117 See, for example, R. M. Nance, *Cornish for All* (2nd edition St Ives 1949).
118 N. J. A. Williams, *Clappya Kernowek: an introduction to Unified Cornish Revised* (Agan Tavas 1997).

In the 1980s two further varieties of revived Cornish were launched by revivalists, both of which gained a certain measure of support from learners. The first of these was based, not on the riches of Middle Cornish, but on the attenuated and imperfect remains of the late seventeenth and eighteenth centuries. This variety of the revived language has been given the misleading name of "Modern Cornish".[119] Although there are a number of serious theoretical and practical objections to it, it is in essence not inauthentic. The same cannot be said for the second new departure, **Common Cornish** or Kernowek Kemyn, which was put forward in 1986 by Ken George. This system departs very seriously from the Cornish texts on which it claims to be based.[120]

As we have seen, one of the most distinctive features of Middle Cornish is the assibilation of Old Cornish /d/ to either <s> or <g/j>. The deviser of Common Cornish noticed the hesitation in Middle Cornish between <s> and <g> in words like *wose/woge* 'after', *kerense/kerenge* 'love' and *ese/ege* 'was'. Drawing some doubtful conclusions from a suggestion made by Loth in 1897, he assumed that behind the variation lay two palatal phonemes /tʲ/ and /dʲ/. He thus wrote <wodja> 'after', <edja> 'was', <adjwa> 'gap', <bohodjek> 'poor', <adjwon> 'know', <gantjo> 'with him', <an tji> 'the house', <kerentja> 'love' and <boluntjedh> 'wish'.[121] In an article published in 1990 I demonstrated why these "phonemes" had never existed[122]—and they were removed from Common Cornish. Spellings with <dj> and <tj> look so alien and out of place in revived Middle Cornish, that I find it hard to believe even now that they were ever put forward.

I hope I have convinced you how important are the Prosodic Shift and vocalic alternation to the understanding of Middle Cornish phonology. It is remarkable that the handbooks of Common Cornish nowhere so much as hint at either. Both are conspicuous everywhere in the Cornish texts. It is thus odd that both the Prosodic Shift and vocalic alternation were missed completely.

Common Cornish does not merely ascribe to Middle Cornish a mistaken phonology, it clothes the questionable sound-system in a newly constructed spelling. This is of mixed origin, being an amalgam of Middle Cornish, Old Cornish, Welsh and Breton spelling conventions but with a number of *a priori* features thrown in. Because Common Cornish erroneously assumes that Middle Cornish had two long *o*-vowels, one of which became /u:/ in Late Cornish, the orthography has to distinguish, for example, the words <bos> 'to be' and <boes> 'food'. The digraph <oe> for /o:/ is virtually unknown in the

---

119 See, for example, R. R. M. Gendall, *A Practical Dictionary of Modern Cornish* (Liskeard 1997). "Modern Cornish" should really be known as "Revived Late Cornish".

120 See pp. 38–64 above.

121 See K. J. George, "The Use of a Mainframe Computer to Analyse Cornish Orthography" in Gordon Maclennan, *Proceedings of the First North American Congress of Celtic Studies* (Ottawa 1986) 89-115; K. J. Gerorge, *The Pronunciation and Spelling of Revived Cornish* (Cornish Language Board 1986).

122 See pp. 1–25 above.

medieval texts but in Common Cornish it is written in all words with /u:/ in Late Cornish, *e.g.* <koes> 'wood', <goes> 'blood', <loes> 'grey' and <troes> 'foot'. It is even written in those words in Late Cornish that exhibit <ô> and where there is not the slightest hint of a raised vowel, *e.g.* <goer> 'knows', <koer> 'wax', <koen> 'dinner', <oen> 'lamb', <doen> 'to carry' and <hwoer> 'sister'.

Common Cornish assumes that the medieval language had half-length, when it did not. In consequence short vowels are distinguished from half-long ones by doubling the following consonant: <penn> 'head', <gwann> 'weak', <tamm> 'bit', etc. The name of the town Camborne in West Cornwall occurs repeatedly in BM where it is spelt <Cambron>, *e.g.*

a wylste gy meryasek
in **cambron** an lagasek
 nyns usy eff malbe dam

[Did you see Meriasek?
In Camborne the sharp-eyed fellow
 is in no damn place].[123]

Some years ago on the advice of users of Common Cornish the town council put up a notice welcoming visitors to **Kammbronn**.[124] Those accustomed to traditional spelling were not happy.

To attempt to resuscitate an extinct language is fraught with difficulty and the end result will perforce be of questionable authenticity. To revive a language with a largely mistaken phonology and an artificial spelling is surely indefensible. Unfortunately Common Cornish has attracted a number of

---

**123** BM 1017-19.

**124** *Cf.* "Kemyn [*i.e.* Common Cornish] is something quite different, an entirely artificial creation which does not resemble Cornish as used by Cornish people at any time in history. To those accustomed to Unified, as indeed to those who prefer Kernuak [*i.e.* Revived Late Cornish] Kemyn has an alien and somewhat sinister appearance, as if the language had somehow been taken over by robots and reduced to the status of a code. Every principle of sound and spelling, claim the supporters of Kemyn, must be followed to its logical end and strictly observed, however weird the outcome. To take a familiar example, the place-name *Camborne* is recorded in several forms during the centuries when its inhabitants spoke Cornish, the most common being *Cambron* and *Cambrone*, the former is found regularly in the medieval play *Bewnans Meryasek*, part of which is set in Camborne, and this has been the form used in Unified Cornish. But when Camborne Town Council wanted to erect signs in Cornish welcoming people to the town, they understandably sought the advice of the Cornish Language Board: the outcome was the appearance of signs welcoming people to *Kammbronn*, a form resembling nothing found in history, and of alien and un-Cornish appearance. What the supporters of Kemyn have thus done to one Cornish place-name, they seek to do to the whole language, and have indeed made some progress in that direction", P. A. S. Pool, *The Second Death of Cornish* (Redruth 1995) 6-7.

adherents over the last decade, a trend which I sincerely hope will not continue.

I mentioned William Bodinar of Mousehole at the beginning of this talk. His letter written in 1776 is the last piece of traditional Cornish we have. It reads as follows:

> Bluth vee eue try egence a pemp. Thera vee dean boadjack an poscas. Me rig deskey Cornoack termen me vee mawe. Me vee de more gen car vee a pemp dean moy en cock. Me rig scantlower clowes eden ger Sowsnack cowzes en cock rag sythen warebar. No riga vee biscath gwelles lever Cornoack. Me deskey Cornoack mous da more gen tees coath. Nag es moye vel pager pe pemp en dreau nye ell clappia Cornish leben—poble coath pager egance blouth. Cornoack ew all neceaves gen poble younk.

> [My age is threescore and five. I am a poor fisherman. I learnt Cornish when I was a boy. I was at sea with my father and five other men in a boat. I hardly heard a single word of English spoken in the boat for a week on end. I never saw a Cornish book. I learnt Cornish going to sea with the old men. There are no more than four or five in our town now who can talk Cornish—old people eighty years of age. Cornish is all forgotten by young people].[125]

Experience shows that once a language has died completely, resurrecting it is very difficult. Manx and Cornish have both become extinct. Manx is nonetheless being successfully revived. Let us endeavour to achieve a strong and unified revival of Cornish.

---

125 Quoted from Loth, "Cornique moderne" 228-29.

# INDIRECT STATEMENT
# IN CORNISH AND BRETON*

## Indirect statement in Welsh: a comparison

Welsh has two main ways of introducing indirect statement. The first involves the verbal noun. When the verb of the main clause and of the subordinate clause are in the same tense, the verbal noun precedes its noun subject. If the subject is pronominal, it appears as a possessive adjective before the verbal noun:

> *Gwn fod John yn athro* 'I know John is a professor'
> *Gwyddwn fod y dyn yn dlawd* 'I knew the man was poor'
> *A ydych yn credu fy mod yn dweud y gwir?* 'Do you believe I am telling the
>     truth?' GCW: 119–20.

If the tense of the main verb and of the verb in the noun clause are different, the subject of the subordinate verb is preceded by the preposition *i* 'to' and followed by the verbal noun:

> *Credaf i'r dyn farw ddoe* 'I believe the man died yesterday'
> *Gwyddoch inni wneud ein gorau* 'You know that we did our best' GCW:
>     120.

This use of the preposition *i* before the subject is very common in Modern Welsh. It is less so in the medieval language, though examples do occur, e.g. *ny thebygaf i y un o hyn uynet ar dy geuyn di* 'I do not think any one of these will go upon thy back' (PKM: 25).

In the second construction a finite form of the verb is used with the preverbal particle *y* or *yr:*

> *Gwyddwn y deuai ef* 'I knew that he would come'
> *Ni chredaf y gwyddant hwy* 'I do not believe that they know'
> *Mae'n dda genyf y bwriedwch ddyfod* 'I am pleased that you intend to
>     come' EGC: 225.

---

\* First published in *Cornish Studies*. Second series: Six. 1998. Exeter: University of Exeter Press. Pp. 172–82. ISBN 0-85989-610-2. A version of this paper was given at the Tionól of the Celtic School of the Dublin Institute for Advanced Studies in November 1997. The Zimmer Collection in the library of University College, Dublin, contains an extensive archive of Breton devotional works. Some of this material has been used here.

## Indirect statement in Breton

In Breton indirect statement is rarely rendered by means of the verbal noun, e.g. *Lavaret en devoa mont* 'He had said he would go' (YBB 408). A trace of this usage is also seen in such common expressions as *bezhañ ouzhoñ* 'I know' (literally 'I know [it] to be'). Indirect statement in Breton is more usually rendered by means of a finite verb introduced by *e, ez,* the equivalent of Welsh *y, yr*:

> *Lennet em eus war ar gazetenn e oa bet ur gwall zarvoud henthouarn* 'I read in the paper that there had been a train crash'
> *Krediñ a ran e teuio an amzer da vrav* 'I believe the weather will become fine'
> *Kavout a ran ez eo kerik an tamm kig-se* 'I find that this piece of meat is rather expensive'
> *Ne gav ket dezhañ e vije bet den ebet ken o chom eni* 'He does not think that anybody else would have stayed there' YBB: 405-07.

This construction is commonplace in Middle Breton also, e.g *pan ho deffoe lauaret an oratoret ez oa un tra imposibl* 'when the orators had said that it was an impossible thing' (VC §15) and *E credaff ivez ferm—Ez eo e Map unic, hon Aoutrou biniguet An eil Person Divin* 'I also firmly believe—That his only Son, our blessed Lord, is the second divine person' (CD: 214).

## Indirect statement in Cornish

Middle Cornish has examples in indirect statement of both the verbal noun and the finite verb. The verbal noun in Cornish is used in two ways: (a) before a noun subject or preceded by a possessive adjective if the subject is pronominal; (b) after the subject (nominal or pronominal) + *the / ʒe* 'to':

(a)
> *ahanas yth ew scrifys bos eleth worth ʒe wyʒe* 'of thee it is written that angels are guarding thee' PA 14b
> *Pan welas an ethewon bos crist au cuthyll meystry* 'When the Jews saw that Christ was doing mighty works' PA 26a
> *lauar annes ow bos vy a'm bewnens* 'say that I am weary of my life' OM 700–01
> *an el thy'n a leuerys sur worth an beth y vos yn ban dasserghys* 'the angel indeed at the tomb told us he had risen up' RD 1062–64.

(b)
> *Lemmyn ny a yl gwelas hag ervyre fest yn ta cryst ʒe woʒaff dre ʒensys mur a benans yn bys ma* 'Now we can see and determine very well that Christ through manhood suffered much penance in this world' PA 60ab

*Pylat yn ta a woȝye y ȝe gusel dre envy* 'Pilate knew well that they were speaking through envy' PA 127a

*preder my the'th whul a dor* 'consider that I made you of earth' OM 67

*na cous ef the thasserghy un ger* 'do not speak a single word [to the effect] that he has risen' RD 59–60

*bytegyns reys yv crygy ihesu cryst the thasserghy* 'nonetheless one must believe that Christ has risen' RD 1016–17.


*Ef the seuel a'n beth men ha'y vos datherys certen y gous ny dal thy'nny ny* 'we ought indeed not report that he rose from the tomb and that he is risen' (RD 566-68) is an example of (b) followed by (a).

The Cornish equivalent of Welsh *y, yr* and Breton *e, ez* is *y, yth*. This particle is used when the indirect statement involves a finite verb:

*yn clewsons ow leuerell pur wyr y fenne terry an tempel cref* 'they had heard him saying that he would indeed destroy the strong temple' PA 91ab

*Rag an traytor a gewsys ha ȝerag leas huny war lyrgh y vonas leȝys ȝen tressa dyth y seuy* 'For the traitor said and in front of many that after being killed he would rise on the third day' PA 240ab

*y'n clewys ov leuerel treydyth wose y terry y wrefe y threhevel* 'I heard him saying that he would build it three days after destroying it' PC 1314–16

*y leuerys ef ynweth datherghy an tressa deth y wre* 'he also said that he would rise on the third day' RD 4–6

*del thethywsys thy'mmo vy y wres yn ban dasfewe* 'as you promised me that you would rise up again to life' RD 450–51

*lemmyn me a grys yn ta y fynnaf vy mos pella esough haneth* 'now I well believe that I will go further than you tonight' RD 1274–79.


## Indirect statement in Cornish introduced by *del* 'as'

Cornish has a further construction, particularly common in Late Cornish, which involves introducing the subordinate clause with *del* 'as'. In such constructions *del* is often reduced to *der, ter, dr* or *tr*. Here are some examples from the seventeenth and eighteenth centuries:

*Pe reege an vennen gwellas tr' o an wethan da rag booze ha der o hi blonk tha'n lagagow* 'When the woman saw that the tree was good for food and that it was pleasing to the eyes' RC 23: 176

*Leben pe reg Jesus clowaz ter o Jowan towlaz tha bressen* 'Now when Jesus heard that John had been thrown into prison' RC 23: 189

*hei a dhalsvaz dha 'wil krei ter dha a thermâz hei deztrîez* 'she began to make a cry that her good man had been murdered' BF: 18

*eue levarraz dr' oua gever ul* 'he said that it was *Goats All*' BF: 25

*buz me a aore hemma urt e hoer an Curnoack dr' uava talvez buz nebbaz* 'but
   I know this from its sister, the Cornish language, that it is but little
   valued' BF: 31

*ha Deu gwellas tr' ovo da* 'and God saw that it was good' BF: 52.

## The origin of Cornish *del* 'that'

George in his article "Which base for Revived Cornish?" suggests an English
origin for the construction with *del*:

> The use of the Late Cornish conjunction *tell* 'as' seems to be taken from
> the use of 'as' instead of 'that' in dialectal English; e.g. in William
> Rowe's translation from Genesis: *Preg laule theeze tell estah en noath* [leg.
> *hoath*] 'Who told thee that thou wert naked?' George 1995: 108.

George appears here to be confusing *del* 'as' with *tel* (< *fatel* 'how') which is also
used in Cornish to introduce indirect speech. A further example of *tel < fatel* is
to be seen in Rowe's *ha angie oyah tel erangye en hoath* 'and they knew that they
were naked' (RC 23: 177), whereas Rowe uses the full form (spelt *fatal*) in *pe rêg
e gwellaz fatal o geaze gwreaze anotha gen an teeze feere* 'when he saw that he had
been mocked by the wise men' (RC 23: 199).

Fatel 'that' is very common indeed in John Tregear's homilies (*c.* 1555),
where it is usually spelt *fatell*. Here are a few examples from the first homily:

*Gothvethow fatell ew du agan arluth ny* 'Know that God is our lord' TH 1
*Rag why a res understondia ha eresy fatell ew an dewses spuris* 'For you must
   understand and believe that the deity is spirit' TH la
*yth ew scriffes in second chapter in Genesis fatell rug du anella in corffe den* 'it
   is written in the second chapter of Genesis that God breathed into the
   body of man' TH 2
*alsan ny predery fatell ylly du gull moy ragan in agen creacion* 'could we
   think that God could do more for us in our creation?' TH2a
*Ith ew the vos consyddres in agan part ny fatell ve mabden dres theworth an
   kyth stat na benegas* 'It is to be considered on our part that mankind
   was brought from that same blessed state' TH 3.

Fatel 'how' itself is etymologically a derivative of *del* 'as', though exactly how
is not entirely clear. I believe that *fatel* may derive from *\*py forth del* 'in which
way' or the like. It is significant that when two instances of *fatel* 'how' occur in
adjacent clauses, the second instance is reduced to *del* 'as': *gans ow thraytor
dyskis fatel dons thov hemeres ha del vezaff hombronkis* 'taught by my betrayer how
they shall come to take me and how I shall be led' PA 61cd. Whether *ter* in
some of the citations from BF above is for earlier *del* or earlier *fatel* is uncertain.

While *del* 'as' might conceivably be a calque on dialectal English 'as' for
'that', *fatel / tel* 'how' is perhaps less likely to be. For this reason alone the

114

hypothesis of an English origin for *del/tel* in indirect speech is questionable. There are, however, two more cogent reasons for doubting the view that we are dealing here with a construction based on English.

In the first place both *del* and *fatel* are used to introduce indirect speech already in Middle Cornish. We have seen some examples of *fatel* 'that' from TH. *Fatel* is also so used in *Beunans Meriasek* (AD 1504):

> *me ages guarnyas fetel ese turant brays er agis pyn drehevys* 'I warned you that a great tyrant had risen against you' BM 3444–46
> *yma ree ov leferel delyfrys der varia fetel ywa dyogel* 'some are saying that he has certainly been freed by Mary' BM 3739–41.

Although the date of the *Ordinalia* is uncertain, the plays are at least as old as the early fifteenth century. They contain examples of both *del* and *fatel* as conjunctions with the sense 'that':

> *why re welas fetel formyas dev an tas nef ha nor* 'you have seen that God the Father created heaven and earth' OM 2825–27
> *the welas fetel sevys cryst mes a'n beth* 'to see that Christ rose from the tomb' PC 3241–42
> *yn ur na y fyth clewys del ony ganse brewys hag elf at es* 'in that hour it will be heard that we have been wounded by them and are ill at ease' RD 572–74
> *ny a fyn leuerel ol yn pow sur the pub den oll fatel wrussyn ny keusel orth an arluth ker* 'we will tell everybody in all the country that we spoke to the dear lord' RD 1339–42.

*Pascon agan Arluth* (PA) is the oldest continuous text of Middle Cornish and the original was probably composed in the early fourteenth century. PA has a number of instances of *del* to introduce indirect statement:

> *par del won lauaraff ȝys yntre du ha pehadur acordh del ve kemerys* 'as I know I will tell thee how agreement was made between God and sinner' PA 8ab
> *lemmyn ny a yll gwelas lauar du maga del wra neb a vynno y glewas* 'now we can see that the word of God nourishes whoever wishes to hear it' PA 12cd
> *ȝen eȝewan dyrryvys del o y fynas synsy* 'he informed the Jews that it was his wish to seize [him]' PA 62c
> *Mam Ihesus marya wyn herdhya an gyw pan welas yn y mab yn tenewyn dre an golon may resas ha ȝen dor an goys han lyn annoȝo dell deveras* 'The mother of Jesus, Blessed Mary, when she saw the spear thrust into her son into his side so that it pierced the heart and that the blood and water dropped from him' PA 221ac

*Un venyn da a welas dell o Ihesus dystryppijs* 'A good woman saw that Jesus had been stripped' PA 177a.

These Middle Cornish examples would seem to contradict the notion that *del/fatel* to introduce indirect speech is a Late Cornish phenomenon and as such is based on dialectal English. On the contrary it appears that *del/fatel* to introduce indirect statement is an intrinsic part of the medieval language.

### Breton *penaos* 'how' in indirect statement

The second reason for questioning an English origin for the *del/fatel* construction is that there appears to be a parallel in Middle Breton with *penaos* 'how' < *pe* \**naoz* 'which manner'):

*hac ez lauar penaux hon doueou ez ynt diaoulou* 'and says that our Gods are devils' VC §12

*ez prouphas deze an guerhes penaux an gentilet hoaz ho deffoy a diaraoc lauaret en tra se* 'the young woman proved to them that the pagans had previously spoken of this matter' VC §15

*gouuez en fat cesar penaux nigun ne gallas biszgoaz resistaff ouzomp* 'know in fact, Caesar, that no one was ever able to withstand us' VC §16

*Chuy a lauar penos ez credit en Doue* 'You say that you believe in God' DC: 12

*Ema hon oll fizians penaus hon avancet* 'All our faith is that you will assist us' CD: 222

*Rac Doué en deveux avouët Penaos é rey d'ar Beleyen Gallout Pezr* 'For God promised that he would give the power of Peter to the Priests' CD: 384

*pe consideraint penaus e uaint priuet Ac er uision a Doué* 'when they consider that they have been deprived of the vision of God' CH: 47.

The construction is also well attested in the modern language:

*mæs avoui a reomp penaus ezomp christenien* 'but we affirm that we are Christians' *Cat.*: 15

*Rac sonjal a reont ervad penaus an den a bropos, ha Doue a zispos* 'For they consider well that man proposes and God disposes' *Imit.*: 43

*S. Frances de Sales a lavar penos nombr a dud demezet a vezo daonet, abalamour da veza profanet ar Sacrament-se* 'St Francis de Sales says that a number of married people will be damned for having profaned this sacrament' *Reg.*: 21

*Va Doue, me gred fermament, Penaoz ezoc'h ama present* 'My God, I firmly believe that thou art here present' *Kantikou*: 22

*hag ec'h anavezjont penaos hen doa bet eur vision en templ* 'and they realized that he had had a vision in the temple' *Testamant* Luc. i 22

*Me a grede d'in penaos ar vuhez a oa beva gant bara sec'h ha taoliou treid* 'It seemed to me that life was to live on dry bread and kicks' *Marvailhou*: 17-18.

Although such syntax is common in Middle and Modern Breton, grammarians condemn it as being un-Celtic. Hemon under the heading "'Penaux; penaos' used as a conjunction" (HMSB 310) says: "It seems to have been originally a device to imitate the structure of foreign languages. The order of words, subject + verb in the subordinate clause is alien to Breton." By "foreign" Hemon presumably means either French or Latin. French does not use *comment* 'how' to introduce indirect statement. It is likely, however, that *penaos* as a conjunction in Breton is a calque on the comparable use of *quomodo* in post-Classical Latin; cf, the following from the Vulgate: *reminiscentis vestrum obedientiam: quomodo cum timore et tremore excepistis ilium* 'as he remembered your obedience how/that with fear and trembling you received him' II *Corinth.* vii 15. The Vulgate also uses *quod* 'which', *quia* 'since' and *quoniam* 'because' to introduce indirect statement.

Kervella dislikes *penaos* as a conjunction even more than Hemon does, for he calls it *boaz argasus* 'a disgusting habit' (YBB: 406). He admits that it is widespread in the spoken Breton of Treguier at least.

There is a significant difference between the Breton use of *penaos* and Cornish *fatel/del* as a subordinating conjunction. In Breton *penaos* is frequently followed by the verbal particle *ez* + verb, In Cornish on the other hand *fatel/del* immediately precede their verb. This means that in Breton *penaos* is sometimes separated from the verbal complex and can even be used to introduce a negative verb, In Cornish *fatel/del* always forms a single unit with the verb and cannot therefore be followed by a negative particle. Nonetheless the very close semantic parallel between *fatel* 'how' > 'that' and *penaos* 'how' > 'that', suggests there is some connection between the Breton and the Cornish constructions.

### The origin of *fatel/del* 'that' in Cornish

From the Norman Conquest until the Reformation there were always many Bretons in Cornwall. Cornish was, not astonishingly, influenced by Breton in a number of ways. The verse literature of Middle Cornish is based on Breton and French models rather than on Middle English ones. Dramatized saints' lives were a marked feature of Middle Breton literature, There is in Britain only one surviving medieval play about the life of a saint, the Cornish *Beunans Meriasek* or 'Life of St Meriasek'.[1] St Meriasek was patron saint of Camborne in Cornwall, but he was himself a Breton and much of the play is set in Brittany. Cornish has lost the inherited names for Jesus and Mary and instead uses *Jesus/Jesu* and *Marya*, both of which are borrowed from Breton. More

---

1    With the discovery of *Bewnans Ke* this is no longer true.

remarkably the Cornish for London is *Loundres,* the French form which was almost certainly borrowed through Breton. One should remember that throughout the medieval period Breton and Cornish were largely, if not entirely, mutually intelligible.

One might argue that the semantic shift 'how' > 'that' is a natural one and that the use of *fatel/del* to introduce indirect statement in Cornish could have arisen spontaneously. On the other hand, the virtually identical usage in Breton suggests strongly that we are dealing here with a common South Brythonic calque on Late Latin. I assume that *fatel/del* 'that' in Cornish is indeed borrowed from Breton. I would suggest moreover that the channel for the introduction of such syntax was the bilingual clergy who were accustomed to preach and write in both Breton and Cornish. One thing is certain: the use of *fatel/del* to introduce indirect statement in Middle and Late Cornish has nothing at all to do with English dialect.

### Further "Anglicisms" in Late Cornish

George also says "The syntax of Late Cornish appears more like English syntax than that of Middle Cornish" (George 1995: 107) and he cites two examples: (a) the widespread use of the verb *gul* 'to do' as a verbal auxiliary; (b) the use of the verb *gasa* 'to let' in imperatives like *gas ny tha vos* 'let us go'.

*Gul* 'to do' as a verbal auxiliary is very widespread indeed in Middle Cornish. Here are some illustrative quotations from the texts.

> *ov arluth pan **wruk** serry, pan **ruk** drys y worhemmyn, ov ertech **gruk** the gylly* 'when I angered my Lord, when I transgressed his command, I lost my inheritance' OM 352–54
>
> *ha gans myyn **gureugh** hy knoukye erna **wrello** tremene; benytha na **wreugh** hethy* 'and with stones strike her until she die; never cease' OM 1694–95
>
> *leuerel thu'm arluth **gura** ihesu na **wrella** dampnye* 'tell my lord that he do not condemn Jesus' PC 1957–58.

Moreover the other two Brythonic languages very frequently use their respective verbs for 'to do' as auxiliaries. Evans speaking of the verbal noun observes, "In M[iddle] W[elsh] it is frequently employed as object of one of the forms of *gwneuthur* 'to do' in abnormal order" (GMW 160). Similarly Hemon in his Middle Breton grammar has a section entitled "'To do' as an auxiliary" (HMSB 249–50).

George claims in particular that the use of *gul* as an auxiliary in interrogative sentences (e.g. *Ra ve moas gena why* 'Shall I go with you?' and *reeg Dew lawle* 'Did God say?') is a distinctively Late Cornish phenomenon. Yet the construction is attested in Middle Cornish: *dar, soposia **a reta** den rych nefra mones then neffa da ny yl?* 'what? do you suppose that a rich man can never go to good heaven?' BM 459–61; *dar seposia prest **a reta** omma settya orth emperour?*

'what? do you indeed propose to attack an emperor here?' BM 2445–46; *Dar, ny* **ren** *ny redya…?* 'Why, do we not read…?' TH 39; and *A* **ra** *tus vsya offra bois ha dewas* 'Do people usually offer food and drink?' TH 52a.

The use of *gasa* in imperatives is already well established in Middle Cornish, e.g. **gesough** *y aga thyr the wrowethe* 'let the three of them lie' OM 2036–37; **gesough** *hy abart malan yn morter skuat the gothe* 'let it for the devil's sake fall, crack, into the slot' PC 2815–16; **geseugh** *y the thysplevyas* 'let them spread out' PC 2832; **gas** *vy lemmyn th'y hure* 'let me now embalm him' PC 3196 and **gays** *thym the ombrene* 'let me redeem myself' BM 1252. The Welsh equivalents of *gas* 'let' and *geseugh* 'let' (pl.) are *gad* and *gadewch* respectively and they have long been used in Welsh to form imperatives, e.g. *gadewch inni fynd* 'let's go'; *gadewch i mi feddwl* 'let me think' and *gad iddo ddod* 'let him come' (MW: 228-29).

There is an important lesson for us here. Before dismissing any aspect of Cornish syntax as a late corruption based on English, we should search the Middle Cornish texts to discover whether the feature in question is attested in the earlier language. We should also examine Welsh and Breton closely to see whether an apparently Late Cornish construction has parallels elsewhere in Brythonic.

George's observations about Late Cornish syntax are the result of his apparent (and unfounded) opinion that Middle and Late Cornish are different languages. From the point of view of phonology, syntax, inflection and vocabulary Middle and Late Cornish are effectively the same. There is nothing in the second which is not already present in the first. Middle and Late Cornish form an unbroken continuum. The only significant difference between the medieval and the later language is the spelling. Arguments about the relative merits of Middle or Late Cornish as a basis for the revival are, therefore, misconceived.

# 'SAINT' IN CORNISH*

## Titles with territories and titles in apposition

In traditional Cornish terms like *myghtern* 'king', *myghternes* 'queen', *duk* 'duke' and *epscop* 'bishop' are frequently followed by a territorial or population name in genitival relation with them. As examples one might cite the following:

> *mygtern ethewon, myghtern yuthewon, myghtern yethewon, myghtern yethewen* 'king of the Jews' PA 187d; PC 982, 1583, 2039, 2066, 2117, 2125, 2797, 2800, 2835
>
> *myghtern israel, myghtern ysrael* 'king of Israel' PC 276, 427, 2879
>
> *myghtern nef* 'king of heaven' RD 926, 1754, 2421, 2523
>
> *myghternes nef, myterness neff* 'queen of heaven' BM 154, 3134
>
> *duk bryten* 'duke of Brittany' BM 1
>
> *war thuk kernow* 'upon the Duke of Cornouaille' BM 2396; *Duk kernov* 'the Duke of Cornouaille' BM 2397
>
> *epscop kernov, epscop kernow* 'bishop of Cornouaille' BM 2860, 2884, 2890
>
> *Ispak Kar-êsk* 'bishop of Exeter' AB: 222.

Compare also *chyff arluth rohan* 'chief lord of Rohan' BM 1936 and *Arlothas Kernow* 'the Duchess of Cornwall' BF: 31.

The same terms *myghtern, myghternes, duk* and *epscop* are also frequently used with a following personal name in apposition, e.g.

> *mytern alwar* 'king Alwar' BM 2463
>
> *mytern casvelyn* 'king Casivellaunus' BM 2465
>
> *mytern connan* 'king Conan' BM 223
>
> *the vyghtern dauid* 'to king David' OM 1929; *Myterne Davith* 'king David' TH 8a
>
> *myghtern erod* 'king Herod' PC 1842
>
> *myghtern ihesu* 'king Jesus' PC 2354
>
> *mytern lucius* 'king Lucius' TH 51
>
> *mytern margh* 'king Mark' BM 2464
>
> *mytern massen* 'king Maximius' BM 3156
>
> *myghtern pharo* 'king Pharaoh' OM 1479, 1712
>
> *myghtern salmon, mytern Salamon* 'king Solomon' OM 2545; TH 31
>
> *duk conan* 'duke Conan' BM 84
>
> *duk magus* 'duke Magus' BM 3920; *duk nobyl magus* 'noble Duke Magus' BM 3930
>
> *ebscop cayphas, epscop cayphas* 'bishop Caiaphas' PA 88b; PC 1201, 1851.

Compare also *arluth costentyn* 'lord Constantine' BM 1739.

---

\* First published in *Cornish Studies*. Second series: Seven. 1999. Exeter: University of Exeter Press. Pp. 219–241. ISBN 0-85989-644-7

The second construction involving apposition rather than genitival relation is commoner in Cornish than the first. It would seem, however, to be the less native of the two. In all the Brythonic languages, when a proper noun follows a noun, it naturally acquires genitival force. Thus Breton *Barzhaz Breizh* means 'the Poesy of Brittany' and Welsh *Plaid Cymru* means 'the Party of Wales'. Similarly in Cornish *carek veryasek* BM 1072, for example, can only mean 'Meriasek's rock'. The expression *map dauid, map daueth* 'son of David' occurs at PC 271, 277, 419 and 423. Taken literally, therefore, *myghtern David* ought to mean 'David's king'—which makes no sense. The Cornish expression *myghtern David* 'king David' is clearly a calque on English 'King David' or Latin *rex David*. The same is true of *Duk Magus* 'Duke Magus' and all the other titles in apposition cited above. Such expressions as *myghtern David, duk Magus* and *epscop Cayphas* do not conform to the natural tendency of the Brythonic languages to understand A + B (where B is a proper noun) as ' the A of B' rather than 'A, the B'.

### "King Arthur is not dead"

In Welsh in order to express apposition with words meaning 'king', 'lord', etc., one originally inverted the word-order and lenited the title, e.g. *Arthur Frenin* 'King Arthur' and *Ioan Fedyddiwr* 'John the Baptist'. A similar word-order is also to be found in Irish, though without initial lenition, for example *Dáibhí Rí* 'King David', *Anraí Rí* 'King Henry' and *Íseáia Fáidh* 'the prophet Isaiah'. In contemporary Welsh, however, the English word-order prevails, though the definite article precedes the title, e.g. *y Brenin Arthur* 'King Arthur', and *y Tywysog Siarl* 'Prince Charles'.

In Welsh the definite article cannot occur before a noun followed by a proper noun in genitival relation to it. This is because the first noun is already definite by reason of the following proper noun. In Welsh, therefore, one says *hanes Cymru* 'the history of Wales', not *\*yr hanes Cymru* and *Eglwys Loegr* 'the Church of England', not *\*yr Eglwys Loegr*. If the article is used, the noun and its following proper noun must be in apposition to each other. This is why the second noun in such phrases *y Brenin Arthur* and *y Twysog Siarl* cannot be understood as genitive. Since *y Brenin Arthur* with the definite article *y* before *Brenin*, cannot mean *\**'Arthur's king' (which would be *brenin Arthur*), it can only mean the King, Arthur', i.e. 'King Arthur'. Similarly *y Tywysog Siarl* cannot possibly mean *\**'Charles's prince'. It can only mean 'The Prince, Charles', i.e. 'Prince Charles'.

In Welsh *Arthur Frenin* and Irish *Dáibhí Rí* the name comes first and the title second. A comparable syntax is sometimes found in Cornish, for example in the expressions *Walter Kembro* 'Walter the Welshman' (CPNE: 48) and *Charles Mightern* 'King Charles' in the Letter of King Charles.

I have noticed no precise parallel in Cornish for *y Brenin Arthur* 'King Arthur' involving the word *mytern* 'king'. The expressions *an emp[r]our costenten* 'the emperor Constantine' BM 1326, *then emperour costentyn* 'to the emperour Constantine' BM 3957 and *then vyternes helen* 'to queen Helena' BM 1158 are, however, exactly comparable. Similarly, the phrase *ov arluth costentyn* 'my lord Constantine' at BM 1527 can also be compared, since the first element *arluth* is rendered definite by the possessive adjective *ov* 'my' and the whole phrase is therefore unambiguous. It can only mean 'my lord, Constantine', i.e. 'my lord Constantine'.

The motto of the Federation of Old Cornwall Societies is *Nyns yu marow myghtern Arthur*. In view of *myterne Davith* 'king David', *myghtern Salmon* 'king Solomon', *mytern Connan* 'king Conan', *mytern Margh* 'king Mark', etc. in the texts, *myghtern Arthur* 'king Arthur' cannot be described as incorrect. Nonetheless *Nyns yu marow Arthur myghtern* (cf. *Charles Mightern*) or *Nyns yu marow an myghtern Arthur* (cf. *then emperour costentyn*) would have been even better Cornish.

### The saint's name without *Sen/Sent*

If *mytern David* 'king David' is based on English or Latin and is not Celtic in origin, it follows that expressions like *Sen Luk* 'St Luke', *Sent Powl* 'St Paul', etc., are similarly calques on English or Latin and are also non-Celtic. It is significant that *Sen/Sent* is common in Cornish only with foreign saints. Celtic saints and some of the commonest saints of the New Testament are usually referred to in Cornish by their Christian names alone.

As examples of the simple Christian name referring to the saint one might cite *Goluan* (< *gol *Yowan*) 'the feast of St John'; *bevnans meryasek* 'the Life of St Meriasek' BM 4550; *maria cambron* 'St Mary of Camborne' BM 2510; *Plêth Maria* 'Our Lady's tresses' AB 245a; *myhall, sera* '[by] St Michael, sir' CW 599; *dugoll myhal, dugol myhall* 'the feast of St Michael, Michaelmas' BM 2077, 2201; *chear pedyr* 'the Chair of St Peter' TH 49 and *re Yîst, re Ist* 'by St Just' AB: 249. Some of these expressions will be discussed in greater detail below.

This use of the Christian name without *Sen* or *Sent* is customary in Cornish toponyms where the saint is a Celtic one. To exemplify this point I give below a brief selection of place-names. The toponyms consist of one of five toponymic elements: A) *eglos* 'church'; B) *fenten* 'well'; C) *lan* 'enclosure'; D) *merther* 'grave, burial place'; E) *plu* 'parish' or F) *porth* 'harbour; gateway', followed by the name of a Celtic saint:

**A**
*Egglous Boryan* 'St Burrian' PNWP: 43 & *Eglez Burian* BF: 27; *Eglosbudock* 'Budock' CLN5: 19; *Egloscraweyn* 'Crowan' CPNE: 91; *Egloscuri* 'Cury' CLN5: 21; *Egloscutbert* 'Cubert' CLN5: 21; *Egloserm* 'St Erme' CLN5: 21; *Egloslagek* 'Ladock' CLN5: 21; *Eglosmadern* 'Madron' CPNE: 91; *Egglostetha* 'St Teath' CPNE: 91; *Eglos Senor, Egglose Zennor* 'Zennor Churchtown' PNWP: 76.

**B**
*Fentyn Carensek* = 'St Carantoc's well' CPNE: 97; *Ventongassick* 'St Cadock's well'; *Ventonberron* = 'St Piran's well'; *Venton East* = 'St Just's well' PNWP: 79;

*Ventonglidder* = 'St Clether's well'; *Fentonladock* = 'St Ladock's well'; *Ventontinny* < *\*fenten Entenin* = 'St Antoninus's well'.

**C**

*Lananta, Lalanta* < *Anta* 'Lelant' PNWP 57; *Lanberan* < *Piran* 'Perranzabuloe' CLN5: 17; *Lantinning* < *Entenin* 'St Anthony in Meneage' CLN5: 17; *Langustentyn* < *Costentyn* 'Constantine' CLN5: 17; *Langoron* 'Goran' CLN5: 17; *Lanhidrock* < *Ydroc* 'Lanhidrock' CLN5: 17; *Lanuah* 'St Ewe' CLN5: 17; *Lawenep* < *Gwenep* 'Gwennap' CLN5: 17; *Lanwethenek* (also *Lodenek*) < *Gwethenoc* 'Padstow' CPNE: 277.

**D**

*Barrymaylor* < *merther Maylor*; *Mertheruny, Mertherheuny* (CPNE: 164) < *merther Euny*; *Merthersithny* CPNE: 164; *Menedarva* < *merther Derva*.

**E**

*Pelynt* < *\*plu Nynt* CPNE: 187; *Plu-alyn* 'St Allen' CPNE: 295; *Plewe-Golen* 'Colan' CPNE: 295; *Plewgolom* '?St Columb Major' CPNE: 295; *Pluysie* 'St Issey' CPNE: 295; *plew Paule* 'Paul' BF: 38 & *pleu Paul* AB: 222; *pleu Yst* 'St Just in Penwith' AB: 222 & *Pleu Êst* JRIC 1886: 12; *Pluvogan* 'St Mawgan' CPNE 295; *plu vuthek* 'Budock' OM 2463.

**F**

*Porthia* 'St Ives' < *porth Ya* CPNE: 299, *Poreeah* BF: 25; *Porthkea* = 'entrance to parish of St Kea'; *Porthleven* < *porth Elvan*; *Porthmawgan* 'St Mawgan in Pydar' CPNE: 300; *Porth Mellin* 'harbour of St Melyan'; *Porth Perane* 'Perranuthnoe' CPNE: 300; *Porthzennor Cove*; *Portsenen* 'Sennen Cove' < *\*porth Senen* PNWP: 68; *Priest Cove* < *\*porth Ust*, i.e. the cove of St Just PNWP: 65 (cf. *Porth East* at Gorran Haven PNWP: 26).

The above list could be considerably extended, particularly as far as toponyms in *Lan-* are concerned. Examples with different first elements include *Altarnun* < *alter Non* 'St Non's altar' and *Luxulyan* < *lok Sulyan* 'place of St Sulian'. This latter was also known as *Lansulien* (CLN5: 18). Some of the above may be uncertain; the important point to notice is that in none of them is the saint's name preceded by *Sen* or *Sent*.

### 'Saint' in Welsh and Irish

In Welsh Celtic saints are usually referred to by the simple Christian name. If necessary the adjective *Sant* 'saint, holy' is added after the name, e.g. *Dewi Sant* 'St David'. Foreign saints are usually introduced by *Sant* before the Christian name. The practice in Welsh is described in the most recent English-Welsh dictionary as follows:

> **saint** … *attrib.* Sant *usua*[*lly*]. *precedes the names of saints of the Roman and Greek calendars, and follows the name of Celtic saints* (WAD: S 1204).

The position is similar in Welsh toponyms. One finds the bare Christian name with *llan* 'enclosure' (cf. Cornish *lan-*), for example, in *Llanfair* < *Mair* 'Mary', *Llandudno* < *Tudno* and *Llanilltud* < *Illtud*. *Ty* 'house' occurs with the bare name, for example, in *Tyddewi* 'St David's'. Notice, however, that in most cases *Sant* before the saint's name is most frequently *Sain* in place-names, e.g. *Sain Ffagan* 'St Fagan's' and *Sain Nicolas* 'St Nicholas'. Welsh is thus broadly similar to Cornish in this respect, since in neither does Welsh *Sant/Sain* or Cornish *Sent/Sen* precede the Christian name of Celtic saints.

It is quite apparent that the use of the simple Christian name is a common Celtic phenomenon and has its origins in the practice of the Celtic church. In Irish St Patrick, St Bridget and St Columba are known as *Pátric/Pádraig*, *Brigit/Bríd* and *Colum Cille* respectively. We thus find such expressions as *Bethu Phátric* 'the Life of St Patrick', *Teampall Phádraig* 'St Patrick's Cathedral', *Bethu Brigte* 'the Life of St Bridget', *Lá Fhéile Bríde* 'St Bridget's Day', *Betha Cholam Chille* 'the Life of St Columba' and *Í Choluim Chille* 'Iona of St Columba'. If it is necessary to distinguish Patrick the saint from a secular character, one can say *Pádraig Naofa* 'Holy Patrick'—an expression reminiscent of *Dewi Sant* in Welsh. The use of the Christian name was taken over into Hiberno-English. St Bridget is sometimes called 'Biddy' and the 17th March is 'Patrick's Day' or even 'Paddy's Day'.

Foreign saints in Irish receive a prefixed *San* before their names, e.g. *San Antaine* 'St Anthony', *San Froinsias* 'St Francis' and *San Caitríona* 'St Catherine'. Even here *San* is not universal. SS Peter and Paul, who are associated with the Apostolic See from the earliest times, are known to the Catholic Irish as *Peadar* and *Pól*. respectively. Certain other nativized saints are referred to without *San*. Thus 26th December, the feast of the proto-martyr and a very important day in the Irish calendar, is called *Lá Fhéile Stiofáin* 'Stephen's Feast Day'. St Stephen's Green in Dublin is in Irish *Faiche Stiabhna* and indeed the place is always referred to as 'Stephen's Green' by Dubliners.

There has been a tendency in Irish since the early seventeenth century to prefix all saint's names with *Naomh* 'Saint', e.g. *Naomh Pádraig*, *Naomh Eoin* 'St John' and *Naomh Pól* 'St Paul'. This practice appears to have arisen first in litanies of the saints that were translated from Latin. More recently English form like St Patrick, St John, etc., have reinforced the tendency. It is even now by no means universal, however. A branch of the Gaelic Athletic Association in South Dublin is known as *Cumann Naomh Eoin* 'St John's Club' where *Naomh Eoin* 'Saint John' is a calque on English. On the other hand the all-Irish secondary school in Dublin bears the more authentic name *Coláiste Eoin*.

### 'Saint' in Breton

Similarly in Brittany one finds toponyms in *Lan-*, e.g. *Lanndevenneg, Landudal,* and *Lannildud*. In Brittany the element *plou* 'parish' (cf. Cornish *plu, plew*) is common with the bare saint's name, e.g. *Plougouloum, Plouizi* and *Plouzeniel*. Further elements immediately followed in toponyms by the simple name include *kastell*, e.g. *Kastell Paol* 'St Pol-de-Léon'; *porzh* 'harbour', e.g. *Porzh-Pêr* 'Port-Saint-Pierre' and *lok* 'place', e.g. *Loctudy* and *Locmélar*. It would seem, then, that in Breton, as in Welsh and Cornish, Celtic saints were originally referred to by use of the Chrisitan name by itself.

In Breton, however, there is a marked tendency, when the name is not preceded by any other element, to prefix Celtic saints' names with *Sant*. This occurs in prayer books, where one finds such expressions as *Sant Michæl Archæl* 'St Michael the Archangel', *Sant Jan-Badezour* 'St John the Baptist' and *an Ebestel Sant Pêr ha Sant Paul* 'the Apostles St Peter and St Paul' *(Cat.*: 263). It also occurs in toponyms, e.g. *Sant-Maodan, Sant Peran, Sant-Wenn* and *Sant-Yust*. Notice also that *Yann*, the equivalent of Cornish *\*Yowan*, appears with *Sant* in the place-names *Sant-Yann-ar-Biz* 'St Jean du Doigt' and *Sant-Yann-ar-C'houenon* 'St Jean-sur-Couesnon'. It should be noted further that in Breton, where male saints have *Sant*, female saints have *Santes, Santez* prefixed to their names. One thus finds forms like *Sanctez Cathell* 'St Catherine', *Buhez Santez Nonn* 'the Life of St Non' and even *Santes Mari* 'St Mary, the Blessed Virgin Mary'.

Collections of saints' lives were always popular in Brittany. In such works Celtic saints always receive *Sant* or *Santes* before their names. In BS, for example, one finds *s[ant] Güénæl* 'St Gwenael' (3 Nov.); *s. Guénolé* 'St Gwenolé' (3 March); *s. Paul, escob a Léon* 'St Paul, bishop of Léon' (12 March); *s. Padern, quetan escob a Huénèd* 'St Paternus, first bishop of Vannes' (16 April) and *s. Mériadec, escob a Huéned* 'St Meriadec/Meriasek, bishop of Vannes' (7 June). Female saints in BS include *Sès Ninnoc, gùérhiès* 'St Ninnoc, virgin' (4 June) and *Stès Noal, gùérhiès* 'St Noal, virgin' (6 July).

The difference between *Sant* with male saints and *Santez* with female ones is reminiscent of Latin saints' names in *Sanctus* and *Sancta* respectively. It is likely, therefore, that the practice of prefixing the name of all saints, Celtic or foreign, with *Sant* or *Santez* is a Latin convention (reinforced no doubt by French *Saint* and *Sainte*) adopted into Breton. A cursory glance at Breton works of popular piety, indicates just how closely such Breton works follow Latin and French models. In the litanies of the saints, for example, it is common to find on one side of the page Latin invocations like the following:

**Sancte Petre**, *ora pro nobis* 'St Peter, pray for us'
**Sancte Paule,** *ora pro nobis* 'St Paul, pray for us'
**Sancte Jacobe**, *ora pro nobis* 'St James, pray for us'
**Sancte Joannes,** *ora pro nobis* 'St John, pray for us'
**Sancte Toma,** *ora pro nobis* 'St Thomas, pray for us',        etc.,

and the equivalent in Breton in the next column:

**Sant Pêr,** *pedit evidomp* 'St Peter, pray for us'
**Sant Paol**, *pedit evidomp* 'St Paul, pray for us'
**Sant Jaques**, *pedit evidomp* 'St James, pray for us'
**Sant Ian**, *pedit evidomp* 'St John, pray for us'
**Sant Thomas**, *pedit evidomp* 'St Thomas, pray for us',     etc. (HBL: 659).

Notice that in the case of *Sant Pêr* and *Sant Ian* the form of the saint's name was inherited from Latin in the early Christian period. With neither would one expect *Sant*.

Female saints, when they occur in litanies, are prefixed by *Sancta* in Latin and *Santes* in Breton. One thus finds the following equivalents, for example:

| Latin | Breton | |
|---|---|---|
| *Sancta Agatha* | *Santes Agata* | |
| *Sancta Lucia* | *Santes Luç* | |
| *Sancta Agnes* | *Santes Agnes* | |
| *Sancta Cæcilia* | *Santes Aziliç* | |
| *Sancta Anastasia* | *Santes Anastas* | (HBL: 660-69). |

If, then, Breton differs from Welsh and Cornish in using *Sant/Santez* indiscriminately with all saints' names, it does so by analogy with Latin. The Bretons, unlike either the Welsh or the Cornish, remained uniformly Catholic at the Reformation. In consequence they maintained their devotion to the saints and were also exposed to a popular piety mediated through Latin models. This is why the Breton treatment of saints' names was so heavily influenced by Latin.

The Irish also remained Catholic and it is remarkable that the use of *Naomh* 'Saint' with all saints' names seems to begin in Ireland at the period of the Counter-Reformation.

## The saint's name as Cornish toponym

Not infrequently in Cornwall the saint's name is used by itself as the name of the parish. Examples of this use of the saint's name by itself from contemporary Cornish place-names include *Breage, Budock, Buryan, Colan, Constantine, Cubert, Degibna, Feock, Gerrans, Gulval, Gwennap, Gwinear, Gwithian, Kenwyn, Ladock, Mabe, Madron, Mawgan, Mawnan, Mylor, Paul, Phillack, Probus, Sithney, Stithians, Wendron* and *Zennor*.

The saint's name without *Sen* before it but with a descriptive element after occurs in *Perranarworthal < Peran \*ar wothel* = 'St Piran facing the water ground'; *Perranuthnoe* = 'St Piran and St Gwethenoc'; *Perranzabuloe < Peran +* Latin *in sabulo* = 'St Piran in the sand' and *Petherwyn < Padarn wyn* 'Blessed St Paternus'.

The use of the name of the saint as name of the parish would seem to have its origins in the practice of Cornish speakers themselves. This can be seen from the following examples from the Cornish texts:

*Kûz karna na huîla en **Borrian*** 'Cornawheely Wood in Buryan' BF: 18
*Mean orrol en **Madern*** 'another stone in Madron' BF: 27
*Tubmas Trythal, **Proanter Sennen*** 'Thomas Trythal, parson of Sennen' Ellis: 98
*Drake **Proanter East*** 'Drake, the Parson of St Just' ACB & Ellis: 98
*Dho **Proanter Powle*** 'the Parson of Paul' ACB
*tha **Pobl Bohodzhak Paull** ha'n Egles nei* 'for the poor people of Paul and our church' BF: 57.

The name *Mevagissey* is for *\*Meva hag Issy* 'St Meva and St Issey', the two saints of the parish. The presence of the Cornish word *(h)ag* in the name would seem to indicate that *\*Meva hag Issy* was a living toponym while Cornish was spoken in the district.

### Sen(t), Synt 'Saint'

As has been suggested *Sen* or *Sent* is common only with foreign saints. Examples from the Cornish texts include the following:

*S Ambros* TH 39, 47, 47a, 49; *S Ambrose* 45a; *S. Ambros* SA 62, 62a x 2, 66
*Sent augustyn* TH 37a; *S Austyn* TH 32; *S Austen* SA 59; *S. Austen* SA 64a, 65a, 66; *S austin* TH 32; *S Agustyn* TH 32a, 37, 56, 58; *S Agustin* TH 32a; *S Augustin* TH 48 x 2; *S Augustyn* TH 37a, 46
*S Bartholomew* TH 37a
*S Basell* TH 51a; *S Basyll* TH 45a
*S Chrisostum* TH 57
*S Ciprian* TH 39a, 42, 45; 48a, 56; *S Cyprian* TH 42a
*S Cyrill* TH 38a; *S Cirill* TH 57 x 2
*s Ireneus* TH 37; *S Yreneus* TH 19a
*S Jherom* TH 47; *S Hierom* TH 49
*sen luk* BM 391; *S Luk* TH 29a; *S luk* TH 38; *S. Luke* SA 64
*S Mark* TH 53
*S mathew* TH 31a; *S Mathew* TH 35a, 43a
*sent sampson* BM 2983
*S Thomas* SA 60a.

It is apparent from this list that the saints whose names are preceded by the title *Sen / Sent (Synt)* are almost invariably foreign ones. The only exception in the above list is the Breton saint Sampson of Dol referred to as *sent sampson* at BM 2983. The author of BM was almost certainly drawing at this point upon a Latin source which spoke of *\*ecclesia Sancti Sampson*. Moreover, as we have seen, the Bretons tended to use *Sant* with the name of all male saints. In either case the use of *sent* in this instance is not remarkable.

### Sen/Sent in toponyms

We have very few examples from Cornish language texts of *Sen/Sent* in toponyms. Two examples known to me are the following:

*Stean* **San Agnes** *an guella stean en Kernow* 'The tin of St Agnes is the best tin in Cornwall' ACB: facing F f
*Gûn* **St. Eler** 'the moor of St Hilary' BF: 17.

In both cases the saints are foreign rather than Celtic ones.

One apparent exception is St Levan in Penwith, e.g. *En Termen ez passiez thera Trigaz en* **St. Levan;** *Dean ha Bennen en Tellar creiez cheir a Horr* 'In tyme that is passed, there Dwelt in St. Levan a man & woman in a place called The House of a Ramm' (BF: 15, 19). St Levan is by *Volksetymologie* for *Seleven < Solomon* (Doble 1960: 3). In the early twentieth century the place was still called *Seleven* by the older people. *St Levan < Seleven* is, despite appearances, a further example of the saint's name used by itself as a toponym.

### SS Jovyn, Malan & Gylmyn
In the Cornish plays the unsympathetic characters not infrequently invoke the pagan "saint" Jovin. The name occurs both with and without the prefix *synt* (a variant of *sent*):

*ef a'n pren re* **synt iovyn** 'he'll pay for it by St Jovin' PC 368

*syr cayfas re* **synt iouyn** *me a wra the gorhemmyn* 'Sir Caiaphas, by St Jovin, I'll do your command' PC 1363-64

**synt iouyn** *whek re'n carro* 'may dear St Jovin love him' PC 1847

*re* **synt iouyn** 'by St Jovin' PC 1962, 2858

*re* **synt iouyn** *whek* 'by dear St Jovin' PC 2537

**synt iouyn** *whek re'th caro* 'may dear St Jovin love you' PC 3016

*me a'n te re* **synt iouyn** 'I swear it by St Jovin' RD 349

*rak coske reys yv thy'mmo re* **synt iouyn** 'for I must sleep by St Jovin' RD 412-13.

*mara'th caffaf re* **iovyn** 'if I catch you, by Jovin' OM 1532

*rag henna thy's my a de gorthye* **iovyn** *beneges* 'therefore I swear to you to worship blessed Jovin' OM 1811-12

*goef nep a worth* **jovyn** 'woe is him who worships Jovin' OM 1889

*re* **iovyn** *arluth an beys* 'by Jovin, lord of the world' PC 449

*re* **iovyn** *drok yv gyne* 'by Jovin, I'm sorry' PC 1292

*wolcum cayphas re* **iouyn** 'welcome, Caiaphas, by Jovin' PC 1687

**iouyn** *roy thy's bos den mas* 'may Jovin grant you to be a good man' PC 1706

*me a'th pys gynes mar plek war* **iouyn** *gylwel mercy* 'I beg you please to call upon Jovin for mercy' PC 1896-97

*kemmys na worthyo* **iouyn** 'as many as do not worship Jovin' PC 1917

*a thev* **iouyn** *luen a ras* 'O god Jovin, full of grace' PC 2989

*gorth quik iovyn ha soly* 'worship Jovin and Sol quickly' BM 1231

*Thum du* **iovyn** *benygas me a offren iij bran vrays* 'to my blessed god Jovin I will offer three ravens' BM 3406-07.

The name *iouyn* is usually translated 'Jove' but it would seem to be a conflation of the oblique stem *Jov-* of *Jupiter* with *Jovinus* or *Jovinius*. The name *iouyn* is clearly a recent borrowing and as such would normally take *synt* before it. The reason for the inconsistency in the use of *synt* is presumably that the dramatists could not decide whether Jovin was a Continental saint who required *synt* or a pagan god who did not.

*Malan* 'Belial, Beelzebub' (< ?*Malignus* ) is less well attested in the texts. He is both a saint: *rak why a scon ahanan the pilat re* **synt malan** 'for you will soon go to Pilate, by Saint Belial' PC 2340-41, and a god: *hou geiler abarth* **malan** 'ho! gaoler, in the name of Belial!' PC 2235; *gesough hy abart[h]* **malan** *yn morter skuat the gothe* 'let it fall, splat, into the mortise, in the name of Belial' PC 2815-16.

*Synt gylmyn* is a hapax legomenon: *syr arluth re* **synt gylmyn** *my a wra the worhemmyn* 'Sir Lord, by St Gylmyn, I will do your command' OM 2413-14. In view of the alternation seen in *synt iouyn* / *iouyn* and *synt malan* / *malan*, it is likely that the expression *\*re gylmyn* also occurred, although we have no instance of it. Since *re* 'by' (in oaths) lenites the following consonant, I suspect that we are really dealing with a basic form *\*Kylmyn*. This, with Lhuyd and Norris, I take to be the Cornish form of *Columbanus*, Irish *Colmán*. The basic form *\*re Gylmyn* 'by St Columbanus' has given rise to a form *Gylmyn* with permanent initial lenition. *Gylmyn* in turn has further been interpreted as a pagan deity.

The adverb *defry* 'indeed' is also made into a saint in the oath *re* **sent deffry** 'by Saint Truly' CW 606. This fictitious saint was believed to be of foreign origin, for he receives the element *sent* before his name.

## *Synta* as the feminine of *Sent/Synt*

*Synta* has long been used by Cornish revivalists as the feminine equivalent of *Sen/Synt*. Nance, for example, used the expression *Synta Brek* to render 'St Breage' (LPMS: 8-9). The element *Synta* is highly doubtful, however.

As far as can be ascertained, *Synta*, or *Synte*, occurs once only in the Cornish texts. In *Resurrexio Domini* St Thomas, doubting the resurrection of Christ, has already rebuked Peter, John and James for their foolish faith. Finally he rounds on Matthew and says:

> *a* **synte mari** *mathew*
> *mara colyth ty a tew*
> > *gans the whethlow*
> *gul ges ahanaf a wreth*
> *marth yv gynef nath ues meth*
> > *ow keusel gow*

> 'By Saint Mary, Matthew
> if you will hearken, you will cease
> > your silly stories.
> You are making fun of me.
> I am astonished you are not ashamed
> > to utter lies'
> > (RD 1387-92).

Three things should be noticed here. In the first place, *synte mari* in this passage is not a specific reference to the Blessed Virgin Mary. St Thomas does not yet believe the resurrection and does not by implication accept the tenets of Christianity. He cannot therefore believe the mother of Jesus to be a saint. In the second place, the form is not Cornish, but French. *Synte mari* is the scribe's spelling of *Sainte Marie*, which is French, not Cornish. Since the present instance is the only example, we can conclude that *Synte, Synta* was never a productive formant in Cornish. In the third place, it is clear from *Stean Sen Agnes an guella stean en Kernow* 'The tin of St Agnes is the best tin in Cornwall', that the feminine form of *Sen* is *Sen*, not *Synta*

*Synta* 'Saint' as a title for female saints is a ghost-word. *Sen* can be used with non-native saints, but when referring to female Celtic saints the Christian name by itself is sufficient. The toponym *Breage* itself indicates that the Cornish for St Breage was *Brek* or *Breg*. This is corroborated by the form *Eglosbrek* 'St Breages's church, Breage' from AD 1181 (CLN5: 19). Forms like *Synta Brek* 'St Breage', *Synta Ya* 'St Ives', etc. are not Cornish, and are best avoided in the revived language. If in Cornish one needs to indicate that Breg and Ya are saints, one can say *Breg Sans* and *Ya Sans* respectively.

### St John

There are two forms of the name 'St John' in Cornish. The first was originally *\*Yowan* and is the direct reflex of Latin *Iohannes* 'John' adopted into the Brythonic languages in the early Christian period. It is therefore the exact equivalent of Welsh *Ieuan* (*Iwan, Ifan*) and Breton *Yann*. As far as I am aware, *\*Yowan* survives in only one place in Cornish, namely in the word *Golowan, Goluan* 'St John's day, Midsummer (24th June)', in the proverb *Guâve en Hâve terebah Goluan* (JRIC 1886: 11), where *Goluan* is from *gol* 'feast' (< Latin *vigilia*) + *\*Yowan* 'St John'. The loss of initial /j/ is quite regular here; compare *eʒewon* 'Jews' PA 126a for *yethewon*; *eghas* 'health' TH 30a for *yehes* and *eyth* 'language' TH 1 for *\*yeth* (Welsh *iaith*). As in the case of *dugol Myhall* 'Michaelmas', the early formation *Goluan* renders the saint's name as the bare name without prefix.

The second form of the name 'St John' is *Sen Jowan, S Johan*. Here are some examples from the texts:

*by sen iowan* BM 2878
*sent Johan* TH 8; *Sent Johan* TH 23a
*S Johan* TH 15, 42a, 43, 51a, 53 x 3, 57 x 2; *S Jowan* TH 39a
*sen iowen baptyst* BM 4450
*S Johan baptist* TH 8
*S Johan evangelist* TH 8
*S Johan an evangelest* TH 20a.

Notice also *Jowan baptist* without *S(ent)* at TH 43a and *Jowan* at TH 44. The form of the Christian name in *Sen Jowan, Jowan, S Johan* is identical with Lhuyd's *Dzhûan* 'John' and Boson's *Jooan* (BF: 16), where the initial is [dʒ]. Indeed Lhuyd is quite unequivocal that the initial of *Jowan* is [dʒ], for he says:

*In the* Cornish, *the Initial* I *before a Vowel, had two pronunciations: For in some words 'tis pronounced as in* English *in the word* Iew: *As* Jowan, *John; and some as* y: *For* yowynk [*young*] *must be read* yunk, *or* yynk (AB: 228: a)

and

ou *and* ow *in the* Cornish, *are also commonly Equivalent to* u *long; as* Gour an Chy [*The man of the House*] *is read* gûr an tshei, *and* Jowan *John*, Dzhûan (AB: 228c).

The English expression *by sen iowan* 'by St John' at BM 2878, is further evidence, that *John* in English and *Jowan* in Cornish were considered interchangable.

The difference between *(Y)owan* and *Jowan* is the same as that between Welsh *Ieuan* and *Siôn*. *Ieuan* is the name of the saint, while *Siôn* is a secular name and never refers to the saint. Comparable also is the Irish *Eoin* (Scottish *Iain*, Manx *Ean*), the name of the saint and *Seán* (earlier *Seaán* < Old French *Jehan*), the boy's name. One thing is apparent, however; *Sen(t)* and *Yowan* never occur together in Cornish.

### Peter, Paul, and Mary
St Peter is, as far as one can ascertain, never referred to in Cornish as anything other than *Pedyr*. I have noticed the following examples from TH:

*pedyr* TH 18 x 2, 24, 43 x 3, 44a x 7, 45, 45a. 46 x 3, 47a, 48, 49 x 3
*pedyr an apostell* TH 49
*Pedyr* TH 42a x 2, 43, 45, 45a x 2, 47a x 3
*the pedyr* TH 43 x 2, 43a x 3, 44 x 2, 44a x 2, 45, 45a, 46
*the Pedyr* TH 43
*worth pedyr* TH 43a
*stall a pedyr* TH 49.

*Pedyr* is a pre-Norman form of the saint's name. This can be seen by the internal -*d*-, which is the lenition product of original -*t*-. *Pedyr* is thus identical in origin with Welsh *Pedr* and Breton *Pêr* < *Pezr*. Had the name been borrowed from English it would have had an intervocalic -*t*-; cf. the common oath *Peter* in Chaucer.

St Paul the apostle is quite different. He is almost always referred to as *S(ent) Paul*. Here are some instances from the TH:

*Sent powle* TH 13
*Sent powl* TH 13
*S paul* TH 16a, 17a, 18a, 33, 53a x 2
*S paule* TH 18, 25, 32a, 33 x 2, 33a x 2, 34, 38, 39, 51a, 57a
*S. Paule* SA 66
*S paull* TH 18a, 41a, 45

*S paulle* TH 42 x 2
*S pawle* TH 14, 33
*S Pawle* TH 4a, 7a, 8
*S poull* TH 14, 31
*S Poull* TH 32
*S poule* TH 25
*S poulle* TH 31
*S powle* TH 33a, 34
*S Powle* TH 4a x 2.

The only instance in TH of the name of the saint without the prefix *S(ent)* occurs in the phrase *Pedyr ha powle* TH 48 where St Paul is linked with St Peter; cf. *Pedyr ha povle* BM 1689. As noted above, St Peter's name is never prefixed by *S(ent)*.

Just as there are two forms of the name of St John in Cornish, so there are two forms of the name St Paul. The apostle and author of the epistles is *Sent Powl*. The Celtic saint, Paul Aurelian (Doble 1960: 10ff) gives his name to Paul in Penwith. In Cornish the toponym is either *plew Paule* (BF: 38), *pleu Paul* (AB: 222) or *pawl* (BF: 10, 12), *Paull* (BF: 57), *Paul* (BF: 60) or *Powle* (ABC). In either case this latter name lacks *Sen(t)*.

The Blessed Virgin Mary is a special case. 'Saint Mary' occurs but in many languages including English the mother of Jesus is frequently known as 'Our Lady', 'Notre Dame', etc., or 'the Blessed Virgin Mary'. Although the equivalent of 'Our Lady' is not usual in Cornish, the expression corresponding to English 'the blessed Virgin Mary' is well attested:

*wyrhes ker maria* 'Blessed Virgin Mary' TH 12a
*an wyrhes ker maria* 'the Blessed Virgin Mary' RD 154; TH 12a
*an wyrhes maria* 'the Virgin Mary' TH 12a, 13, 13a, 52a
*han wyrhes maria* 'and the Virgin Mary' BM 756
*in wyrhes maria* 'in the Virgin Mary' TH 13a
*an werthias marya* 'the Virgin Mary' SA 59
*an worthias maria* 'the Virgin Mary' SA 61
*an Worthias Maria* 'the Virgin Mary' SA 61a
*an werthias Marya* 'the Virgin Mary' SA 64a.

The name *Maria, Marya* is itself borrowed from Breton or Middle French *Marië*. The original name of the Blessed Virgin Mary direct from Latin *Maria* in the early Christian period would have been *\*Meyr*, *\*Myr* or *\*Mer* in Cornish. Although this is not attested in the literature, Padel suggests that *Venton Veor* (< *fenten ?\*Veyr*) in Liskeard may conceivably contain the earlier name for Mary (CPNE: 97).

*Maria, Marya* in Cornish behaves as though it were an early Celtic name. This is perplexing, given that 'St Mary' is common in English expressions like 'St Mary the Virgin' (and indeed St Mary Magdalene, etc.). Moreover *Sancta Maria* and *Sainte Marie* are common in Latin and French respectively. In

Cornish, however, *Marya* is never prefixed by *Sen(t)*. Instead one finds that her name alone is sufficient in such expressions as *plêth Marîa* 'lady's tresses' (AB: 245a), *chy maria* 'the house/church of Our Lady' BM 640 and even the oath *re Varîa* 'by Our Lady' (AB: 249c).

## The date of the title *Synt/Sent/Sen*

TH and SA for the most part use the abbreviation *S* or *S.* for the word meaning 'saint'. On occasion, however, TH writes *Sent*, e.g. *Sent augustyn* , *Sent powle* and *Sent powl*. BM writes *sen luk* but *sent sampson*. The Ordinalia have *synt iouyn* and *synt gylmyn*. It is not entirely clear, therefore, what was the pronunciation of *synt/sent/sen*. Given that *sen(t)*, *synt* would have been weakly stressed, it is likely that the title was most commonly pronounced [sən]. In more deliberate enunciation, however, the final group [nt] may well have been sounded. If this was so, we can be sure that the title *sent* was not adopted into Cornish until after the shift of final /nt/ > /ns/. *Sent /Synt* is from Old French *saint* or Middle English *saint*, the English itself being a borrowing from French. French *saint* is ultimately from Vulgar Latin *santus* < Classical Latin *sanctus*. *Santus* was borrowed directly in British in the early Christian period and appears with assibilation of the final /nt/ as *sans* 'holy' in Middle Cornish. Cornish *sent /synt* 'saint' and *sans* 'holy' are thus doublets.

In the Old Cornish Vocabulary final /nt/ has already been assibilated to /ns/, for example in *dans* 'dens; a tooth' (cf. Welsh and Breton *dant*). Final /nt/ was already /ns/ in Cornish therefore by the first half of the twelfth century. It follows that the title *sent/synt* could not have been part of the Cornish language until the mid-twelfth century at the earliest. By this period many of the Celtic toponyms of Cornwall were already in place. Any toponym involving a pre-Norman saint, therefore, would of necessity lacked the element *Sen(t)*. This is one reason that *Sen(t)* and *\*Yowan* do not occur together.

## 'Saint' in the English forms of toponyms

There are a number of toponyms that present a striking contrast between the Cornish form without a word for 'saint' and the English form with it, e.g.

| Cornish | English |
|---|---|
| *Lanuste* | *St Just in Penwith* |
| *Plu-alyn* | *St Allen* |
| *Plugolom* | *? St Columb Major* |
| *Pluvogan* | *St Mawgan in Meneage* |
| *Pluyust, Pleu Yst* | *St Just in Penwith* |
| *Pluysie* | *St Issey* |
| *Porthia, Poreeah* | *St Ives* |
| *Porthkea* 'entrance to St Kea' | *St Kea.* |

Contrast also the Cornish name *Melyn Myhall* 'St Michael's Mill' from 1464 without the word for 'saint' with the Latin form of the same place-name from 1258 *Molendium Sancti Michaelis*, which contains *Sancti* 'saint' (Doble 1931: 67).

The majority of forms of the names for St Just in Penwith cited by Pool from historical documents contain the element 'Saint': *St Just* 1291, 1351, 1440; *St Yuste* 1523; *St Ewste* 1558 and *St Just/St Towst* 1581. The only form cited by him that does not contain the element 'Saint' is *Lanuste* from 1396 (PNWP: 54). It is nonetheless clear from the sixteenth-century form *Pluyust*, from Lhuyd's *Pleu Yst* and Pryce's *Pronter East*, that as long as Cornish survived, the name of the town in Cornish was *Lan Ust, Plu Ust* or plain *Ust*. The forms with a word for 'Saint' are from Latin and English documents (in particular registers of the bishops of Exeter). They should not be confused with genuine Cornish-language forms.

The same can be said of the attested names of St Ives. It is apparent from Nicholas Boson's *Poreeah* and indeed from earlier forms *Porthya* 1284; *Porthia* 1291, 1337; *Porthye* 1313 and *Porthea* 1472 (PNWP: 65), that *Porth Ya, Por' Ya* without the element 'Saint', was the Cornish form of the name. Yet the bulk of the forms cited by Pool contains 'Saint': *St Ya* 1283, 1468, 1523; *St Ye* 1283, 1327, 1473; *St Hye* 1342; *St Eye* 1380; *St Ies* 1503; *St Ia* 1540; *St Yes* 1550; *St Yees* 1576 and *St Yves* 1579 (PNWP: 54). These forms with 'Saint' are English, not Cornish.

The contrast between the forms used in English documents and the Cornish form of the same names should be constantly in the minds of revivalists as they attempt to reestablish the Cornish toponymy of Cornwall. Unfortunately, the distinction appears to have been forgotten by some.

## *Henwyn Tylleryow Kernewek*

In December 1995 the Cornish language magazine *An Gannas* published a supplement *Henwyn Tylleryow Kernewek* 'Cornish Place-names' (HTK). This consists of a list of over 500 Cornish toponyms in Cornish with the English equivalents. There were four compilers: Graham Sandercock, Julyan Holmes, Pol Hodge and Ken George. The spelling system and phonology used is Kernowek Kemyn, a form of revived Cornish devised by Ken George, one of the four authors. Kernowek Kemyn or Common Cornish is the form of revived Cornish currently preferred by *An Gannas*.

I have explained in detail in several places (CT, 2001, and see now pp. 36–37, 38–64, and 93–110 above) why the phonology and spelling of Common Cornish are mistaken. In my view Common Cornish is not a legitimate form of the revived language and should be abandoned.

The inauthenticity of Common Cornish can readily be seen from HTK. Noteworthy, for example, is the way 'wood, forest' is invariably written *koes*, the graph <oe> representing a long closed */oː/. Cornish never possessed a long */oː/ separate from an equivalent open vowel /ɔː/. The vowel in the word for 'wood' was originally a diphthong /ui/ which developed via /oi/

into an undifferentiated long /oː/. In some western parts of the Cornish speaking area /ui/ developed as /uː/. In our surviving remains of Cornish, therefore, 'wood' is *coys* (e.g. *Coysbesek, Coyseglase, Coyse Laydock, Coysfala, Coyskentueles* CPNE: 257; *coys* BM 1618) or *cos* (e.g. *Cosesawsyn* CPNE: 257; *cosow* pl. CW 1495) in Middle Cornish, and *kûz* in Late and Western Cornish (e.g. *Kûz* BF: 18, 44). In some toponyms the dialectal form *cous* shortens to *cus-* (e.g. *Cusgarne; Cusveorth* and *Cusvey*). Common Cornish *koes* is without phonetic or orthographic justification.

HTK leaves much to be desired in other respects. Indeed the faults of Common Cornish itself are only one aspect of the problems in the work. The compilers seem in many places to have taken forms of toponyms occurring in Latin and English documents as genuine Cornish. Since the purpose of this article is to examine the way in which the English term 'Saint' is rendered in Cornish, I shall confine myself in my discussion of HTK to those toponyms with hagiographical connections only.

## Anthroponym as toponym

We have seen that in Cornish a saint's name was often used by itself as a place-name. As noted above, examples from Cornish language sources include *Pawl* 'Paul', *Borrian* 'Buryan' and *Sennen* 'Sennen'. In their recommendations for these three place-names in Cornish the compilers of HTK are oddly inconsistent. They suggest *Pawl* for 'Paul', *Eglosveryan* for 'Buryan' but *Sen Senan* for 'Sennen', i.e. the simple name in the first, *Eglos* 'church' + the saint's name in the second but *Sen* + the saint's name, but without any toponymic element in the third. *Eglosveryan* is perhaps justified by the form *Egglous Boryan* from 1588, though *Burrian* from 1593 (PNWP: 43) is identical with the spoken form in Late Cornish (i.e. *Borrian*) and might have been preferable. *Sen Senan*, however, where the native saint has *Sen* before his name, seems wholly unmotivated. Presumably *Sen Senan* is recommended for 'Sennen' because *St. Senane, St. Senan* are attested in early documents (PNWP: 68). These forms are not in Cornish, however. They are English forms of the name, and as such are irrelevant to the establishment of the Cornish toponym.

*St. Paulus* and *St. Paulinus* are attested for the place-name 'Paul' from the thirteenth to fifteenth centuries (PNWP: 62). Doble tells us that the church of Paul is called both *Ecclesia S. Pauli* and *Ecclesia S. Paulini* in the registers of the bishop of Exeter (Doble 1960: 33). It is difficult to understand therefore why the compilers of HTK did not recommend *\*Sen Pawl* as the Cornish form of the name. Perhaps they felt they really could not fly in the face of the evidence of our Late Cornish texts—which invariably call the place *Pawl* or *Paul*. Which being so, it is curious that they did not embrace spoken Cornish forms throughout and recommend *Senan* and *Beryan* as well.

It would appear, for example, from *Eglosveryan* < *eglos* + the saint's name that the compilers of HTK believe the simple name to suffice for Celtic saints

135

in some contexts. Compare further the following place-names in *Eglos-* and *Lan-* from HTK (CSN = saint's name):

*Eglosalan* < *eglos* + CSN 'St Allen'
*Eglosenoder* < *eglos* + CSN 'St Enoder'
*Eglostedha* < *eglos* + CSN 'St Teath'
*Eglostudi* < eglos + CSN 'St Tudy'
*Lannentenin* < *lan* + CSN 'St Anthony'
*Lannewa* < *lan* + CSN 'St Ewe'
*Lannyust* < *lan* + CSN 'St Just in Penwith'.

In all these names the English form contains 'Saint' yet the Cornish form recommended by HTK appears tacitly to accept that after *Eglos-* and *Lan-* the saint's name by itself is used. In other toponyms they are prepared to use the saint's name without either *Sen* before it on the one hand or *Eglos-*, *Lan-*, or whatever in front of it on the other. We have already noted *Pawl* in HTK. Other saint's names/toponyms from HTK without any element before them include *Pyran ar Woethel* 'Perranarworthal', *Pyran yn Treth* 'Perranzabuloe' and *Pyranudhno* 'Perranuthnoe'. Here St Piran, and in the last name, St Wethenoc, appear without the element *Sen*.

Given that the names of some Celtic saints recommended in HTK appear in unadorned form, it is difficult to understand why the compilers should insist on putting *Sen* before other names to produce a host of unwarranted forms: *\*Sen Endelyn* 'St Endellion'; *\*Sen Erven* 'St Ervan'; *\*Sen Gwenna* 'St Wenna'; *\*Sen Kolomm Veur* 'St Columb Major' and *\*Sen Mawgan* 'St Mawgan', for example. *Sen Kolomm Veur* is particularly unhappy when *Plewgolom* is attested from 1543 (CPNE: 295). Furthermore, in the light of *Pluvogan* (CPNE: 295) there seems to be little justification for *\*Sen Mawgan*.

Perhaps the compilers of HTK might explain their having added *Sen* to *\*Sen Endelyn*, *\*Sen Erven*, etc., by pointing out that in each case the English forms contain the element 'Saint'. This, however, does not justify *Sen* in *\*Sen Senan*, since there is no 'Saint' in the English form of the place-name. If *\*Sen Senan* 'Sennen' is unmotivated, so also are the following from HTK:

*Sen Goedhyan* 'Gwithian'
*Sen Gwynnyer* 'Gwinear'
*Sen Ke* 'Kea'
*Sen Mowgan* 'Mawgan'
*Sen Mownan* 'Mawnan'
*Sen Senar* 'Zennor'
*Sen Sydhni* 'Sithney'.

Here the English versions of the name lack 'Saint' and thus preserve the authentic Cornish forms. It is a pity that the compilers of HTK have added an unhistorical *Sen* to each of the toponyms. A transliteration of the current English place-names would have given a more authentic Cornish name.

## Two further names in HTK

We have seen that the place-name St Levan contains the name *Seleven* < *Solomon*. The original form of the name is thus the name of the saint by itself. It is noteworthy that *Selevan* is a form of the place-name recorded from 1523 (PNWP: 57). The same personal name is also to be found in the Penwith toponym *Bosliven* < *bos Seleven* 'the settlement of Solomon'. The first unstressed syllable in *Seleven* was subsequently reinterpreted as *Sen* 'Saint'. This in turn gave rise to the English form *St Levan*. Nance in his Unified Cornish version of *Jowan Chy an Horth* recommended *Plu Seleven* (Nance 1949: 37). Though unattested, such a form would be unobjectionable. The compilers of HTK, however, recommend the remarkable form *Sen Seleven* (cf. LPMS: *passim*). In English this could be rendered literally as 'St St Levan'—a place of double sanctity!

The toponym *St John* is rendered by HTK as *Sen Yowann*. This combines the early form *Yowan* (which is attested only in *Goluan*) with the later element *Sen*. *St John* in Cornish, as we have seen above, is invariably *Sen(t) Jowan* with <J> [dʒ]. *\*Sen Yowann* is without historical basis and cannot possibly be justified.

## HTK: conclusion

HTK is doubly inauthentic. In the first place the orthography used is spurious. This is because the inventor of Common Cornish mistakenly believed that Middle Cornish was very close to Welsh and Breton and constructed his spelling in the light of his mistaken opinion. Breton in particular was the model both for the phonology and orthography of Common Cornish—with unfortunate results.

In the second place, the hagiographical toponyms in HTK are inconsistent in themselves. In particularly such place-names are vitiated by the compilers' unwarranted practice of equating 'Saint' in English with *Sen* in Cornish. The compilers take toponyms from non-Cornish sources that exhibit 'Saint' (or *Sancti, Sanctae*) and by translating 'Saint' as *Sen* appear to believe that they are producing a genuine Cornish place-name. It is also probable that Breton toponyms in *Sant* have also served as a model for some of their recommended forms. Whatever the reasons for it, the policy of the compilers of HTK is ill considered. They would have been better advised to pay greater attention both to the toponyms that are actually attested in the Cornish texts on the one hand and to the Welsh, early Breton and other Celtic parallels on the other. As it stands, HTK is very unsatisfactory and cannot be recommended.

# "A MODERN AND SCHOLARLY CORNISH-ENGLISH DICTIONARY": KEN GEORGE'S *GERLYVER KERNEWEK KEMMYN**

## Introduction

In 1993 George published his *Gerlyver Kernewek Kemmyn* [GKK], a book which is described on the back cover as "A modern and scholarly Cornish-English dictionary". The Cornish used is Kernowek Kemyn or Common Cornish, a system of George's own devising. George claims that the orthography of Kernowek Kemyn and its underlying sound system reflect more accurately than Unified Cornish the phonology of the traditional language. George also claims that his orthography is phonemic. The term "phonemic" means that any one sound in the language is always represented by the same letter or group of letters. It is not necessary to scrutinize GKK thoroughly to realize that the claims of the orthography to be phonemic are unwarranted. In the following list of words from GKK, for example, the same "phoneme" is spelt differently:

> *kavoes* 'to get' (< OC -*uit*) but *eglos* 'church' (< OC -*uis*)
> *prena* 'to buy' (W. *prynu*), *krena* 'to tremble' (W. *crynu*) but *warlyna* 'last year' (W. *y llynedd*)
> *bywek* 'lively' (W. *bywiog*) but *Kernewek* 'Cornish' (W. *Cernyweg*)
> *defendya* 'to defend' but *diformya* 'to deform'
> *politek* 'politic' (< Greek *politikos*) but *krytyk* 'critic' (< Greek *kritikos*)
> *epystyl* 'epistle' (W. *epistol*) but *pistyll* 'spout' (W. *pistyll*)
> *kyst* 'box' (W. *cist*) but *trist* 'sad' (W. *trist*)
> *arsmetryk* 'arithmetic' but *eretik* 'heretic'
> *gwerthys* 'shuttle' (B. *gwerzhid*) but *gonis* 'work' (B. *gounid*)
> *chalys* 'chalice' but *servis* 'service'
> *palys* 'palace' (W. *palas*) but *solas* 'solace' (W. *solas*)
> *jentyl* 'well-born' (< OF *gentil*) but *sivil* 'civil' (< OF *civil*)
> *favour* 'favour' but *sokor* 'succour'
> *diskarga* 'to discharge' (B. *diskargan*) but *dyskybel* 'disciple' (B. *diskibl*)
> *edifia* 'to edify' but *justifya* 'to justify'
> *frya* 'to free' but *fia* 'to flee'
> *annia* 'to vex' but *agrya* 'to agree'
> *gokki* 'foolish', *gokkineth* 'folly' but *gokkyes* 'fools'
> *trynyta* 'trinity', *cheryta* 'charity' but *antikwita* 'antiquity'
> *konviktya* 'to convict' but *vyktori* 'victory'

* First published in *Cornish Studies*. Second series: Nine. 2001. Exeter: University of Exeter Press. Pp. 246–311. ISBN 0-85989-702-8. The version of this review here is slightly revised and expanded from the first publication.

*kemmyska* 'to mix' (< *ken* + *mysky*; cf. W. *cymysgu*) but *kemusur* 'symmetry' (< *ken* + *musur*; cf. W. *cymesur*)

*demondya* 'to demand' (< OF *demander*) but *kommondya* 'to command' (< OF *comander*)

*gwannder* 'weakness' (B. *gwander*) but *glander* 'cleanness' (B. *glander*)

*klyket* 'clicket' but *boekket* 'bucket'

*fashyon* 'fashion' but *passhyon* 'passion'

*dessayt* 'deceit' (< ME *deceite*) but *resayt* 'recipe' (ME *receite*)

*nesa* 'to approach' (W. *nesu, nesau*) but *nessa* 'next' (W. *nesaf*)

*klokk* 'clock' but *luk* 'luck'

*charet* 'chariot' but *gargett* 'garter'

*fyttya* 'to fit' but *akwitya* 'to acquit' (*aquyttya* in the texts)

*plattya* 'to crouch' but *skwatya* 'to squash'

*hwypp* 'whip' but *skryp* scrip'

*botell* 'bottle' but *sotel* 'subtle'

*referya* 'to refer', and *preferya* 'to prefer' but *konkerrya* 'to conquer' and *gwerrya* 'to wage war'

*sertan* 'certain' but *bargen* 'bargain'

*fesont* 'pheasant' and *plesont* 'pleasant' but *remenant* 'remnant' and *semlant* 'appearance' (< ME *semlant*)

*pemont* 'payment' (< ME *paiement*) but *fisment* 'face' (< ME *visement*)

*tulyfant* 'tulip' but *olifans* 'elephant.'

GKK writes *kons* 'pavement' with a long vowel but *kons* 'vagina' and *pons* 'bridge' with a short one. Why do we not find *kons*, *\*konns* and *\*ponns*? Similarly GKK has *fondya* 'to found' with a long vowel but *londya* 'to land' with a short one. Why is it not *fondya* and *\*lonndya*? GKK writes *tont* 'impertinent' with a long stressed vowel but *marchont*, etc., with a short unstressed one. GKK geminates after unstressed vowels in *kribenn, eythinenn, linenn*, etc. Why, then, does it not write *\*marchonnt, \*fesonnt, \*plesonnt, \*serponnt*, etc? Perhaps the most bizarre departure from a 'phonemic' spelling in GKK occurs in the derivatives of **naw** 'nine'. We find *naw* 'nine', *nawves* 'ninth' but *nownsek* 'nineteen' and *nownsegves* 'nineteenth.'

Unified Cornish spelling does not claim to be phonemic, but it is firmly rooted in Middle Cornish scribal practice. The spelling of GKK on the other hand is hypothetical and often confused. Phonemic it is not.

### The accuracy of George's database

The question remains how George's revised phonology and orthography came to be so inconsistent. Kernowek Kemyn is, we are told, based on a computer analysis of the tradtional Cornish texts. George's database is not in the public domain and it is impossible, therefore, to submit it to scrutiny. In GKK, however, each headword is accompanied by authentication and frequency codes, themselves based upon George's computer analysis of the Cornish texts. By comparing these codes with the actual attestation of words in traditional Cornish, we can assess the accuracy or otherwise of George's Cornish database.

George's frequency and authentication codes are explained in the introduction to GKK, pp. 8 - 17. In the body of the dictionary the codes are given within curled brackets. The codes {4: M: 1 (BM. 3220)}, for example, after **greons** 'greyhound', mean that the word in question is a loanword assimilated to Cornish phonetic type {4}, is confined to Middle Cornish {M} and occurs once only {1}, the occurrence being cited as line 3220 of *Beunans Meriasek*. The codes {1: D: 0 (38)} after **gwalgh** 'glut' mean that the word is a native one {1}, that it occurs in Cornish English dialect {D}, is unattested in any traditional Cornish text but has been taken from Nance's 1938 dictionary {0 (38)}. The codes after the verb **diskevera** are {4: L: 2}. Here again {4} means the word is a loan that has been assimilated to Cornish phonology, {L} means that the word is exclusively Late Cornish, while {2} suggests that the etymon occurs 2-3 times.

It will be seen that the figure given in third place in George's authentication and frequency codes represents the number of times that any etymon is said to occur. The numbers used are to be interpreted as follows: 0 = unattested; 1 = occurs once only; 2 = occurs 2 or 3 times; 3 = occurs between 4 and 9 times; 4 = occurs between 10 and 31 times; 5 = occurs 32 to 99 times. The highest frequency code given is 9, which means that an item occurs more than 3162 times. In the following pages we will not concern ourselves with any etymon that bears a frequency code higher than 5. We will see below, however, that there are many discrepancies between the frequencies given in GKK and the actual occurrences of the corresponding words in the Cornish texts themselves. This and further notable inaccuracies in the codes would lead the impartial observer to suspect that George's database of Cornish is less than perfect. In that case the statistics in any of George's published works on Cornish should be treated with caution.

Notice that in the following list headwords are given in Kernowek Kemyn followed by UC(R) in square brackets.

**abas** [abas] 'abbot': GKK says this word is confined to a single instance in OCV. This is incorrect: *Corn[ish] **Abaz** glossing An Abbot* AB: 270a.

**aghskryf** [aghscryf] 'pedigree': GKK says this is a modern neologism taken from Nance's 1955 dictionary. This is incorrect: *ple ma faut a Koth **ahskref*** AB: 224; *dho'n **Ah-skrefo** Zouznak* AB: 224.

**akordya** [acordya] 'to agree': GKK says this verb is confined to a single instance in PA. This is incorrect: *trest am bus boys **acordys*** BM 494.

**akusashyon** [acusacyon] 'accusation': GKK says this word does not occur in the texts but has been taken from Nance's 1938 dictionary. This is incorrect: *oppressys gans fals **accusacion*** TH 25.

**akusya** [acusya] 'to accuse': GKK says this word is confined to one instance in PC. This is incorrect: *may hyllyn y **acusye*** PC 1625; *pan fue genough **acusyys*** PC 1859; *kepar del fus **acusyys*** PC 1999; *pan fue **acussys*** PC 2386; *a **akiuzya** ha damnya* AB: 224.

**alhwedha** [alwhedha] 'to lock': GKK says this verb is confined to a single instance in Lhuyd: *Dho lyhuetha* glossing *Claudo, To shut; to lock* AB: 48b. This is incorrect: *in ov cofyr sur gorys oma alhwethys certeyn* BM 3643-44.

**alow** [alaw] 'water lily': GKK says this word occurs in place-names but is otherwise unattested. This is incorrect: *Nymphaea, Alau. White water-lily.* AB: 101c; *Alau, White Water Lillies* Borlase 376c.

**-ama** [-ama] 'me': GKK says this is a Late Cornish pronominal form that arose when "a phrase like *gene' mevy* 'with me' was re-interpreted as *gen ama vy*". This is incorrect: *–ama* is already a Middle Cornish form: *te a vyth yn keth golow yn paradis genama* PA 193d.

**amontya** [amontya] 'count': GKK says that this word is confined to two instances in PA (i.e. *ny yl den vyth amontye* PA 40b; *den vyth ny yl amontye* PA 59c). This is incorrect: *pandra amount thy'n gonys* OM 1223; *ny amont travyt* PC 439; *tra uyth ny amont* RD 559; *rag thym ny ammont defry* BM 2055; *ny ammont ov peiadov* BM 3624; *ny amownt whelas mercye* CW 527; *ny amownt gwythell duwhan* CW 1712; *ny amownt thymma resna* CW 2395.

**anella** [anella] 'to breathe': GKK says this verb is confined to two instances in TH. This is incorrect: *fatell rug du anella* TH 2; *Ha wosa anella* TH 36; *hag a rug enella warnetha* TH 38a.

**angra** [angra] 'to anger': GKK claims that this word is confined to a single instance in PA. This is incorrect: *hag a angras du* TH 7a; *me a angras* CW 1683; *Nena Herod…yw engrez* RC 23: 199. GKK cites *engrez* as a separate headword.

**anhedhek, anhudhek** [anhedhek]: GKK has two separate headwords. The first, we are told, is an adverb meaning 'incessantly' which occurs once in BM, the second is an adjective meaning 'easeles' and occurs twice in BM. This is incorrect. The two are, of course, the same word. *Anhedhek* is a compound of *hedhy* 'to cease' and means either 'without respite, afflicted' (adj.) or 'without respite, unceasingly' (adv.). See Nance's 1938 dictionary s.v. There are *four* examples in BM: *kynth este claff anhethek* BM 1853; *me yv vexijs anhethek* BM 2630; *drefen ov boys anhethek* BM 3072; *assoff guan hag anhethek* 4181.

**anhweg** [anwhek] 'bitter, grim': GKK claims that this word has been taken from Nance's 1938 dictionary, being unattested in the texts. This is incorrect: *cachaf y ben pur anwhek* OM 2816; *me a's doro pur anwhek* PC 2332; *mar anwhek dyghtys* PC 3188-89; *lavyr pur anwek* BM 451; *peynis anwek* BM 2380; *Anwhek, unsweet, unsweetly* ACB: folio after K 2.

**arader** [arader] 'plough': GKK says this word is confined to OCV and a single instance in Lhuyd (i.e. at AB: 43b). This is incorrect: *W. Aradr, Corn[ish] Ardar, A Plow* 7b; *Dean ardar, †tardhur* glossing *Arator, A Plow-man* 43b; *Ardar* glossing *Aratrum, A Plow* 43b; *Dorn ardar* glossing *Stiva, The plough-tail or handle* AB 155a; *Ardar and aradr, A plow; Aratrum* AB: 241a; *Ardar* glossing *ARATRUM* AB: 290a; *Gora an ohan en arder* translated as *put the oxen to the plough* ACB: F f 2.

**arbennik** [arbennek] 'special': GKK's headword on page 34 is <arbennik> and the compiler has a note: 'The suffix is -IK, not -EK'. Under **speshyal** on page 295 the compiler has a note: 'Use **arbennek** for the aj.' [with -EK rather than the recommended -IK]. On page 34 also the word <arbennik> is described as a modern invention, unattested in the texts. This is incorrect: *yu'n arbednek ha'n ydnek* AB: 224; *ARBEDNEK, usual, customary* ACB: folio after K 2; *Arbednek, used, customary* Borlase 377.

**arghel** [arghel] 'archangel': according to GKK the plural is not attested until **arthelath** at CW 61. This is incorrect: *neg esa ow desuethas theugh elath nanyle* **arthelath** SA 60a.

**argument** [argument] 'argument': GKK says this word is confined to a single instance at PC 1661. This is incorrect, since the plural **argumentys** is attested at SA 61a.

**arloedhes** [arlodhes] 'lady': GKK says this word is confined to Old Cornish and place-names. This is incorrect. It is attested in both Middle and Late Cornish: *meystres hedyr vywy hag* **harluzes** CF; *arlothes ker my a wra* PC 1965; *ov* **arlothes** *sur gyne* PC 2194; *hag* **arluthes** *a vyth gurys* RD 1701; *lowena ʒyvgh* **arlothes** BM 237; *neb* **arlothes** *worthy* BM 330; *Rag an* **Arlothas** *an wolas Kernow* BF: 9; *rag gun* **Arlothas** *da* BF: 11; *lever bean rebbam dro tho an* **Arlothas** *Curnow* BF 37; *lever an Have an* **Arlothas** *Kernow* BF: 37.

**askal** [ascal] 'thistles': GKK gives this as the collective plural of *ascallen* 'thistle' but says the form (as distinct from the singular) is not attested. This is incorrect: *Spearn ha* **askal** *ra e dry rag theeze* RC 23: 182; *Askallen* [*pl.* **askal**] glossing *Carduus, A Thistle* AB: 46b. Cf. †*ASKELLEN, Askallen, pl.* **Askal**, *a thistle* ACB: folio after K 2 verso.

**askus** [ascus] 'excuse': GKK says this noun is not attested. It is likely, however, that [əsˈkuːs] is the pronunciation of <excus> in the two following examples: *oll* **excuses** *a'n par na* TH 14; *yth ethans y heb* **excusse** TH 14.

**assaya** 'to try': GKK says this verb is confined to a single example each in RD and CW. This is incorrect: *tra vyth* **assaye** OM 2477; **asaye** *ow arluth ker* RD 2051; *dus nes hag* **assy** *an poyt* BM 3325; **assays** *ha teball pynchis* TH 34; *gwraf* **assaya** CW 201; *manaf* **saya** CW 472.

**assendya** [ascendya] 'to ascend': GKK says this word is confined to a single instance in TH. This is incorrect: *agan lef yn* **ascendys** RD 174-75; **assendijs** *the'n neff in ban* BM 4052; *then neff* **assendias** *inweth* BM 4084; *fatell rug Crist* **assendia** *thy'n neff* TH 33a; *agyn Arluth ha'n Saviour ew* **ascendis** *the'n nef* SA 59; *mas Dew* **ascendias** *the'n neff* SA 60. The word **ascensyon** is not listed by GKK but it occurs at TH 36, 37a, 44a and 52.

**assentya** [assentya] 'to assent': GKK says this verb is confined to two instances in the *Ordinalia*. This is incorrect: *a vynnegh ol* **assentye** PC 2037; **assentye** *ol the henna* RD 583; *ha myns* **assentyas** *genas* CW 247; **assentyes** *yth yns sera* CW 272; *yn* **assentys** *te a glow* CW 654.

**avisia** [avysya] 'to take note': GKK says this is confined to a single instance in CW. This is incorrect: *an beth me re* **avysyas** RD 399; **avesijs** *off* BM 577; *beth* **avysyys** BM 840; **avesyans** *eff a hena* BM 1031; *byth* **avysshes** CW 1755; **avice** *pub tra* CW 1799; *me a vyn skon* **avycya** CW 1803; *bethowgh* **avysshes** CW 2367.

**avisment** [avysment] 'advise, counsel': GKK says this word does not occur in the texts but has been taken from Nance (1955). This is incorrect: *rag nyna tus a gymmer* **advisement** *bras* TH 1.

**avowa** 'to avow, admit': GKK says this verb is confined to a single instance in PC. This is incorrect: *myns a wruk me a'n* **avow** PC 1301; *ma na veath y* **avowe** PC 1783; *me a'nn* **avow** *dyougel* RD 2120; *hager lower os me an* **avow** CW 480; *me an* **advow** CW 2353.

**awelek** [awelek] 'windy': GKK says this is unattested, being taken from Nance's 1955 dictionary. This is incorrect: **Auelek**, *windy* Borlase 378.

**aweyl** [awayl] 'gospel': GKK gives as the plural *\*aweylyow*, which is not attested. The compiler does not seem to have noticed that there is a plural in the texts: *a scryffas* **aweylys** TH 37a; *a thyscas y* **aweylys** TH 38; *aga* **aweylys** TH 52a.

**aweyler** [aweyler] 'evangelist': GKK says that the plural is *aweylers*, and says it confined to 2-3 instances in TH. This is incorrect: *ran* **aweilers** TH 33a; *ran* **aweylers** TH 42; *appostres,* **aweilers** TH 42; *Ran an* **Aweylors** TH 53; *onyn vith an* **Aweylers** TH 53; *onyn* *vith an **aweylers** TH 53a; dell vsy an **Awaylers** TH 53a onyn vith an **Aweylers** TH 53a; onyn vyth an **Aweylers** TH 54.*

**aysel** [aysel] 'vinegar': GKK says this is confined to a single instance in the *Ordinalia* (i.e. PC 2978). This is incorrect. The word also occurs in PA: *eysyll bestyll kemyskis* PA 202b.

**banadhlek** [banallek] 'place of broom': GKK says this is unattested outside place-names. Note, however, *...whence our bannal, **banathlek**, **bennathlick**, a place in Constenton; also the proper name **Bennalack** ACB: opposite L.*

**banadhlen** [banallen] 'broom (plant)': GKK says the singular is confined to a single instance at AB: 240c. This in incorrect: *Banhadlen in Welsh, signifies Broom; Corn[ish] **Bynollan**, A Beesom AB: 3a; Scopa...A beesom. C[ornish] **Bynolan** AB: 146b; **Bannolan**, A broom AB; 240c. Cf. also **Bynollan**, a Beesom; Broom Borlase 380; **BANNOLAN**, a broom ACB: opposite L.* GKK says that the collective *banal* occurs in dialect, in place-names and once in OCV but not elsewhere. This is also incorrect: *S.W. & Corn[ish] **Banal**. Arm. Balan, Broom AB: 7c; Genista...Broom. C[ornish] **Banal** AB: 63a.*

**bargenya** [bargynya] 'to bargain': GKK suggests that the verb is confined to a single instance in Lhuyd. This is incorrect: *Dho **bargidnia** glossing Consentio, To consent AB: 50c; **Bargidnias** glossing Pactus AB: 111a; chei a **varginiaz** rag trei penz BF: 15; Nenna chei a **varginiaz** rag vlethan moy BF: 15; Enna chei a **varginiaz** rag blethan moy BF: 16; **BARGIDNIA**, dho **bargidnia**, to bargain, to contract ACB: L; **Bargidnia** gen dean da mose da whele sten ACB: opposite F f 2.*

**barr** [bar] 'branch, top': GKK says the plural **barrow** is unattested. This is incorrect: *an wethan han **barrow** TH 4a; an buddes, an **barrow** TH 8a; oll thyn **barrow** TH 39a.*

**basket** [basket] 'basket': GKK says this word is confined to a single instance in Lhuyd. This is incorrect: ***Basket** glossing Calathus, A Basket, a hampier or pannier AB: 45b; **Basket** dorn, a hand-basket s.v. Corbis AB: 51c. Cf. **BASKET**...a basket ACB: L.*

**bejeth** [bejeth] 'face': GKK suggests that the word is confined to a single instance in Late Cornish, i.e. in Keigwin. This is incorrect. In the first place the author is Chirgwin, not Keigwin. In the second place there is more than one source. In the third place there are at least four examples: *ha spiriz Deu reeg guaya var **budgeth** an dour BF: 51; Gen agaz **bedgeth** gwin, ha agaz blew mellyn x 3 ACB: opposite G g.*

**benfis** [benfys] 'benefice': GKK says this is confined to a single occurrence at OM 2612. This is incorrect: *pan lafuryens rag **benefys** BM 2827.*

**besydh** [besyth] 'baptism': GKK suggest that this word is unattested, being derived from Nance (1938). This is incorrect: *Solem ro in aga **begeth** the cresy TH 20; ow cows a'n **beseth** a'n flehis TH 37.*

**bleydh** [bleydh] 'wolf': GKK says the plural <bleydhi> occurs in BM. This is incorrect. *Blythy* in BM is the plural of *bledhen* 'year': *kuntullugh an flehysygyov a vo pur certen achy the try **blythy** 'gather the children, that may be right certainly at home within three years' BM: 1535-37.* The only plural of the word 'wolf' attested in the texts is Tregear's *blythes*. GKK mentions this form and says it occurs once. This in incorrect. It occurs twice: *yth yns y in golan ramping **blythes**, settys rag devorya. yma agan Savyour worth aga gylwall y **blythes** TH 19a.*

**blydhen** [bledhen] 'year': GKK tells us that the plural is *blydhynyow*. The compiler adds a note: 'for <y> in plural cf. *fentynyow*'. He is apparently unaware that a plural without <y> is well attested: in *nep dew cans a **vlethynnow** OM 657; Ober **bledhynno** yu AB: 223.*

**berlewen** [borlewen] 'morning star': GKK says this is confined to a single instance in Lhuyd. This is incorrect: *ha'n* **vurluan** *agery in agys colonow* TH 18. Cf. *BYRLUAN, the morning star* ACB: two folios after L 2; *Byr-luan, the Morning Star* Borlase 380.

**bogalenn** [vogalen] 'vowel': GKK ascribes it to K[en] J. George. This is incorrect. With initial <v> it was already in use in the 1940s. Note these instances from ALK: *An* **vogalennow** *Y hyr ha Y cot yu kemmyskys* ALK 57 (1957); *vogalen - vowel* ibid.

**bowji** [bowjy] 'cow-shed': GKK says that apart from toponyms this word is confined to two instances in Lhuyd. This is incorrect: *W. Boydy & Beydy, A Cow-house; Corn[ish]* **Boudzhi** AB: 10b; **Boudzhi**, *a Fold* glossing *Caula* AB: 47a; **Boudzhe** *devaz* glossing *Ovile, A sheep-coat, a fold, a sheep-house* AB: 110c. Cf. **BOUDZHI**, *a fold; boudzhi devez, a sheep fold* ACB: L 2 verso.

**bragya** [bragya] 'to threaten': GKK says this word is confined to BM, where it occurs once. This is incorrect on both counts: *na* **vrakgy** *e rak ef a sur* RD 2018; *Ty horsen* [*n*]*agen* **brag** *ny* BM 1228; *na* **vragyogh** *brays lafarov* BM 1597; [*n*]*am* **brag** *vy* BM 3491; *neb ur* **braggye** BM 3507; *ef a's* **braggyas** *y'n vaner ma* TH 40.

**Breton** [Breton] 'Breton' [inhabitant]: GKK says that this word is unattested and has been taken from Nance's 1938 dictionary. Nicholas Boson writes: *an* **Bretten** *ha an Kembreeanz ha an Curnowean* BF: 29; *rag an* **Bretten** *ha an Curnowean* BF: 29.

**brin** [bryn] 'brine': GKK says this word is unattested being taken from Nance's 1955 dictionary. This is incorrect. Lhuyd gives Cornish **Bryn** glossing *Muria, Brine* AB: 96a.

**broennenn** [bronnen] 'rush (*Scirpus*)': according to GKK this singular is attested three times, once each in OCV, RD and Lhuyd (AB: 146b). This is incorrect, since Lhuyd cites it twice: *W. Bruynen, A Rush; Corn[ish]* **Brydnan** AB: 10b; †**Brunnen, brudnan** glossing *Scirpus, A rush without a knot* AB: 146b.

**brottel** [brottel] 'frail, brittle': GKK says this word is from Middle English 'with change of vowel'—which the dictionary does not attempt to explain. GKK does not seem to have noticed that the word occurs in Cornish with an unrounded stressed vowel: *the'n dore* **brytyll** *prye* TH 9; **Brettal**, *Brittle* (in a list of Cornish words agreeing with English) AB: 33c.

**brys** [brys] 'womb': GKK says the word is confined to a single instance in BM. This is incorrect: *creator a* **brys** *benen* RD 191; *deuones a* **brys** *benen* RD 1350; *in* **breys** *benen* BM 846; *a thuth in* **breys** *Maria* BM 856; *a ve benegas in* **breis** *y vam* TH 8.

**Brythonek** [Brethonek] 'British': GKK says that the word is taken from Nance's 1938 dictionary, being unattested in the texts. This is incorrect: *an Tavaz* **Brethonek** AB: 222; **Brethonek** *Kembrian* AB: 222; *Dialeksho* **Brethonek** AB: 222; *Skot-***Vrethonek** AB: 222; *lavarnanz priez an Tavas* **Brethonek** AB: 222; *Gal-***Vrethonek** AB: 222; *an gerlevran bian* **Brethonek**-*ma* AB: 222; **Brethonek** *Pou Lezou* AB: 222; *gerrio* **Brethonek** AB: 223; **Brethonek** *Kernou* AB: 223; *an Mytern* **Brethonek** AB: 224; *gen Tiz* **Brethonek** AB: 224; *uar anuo* **Brethonek** AB 224. Cf. also **BRETHONEK** *British; Brethonek Kembrian Welsh British* ACB: folio after L 2, and **Brethonec**, *adj. British, the British or Welsh language* LCB s.v.

**bryvya** [bryvya] 'to bleat': according to GKK this verb is confined to a single instance in Lhuyd. This is incorrect: *Dho* **privia** glossing *Balo, To Bleat* AB: 44b; *Ma'n dhavaz a* **privia**, *The sheep bleats* AB: 230c; *A* **privia**, *Bleating* AB: 248a. CF. **PRIVIA**, *dho privia, to bleat* ACB: opposite X 2.

**byrla** [byrla] 'to embrace': GKK says this is attested once. This is incorrect: *Amplector, To Embrace; C[ornish]* **Byrla** AB: 2c; *Kensa blethan,* **byrla** *a' baye* ACB: F f. Cf. **BYRLA**, *to embrace* ACB: two folios after L 2.

**chast** [chast] 'chaste': GKK says this word is confined to a single example in TH. This is incorrect: *an chast spowse a crist* TH 33; *in chast gwren ny kesvewa* CW 1314.

**chastia** [chastya] 'to chastise': GKK says that the verb is confined to a single instance in BM. This is incorrect: *me an chasty* PA 127c; *mar ny vethe chastijs* BM 810; *rag chastya an crustunyon* BM 1180.

**chasya** [chassya] 'to chase': the frequency code {2} for this word in GKK implies that it occurs three times at the most. This is incorrect: *rag y chasye* PA 163d; *pan vef chacys* OM 706; *me a's chas yn mes* PC 317; *chasshes on a baradice* CW 1764; *alena aga chassya* CW 1823; *Chacyes, pursued* AB: 226c. Cf. *CHACY, to chase, to pursue; chacyes, chased pursued* ACB: M.

**chayn** [chayn] 'chain': GKK says the singular is not attested. This is incorrect: *gans chayne tane adro thymo* CW 331.

**chaynya** [chaynya] 'to chain': GKK says that this word is unattested in traditional Cornish and has been derived from Nance's 1938 dictionary. This is incorrect: *pur fast yth os chenys* BM 3809; *cheynys in keth vaner ma* BM 3825; *Awoys ov bones cheynys* BM 3826.

**chyften** [chyften] 'chieftain': GKK says this word is confined to a single instance at OM 1445. This is incorrect: *war an gwlascur cheften* BM 3.

**daffar** [dafar] 'apparatus, receptacle': GKK's frequency code {2} means that this word is attested at most three times. This is incorrect: *daver vyth wy ny ʒecsyugh* PA 50b; *cafas daffar pur parys* PA 105d; *dafyr lathva* [= ammunition] Keigwin (King Charles's Letter); *Daver, a script, a pouch, a budget* ACB: opposite N; *Daffar, Conveniences, Furniture* Borlase 383.

**damma-wyn** [dama wyn] 'grandmother' (why the hyphen?): GKK says the word is confined to a single instance in Lhuyd. This is incorrect: *Corn[ish] Taz gwydn [& Sira wydn] a Grand-father, and Dama wydn, a Grand-mother* AB: 3b; *Dama widn, i.e. W. Mam wen* glossing *Avia, A Grand-mother* AB: 44a. Cf. *dama uidn, a grandmother* ACB: two folios after M.

**darn** [darn] 'piece': GKK says the plural *darnow* is unattested anywhere. This is incorrect: *dywolow yfarn a squerdyas corf iudas ol ʒe ʒarnow* PA 106c.

**dasserghyans** [dasserghyans] 'resurrection': GKK says there are at most three examples of this word in Middle and Late Cornish together. This is incorrect: *na vyth moy a'th daserghyans* RD 2545; *a thasserghyens cryst* RD 2632; *wosa y thethyrryans* TH 49; *Thasurrans an Corf* BF: 56; *thethoryanz a'n corf* ACB: two folios after E e; *dedhoryans an corf* LCB: 396. Cf. *dasserghyans, a resurrection* ACB: opposite N.

**deboner** [deboner] 'debonair': GKK implies that the two instances of this word are from PA. This is incorrect. There is one instance at PA 129c: *a gewsys dyboner*. The other example is from the Charter Fragment: *curtes yw ha deboner* (quoted in LAM: 30).

**dehweles** [dewheles] 'to return': GKK says this verb is confined to one instance in the *Ordinalia*. This is incorrect: *kyns dewheles my a'd pys* OM 728; *an varghvran na thywhele* OM 1105; *sav byner re thewhylly* OM 2196; *may tewhyllyf arte thu'm gulas* RD 879; *rag bener re thewellen* BM 3439; *na byth moy na ʒewylly* BM 4146.

**dekkweyth** [degweyth] 'ten times': GKK says the word is unattested. This is incorrect: *Deguyth, Ten times* AB: 248c; cf. *Deguyth, ten times* ACB: opposite N. KK's <-kkw-> for *-gw-* in this word is pure invention.

**delyow** [delyow] 'leaves': GKK says the word is found as *delkiow* in Late Cornish. This is only partially true. *Delkiow* is cetainly well attested in Late Cornish, e.g. *Delkiou,*

*Leaves* AB: 243b; *delkyow* RC 23: 177; *delkiow sevi* x 6 Chirgwin (LAM: 228-30), but *delyow* also occurs in the later language: *delyow* AB: 243b and *dellyow* CW 93.

**dena** [dena] 'to suck': GKK says the word is confined to a single instance in Lhuyd. This is incorrect: *hag ef gensy ow tene* PA 161c; *na ve ʒeʒe denys bron* PA 169d; *pan denys bron* OM 1755; *an bronnow na thenes flehesyggow* PC 2649; *ha specyly re ov tena* BM 1509; *Dho tena* glossing *Sugo, To suck* AB: 158. Cf. *TENA, dho tenna, to draw; also to suck; denys, suck'd; ow tenne, sucking; fleghys menys ow tenne, small children sucking* ACB: Z.

**densek** [densek] 'toothy': GKK correctly points out that this word occurs in OCV (*denshoc dour* glossing *luceus* ['pike']). The dictionary fails to mention, however, that Borlase gives *denjack* 'hake' and that *tinsack* 'hake' survived in dialect at St Ives (GCSW: 72). Cf. also *DENSHOCDOAR, a lucy fish, a hake fish.— Denshocdour. hod*[*ie*] *Denjack* ACB: N. GKK adds a note that there is no need for *i*-affection in *densek*. This is incorrect, since there is *i*-affection in OCV; *denshoc* is a compound of *dens* 'teeth' + *oc* rather than *dans* 'tooth' + *-oc*.

**derwenn** [derowen, derwen] 'oak tree': GKK says the word, the singular of *derow* 'oaks' is unattested. This is incorrect: *Derven, an oak* Borlase 383.

**despitia** [despytya] 'to insult': GKK says the word is unattested in the texts, being derived from Nance's 1938 dictionary. This is incorrect: *gureugh y thyspytye* PC 1397.

**destryppya** [dystryppya] 'to strip': GKK says this verb is confined to one example in PA (i.e. *Whare y an dystryppyas* PA 13a). This is incorrect: *me a thystryp ow dyllas* PC 250. In view of <diruska> it is difficult to see why GKK does not spell this word <distryppya>.

**desygha** [deseha] 'to dry': GKK says the word is confined to a single example in the *Ordinalia*. This is incorrect: *pan vs gveyth ov tesehe* OM 1128; *dor dyseghys* OM 1144; *may fens y dysehys* OM 1833; *pan vons dysehys gulan* OM 1838.

**devorya** [devorya] 'to devour': GKK says this word is confined to 2-3 instances in TH. This is incorrect. It does indeed occur once at TH 4 and twice at TH 19a. GKK is apparently unaware, however, that the verb also occurs in BM: *lues oma deworijs* BM 4178.

**dewdhegves** [dewdhegves] 'twelfth': GKK says that this word is confined to a single instance in TH. I am unable to find it. The only example of 'twelfth' known to me is *Dow dêgvas, the twelfth* ACB: F f 2 verso.

**Dewnens** [Dewnans] 'Devonshire': GKK says the form is confined to a single instance in Lhuyd. This is incorrect: *Kernou ha Deunanz* AB: 224; *auoz an dzhyi rygkuitha Deunanz* AB: 224; *ha liaz en Deunanz* AB: 224. Cf. *DEUNANZ, Devonshire* ACB: N verso.

**diank** [dyank] 'to escape': GKK says this verb is confined to one occurrence (i.e. PC 1180). This is incorrect: *y ʒe ʒeank yndella* PA 251b; *mars yv dyenkys* RD 520; *maras ywe dyenkys* BM: 3732.

**dibenna** [dybenna] 'to behead': GKK says the word is confined to a single instance in Lhuyd. This is incorrect: *ran cregys ran debynnys* BM 1351.

**diber** [dyber] 'saddle': GKK tells us this word is attested in Old, Middle and Late Cornish and in toponyms. The frequency code given is {5}, which suggests that the word occurs between 32 and 99 times. This is incorrect. According to Padel it is attested in the single place-name *Carrack an deeber* (1613) in Zennor. Apart from that I have collected the following instances: *diber* glossing *sella* 'saddle' OCV 955; *deeber* Richard Symonds *c.* 1644; *Dibre* [*a saddle*] glossing *Dorsuale* AB: 55c; *Debr* *dour* [*i.e. sella pluvialis*] s.v. *Galerus, A hat* AB: 62b; **Diber** glossing *sella equina* AB: 148a. Cf. *DEBRDOUR, a hat.—see DIBER. This is pronounced, Deberdower* ACB opposite N; †*DIBER, a saddle; debr-dour, a hat, a water saddle* ACB: folio after N. The frequency code should be emended.

**diek** [dyek] 'lazy': GKK says this word is confined to a single occurrence each in OCV and BM. This is incorrect: *nyng o dyag the wull* TH 2a.

**difyga** [dyfygya] 'to fail, to tire': GKK says this word is unattested. This is incorrect: *an ioy na thyfyk nefra* OM 517; *byth na thyfyc* RD 76; *ioy na thyfyk* RD 1310; *byth na thyfyk* RD 1434. GKK implicitly criticizes Nance for having written the verbal noun <dyfygya>. Nance was, it seems, more right than GKK: *Tefigia, To tire, W. Dyffygio* AB: 245a. Cf. *TEFIGIA, to fire* (leg. *tire*) ACB: opposite Z; *Tefighia, to tire; Tevigia, id.* Borlase 408; *Tefigia v.n. To tire, to be tired. Llwyd*, 245. *W. difygio* LCB.

**digesson** [dygesson] 'discordant': GKK says this word is unattested in the texts and has been taken from Nance's 1938 dictionary. This is incorrect: *an laveryanz anydha yu muy kalliz ha dygesson* AB: 223.

**dinas** [dynas] 'city': GKK says this word is unattested except in toponyms and has been taken from Nance's 1938 dictionary. This is incorrect: *Dinaz,* †*brenniat* glossing *Propugnaculum, A fortress, a bulwark, a rampart* AB: 130; *Urbs … A city, a wall*[']*d town. C*[*ornish*] *Dinaz* AB: 177c; C[*ornish*] *Dinas* glossing *URBS* AB: 298b. Cf. *DINAZ, Dinas, a bulwark, a fortress; also, a city, a walled town* ACB: folio after N verso.

**dinerenn** [deneren] '(single) penny': GKK says the word is confined to a single instance in BM. Lhuyd, however, writes: *A Penny, C*[*ornish*] *Dinar & Dinaryn* AB: 283a.

**dineythi** [denethy] 'to give birth': GKK says this word occurs at most three times in Middle and Late Cornish together. This is incorrect: *mar quren flogh vyth denythy* OM 390; *na caym pan yu dynythys* OM 618; *ef a wra dynythy* OM 638; *ny a thynyth vn flogh da* OM 664; *gans y gorf a'm dynythys* OM 863; *a dor ov mam dynythys* OM 1754; *a vaghteth gulan dynythys* PC 1727; *ty a vyth mabe denethys* CW 1323; *flehys am bef denethys* CW 1979; *Denethes Dar an Speris zance* BF: 41; *Denethes der Spiriz Sanz* BF: 56; *DENETHYS, born, come forth* ACB N; *DYNYTHY, to bear; dho dynythy map, to bear a child; dynythys, born, produced; dho dynythy, to come; dynythys, come forth* ACB: opposite O; *than fleghys tha denethy* Keigwin (King Charles's letter).

**diruska** [dyrusca] 'to peel, scrape off skin': GKK says the verb is unattested in traditional Cornish. This is incorrect: *ha hy warbarth dyruskys* OM 787; *trogh ha dyruskys* PC 2687.

**disesya** [dysesya] 'to discomfort': GKK says that this verb is unattested and has been derived from Nance's 1938 dictionary. This is incorrect: *ragh ovn the vos desesys* PC 97; *desesijs bras off deffry* BM 1771.

**diskrysi** [dyscrejy] 'to disbelieve': GKK says the verb is confined to a single instance in Middle Cornish. This is incorrect: *na thyscryssough dev a nef* OM 1657; *kafus ken the thyscrysy* OM 1826; *yn sur re re thyscryssys* RD 1040; *Dezkrissa, To distrust* AB: 249c. Cf. *DEZKRIZA, to distrust* ACB: N verso.

**diskudha** [dyscudha] 'to uncover': GKK says the verb is confined to one instance in Middle Cornish. This is incorrect: *an gorhel gvren dyscuthe* OM 1146; *me a vyn y thyscuthe* PC 1393; *lemmyn dyskuth ha lauar* PC 2852; *awos descotha* CW 1369; *As Dizkuedha and Dyzkydha, To discover* AB: 249c. Cf. *DISCUTHE, to uncover* ACB: folio after N verso.

**displesya** [dysplesya] 'to displease': GKK says this verb is confined to a single instance in TH. This is incorrect: *na vewy dysplesys* BM 119; *na vewy dysplesijs* BM 322; *genes* *yth off* **dysplesijs** BM 400; **dysplesijs** *purguir genas* BM 490; *Kynth ogh geneff* **dysplesijs** BM 492.

**disprevi** [dysprevy] 'to disprove': GKK says that this a modern neologism unattested in the texts. This is incorrect: *inweth the prevy ha the **dhisprevy** pup tra scriffis* TH 36.

**diveth** [dyveth] 'shameless': GKK says this word is not attested and has been taken from Nance's 1938 dictionary. This is incorrect: *bost a wrens tyn ha **deveth*** PA 242d.

**diwoesa** [dewosa] 'to bleed': GKK spells says that the word is confined to BM where it occurs 2-3 times. This is incorrect: *may hallons boys **dewogys*** BM 1556; *parys thage **dewosa*** BM1575; *gruegh scon age **dewose*** BM 1584; *hag a'n **dewoys** knak oma* BM 1652.

**diworth** [deworth] 'from': GKK gives this word a frequency code of {5}, i.e. between 32 and 99 times. As Ray Edwards has pointed out (*Notennow Kernowek* 3 (1999)) *dyworth* occurs 7 times in the texts. *Athyworth* is less common, occurring 6 times. The most frequent form is *thyworth, theworth* which occurs 167 times. Under *dhiworth* GKK says: 'commoner than *diworth*', but gives no figure for its frequency. The two entries in GKK, therefore, are misleading and the frequency code given is not accurate.

**dons** [dons] 'dance': GKK says the word is unattested outside toponyms. This is incorrect: *high stones (called **Daunce** mine)* BF: 10; *...the name they go by most commonly that that of **Dawns**-men, that is, the Stone-Dance* Borlase 183; ***Dawnse** in Cornish, signifies a Dance* Borlase 183; ***Dawns**, a Dance* Borlase 383.

**dotya** [dotya] 'to dote, to rave': GKK says this verb is confined to a single instance in BM. This is incorrect: *mar mynnyth **dotya*** BM 346; ***dotyys** oys vyl* BM 462.

**downder** [downder] 'depth, deep': GKK says this occurs 2-3 times in Late Cornish. This is incorrect: *W. Dyvnder, Depth; C[ornish]* **Dounder** AB: 19b; **Dounder** *glossing Profundum, A gulf, a bottomless pit, the deep, the sea* AB: 129c; **Dounder**, *Dep[t]h* AB: 240b; *rag mer a **dounder*** BF: 51; **downder**, *a gulf, a bottomless pit, deepness, depth* ACB: *two folios after N; ha tewolgow ese war enep an **downder*** LCB: 395.

**dreysenn** [dreysen] 'brambles': GKK says that this word is confined to a single instance in Lhuyd. This is incorrect: *C[ornish]* **Dreizan** *glossing Rubus, A bramble, a bush* AB: 141c; *C[ornish]* **Dreizan** *glossing A Bramble* AB: 272b. Cf. **DREIZAN**, *a raspberry tree, or bush* ACB: two folios after N verso.

**drivya** [dryvya] 'to drive': GKK says this verb is confined to a single instance in TH. This is incorrect: *aga **dryvya** in mes* TH 13; *Eff a ve **dryvys** war theller* TH 49a.

**drokpollat** [drogpollat] 'scoundrel': GKK spells this word <drokpollat> and tells us (page 84) that this word is from *drog* + *pollat*, with a geminate <ll>. The simplex *pollat*, however, is given as a separate headword on page 257, where it is spelt with a single <l> as <polat>.

**dughanhe** [duhanhe] 'to grieve, afflict': GKK says that this verb is confined to a single instance in the *Ordinalia*. This is incorrect: *yth oma pur **dewhanhees*** CW 1225.

**dyerbyna** [dyerbyn, dyerbyna] 'to meet': GKK is apparently unaware of *dyerbyn* as a verbal noun. It also says that the verb is attested once only in Middle Cornish. This is incorrect: *arte 3y **dyerbyne*** PA 167c; *Vn den as **dyerbynnas*** PA 174a; *why a **thyerbyn** wharre* PC 628; *a's **dyerbyn** dyougel* PC 897; *ny alsen y **thyerbyn*** PC 2276; *eff a **deerbyn** trestyns* BM 2255. As is clear from the above examples, the verb is always transitive. GKK's distinction between *dyerbynna gans* 'meet' (going in the same direction) and *dyerbynna orth* 'meet' (going in opposite directions) is both ungrammatical and entirely without foundation.

**dynnerghi** [dynerhy] 'to greet': GKK says this verb is confined to a single occurrence in Lhuyd. This is incorrect: *herodes reth **tenyrghys*** PA 115b; *a'th **dynyrghys** hag a'th* *pys* PC 565; *genef ythos* **dynerghys** RD 1628; †*Dynerxy* [*or* ‡*Dynerhy*] *To Greet or Salute* AB: 249c. Cf. *DINYRGHY, to send for; also to greet* ACB: folio after N verso.

**dyssembla** 'to dissemble': there are several occurrences of this verb: *Na rewgh dyssymbla* TH 40a; *Dho* **dissembla** glossing *Simulo, To feign, to counterfeit* AB: 150c. Cf. *DISSEMBLA, dissemble* ACB: two folios after N verso. Curiously, the word appears to be wanting from GKK.

**dyssipel, -plys** [dyscypyl, -plys] 'disciple': GKK says that the word is unattested outside TH. This is incorrect: *ha'y* **ȝyscyplys** *a'n sewyas* PA 52b; *ȝ'y* **ȝyscyplys** *y trylyas* PA 55c.

**dyw** [dew] 'god': GKK says the plural is unattested outside toponyms. This is incorrect: *y fyeugh yn surredy yn ur na avel* **dewow** OM 177-78; *a worth* **dewow** *tebel* OM 1818; *fals* **duwow** OM 1882; **dewov** *nowyth* OM 2732; *thum* **dewov** *tek* BM 914; *theth* **dewov** *try mylwyth fy* BM 915; *ov* **dewov** *flour* BM 922; *nyns o an re na* **dewov** BM 1801; *naha dewov nag yv vas* BM 2519; *why a vith kepar ha* **duow** TH 3a; *saw a pony* **dewyow** *gwryes* CW 812; *For we read* **Deuon** *and* **Deuou**, *Gods* AB: 243b; **Deauon**, *Gods;* **Deuiou** *id.* Borlase 383; *Ty nyn vyth thy* **Dewyow** *eraill mez me* x 2 ACB: two folios after E e. Cf. *DEU, God; pl.* **Deuon, deuou**, *Gods* ACB: N verso.

**dywolow** [dewolow] 'devils': GKK says that this form occurs twice, once in TH and once in CW. This is incorrect: **dywolow** *yfarn a squerdyas* PA 106c; *ena golmas* **dewolow** PA 212b; *ha* **dewolow** *hep nyuer* OM 569; *ha fethys an* **dywolow** PC 77; *an* **thewolow** PC 3057; *pryncys a'n* **dewolow** RD 97; *er bos* **dywolow** RD 301; *re'n kergho an* **dewolow** RD 2277; *rak deuones* **dewolow** RD 2302; *ow* **dewolow** *duegh gynef* RD 2307; *skrymba bras a'n* **dewolow** RD 2344; *orth temtacyon* **dewolow** BM 145; *sur* **dewolov** *ens y* BM 916; *warbyn an* **dywolow** TH 28; *oll an* **thewollow** CW 481; *an* **thevllow** *pub onyn* CW 2010; *yma an* **thewollow** CW 2021; *comerez gen an* **Jowlov** RC 23: 193 (and see emendation in RC 24: 100); *DEWOL, the devil; pl.* **Dewolow** ACB: N verso.

**Ebrow** [Ebrow] 'Hebrew': GKK says that this word is confined to a single instance in the *Ordinalia* (i.e. *fleghes* **ebbrow** PC 239). This is incorrect: *En Tavaz Greka, Lathen ha'n* **Hebra** BF: 59. Notice further: *in second chapter thyn* **hebrues** TH 13; *tha Greckian,* **Hebran** BF: 27.

**edifia** [edyfya] 'to edify, to build up': GKK says this word is confined to a single instance in TH. This is incorrect: *rag* **edifia** *corfe crist* TH 31; *rag* **edyfya** *an corfe a crist* TH 42; *Rag* **edyfya** *spiritually* TH 42.

**eksperyans** [experyans] 'experience': GKK says that this word is confined to a single instance: BM 4318 [recte 4391]. This is incorrect: *Ith esa dhe'n profet Job* **experience** TH 7; *na ve an catholyk egglos the ry thym* **experiens** TH 37a; *an pith a ren ny the aswone dre* **experiens** TH 40.

**ekwal** [equal] 'equal; equivalent': GKK says this word is confined to two instances in CW (i.e. at 604 and 2198). This is incorrect: **equall** *recompens* TH 24; *war y wull* **equall** *ha kepar* TH 28a.

**enep** [enep] 'face': GKK says that this word is attested 2-3 times in OCV and Lhuyd. This is incorrect: **eneb** glossing *pagina* OCV 754; †*Enap* glossing *Facies, A face, a visage* AB: 58a; *Tyrnehuan liven,* †*Enep* glossing *Pagina, The side of a leaf or page* AB: 111b; *C[ornish]* †*Enep* glossing *A Face* AB: 276; *agas* **enep** 'your face' quoted from Borlase MS by Nance (1938) s.v. Cf. *ENAP, Enep, the face, the countenance* ACB: O 2.

**entent** [entent] 'intent': GKK says this word occurs is confined to a single instance at CW 496. This is incorrect: *heb colynwall gans* **intentys** *ha ordynans anethe* TH 40a; *rag an* **entent** *neb a ve an pen ha'n dalleth* TH 47-47a; *nyng ew thyn* **entent** TH 55a.

**er** [er] 'heir': GKK says that this word is confined to a single instance at BM 372. This is incorrect: *neg ew ef ow kill* **heare** *nep ne theffa regardya an keth gyrryow ma* SA 59.

**erba, -bys** [erba, -bys] 'herb': GKK says that neither the singular nor the plural is attested. This is incorrect: *palm ha bayys, byxyn* **erbys** PC 261; *hag* **erbys** *an goverou* BM 1971; *ha'n* **earbes** *a'n keth dor na* CW 948

**eretons** [eretons] 'inheritance': GKK says the word is confined to two instances in BM (i.e. at 1953 and 3469). This is incorrect: *in ov* **hertons** *deth ha nos* BM 2452; *ha ry then ny an* **herytans** *in gwlas neff* TH 41.

**ermit** [ermyt] 'hermit': GKK says this word is confined to Old Cornish, occurring once in OCV (as *hermit*). This is incorrect. The word is also attested in Middle Cornish: *ena* **ermet** *purguir boys* BM 1133; *avel* **hermyt** *pur thevry* BM 1948; *avel* **hermyt** *in guelfos* BM 1964.

**ervira** [ervyra] 'to decide': GKK says this verb is confined to two instances in PA. This is incorrect: *my a* **yrvyr** OM 1229; **yrverys** *eu ru'm levte* OM 2611; *del of* **yrvyrys** PC 493; *war veyns ol of* **yruyrys** PC 854; *rak satnas yv* **yrvyrys** PC 880; *an porpos yv* **erverys** BM 988.

**eskerens** [eskerens] 'enemies': GKK's authentication code {I} for *eskerens* the plural of *escar* 'enemy' suggests that the form is unattested and has been inferred from 'derivatives and the rules of grammar.' This is incorrect: *nan kemerre y* **yskerans** PA 241b; *tho'm* **yskerens** PC 737; *tha* **eskerans** BM 1176; **eskerams** *ov du soly* BM 1197; *gwregh cara agys* **yskerens** TH 22; *ow exortya y* **yskerens** TH 22; *mas inweth y* **yskerens** TH 22a; *pan en ny y* **yskerans** TH 24; *the cara agan* **yskerans** TH 24; *So the cara agan* **yskerens** TH 24; *dre y* **yskerans** TH 24; *the gara y* **yskerens** TH 24; *theworth aga* **yskerens** TH 25; *cothmans hag* **yskerenns** TH 26; *warbyn agan gostly* **eskerens** TH 28; *warbyn y* **yskerens** *ha* **yskerens** *a onyn vith* TH 50a.

**eskisyow** [eskyjyow] 'shoes': GKK says this, the plural of *eskys* 'shoe', is confined to OCV and Lhuyd. This is incorrect: *dysk the* **skyggyow** *quyk the ves* OM 1406; *unworthy rag bocla y* **skyggyow** TH 8.

**Est** [Est] 'August': the compiler asserts on page 92 that *Est* 'August' is confined to a single instance in Gwavas. This is presumably a reference to *Durt Newlin in Bleau Pawle 22* **East***, 1711* (LAM: 238). The compiler's observation in incorrect. *Est* 'August' is attested elsewhere: W. *Aust, August; Corn[ish]* **East** AB: 14c; cf. **East**, *August* ACB: folio after T 2. He further claims on p. 222 that *mis-Est* (why the hyphen?) is a recent invention. This is also incorrect: *in* **meys est** *an viijves deth an secund feer sur a veth sensys in pov benytha* BM 2197-99; *Adheworth Newlyn, a'n Blew Paul, on 22ves* **mys Est***, 1711* (Gwavas, LAM: 238); *Miz-East* (*August*) ACB F f 2 verso; *Ni trehes e bigel en* **miz-east** ACB: two folios after F f 2.

**Est** [Yst] 'East': GKK says that this word is confined to BM 664 and CW 1742. This is incorrect: *Wor duath Gwra gwenz Noor* **East** *whetha pell* BF: 44; *a reeg doaze teeze veer thor an* **Est** (Rowe) RC 23: 194; *Rag ma gwellez genani e steran en* **Est** RC 23: 194; *ha pel da* **East** *ev a Travaliaz* BF: 15; *EST, the East* ACB: O 2 verso.

**estren** [estren] 'stranger': GKK says that the word is unattested. This is incorrect: *geffya e foto dho* **Estren** *pel-pou* AB: 222.

**ewinas** [ewynas] '(finger)nails': GKK says that the plural is confined to a single instance in Lhuyd. This is incorrect: W. *Ewinedh, Nails; C[ornish]* **Winaz** AB: 28a; *Unguis...A nail, a claw, a talon...C[ornish] Euin & iuin, plur. iuinaz* AB: 176b.

**eyrin** [eyryn] 'sloes': GKK says this word is unattested. This is incorrect: W[elsh] *Eirin, Plums; Corn[ish]* **Aeran** AB: 15c; and cf. **Aeran**, *Plumbs* Borlase 376; **Aeran**, *a plumb, a prune* ACB: K 2 verso.

**eythinen** [eythynen] 'gorse bush': GKK says the singular is confined to a single instance in OCV. This is incorrect: *glastanen, **eithinen**, brox* AB: 223; *Eithinan, A furze-bush* AB: 240c; ***EYTHINNEN**, furze. Hod[ie] **Eithin**, and Ython* ACB: folio after O 2. GKK also claims that apart from toponyms the collective *eythin* [eythyn] is attested twice only. This is also incorrect: *Bagaz **eithin**, a Bush of furze* AB: 33c; *bagaz **eithin**, a bush of furze* glossing *Dumus* 56a; ***Eithin*** glossing *Genista spinosa* AB: 63a; *Tskekke'r **eithin*** glossing *Parus, A titmouse, a muskin* AB: 113c; *Whelas poble tha trehe **ithen*** ACB: F f 2. According to Nance, Gwavas gives *cromman **eythyn*** 'furze-hook' (1938, p. 30; *crobman **ithen*** according to Gendall) and Pryce's MS gives in a note *begh **eythyn*** 'a burn [load] of furze' (Nance 1938: 10).

**favera** [favera] 'to favour': GKK says this verb is confined to one instance in TH (i.e. TH 51). This is incorrect: *a ser arluth **faverugh** ny* BM 3349.

**figura** [fygura] 'to figure': GKK says the word is unattested and has been taken from Nance's 1938 dictionary. This is incorrect: *kepar del ve va **fuguris** in la goyth* TH 38a; *han dra a ve **figurys** in pascall oyen in la coith* TH 52a.

**fisyshyen** [fysycyen] 'physician': GKK says this word is confined to single instance in BM. This is incorrect: *ov boys **fecycyen** connek* BM 1421: ***fecessyon** ny thereff nefra* BM: 1482; *in bys ma rag **fecycyen*** BM 1484; *Eff ew an **phisicion** ha'n metheg a rug sawya oll agan deseyses* TH 11.

**flourenn** [flowren] 'flower': GKK cites this *hapax legomenon* from TH and glosses it 'fine specimen.' This is incorrect. The word means 'flower' in the botanical sense: *eff a deffe in ban kepar ha **flowren**, eff a clomder* 'he grows up like a flower, he withers' TH 7.

**foly** 'folly': this word is well attested: *mvr a **foly** ew thotho* OM 191; *rag gul **foly*** OM 708; *me ny wruk **foly*** PC 1295; *yth apyas thy'm gul **foly*** PC 1438; *myns a geusys **foly*** PC 1782; *na temptyogh vy the **foly*** BM 501; *ow **foly** ʒ[y]mmo gava* CW 429; *henna yth o tha **folly** gye* CW 1013; *ow **folly** yth ew mar vras* CW 1522. The word does not appear to be in GKK.

**fondya** [fundya] 'to found': GKK says that this verb is confined to a single instance in BM. This is incorrect: *omma lemmen **fondya** plays* BM 720: *Omma me re **fundyas** plas* BM 990; *ov chy **fundia*** BM 1150; *Eff a **fowndyas** y egglos* TH 45a; *fatel ve hy **foundyes** dre an auncient appostles* TH 47a

**form, -ys** [form, -ys] 'bench': GKK says this word occurs in Cornish English but is not attested in the texts. This is incorrect: *me a's ordyn though wharre, cheyrys ha **formys** plente; ysethough syre iustis* 'I'll order them for you immediately, chairs and plenty of benches; be seated, sir justice.' PC 2228–30.

**forsakya** [forsakya] 'to forsake': GKK says that this word is confined to two instances in in TH. This is incorrect: ***forsakyans** byen ha muer* BM 384; *ny **forsakyn** y hanow* BM 1212; ***forsakis** y das hay vam* BM 1941; *the **forsakya** pub tra* TH 21a; *deneya ha **forsakya*** TH 33a; *an ledran a **forsakiaz** an Vertshants* BF: 17.

**fowt** [fowt] 'error': GKK suggests that the plural *fowtow* is a recent coinage, given by Nance (1938), but otherwise unattested. The compiler of GKK adds a note: 'NB MidC *fawtys* is the attested plural occurring twice in TH, but Nance gave *fowtow* and this is in common use.' Both main entry and note are incorrect. The plural form *fowtys* occurs *three* times in TH: *ow rebukya aga **fautes*** TH 22a; *an offences ha **fawtys*** TH 25; *ha kemeras sham a'ga **fawtys*** TH 29a. Moreover *fowtow* is attested: *geffya y **foto** dho Estren pel-pou* AB: 222; *try **fotou** idzhanz* AB: 223; *an **fotou** erel* AB: 223.

**Frynk** [Frynk] 'France; French': GKK's treatment of this word is very misleading. The basic form is *\*Frank* 'a Frank, a Frenchman' < Latin *Francus*. Because the Frank was a freeman, unlike the subject Gauls, the word also came to be an adjective meaning 'free'. This is seen in Cornish in the Godolphin motto *Frank ha leal etto ge* 'Free and loyal art thou' ACB: opposite F f. The Latin plural *Franci* became *Ffrainc* 'Franks, French people, France' in Welsh and *Frynk/Frenk* in Cornish. With the use of the plural of the population name to mean the country, cf. *Cymry* 'Welshmen' and *Cymru* 'Wales', both from *\*Kombrogi* 'fellow-countrymen, Welshmen', the difference between *Cymry* and *Cymru* being one of spelling only. The Cornish form was originally *\*Kembry* 'Wales', but this was reduced to *Kembra, Kimbra*. The original <y> is seen in the recharacterized plural *Kembrian* 'Welshmen' (AB: 222, 223, 242c) < *\*Kembry + on*. GKK says the <y> in *Frynk* 'is unexpected but is found twice in Late Cornish'. This is incorrect on both counts: *ha ugge hedda mose tho* **Frenk** N. Boson, BF: 29; *Pou Lezou en* **Vrink** AB: 222; *Kynyphan* **frenk** 'nut of France, walnut' AB 74a; *Pokkys* **Frenk** 'pox of France' AB: 82a; *Nenna e eath car rag* **Frink** Tonkin (LAM: 226); *Materen* **Frink** Tonkin (LAM: 226); **VRINK**, *France; also a Frenchman, or French.* **Frink**, id. ACB: folio after A a 2 verso. Cf. *kynyphan* **frenk**, *a French, or wall nut* ACB: S 2; *POKKYS* **FRENK**, *the pox* ACB: opposite X. The hesitation between *y* and *e* is regular in Cornish; cf. *\*santi > sens/syns* 'saints' and *\*danti > dens/dyns* 'teeth'. George says the vowel *y* is unexpected, presumably because he would have expected *a* in the singular *\*Frank*. As we have seen *Frynk/Frenk* is a plural and always means 'France' or 'the French' (pl.). A plural *Frankaz* 'Frenchmen' based on the singular *\*Frank* 'Frank, Frenchman' is used by Gwavas (cited by Gendall). GKK's main mistake here is to attempt to treat *Frynk* 'France' and *\*Frank* 'Frenchman' under the same heading. Notice incidentally that Pryce cites the word *FRANK* 'free at liberty' ACB: opposite P, and in his lament for William III Lhuyd uses *Frank* to mean 'France': *Dhort henna war* **Frank** *ha war Span* Lhuyd (LAM: 234). Moreover Nicholas Boson writes **Francan-belgan** 'Franco-Belgian' BF: 31.

**Frynkek** [Frynkek] 'French language': GKK says this is 'actually found as **Frencock** in Late Cornish.' This is incorrect. Nicholas Boson writes *an* **Frenkock** (not *\*Frencock*) *feen* BF: 29 and John Boson writes *En* **Frenkock** *ha Carnoack* BF: 59. One also finds **Vrinkak** glossing *Gallica lingua, The French Tongue* AB: 223; *Arvorek ha* **Frenkek** AB: 222; *avez a* **Frenkek** AB: 223; cf. **VRINKAK**, *the French tongue* ACB: folio after A a 2 verso. Welsh *Ffrangeg* 'French language' is from *\*Ffrank* singular + *eg*. Cornish *Frynkek* is from *Frynk* plural + *ek*, hence the difference in vocalism.

**gast** [gast] 'bitch': GKK says this is confined to a single instance in Lhuyd. This is incorrect: *W. Gast, A Bitch; Corn[ish]* **Gest** AB: 14c; **gest** AB: 46a (s.v. *Canis*); **gest**, *A bitch* AB: 241b; *CANIS ...Kei, ǂki,* **gest** AB: 291a. Cf. **GEST, GYST**, *a dog; properly, a bitch* ACB: P 2.

**gaver** [gavar]: GKK gives *gever* on p. 108 as the plural of *gaver* 'goat' and implies that the form is confined to place-names. This is incorrect: *eue a reeg pederre war* **Gever**, *ha meskeeges dro tho Anko, eue levarraz droua* **Gever** *ul* BF: 25; *Devas, ean,* **gever** *ha menas* Bilbao MS; *Gavar, A goat,* **Gever** AB: 243a. Cf. *ǂGAVAR, a goat, pl.* **Gever** ACB: opposite P 2. GKK does not mention the earliest instance of the plural of *gavar*, i.e. *gyfras: na the offra in ban the Thu ley, oghan, devas ha* **gyffras** TH 27a.

**gaver mor** [gavar mor] 'crayfish; spider crab': GKK cites this s.v. *gavar* <gaver> and arbitrarily lenites the initial consonant of *mor* to give *\*gaver vor*. The dictionary also asserts that apart from Cornish dialect the word is confined to Lhuyd, who cites it once only. This is incorrect: *...called otherwise by the Cornish* **Gavar mor** s.v. *Legast, a Lobster* AB: 5a; *Corn[ish]* **Gavar mor** *[i.e. Sea-goat] A sort of Lobster, so call'd from its* *long horns* AB: 34b; ***Gavar mor*** glossing *Locusta, A lobster* AB: 81a; ***Gavar mor**, A segar or long oister* AB: 241bc.

**gedya** [gedya] 'to guide': GKK says that this verb is confined to one instance in BM. This is incorrect: *the teller da rum* ***gedya*** BM 629; *grua ov* ***gedya*** *vy* BM 637; *me agis* ***gyd*** BM 981; *rum* ***gedya*** *in forth wella* BM 1099; ***gedyogh*** *dymo* BM 2089; *ov bevnans oma* ***gedya*** BM 2541; *reth* ***gedya*** *del vo plesijs* BM 3015.

**gedyer** [gedyer] 'guide': GKK says that this word is derived from Nance (1955), being unattested in the texts. This is incorrect: *ow tristya fatell ota* ***gydyar*** *the'n re ew dall* TH 14a.

**genesigeth** [genesygeth] 'birth': GKK says this is confined to 2-3 instances in BM and TH. This is incorrect: *ay* ***genesygeth*** BM 4387; *mortall* ***genesegeth*** TH 6a; *then* ***genesegath*** TH 8; *dre* ***genesegeth*** TH 26; *ha '****enegegath*** SA 61a.

**genn** [gen] 'wedge, chisel': GKK says this word is confined to a single instance in Lhuyd. This is incorrect: *A Wedge; Corn[ish]* ***Gedn*** AB: 14c; ***gedn*** glossing *Cuneus, A Wedge* AB: 53a; ***Gedn*** *is Cornish for a wedge* Pryce 1778 (LAM: 308); ***GEDN**, a wedge* ACB: opposite P 2.

**gerlyver** [gerlyver] 'dictionary': GKK says that this word is confined to a single instance in ACB (1790). This is incorrect: *neb 'ramatek ha* ***gerlevar*** AB: 222; *mar peue* ***gerlevar*** AB: 222; *hay* ***gerlevro*** *e honan* AB: 222; *e '****erlevar*** *Kembrian* AB: 223; *en an* ***ger-levar*** *Ladin ha Keltek* AB: 223.

**gerlyvrynn** [gerlyvryn] 'glossary, short dictionary': GKK says this word is confined to a single instance in Lhuyd. This is incorrect: ***ger-levran*** *Kernuak* AB: 222; *na huath* ***gerlevran*** *veth* AB: 222; *ha'n* ***gerlevran*** *Arvorek* AB: 222; *neb '****Erlevran*** *Brethonek* AB: 222; *e* ***gerlevran*** *Kembrian* AB: 222; *mez* ***gerlevran*** *Kernuak* AB: 222; ***gerlevran*** *bian Brethonek* AB: 222; *an* ***gerlevran-na*** AB: 223; *an* ***gerlevran-ma*** AB: 223; *vez a'n hoth* ***Erlevran-ma*** AB: 223; ***gerlevran*** *Kernuak Levarva Cotton* AB: 223; *en an* ***gerlevran*** *Kernuak-ma* AB: 223; *en an* ***gerlevran-ma*** AB: 223.

**gil** [gyl] 'deceit, guile': GKK says that this word is confined to a single instance in the *Ordinalia*. This is incorrect: *rag ovn genes bones* ***gyl*** OM 196; *seruont hep* ***gyl*** OM 2402; *hep toll na* ***gyl*** OM 2559; *deceypt vith na* ***gyll*** TH 11.

**glanhe** [glanhe] 'to clean': GKK says that this verb is confined to two occurrences in TH. This is incorrect: *yth ough* ***glanhys*** PC 865; *genen yv* ***glanheys*** BM 4523; *an nenaf a veth* ***glanhis*** SA 60a.

**glena** [glena] 'to stick': GKK says that this verb is confined to two instances in TH. This is incorrect: *orto fast navng o* ***glenys*** PA 176c; *th'y thyller arte* ***glenes*** PC 1154; *worto an kyc a* ***glene*** RD 2594; *y* ***glynes*** *hardlych* RD 2597; *a russa* ***glena*** TH 19a; ***glena*** *agys honyn* TH 58; *Dho* ***glenys*** [sic] glossing *Haereo, To stick, to cleave,* etc. AB: 65a. Cf. ***GLENAZ***, *dho glenys, to cleave to, to stick to* ACB: P 2 verso.

**glew** [glew] 'sharp, penetrating': GKK says that this word is confined to three instances, in the *Ordinalia* (i.e. OM 2062, PC 2088 and RD 2582. This is incorrect: *y astevyth peynys* ***glu*** BM 765.

**glyb** [glyb, gleb] 'wet': GKK says that apart from dialect survivals this word is confined to two examples in Lhuyd. This is incorrect: ***Gleab*** glossing *Fluidus* AB: 60b; ***Gleb*** glossing *Humidus* AB: 66b; ***Gleb*** glossing *Madidus* AB: 83c; *Dedh* ***gleb***, *A wet day* AB: 243c; *Keuar '****leb***, *Wet weather* ibid. Cf. ***GLEAB***, *wet, moist* ACB: P 2 verso.

**glybya** 'to wet, to moisten': GKK says that this verb is confined to a single instance in BM (line 3276). This is incorrect: *yma daggrow ow* ***klybye*** *the dreys* PC 482-83. Cf. *dho* ***glybye***, *to wet, to moisten* ACB: P 2 verso.

**godra** [godra] 'to milk': GKK says this word is confined to a single occurrence in Lhuyd. This is incorrect: *W. Godro, To Milk; Cor*[*nish*] **Gudra** AB: 17b; *Buket* **gudra** glossing *Mulctra, A milk-pail* AB: 95a; *dhort* **gudra** *an devaz han gour* AB: 240b. Note also **Gudra**, *to milk or milch* Borlase 390; **GUDRA**, *dho* **gudra**, *to milk; buket* **gudra**, *a milk pail* ACB: opposite Q 2.

**godrevedh** [godreva] 'third day hence': GKK says the word is taken from Nance's 1955 dictionary, being otherwise unattested. This is incorrect: **gydreva**, *The third day hence* AB: 249a. Cf. **GYDREVA**, *the third day hence* ACB: two folios after Q 2 verso; **Gudreva**, *the third Day hence* Borlase 390; **gydreva**, *adv. The third day hence* LCB. GKK implicitly criticizes Nance for spelling the word <godreva>. It is GKK's <godrevedh> that is unjustified.

**goel** [gol] 'sail': GKK says that this word is confined to three instances (i.e. OCV, RD 2331 and BM 1085). This is incorrect: *tenneugh a thysempys y* **goyl** *yn ban* RD 2291-92; *tennogh dyson an* **goyl** *thym in ban lemen* BM 597-98; *Guelan* **gol**, *the sail-yard* AB: 3a; *C*[*ornish*] **Gol**, *Velum* AB: 33a; **Gol**, **guyl** glossing *Velum, A veil, a curtain or sail* AB: 170c. Cf. **GOIL**, **Gol**, *a sail; also a vail* ACB: folio after P 2.

**goellys** [gullys] 'gulls': GKK says that this word, the plural of *goella* [gulla] 'gull' is confined to a single instance in Lhuyd. This is incorrect: **gulles**, *Guls* AB: 243a; *an* **gullez** *ha'n idhen mor aral* AB: 245a.

**Goelowann** [Golowan] 'St John's Eve, Midsummer': GKK says this is confined to one instance in Late Cornish. This is incorrect: *Guave en Have terebah* **Goluan** Ustick MSS; *…Midsummer is thence, in the Cornish tongue, call'd* **Goluan**… Borlase 130.

**goen** [gon] 'sheath': GKK says that this word is confined to Old and Middle Cornish. This is incorrect: **Gun**, †**guain** glossing *Vagina, A sheath or scabbard* AB: 169a. Cf. **GÛN**, *a gown; also, a sheath* ACB: folio after Q 2.

**goesogen** [gojogen] 'black pudding': GKK says this word comes from Nance (1955) being unattested in the texts. This is incorrect: **Gudzhygan**, *A black Pudding, from the old word guaedogen, of the same signification* AB: 4c; *W.* †**gwaedogen**, *A Pudding*; *C*[*ornish*] **Gudzhygan** AB: 10b; **Gudzhygan** *(a black pudding)* s.v. *Fartum, A pudding, a farce* AB: 58c. Cf. **GUDZHYGAN**, *a blood pudding* ACB: Q opposite.

**gokkyes** [gockyes] 'fools': GKK cites this as a separate headword distinct from *gokki* [gocky] and says that the word is unattested. This is doubly incorrect. *Gockyes* is merely the plural of *gocky* 'foolish, foolish person' and means 'fools'. It is attested: *gorteugh lymmyn* **gockyes** 'stay now, you fools' PC 1149; *nyns ough lemmyn* **gokyes** 'you are nothing but fools' RD 1136.

**golowi** [golowy] 'to lighten': according to GKK this is confined to one instance each in BM, CW and Lhuyd. This is incorrect: *re* **woloways** *ov skyans* BM 213; *han presan ov* **colowhy** BM 3714; *an kigg ew touchis gans dowla rag malla an nenaf bos* **golowis** *gans an Spiris Sans* SA 60a; *ow* **collowye** CW 125; *Dho* **gylyua** glossing *Fulgeo, to shine, glister or glitter; to lighten* AB: 61c-62a; *Dho* **Gouloua** glossing *Lumino, To light, to enlighten* AB: 82b; **Kylyui**, *To lighten* AB: 245b; *Patl yzhi a* **kylyui** *ha trenna* AB: 248. Cf. also *Karn-***Gollewa**, *that is, the Karn of Lights* Borlase 131 and **GOLOUA**, *dho* **goloua**, **gouloua**, *to light, to enlighten* ACB: folio after P 2.

**golvan** [golvan] 'sparrow': GKK says this word occurs twice, once in OCV and once in Lhuyd. This is incorrect: **goluan** glossing *passer* ['sparrow'] OCV; *Arm. & Corn*[*ish*] **Golvan** [*a Sparrow*] AB: 38a; **Gylvan** *ge* glossing *Curruca, A hedge-sparrow* AB: 53b; *Passer…A sparrow…C*[*ornish*] **gylvan**, †**golvan** AB: 114a; **Golvan**, *A sparrow* AB: 241b; *A Sparrow, C & Ar.* **Golvan** AB: 286b. Cf. †**GOLVAN**, *a sparrow*; **golvan-ge**, *an hedge-sparrow. Hod*[*ie*] **Gylvan**, *and* **Gylvan-ge** ACB: folio after P 2 verso.

**gorheri** [gorhery] 'to cover': GKK says this verb is confined to a single instance in the *Ordinalia*. This is incorrect: *tha'gas **gorhery** hep gow* PC: 2655; *goole powze crohan ha ez **goreraz*** RC 23: 183; ***GORHERY**, to cover, to hide* ACB: two folios after P 2 verso; *Ha **gwarrow** goz pennow genz lidziw glaz* ACB: two folios after G g 2.

**gorlewin** [gorlewen] 'west': GKK says that this word is confined to a single instance Lhuyd. This is incorrect: *an bôbl en **Gorleuen** Kernou* AB: 222; *en **uorleuen** an G'laskor-ma* AB: 224; *kenza **gorleuen** an 'Ulaskor-ma* AB: 224. Cf. ***GORLEUEN**; bobl en **gorleuen** Kernou, people in the western part of Cornwall* ACB: two folios after P 2 verso.

**gossen** [gossen] 'rust, ferruginous earth': GKK says that appart from English dialect this word is unattested. This is incorrect. Pryce writes: ***GOZAN**, **Gossan**, rust, iron ochre, ferruginous* [sic] ACB: opposite Q.

**gour-gath** [gourgath] 'tomcat': GKK says this word, which is otherwise unattested, has been derived from Nance's 1952 dictionary. This is incorrect: ***Gurkath**, A he-cat* AB: 241b. Moreover the word is already in Nance's 1938 dictionary s.v. *cath* 'cat' on page 21.

**governya** [governya] 'to govern': GKK says that this verb is confined to 2-3 examples in the *Ordinalia* and CW and adds a note that the variant *governa* occurs in TH. In fact *governya* is confined to the *Ordinalia*: *rag **governye** ow bewnans* OM 89; *rak **governye** oll an beys* PC 930. CW has *governa*, i.e. the same form as in TH: *omma thagan **governa*** CW 181. GKK fails to mention that the word is cited by Lhuyd: ***Govarna**, Govern* AB: 248a.

**gramasek** [gramasek] 'grammar': GKK asserts that this word is unattested in the texts, being derived from Nance's 1952 dictionary. George adds a note: 'Nance's Cornicisation of E. *grammatic(al)*'. None of this is really correct. Lhuyd uses the term *gramatek* (e.g. ***Gramatek** ha ger-levran Kernuak* AB: 222) of which *gramasek* is Nance's more fully Cornicized form. *Gramatek/gramasek* is based on Welsh *gramadeg* 'grammar', itself the regular development of Latin *grammatica* (cf. Irish *gramadach*). English *grammatical* is irrelevent.

**Grekys** [Grekys] 'Greeks': GKK's code {I} means that this is deduced from the singular *Greca* 'Greek' and that *Grekys* itself does not actually occur. This in incorrect. The plural occurs twice: *Oecumenius, den auncient in egglos an **Grekys*** TH 26a; *athea'n egglos a'n **Grickys*** TH 56.

**grevons** [grevons] 'grievance: GKK says that this word is confined to a single instance in BM. This is incorrect: ***Grefons** ha cleves seson* BM 1000; *y **grefons** sewagya* BM 1004; *nyns yv **grefons** me an geyl* BM 1438.

**grondya** [grondya] 'to found': GKK says this word occurs 2-3 times in Middle Cornish. This is incorrect: *war fals y3 ens **growndys*** PA 118b; *Nans yw **groundyys** genef vy* OM 2321; *sur ha **grondya*** BM 1151; ***groundya** aga honyn* TH 32a; *a res bos **groundys*** TH 51a.

**grugyerik** [grugyeryk] '(young) partridge': GKK says that the word is confined to a single instance in Lhuyd. This is incorrect: ***Gyrgirik**, A Partridge* AB: 5a; ***gyrgirik*** glossing *Perdix, A partridge* AB: 117b; ***Gyrgirik**, A Partridge* AB: 241b.

**gwaneth** [gwaneth] 'wheat': GKK says this word is confined to three instances in Late Cornish. This is incorrect: *kerth, barlys ha **gwaneth*** CW 1066; *Barles **gwanath** ha keer* Bilbao MS; *W. Guenith, Wheat; Corn[ish] **Guanath*** AB: 15b; ***Guanath*** glossing *Triticum, Wheat* AB: 167a; *C[ornish] **Guanath*** glossing *TRITICUM* AB: 297b; ***Guanath**, wheat; bara **guanath**, wheaten bread* ABC: Q.

**gwannder** [gwander] 'weakness': GKK says this word is unattested in the texts, being derived from Nance's 1938 dictionary. This is incorrect: *rag **gwander** y a go3as* PA

68c; *Rag **gwander** war ben dowlyn* PA 171c; *doun an grows rag **gwander*** PA 173d; *rag **guander** ef re cothas* PC 2618; ***Guander**, Weakness* AB: 240b. Cf. ***Guander**, weakness* ACB: Q.

**gwary-myr** 'play, pageant': this word is cited as ***guirremear*** by Scawen (Nance 1938 s.v. *gwary-myr*); ***Guirimir*** by Borlase 196 and cf. ***guary-meers**, interludes played in the rounds; amphitheatres* ACB: Q 2. It appears to be wanting from GKK.

**gwaynya** [gwaynya] 'to gain': GKK says this word is confined to one instance in Lhuyd. This is incorrect: *hag eff a **gvayn** roov cans* BM 388; *hag a **guayn** pur sempellos* BM 2256; *Dho **guaynia** glossing Lucror, To gain, to win* AB: 81c; *To Win or Gain, C[ornish] **Guaynia** AB: 289b.

**gwaytya** [gwaytya, gwetyas] 'to expect': GKK says the verbal noun is not attested. This is incorrect: *pan a dra a ren ny **gwettyas*** TH 15a; *fatell yllans **gwetias*** TH 55a; *uz na ellen skant **quatiez*** BF: 25; *Mattern James rig **quachas** e stoppia* LAM: 224; *Eva rig **quachas** moaze* LAM: 224.

**gwenenenn** [gwenenen] 'bee', **gwenen** [gwenyn] collective 'bees': GKK follows Nance in making *gwenenen* the singular and *gwenyn* the plural. ***Guenenen** 'apis'* [i.e. 'bee' singular] occurs in OCV. Lhuyd, however, makes *guanan* his singular: *W. **Guenynen**, A Bee; Corn[ish] **Guanan** AB: 13c; W. Guenynen, A Bee; Corn[ish] **Guanan** AB: 15b; Apes vel apis, Guenynen, A Bee; C[ornish] **Guanan**, [pl. **guenyn**] AB: [4]3a; **Guanan**, A bee* AB: 240c. The plural *gwenyn* occurs in *Kaual **guanan** glossing Alveare, A Bee-Hive* AB: 42b; *Ha ma leiaz bennen Pokare an **guenen*** ABC: folio after F f 2; *Corgwenyn Beeswax* Borlase 382b. It would seem, then, that in Late Cornish *gwenen/gwenyn* was both singular and plural. According to GKK *gwenen* occurs twice. We have noted above eight examples.

**gwenton** [gwaynten] 'spring': GKK says this word is confined to OCV and Lhuyd. This is incorrect: *Houl sooth, Tor lean, paravy an **gwaynten*** Scawen MSS. Cf. also ***GUAINTOIN**, the spring. Hod[ie] **Guainten, Gwainten** ABC: Q.

**gwiader** [gwyader] 'weaver': GKK says that this word is confined to Lhuyd. This is incorrect, since Gwavas writes: *Why ladar **gweader**, Lavarro guz pader* LAM: 242 (also in ACB: two folios after F f 2).

**gwibenn** [gwyben] 'fly': GKK says that this word is confined to a single instance in Lhuyd. This is incorrect: *A Flie; Corn[ish] **Guiban** AB: 13c; **Guiban** glossing Insectum, A Fly, an Insect* AB: 71b; ***Guiban** glossing Musca, a fly* AB: 96a. Cf. *GUIBAN, a fly, an insect* ACB: Q 2 verso.

**gwikoryon** [gwycoryon] 'merchants': GKK says that this plural is confined to two instances in PC. This is incorrect: *crist a gafas **gwycoryan*** PA 30c.

**gwius** [gwyus] 'winding': GKK says that this is unattested in the texts and has been taken from Nance's 1955 dictionary. This is incorrect: *the belha ha the **weusa** a vova ow mois in rag* TH 17a.

**gwlesik** [gwlesyk] 'leader': GKK says this word is confined to place-names. This is incorrect. Lhuyd writes: *en termen Maksen **Ulezek*** AB: 224.

**gwragh** [gwragh] 'old woman': GKK says that this word is confined to Old Cornish and place-names. This is incorrect: *Anus...An Old Woman...C[ornish] Bennen goath; **gurah** AB: 3a; Vetula...An old woman or wife. C[ornish] Benyn goth, †**gurah** AB: 173a; Cf. also ***GURAH**, an old woman* ACB: folio after Q 2. It also occurs in dialect as *wrah, wraugh, wraff* with the sense 'wrasse', a fish with hag-like features GCSW: 174.

**gwrannenn** [gwrannen] 'wren': GKK says this word is attested 2-3 times in Lhuyd who, we are told, spells it <gwradnan>. This is incorrect on both counts: *English. A Wren, Corn[ish] **Guradn** AB: 9c; **Guradnan**, A Wren* AB: 33c; ***Guradnan** glossing Troglodytes,*

*A wren* AB: 167a; **Guradnan**, *A wren* AB: 241b; cf. also **GURADNAN**, *a wren* ACB: folio after Q 2. Nowhere does Lhuyd spell the word with initial <gw>.

**gwreydhenn** [gwredhen] 'root': GKK says that this singular in -*enn* [-en] is confined to OCV and Lhuyd. This is incorrect: *dell ons y aga dew an* **wrethyan** *dretha mayth o res the lynyath mab den dos, han* **wreythan** *unwith o corruptys ha nyns o vas, fatel ylly an wethan ha'n barrow ow tos mes a'n* **wreythan** *na bos vas?* TH 4a; *theworth an* **wreythan** TH 8a. GKK suggests that TH contains two instances of a word *\*gwredhyans* 'foundation'. I am unable to locate either of them.

**gwreydhya** [gwredhya] 'to take root': GKK says the word is unattested. This is incorrect: **gurythyoug** *ha tyvoug arte* OM 1894; *yn dor ymons ol* **gurythyys** OM 2084.

**gwrys** [gwrys] 'crystal'. GKK says that no cognates have been identified. This is incorrect. In his glossary to *Beunans Meriasek* (*Archiv für Celtische Lexikographie* 1 (1900): 121) Stokes suggested that *grueys* at BM 1288 was from *\*gwysr < uitrum*. I would suggest further that *gwrys* represents the regular Cornish development of *\*uritu-*, an early British metathesis of Latin *uitrum* 'glass.' The unmetathesized variant *uitru-* developed regularly in Cornish as *gweder*.

**Gwydhelek** [Godhalek] 'Irish, Gaelic': GKK says that the word has been taken from Nance's 1938 dictionary, since it is unattested in the texts. This is incorrect: *ha gerlevar rag oz Tavaz huei ha rag an* **Godhalek** AB: 222; *mar peue gerlevar &c Kernuak ha* **Godhalek** AB: 222. Cf. **GODHALEK**, *Irish* ACB: folio after P 2.

**gwyr** [gwer] 'green': GKK says this word is confined to two instances in Lhuyd. This is incorrect: *W. Guyrdh, Green; Corn*[*ish*] **Guer**. AB: 12b; *W. Guyrdh, Green; Corn*[*ish*] **Guer** AB: 18c; *C*[*ornish*] *Delkio* **guer** glossing *Frons* AB: 61c; *C*[*ornish*] **Guer**, *guirdh* [*guirt*] AB: 174c; *Ky* **guer** *vel an guelz, As green as grass* AB: 248c. Cf. **GUER**, *green, lively, flourishing* ABC: Q 2.

**gwyrgh** [gwergh] 'virginal, pure, innocent': GKK says the word is unattested in the texts. This is incorrect: *dre'n pyte a gemeras orth flehys* **gruegh** *ha byen* 'through the mercy he showed to children innocent and small' BM 1691-92; *drefen kemeres pyta a'n flehys* **gruergh** *del rusta* 'because of taking pity upon the innocent children as you did' BM 1704-05; *tremmyl flogh* **gruergh** *the latha* 'to kill three thousand innocent children' BM 1776.

**hager-awel** [hager-awel] 'storm': GKK cites this under *hager* and says that it is confined to a single instance in ACB. This is incorrect: *Kensa, vrt an* **hagar auall** *iggeva gweell do derevoll* BF: 9; *Kensa, urt a* **hagar-awal** *iggeva gweel do derevoll* BF: 12; *Keuar,* **hagar-auel** glossing *Tempestas, A tempest or storm* AB: 161c; **haga**[r]**-auel**, *bad weather, a storm* ACB: two folios after K 2; **Hagar awell**, *ha auel teag* ACB: opposite F f 2.

**hanasenn** [hanajen] 'sigh': GKK tells us the word is confined to a single instance in Lhuyd. This is incorrect: *A Sigh. Arm. Huanal. Corn*[*ish*] **Hanadzhan** AB: 8c; *Suspirium...A sigh; A short breathing. C*[*ornish*] **Hanadzhan** AB: 159c. It is probable also that **Hynadzhas** glossing *Gemitus, a groan or sigh* at AB: 62c is a misprint for *\*Hynadzhan*. Cf. **HANADZHAN**, *a sigh* ACB: opposite R.

**handla** [handla] 'to handle, to touch': GKK says this verb is confined to a single instance in BM. This is incorrect: *drok* **handle** *del om kyry* PC 991; *ny alla* **handle** *toul vyth* PC 2678; *gesough vy th'y* **handle** PC 3165; *galles* **handle** PC 3194; *erna* **hyndlyf** *y golon* RD 1531; *thy* **handla** *sur eff am gays* BM 1113; *le mayth eua* **drokhendelys** BM 3760.

**hangya** [hangya] 'to hang': GKK says that this verb is confined to a single instance at BM 1245. This is incorrect: *oll an la ha'n prophetys ow* **hangya** TH 20a.

**hansel** [hansel] 'breakfast': GKK says this word is confined to two instances in BM (i.e. at lines 110 and 960). This is incorrect: *Jentaculum...A break-fast. C*[*ornish*] **Haunsel**

AB: 67b; *Haunsel, a Breakfast* Borlase 392; *HAUNSEL, a breakfast* ACB: opposite R; *Gwag o ve, ra ve gawas* **haunsell**? *I am hungry, shall I have breakfast?* ACB: opposite F f 2.

**hanter-kans** [hantercans] 'fifty': GKK says that this word is attested 2-3 times in Middle and Late Cornish. This is incorrect: *ha* **hanter** *cans keuelyn* OM 957; *ha* **hanter** *cans y gyle* PC 506; *ha* **hantercans** *kevellen* CW 2262; *C[ornish]* **Hanter** *kanz* glossing *Quinguaginta* AB: 135a; *hanter-canz, fifty* ACB: opposite M.

**harber** [harber] 'refuge': GKK says this word has been taken from Nance's 1938 dictionary, being unattested in the texts. This is incorrect: *ena purguir an poddren thotho prest re ruk* **harber** BM 2290-91; *malbe yeman in* **harber** BM 3303. *Erberow* OM 32 is probably the plural. Cf. *ERBER, a garden; pl. Erberow* ACB: O 2 verso.

**heligenn** [helygen] '(single) willow tree': GKK says the singular in *-enn* [-en] is unattested apart from toponyms. This is incorrect. We find *heligen: salix* at OCV 707 and Lhuyd gives *Salix...A willow or sallow tree, an osier. C[ornish]* **Helagan**, †*heligen* AB: 143c; Cf. †*HELIGEN, a willow; Helak, Hellik,* **Helagan**, *id.* ACB: R.

**hembronk** [hembronk, humbrank] 'to lead, to conduct': GKK gives this word the codes {M: 2}, by which is meant that the word is confined to Middle Cornish and occurs between two and three times. This is incorrect: *y'n* **hombronkyas** PA 16a; **hombronkis** PA 61c; *e'n* **hombronky** PA 62b; *y a'n* **hombronkyas** PA 76c; *a'n* **hombronkyas** PA 114c; *a ve* **hombronkis** PA 163c; *a's* **hembronk** OM 1874; *may feen* **hembrynkys** OM 1973; *yth* **hembrenkygh** PC 204; **hembrynkys** PC 584; **hembrynkeugh** PC 1195; *a'm* **hembroncas** PC 1205; **humbrak** *mab den in mes* TH 3; **humbrynkes** *the beha* TH 3a; *agan* **humbrag** *ny* TH 11a. Moreover the word is attested in Late Cornish: *a ve Jesus* **humbregez** RC 23: 185. Cf. also *HEMBRYNKY, to lead, to bring along* ACB: R.

**hernya** 'to shoe a horse'. This word is cited by Pryce: *Moas tha an gove tha* **herniah** *an verh To go to the smith to shoe the horses* ACB: F f 2. It appears to be wanting in GKK.

**hora** [hora] 'whore': GKK suggests that this word is attested in Late Cornish only (i.e. as *hora* by Lhuyd and *whorra* by Carew). This is incorrect: *gas vy the thehesy gans morben bom trewysy the'n vyl* **hora** *war an taal* OM 2703-05.

**howlsedhes** [howlsedhas] 'sunset, west': GKK suggests this word is confined to a single instance in Lhuyd, **Houlzedhas** glossing *Occasus,...sun-setting, The west* AB 104c. This is incorrect: *na oren pana tu, Thuryan,* **houlzethas**, *po Gleth po Dihow* ACB: opposite F f. Cf. *houl zedhaz, sun setting* ACB: opposite R 2.

**hurtya** 'to hurt': this verb occurs three times in TH: *the lee* **hurtys** TH 26; *theth* **hurtya** *ge* TH 48 x 2 and is attested by Lhuyd as *dho* **hertia** glossing *Laedo, To hurt* AB: 75b; cf. *HERTIA, dho hertia, to hurt, or wound* ACB: opposite R 2. It does not seem to be in GKK.

**hwaff** [whaf] 'blow': GKK suggests that this word is confined to three instances in OM (i.e. OM 2711, 2747 and 2755). This is incorrect. The word is also attested in TH with the sense 'gust of wind': *ledys gans pub* **wave** *ha cowas gwyns* TH 31; *ow shackya gans pub* **waffe** TH 42.

**hwedner** [whednar] 'sixpence': GKK says this is known only from Borlase. This is incorrect: **Hue dinar** glossing *Semisolidus, Sixpence* AB: 148a; **hue dinair**, *six-pence* ACB: folio after N verso.

**hwetegves** [whetegves] 'sixteenth': GKK says that this word is confined to a single instance in TH. This is probably an allusion to *in* **xvi-as** *chapter* TH 43a, which hardly counts. The only occurrence of the word known to me is *Whe* **degvas**, *the sixteenth* ACB: F f 2 verso.

**hwiogenn** [whyogen] 'dinner cake': GKK says that this word is not attested, being taken from Nance's 1938 dictionary. GKK also gives as a separate headword *hogenn* [hogen] 'pastry', which is, according to GKK, similarly not attested. This is all incorrect. *Whyogen* and *hogen* are variants of the same word. The item is attested: *Huigan, medulla panis* ['dough, pastry'] AB: 87c; *HOGAN, hogen... also,... a pork pasty* ACB: R 2. Cf. *hot fuggans* (cakes) Bottrell (LAM: 328).

**hwithra** [whythra] 'to examine': GKK asserts that this word is confined to a single instance in OM. This is incorrect: *whythyr pup tra* OM 748; *a whythre warnas* OM 1414; *whythrough hetheu* PC 1113.

**hwithrans** [whythrans] 'research': GKK ascribes this modern coinage to K[en] J. G[eorge]. This is incorrect. The word was in use in the nineteen-sixties: *rak dysquedhes dhe'n bys deweth whythrans byghan* 'to show to the world the end result of a small amount of research' ALK 87 (1964).

**hynsa** [hynsa] 'peers': GKK says this word is confined to a single instance each in OM and BM. This is incorrect: *ha the oll aga hynsa* TH 44; *a ugh aga hensa* TH 44a; *ugh oll aga hensa* TH 45a; *uth oll aga hensa* TH 49a.

**igolenn** [agolen] 'whetstone': GKK says that this word occurs the place-name *Nancegollan* and is otherwise confined to a single instance in Lhuyd. This is incorrect: *W. Galen* [r. *Hogalen*] *A Whet-stone; Corn*[*ish*] *Agolan* AB: 15a; *W. Hogalen, A Whet-Stone, Cor*[*nish*] *Agolan* AB: 16c; *Agolan* glossing *Cos, A whetstone* AB: 51c. Cf. *AGOLAN, a whetstone* ACB: K 2.

**igor** [ygor] 'open': GKK's code {ML: 3} suggests that this word is well attested in both Middle and Late Cornish. This is incorrect. The word is not attested anywhere in the texts, being replaced by *opyn*. If he had looked at Nance (1938), the compiler would have seen that Nance derived the word from Breton (*d*)*igor*.

**istori** [ystory] 'history': GKK says this word has been taken from Nance's 1938 dictionary, being unattested in the texts. This is incorrect: *in seconde lever a Eusebius, Ecclesiastical Historye* TH 46a; *an lever a Eusebius, Ecclesiastical History* TH 47a; *yma S Jherom ow recordya in dalleth a'y story De Ecclesiasticis Scriptoribus* TH 47.

**jarn** [jarn] 'garden': GKK says this word is confined to a single occurrence in Lhuyd. This is incorrect: *Dzharn, An Orchard* AB: 33c; *Luar, Dzharn* glossing *Hortus, A garden or orchard* AB: 66a; *Dzharn* glossing *Pomarium, An orchard* 123b. Cf. *DZHARN, a garden, an orchard* ACB: O.

**Jentilys** [Jentyls] 'Gentiles': GKK says that the word is confined to Late Cornish where it occurs once. This is incorrect: *in myske an Jentyls* TH 14a; *in mysk an Gentyls* TH 45a; *Allale an Gentelles* RC 23: 190.

**Kablys** [Cablys] 'Maundy Thursday': GKK says that this word is confined to a single instance in Middle Cornish (i.e. PC 654) where it is spelt *duyow hamlos*. This is incorrect: *en gyth o deyow hablys* PA 41c; *nyng egy cowse vith a deow habblys* SA 66.

**kachya** [cachya] 'to catch, to seize': GKK says that this verb is confined to a single instance in PC. This is incorrect: *ha chechys yntre dewla* PA 48d; *cachaf y ben* OM 2816; *y cachye* PC 55; *a'n chache uskys* PC 615; *me a cache* PC 452; *yn cacher wythovte nay* PC 987; *kychough ef yn vryongen* PC 1007; *hag a cach an cercot bras* PC 2074; *y a yl bones kechys* PC 2293; *kycheugh ef* PC 2523; *war skwych kychys the ves gans dywthorn* RD 2595-96; *Mose tha an mor tha catchah pyzgaz* ACB: F f 2; *ketchys, taken* Borlase 395.

**kalgh** [cal] 'penis': GKK says this word is confined to one instance each in Lhuyd and John Boson. This is incorrect: *C*[*ornish*] & *Arm. Kal* glossing *Mentula, a Man's privy member* AB: 89a; *Lost, kal* glossing *Penis, A tail, a man's yard* AB: 116c; *Kal* glossing

*Veretrum, A man's privy member* AB: 171c; *Komero 'vyth goz* **Kal** BF: 58; **KAL**, *membrum virile* ACB: folio after R 2 verso; *Komero 'wyth guz* **kal** ACB: folio after F f 2 verso.

**kala** [cala] 'straw': Although it cites OCV and PC 680, GKK says that this word occurs once only. This is incorrect: The word is common: *marnes in* **cala** *garov* BM 4447; *me ny settyaf gwaile* **gala** CW 1355; **Kala**, *Straw* (in a list of current Cornish words) AB: 4c; *moran* **kala** [& *sivi*] *a Straw-berry* AB: 44b; **Kala**, *straw* glossing *Culmus* AB: 53a; **Kala** glossing *Stramen, Straw, litter, stubble* AB: 155b; *Straw, C[ornish]* **Kala** AB: 287a; *gorah an vose tha shakiah an* **kala** ACB: opposite F f 2. Cf. †*KALA, straw* and †*KALA GUELI, a mattress of a bed* ACB: two folios after R 2 verso.

**Kalann** [Calan] 'first day of month': GKK's discussion of this word is not entirely clear, since the dictionary suggests erroneously s.v. <Halann> that the etymon occurs in CW. Under *Kalann* we are told that the word is attested exclusively in Late Cornish and occurs 2-3 times. This is incorrect. The word is attested twice in Middle Cornish: *ix nobyl a* **Cala** *Me* BM 3338; *dew* **whallon** *gwa metton in eglos de Lalant* Consistory Court Deposition 1572 (Wakelin: 89). Under *Calendae* Lhuyd writes **Kalan**; *halan*; *Deu* **halan** *guav, All Saints Day* AB: 45c. Taking all these instances together, we have five examples.

**kammdybyans** [camdybyans] 'mistake': GKK says this word has been taken form Nance (1938) and is not attested in the texts. This is incorrect: *Mez an* **kabmdybianz** *hedda eu gorryzz ker* AB: 223.

**kampoella** [campolla] 'to mention': GKK says that this verb is confined to a single instance in the seventeenth century. This is presumably a reference to *Ha me reeg clowaz an poble* **compla** by James Jenkins (LAM: 230). The assertion in GKK is incorrect, however, since the verb is well attested: *Vn ger na* **campol** *a gryst* BM 903; *purguir* **campollys** BM 2204; *na* **gampol** *crist* BM 2439; *pan* **gampollys** BM 2791.

**kankweyth** [canqueyth] 'a hundred times': GKK says this is confined to a single instance in the *Ordinalia* (a reference to *dek* **canquyth** *thy's lowene* PC 574). This is incorrect: **canquith**, *an hundred times*; *deh* **canquith**, *ten hundred times* ACB: *opposite* M. The variant *kanzuyth* is cited by Lhuyd, AB: 248c. Cf. **Kanzuyth**, *a hundred times* ACB: folio after R 2 verso.

**Karesk** [Keresk] 'Exeter': GKK omits to remark that this toponym is stressed on the second syllable. The dictionary says the toponym is confined to 2-3 instances. This is incorrect: *toaz dre mez an fear* **Ka'r Esk** BF: 16; *dre mes an fer* **Karesk** BF: 17; *ha tha vethes tha* **Careesk** LAM: 224; **Kaer Esk**, *the City of Exceter* [sic] AB: 5a; *Ispak* **Kar-esk** AB: 222; *gorra emez a'n* **Kar-esk** AB: 224; *mez an fêr* **Karêsk** AB: 252a; **Karesk**, *Exeter City* Borlase 394.

**karg** [carg] 'load, burden': GKK says this is a recent coinage taken from Nance (1938), but is otherwise unattested. This is incorrect: *Ha rag hedda an* **karg** *a kodhaz uarnav* AB: 222.

**karoli** [caroly] 'to dance': GKK says the word is unattested. This is incorrect: *C[ornish]* **Korolli** glossing *To Dance* AB: 274c; **COROLLI**, *to dance* ABC: folio after M.

**kav** [caf] 'cave': GKK says the word is confined to a single instance in BM. This is incorrect: *in* **caff** *oma rebon ny* BM 3906; *an dragon vrays us in* **caff** BM 3965.

**kegis** [kegys] 'hemlock; umbellifer': GKK says that this word is confined to a single instance in Lhuyd. This is incorrect: *W.* **Kegid**, *Hemlock; Corn[ish]* **Kegaz** AB: 16b; *W.* **Kegid**, *Hemlock; C[ornish]* **Kegaz** AB: 28a; **Kegaz** glossing *Cicuta, Hemlock* AB: 47c. Cf. **KEGAZ**, *hemlock* ACB: folio after R 2 verso.

**Keltek** 'Celtic': GKK says this word is a modern neologism taken from Nance's 1938 dictionary. This is incorrect: *ger-levar Ladin ha* **Keltek** AB: 223.

**kelynenn** [kelynen] '(single) holly tree': GKK says the singular is not attested. This is incorrect: *Kelinen, Holly* AB: 241c.

**Kembra** [Kembra] 'Wales': GKK says this word is confined to a single example in Late Cornish. This is incorrect: *ha pednzhivikio* **Kembra** AB: 222; *gen a nei en* **Kembra** AB: 222; *emesk nei Tîz* **Kimbra** AB: 222; *Tîz* **Kembra** AB: 223; *Tîz Guenez* **Kembra** AB: 223; *por uir en* **Kembra** AB: 224. [N.B. Since the discovery of the play *Bewnans Ke*, we now have two examples of *Kembra* 'Wales' from the Middle Cornish period.]

**Kembryon** [Kembryon] 'Welshmen': GKK suggests that this, the plural of *Kembro*, is attested 2-3 times in Late Cornish. This is incorrect: *ha an* **Kembreeanz** *ha an Curnowean* BF: 29; *drel an* **Kembreean** BF: 31; *Brethonek* **Kembrian** AB: 222; *Tavaz* **Kembrian** AB: 222; *e gerlevran* **Kembrian** AB: 222; *den veth* **Kembrian** AB: 223; *mar peva e* **Kembrian** AB: 223; *e 'rlevar* **Kembrian** AB: 223; *re* **Kembrian** AB: 223; *Dialek* **Kembrian** AB: 223; *liaz pednzhevik* **Kembrian** AB: 224; **Kembrion**, *The Welsh* AB: 242c. Cf. *Brethonek* **Kembrian**, *the Welsh British* ACB: folio after L 2.

**kemmyn** [kemmyn] 'legacy, testament': GKK says this word is not attested anywhere in the texts but has been taken instead from Nance's 1938 dictionary. This is incorrect: *An* **gymmyn** *ma Luther a leverys* TH 50a, where it appears to be feminine.

**kemmynna** [kemmynna, kemmyn]: GKK says this verb is confined to a single instance in CW. This is incorrect: *ov map gruaff the* **kemynna** BM 503, *me a* **gemen** BM 1263; and once in TH: *the'n re na neb a wrussens* **kymmyn** *an egglos* TH 37.

**kendon** [kendon] 'debt': GKK says this word is confined to a single instance in Lhuyd. This is incorrect: *Dho bos en* **kyndan** glossing *Debeo* AB: 53c; **Kyndan** glossing *Debitum* AB: 53c; *bos mer an* **gyndan** *uarnav* AB: 222; *Ni vedn e nevra dos vez a* **gyndan** AB: 230c. Cf. **KYNDAN**, *a debt; dha bosen* **kyndan**, *to be in debt* ACB: S 2.

**Kernewek** [Kernowek] 'Cornish': GKK states that this word is not attested in Middle Cornish. This is incorrect. The first attestation of the word is as *Cornowok* from 1572 (Wakelin: 89; LAM: 268). Since George dates Late Cornish from 1575-1800, *Kernewek* [Kernowek] ought to be considered Middle Cornish.

**kesen** f., pl. **kesow** 'turf': this word is cited as *kezan* [pl. *kezau*] by Lhuyd s.v. *Caespes* AB: 45b. Cf. **KEZAN**, *a clod or turf; pl.* **Kezau** ACB: opposite S. The word appears to be wanting in GKK.

**kesson** [kesson] 'consonant; harmonious': GKK distinguishes the adjective *kesson* from the noun *kessonenn*. Neither is attested, according to GKK. This is incorrect, since Lhuyd uses the first as a noun: *an re Kernuak a kuitha an* **Kessonnyo** *hedda* AB: 223.

**keth** [keth] 'servile, base; dependent': GKK claims that this word is confined to two instances in OCV. This is incorrect: *an iovl* **keth** BM 159; *ol the varogyen* **keth** BM 2433. Nance translates *marogyen* **keth** as 'liege knights.'

**keus** [cues] 'cheese': GKK says that this word is attested only three times in Cornish. This is incorrect: *caus* and *cos* glossing *caseus* [cheese] OCV; *W. Kaus, Cheese; Corn[ish]* **Kez** AB: 14c; *Caseus...Cheese; C[ornish]* **Kez** AB: 46c; **Kez**, *Cheese; Caseus* AB: 241a; **KEZ**, *cheese; now gereally written and pronounced* **Keas** ACB: opposite S; *Ez* **Kez**? *ez, po neg ez; ma sez* **kez**, *Dro* **kez**; *po negez* **Kez**, *dro peth ez* ACB: F f; *a* **kes** *glas, out of green cheese* Borlase 376.

**kewargh** [kewargh] 'hemp': GKK says this word is confined to a single instance in Lhuyd. This is incorrect: *W. Kyuarx, Hemp; Corn[ish]* **Kuer** AB: 12a; **Kuer** glossing *Cannabis, Hemp* AB: 46a; **Kuer** glossing *CANNABIS* AB: 291; **CUER**, *hemp* ACB: two folios after M verso. Cf. **KUER**, *hemp* ACB: S verso.

**klamder** [clamder] 'faintness, swoon': GKK says that this word is confined to the two instances of PC 2593 and TH 7. This is doubly incorrect. In the first place there are two occurrences (not one occurrence) at TH 7: *an flowre a **glomder*** and *eff a **clomder** hag a in kerth*. In the second place, both forms in TH are the third person singular of the present-future of the verb *clamdera* 'to faint'; neither is a noun. The only instance of the noun *clamder* is the example in PC.

**klerhe** [clerhe] 'clear, brighten': GKK says that this word is unattested in the texts having been taken from Nance (1938). This is incorrect: *hagys lagasow a vith **clerys** ha why a vith kepar ha duow* 'and your eyes will be brightened and you will be like gods' TH 3a.

**kloesya** [clojya] 'to harrow': GKK says that this word has been taken from Nance (1938), being unattested in the texts. This is incorrect: *Dho **klodzha** glossing Occo, To harrow, to break the clods in a plough'd field* AB: 104c. Cf. *KLODZHA, dho klodzha, to harrow the clods* ACB: S.

**klos** [clos] 'close, closely': GKK includes the noun **klos** 'enclosure, close, precinct' which is not attested in the texts. It omits the adjective/adverb **clos** 'close; closely' which is well attested: *the'n beth men yv **clos*** RD 389; *degeys an darasov **cloys*** BM 1728; *aban oma **close** entrys* CW 529; *agen prevetta pur **glose*** CW 859.

**knowenn** [knofen] 'nut': GKK says this word is confined to two instances in Lhuyd. This is incorrect: *W. Kneyen, A Nut, Corn[ish] **Kynyphan*** AB: 8c; *Guedhan **knyfan** glossing Corylus, An hasle-tree* AB: 51c; ***Kynyphan** frenk glossing Juglans, A Wall-nut* AB: 74a; ***Kynyfan** glossing Nux, a nut* AB: 101a. Cf. *KYNYPHAN, a nut; kynyphan frenk, a French or wall nut; **kynyfan** ACB: S 2.

**knyv** [knew] 'fleece': GKK says this word is confined to a single instance (i.e. TH 23). This is incorrect: ***Kneu** glan glossing Vellus, a fleece of wool* AB: 170c. Cf. *KNÊU GLÂN, a fleece, a fell* ACB: S.

**knyvyas** [knyvyas] 'to shear': GKK says this verb is confined to a single instance in Lhuyd. This is incorrect: *the vos **knevys** y knew the ves* TH 23.

**kober** [cober] 'copper': GKK says this word is confined to a single instance each in OCV and Lhuyd. This is incorrect: *Corn[ish] **Kober**, Copper* AB: 21b; *Brest, **Kober** glossing Aes, Brass, Copper* AB: 41c; ***Kober** glossing Cuprum, Copper* AB: 53a; *Copper C[ornish] **Kober*** AB: 274b. Cf. *KOBER, copper* ACB: S; *wheal **cober**, a copper work* ACB: opposite B b 2.

**koen** [con] 'supper': GKK says this word is confined to a single instance in Lhuyd. This is incorrect: *crist worth an **goyn** a warnyas* PA 42c; *bener re gyffy the **con*** BM 1020; *CÔN, Coon, a supper* ACB: folio after M; *KOYN, a supper; Kon, id.* ACB: opposite S 2.

**koer** [cor] 'wax': GKK says this word is confined to one instance each in OCV, PC 2723 and Lhuyd. This is incorrect, since Lhuyd cites the word more than once: *W. Kuyr, Wax; Corn[ish] **Kor*** AB: 18a; *C[ornish] **Kor**, †koir glossing Cera* AB: 47b. Notice also *Corgwenyn Bees-wax* Borlase 382.

**kofer** [cofyr] 'coffer, strong-box': GKK says this word is confined to two instances in Lhuyd. This is incorrect: *in ov **cofyr** sur gorys* BM 3643; *COFER, a chest, coffer* ACB: M verso.

**kog** [cog] 'cuckoo': GKK says this is confined to two instances (i.e. PC 2890 and Lhuyd 52c). This is incorrect: ***Kog**, A cuckoo* AB: 241b. The word is further attested in the proverb *Ma an **Gog** a'n Luar wartha* from the Ustick MSS.

**kommen** [comen] 'common': GKK asserts that this adjective occurs only in the phrase ***comen** voys* BM 2710. This is incorrect: *not **commyn** the vab den* TH 5; ***commine** la a nature* TH 14a; *in agyn **comyn** talke* TH 21a; *an **common** welth* TH 25, 26; *yn **common** welth* TH 40a; *yn agan **commyn** eyth* TH 57a; *eth ew **commyn** trade* TH 57a; *rag **common** bara ha dewas* SA 63a.

**konfondya** [confundya] 'to confound': GKK says this verb is confined to a single instance in TH. This is incorrect: *dretho a veth **confundijs*** BM 2033.

**konsekratya** [consecratya] 'to consecrate': GKK says this word is confined to a single instance in BM. This is incorrect: *may halla an nenaf bos **consecratis*** SA 60a; *Rag henna tha orybe gee: nyng o corf Christ kyns ef the vos **consecratis**, bus osa the vos **consecratis** me a laver the gee, eth ew lymmen corf agen Arluth Jesu Christ* SA 62; *an bois the vos **consecratis*** SA 63; *Kyns an bara the vos **consecratis** ith thew bara* SA 62; *ny pan vo va **consecratis*** SA 63a.

**konsevya** [concevya] 'to conceive': GKK says that this word is confined to a single instance in TH. This is incorrect: *bones flogh vyth **concevijs*** BM 846; ***concevijs** y fue the guir* BM 859; *an map a fue **concevijs*** BM 887; ***conceyvys** yn mostethes* TH 7; *me a ve **conceviis*** TH 8a; ***conceviis** secretly* TH 28; ***concevya** anger* TH 28a.

**kontentya** [contentya] 'to content': GKK says this is confined to a single instance in CW. This is incorrect: *satisfies ha **contentys** gans mab den* TH 10a.

**kornhwilenn** [cornwhylen] 'lapwing': GKK says that the plural of this word is unattested except in place-names and alludes to Padel. GKK does not mention the occurrence of the name in 'Jowan Chy an Horth'; Lhuyd writes *dho Kuz **karn na huila** en Borrian* at JCH § 37 (AB: 253a). Nance renders this *dhe Gos **Kernwhyly** yn Beryan* 'to Cotnewilly Wood [the wood of the desolate place; lit. of the lapwings] in Buryan' Nance 1949: 45.

**kortesi** [cortesy] 'courtesy': GKK suggests that this word is confined to a single example in CW (i.e. *in **curtessye*** CW 763). This is incorrect: *mar luen oys a **corteysy*** BM 299.

**kosel** [cosel] 'quiet, peaceful': GKK tells us that this word confined to two examples, one each in BM and Lhuyd. This is incorrect: ***Cosel** my re bowesas* OM 2073; *purguir sevel in **cosel*** BM 2426; ***Kozal** glossing Piger, Slow, slothfull, etc.* AB: 120b; ***Kuzal** glossing Serenus, Clear, quiet, etc.* AB: 149a; ***COSEL**, softly, quietly* ACB: folio after M verso; ***CUSUAL**, softly, quietly…**cusual** ha têg, Sirra wheage, moaz pel, soft and fair, sweet Sir, goes far* ACB: two folios after M verso; ***CUZAL**, clear, serene* ACB: two folios after M verso; ***Cusal** ha têg, sirra wheage, Moaz pell* ACB: F f.

**kost** [cost] 'coast': GKK says this word is taken from Nance (1938) and is otherwise unattested. This is incorrect: *py **cost** yma trygys* OM 1552; *Jhesus a theth then **costes** a Cesarye Philippi* TH 43a; *eff a gemeras owne a drega na fella in **cost** na* TH 46a.

**kostenn** [costen] 'shield, target': GKK says that this word is confined to a single instance in Lhuyd. This is incorrect: ***Kostan** glossing Clypeus, A shield, buckler or target* AB: 48a; ***Kostan** glossing Parma, A little round shield, target or buckler* AB 113b; ***Kostan** glossing Scutum, A buckler, a shield, a target, a scutcheon* AB: 147a; *C[ornish] **Kostan** glossing SCUTUM* AB: 297a; ***COSTAN**, a bucker, shield or target* ACB: two folios after M verso.

**kowl** [cowl] 'soup': GKK says this word is confined to OCV. This is incorrect: *bynytha ny efyth **coul*** OM 2701; *bynytha na effo **coul*** PC 1610; *the guthel **covle*** BM 2392; *As Evos **kowl**, Sup up your broth; for Evough agos **kowl*** AB: 231c; ***Kaul**, Broth from Caulis* AB: 241a; ***COUL**, broth, porridge* ACB: folio after M verso.

**kowsesyow** [cowsesow, cowsejyow] abstract pl. 'heart, conscience': GKK says the word is confined to a single instance in BM. This is incorrect: *na dreyle y **gousesow*** PC 885.

**krakkya** [crackya] 'to crack': GKK says that this word is confined to two instances in PA (i.e. PA 139a and 164b). This is incorrect: *ran a **crakkyas*** BM: 1582.

**krambla** [crambla] 'to climb': GKK says this verb is confined to one occurrence in Lhuyd. This is inocrrect: *Dho **grambla** glossing Ascendo, To Climb, to Ascend* AB: 43c;

*Dho* **grambla** glossing *Scando, To mount, to climb or get up* AB: 145b. Cf. *GRAMBLA, dho* **grambla***, to climb, to scramble* ACB: opposite Q.

**kreghyn** [crehyn] 'skins': GKK says this, the plural of *kroghen* [crohen] 'skin', is confined to a single instance in CW (i.e. line 1477). This is incorrect: *fatell rons y dos in crehyn devas* TH 19a.

**kreupya** [cruppya] 'to creep': GKK says that this word is confined to one instance in CW. This is incorect: *a wra cruppya ha slynckya* CW 912-13; *me a vyn dallath cruppya ha slyncya* CW 923-24.

**krevhe** [crefhe] 'to strengthen': GKK says that this verb is confined to a single instance from the writings of Nicholas Boson. This is incorrect: *A ra creffe an collonow* TH 52; *sertifyes* (*vel crefeis*) TH 56; SA: *the creffe agen corfow* SA 63a.

**kria** [crya] 'to cry': GKK says this verb is confined to a single instance in the *Ordinalia*. This is incorrect: *ov crye* OM 1418; *ha mercy crye* PC 2062; *ow crye* PC 2242; *the crye* PC 2249; *warbarth ol sur crye* PC 2475; *cryeugh fast* PC 2477; *pup ol ese ow crye* PC 3127; *ymons ow crye* RD 2304; *mar creya war crist* BM 617; *cryaff warnogh* BM 1047; *agen creya* BM 1531; *war crist y creya* BM 1816; *ha creya pup vr* 1825; *na ve creya warnogh why* BM 2169; *am creya vy* BM 3620; *ny a cry* BM 3961; *mercy creyays* BM 4432; *crya mercy* TH 9a; *ow crya out* TH 40a; *creiez chei a Horr* BF: 15; *Ha Deu kries an ebron neve* BF: 52; *Ha Deu kriez an teer zeth* BF: 52; *Adam a gryaze* RC 23: 185; *e griaz thonze* RC 23: 192; *kreiez en Ladin* AB: 223; *CRIA, to call; ha Dew a criaz, and God called* ACB: two folios after M. Cf. *dho* **kreia***, to name, to invite;* **kreias, kreies, kreiz***, called, invited* ACB: opposite S 2.

**kribenn** [cryben] 'comb': GKK says the word is confined to a single instance in Lhuyd. This is incorrect: *W. Krib, A Comb; Corn*[ish] *Kriban: Kriban kuliog, a Cock's Comb* AB: 13c; *Kriban* glossing *Crista, A crest* AB: 52b; *Kriban mel* glossing *Favus, A honey-comb* AB: 59a; *Kriban, A birds crest* AB: 240c; *CRIBAN, a comb, crest or tuft, as of a lapwing, &c.* ACB: two folios after M.

**kristonya** [crystonya] 'to christen': GKK says this verb is not attested in the texts but has been taken from Nance's 1955 dictionary. This is incorrect: *an re na a throlla an flehis the vos besitthis ha cristonys* TH 37a.

**kriv** [cryf] 'raw, unripe': GKK says this word is derived from Cornish English dialect, since it is not attested in the texts. This is incorrect: *Bara ew trylys theworth ann eyl elyment th'e gela rag an vosan ny mar gwan ow kemeras skruth tha thybbry kygg kreff* 'bread is converted from one element to another because we are so weak as to shudder at eating raw flesh' SA 66a; *Kriv* glossing *Crudus, Crude* [or cold] *raw; green or new made; unripe* AB: 52c; *CRIV, crude, raw* AB: two folios after M verso.

**kroenek** [cronek] 'toad': GKK says that this word occurs between 4-9 times. This is incorrect: *croinoc* glossing *rubeta* [toad] OCV 619; *may 30 gweth agis cronek* PA 47d; *gans cronek dv* OM 1778; *the weth vythons the'n cronek* PC 2732; *Latin. Rana, Corn*[ish] *Kranag, A Frog* AB: 9b; *Corn*[ish] *Kranag, A Frog* AB: 11c; *C*[ornish] *Cranag, Rana* AB: 33a; *Kranag diu* glossing *Bufo, A Toad* AB: 45a; *Kuilken, kranag melyn; pedn diu.* †*Guilskin,* †*kroniok* glossing *Rana, A frog, a paddock* AB: 136b; *Kranag, A frog or toad;* AB: 240c; *C*[ornish] *K-ranag* glossing *A Frog* AB: 277a; †*CROINOC, a lizard; cro nekdu* [sic]*, a toad* ACB: two folios after M verso; *Croinoc, a Land Toad...Cronek, id.* Borlase 382.

**krommenn** [cromman] 'sickle, hook': GKK says this word is confined to a single occurrence in Lhuyd. This is incorrect: *Krymman, A Hook; Corn*[ish] *Krobman* AB: 9b; *krobman...kromman* AB: 223; *CROBMAN, a brook, a hook* ACB: two folios after M; *Krobman, a Hook* Borlase 396.

**kronk, -ys** [cronk, -ys] 'blow': according to GKK the word unattested in the texts. This is incorrect: *eff a suffras ragan ny lyas rebuk, keffrys cronkys ha'n moyha cruell myrnans* TH 24.

**kropya** [cropya] 'to penetrate': GKK claims that this wrord is confined to a single instance in PA and CW. This is incorrect: *ha dreyn lym ha scharp ynne a grup bys yn empynyon* PC 2119-20.

**krothaek** [crothak] 'big-bellied': GKK says this word is not attested. This is incorrect: *te foole crothacke* 'you big-bellied fool' CW 1105.

**kroust** [crowst] 'picnic lunch': GKK says this word is confined to the *Ordinalia* and Lhuyd and occurs 2-3 times. This is incorrect: *kemeres croust hag eve* OM 1901; *Krust* glossing *Merenda, A beaver or afternoons nuncheon* AB: 89b; *CROUST, an afternoon's nuncheon; a beaver* ACB: two folios after M; *Crwst, Eating between Meals* Borlase 382; *Krust, An Afternoon's Luncheon* Borlase 396;.

**krowsvaner** [crowsvaner] 'banner with cross': GKK says that this word is not attested in the texts. This is incorrect: *ganso del fethas yn cas worth crousbaner* RD 579-80.

**krowsya** [crowsya] 'to crucify': GKK says this verb is confined to 2-3 instances in the *Ordinalia*. This is incorrect: *rag an keth re ren crowse* PA 185b; *rag bos Ihesus crist crowsys* PA 189c; *crousyough ef* PC 2166; *the'th crousye* PC 2184; *agas myghtern crousys* PC 2360; *bos crousys* PC 2390; *may fo an ihesu crousys* PC 2478; *ha crous ihesu an fals guas* PC 2486; *may fo crousys* PC 2504; *pren th'y crousye* PC 2535; *kepar hag ef on crousys* PC 2900; *a fue crousys* RD 737; *the vos crowsyys* TH 47. Cf. *CROUSE, to crucify; crousys, crucified* ACB: two folios after M.

**kryjyans** [crejyans] 'faith, belief: GKK criticizes Nance for taking this word to be feminine and cites the line *helma ov cregyans yth yv* BM 838 as proof that the word is masculine. As contrary evidence one might cite *mar tregowhe in gregyans na* CW 176. It is true that most words in *-ans* are masculine, but is quite likely that *crejyans* in some forms of Cornish had attracted to itself the gender of *feth, fyth* 'faith.'

**krytyk** [crytyk] 'critic': GKK says this word is unattested and has been taken from Nance (1955). This is incorrect: *ha frederyanz an Creteco ha'n Koth-skreferyon* 'and the opinion of the critics and the historians' AB: 224.

**kulyek-kenys** [culyek kenys] '*cock-crow': GKK says that this term means 'cock-crow' but is not attested in the texts, being taken from Nance's 1938 dictionary. This is doubly incorrect. The phrase is attested but has been misunderstood. (Nance gives *culyek-kenys* 'cock-crow' without an asterisk, implying that the term is attested). Jesus says to Peter at the last supper: *peder, me a leuer thy's kyns ys bos kullyek kenys terguyth y wregh ov naghe* PC 901-03. *Kenys* here is not a noun, but the verbal adjective *kenys* of *cana* used actively. One should translate: 'Peter, I say unto thee: before that cock shall have crowed, three times thou shalt deny me.' The active use of the verbal adjective is common in Middle Cornish, particularly with *devethys* 'come', *gyllys* 'gone', *cothys* 'fallen', etc.

**kuruna** [curuna] 'to crown': GKK says this verb is confined to 2-3 instances in Middle Cornish. This is incorrect: *te yw mygtern cvrvnys* PA 136c; *gans spern curunys* PA 165b; *salmon ov map koroneugh* OM 2347; *may hallo bos kerenys* OM 2374; *ha kerenys a ver dermyn* OM 2381; *whare myghtern kervnys* OM 2391; *rag why thu'm kerune* OM 2398; *guregh y curene* PC 2064; *me a vyn y curune* PC 2116; *nowyth curunys* PC 2124; *emperour curunys* BM 2515; *gans curen sperne curuneys* BM 3037.

**kusulya** [cusulya] 'to advise, take counsel': GKK's attestation code suggests that this verb is attested in Middle Cornish only. This is incorrect: *ny vynsan theth cossylya* CW 670; *hag a'the cossyllyas* CW 771; *hei a kynsiliaz gen nebyn vanah* AB: 252a.

**kykesow** [kekesow] 'Cornish heath (*Erica vagans*)': *E. vagans* is very rare in Cornwall except on the Lizard peninsula. The name *kekesow* occurs in Cornish dialect as *kekezza*. GKK says the word is a late form because *-k-* is not Cornish. This is incorrect. *Kekesow* is almost certainly in origin two words. The second element I take to be *kesow* 'turf, peat' (cf. *Whelas tees tha trehe kesow* 'To seek for people to cut turf' ACB F f 2). The first element may be *cuf* 'dear one' or *cugh* 'hood'. Most probably, however, it is *clegh* 'bells' and *\*clegh kesow* 'bells of the turf' has been simplified (probably in English dialect) to *\*ke' kesow*. With the name cf. the vernacular term for *Erica cinerea* 'bell-heather'. *Kekesow* is not a late form', but rather a noun phrase.

**kystven** [kystven] 'stone coffin': GKK correctly says word is from Borlase. The dictionary suggests, however, that the word is attested once only. This is incorrect. In the form **Kist-vaen** the word is used by Borlase on pp. 151, 182, 197 x 3, 214 x 2. 217 and 218 x 5.

**lafyl** [lafyl] 'lawful': GKK suggests that this word is confined to a single instance at BM 3401 [recte 4301]. This is incorrect: *an pith nag o ragan* **leafull** TH 10; *an pith a rella desyrya theworta* **lafull** TH 39a; *nyns ew* **lawfull** *folysly the wull resystens* TH 50a

**latimer** [latymer] 'translator': GKK says this word is a modern coinage taken from Nance's 1938 dictionary. This is incorrect. William Hals (1655-1737?) of Ventongimps wrote a Cornish vocabulary variously called *An* **Ladymer** *ay Kernow*, *An* **Latimer** *ay Kernou* or *An* **Lhadymer** *ay Kernou*, which is now in the National Library of Wales (see Ellis: 105-06). In a note on a letter he received from Lhuyd Thomas Tonkin writes: 'I likewise sent [Lhuyd] a specimen of Mr. *Hals's* **Latimer** *ay Kernow* of all the letter A, and part of B.' ACB: folio after H h 2 verso. Cf. Jenner's comments in his discussion of the Bilbao MS, where he suggests that Hals made up the word *Ladymer* from Welsh *Lladmer*.

**lemmel** [lemmel] 'to leap': GKK says that the word is confined to a single occurrence in Lhuyd. This is incorrect: *Dho* **lebmal** glossing *Salio, To leap, dance, hop*, etc. AB: 143c; *Dho* **lebmal** glossing *Salto To dance, hop or skip* AB: 143c; †*lemal, To leap, now* **Lebmal** AB 231b; †**Lemmel** †**lebmal**, *To leap* AB: 245b; *reys yw meeras dueth, ken* **lemmel** *uneth* Scawen MSS. Notice also *drizlebmal* AB: 222; *DRIZ-LEBMAL, to leap over* ACB: folio after N verso; *LEBMAL, dho* **lebmal**, *to leap, dance, skip about* ACB: folio after S 2.

**leswedh** [lejer] 'frying pan': GKK claims that this word is confined to a single instance in Lhuyd. This is incorrect: **Letshar** glossing *Frixorium; A frying-pan* AB: 61c; **Letshar** glossing *Sartago, A frying-pan* AB: 144. Cf. *LETSHAR, a frying-pan* ACB: folio after S 2 verso. The etymology is uncertain. Perhaps we should spell the word <lecher>.

**leveryans** [leveryans] 'pronunciation': GKK says that the singular of this word is unattested. This is incorrect: *uar lerh* **Laveryanz** *an Termen nei* AB: 223; *ha aban yu an* **laveryanz** *anydha*, **laverryanz** *kergorryz* AB: 223; *Enradn rag bos an* **laveryanz** *anydha hedh lauer* AB: 223; *uel an* **laveryanz** *ney ha* **laveryanz** *Tiz Lezou* AB: 223.

**lieskweyth** [lyesgweyth] 'many times': GKK says this word comes from Nance (1952), since it is not attested in the texts. This is incorrect: **lyes guyth** *me re bysys* PC 884; *mes company* **leasgwyth** *a bub beast* CW 1673. The word is already in Nance (1938), where he cites PC as his source.

**Lostwydhyel** [Lostwydhyel] 'Lostwithiel': GKK says the toponym is confined to a single instance in BM. This is incorrect. The name occurs not in BM, but in OM: **lostuthyel** *ha lanerchy* OM 2400.

**Loundres** [Loundres] 'London': according to GKK this place-name occurs 2-3 times in the texts. This is incorrect: *Pes myllder eus alemma de* **Londres** *Borde; Senezeriou Pou Kernou en* **Loundrez** AB: 222; *Leverva Cotten en* **Loundrez** AB: 222; *reb vor* **Loundres**

*Tur* BF: 58; *Mee rese mos tha* **Loundres** *mes a thorow* Bilbao MS; *an Tempel K'res en*
**Loundres** LAM: 238; *an tiz a* **Loundrez** *a credgi boz gwir* Gwavas (quoted in Ellis: 96);
*LOUNDREZ, London* ACB: two folios after S 2.

**lughesenn** [luhesen] 'lightning': GKK says this word is confined to a single instance in
BM. This is incorrect. The single instance is in RD: *th'y lesky vn* **luhesen** RD 293.

**luk** [luck] 'luck; enough': GKK says that this is both a noun meaning 'luck' and an
adjective meaning 'enough'. It not an adjective, but an adverb. Curiously GKK,
without specifying which sense is involved, says that the word is confined to a
single instance in Lhuyd. This is incorrect. The adverb is common in Late Cornish:
*Satis... sufficiently, enough.* C[*ornish*] **Lyk**, *laur* AB: 144c; *The Adverbs* **Lyk** *and Laur or*
*laver* [*enough*] *are placed contrary to what we use, after the Noun:... They say Pysgoz* **lyk**
*and pysgoz laver* AB: 248c; **Lyk** *laur and lauer, Enough* AB: 249a; *Ha skienz* **lyk** *en Tavaz*
*Pou* BF: 46; *LUCK, enough—Luk,* **Lyk** ACB: opposite T; *En* [leg. *eu*] *an bara pebes* **luck**?
ACB: opposite F f 2; *Ese leath* **luck** *gen veu?* ACB: F f 2. I can find only one example
of the noun: *ma kalliz* **luk** *dha nei* BF: 18.

**lymma** [lemma] 'to sharpen, to whet': GKK says this word is derived from Nance
(1938), being unattested in the texts. This is incorrect: *gans ow boell nowyth* **lemmys**
CW 2282; *Dho* **lebma** glossing *Acuo, To Whet or Sharpen* AB: 41b. Cf. *LEBMA, dho*
**lebma**, *to whet, sharpen;* **lebmys**, *sharpened* ACB: folio after S 2.

**lytherenn** [lytheren] 'letter': GKK says this word is confined to 2 instances in OCV and
Pryce. This is incorrect: *gorra an* **litheren** *b, arag an* **litheren** *m* AB: 223; *gorra an*
**letheren** *d, arag an* **letheren** *n* AB: 223; *gorra an* **letheren** *d arag s* AB: 223; *an uynyn*
**letheren** *g* AB: 223; *an* **letheren** *t, rag ch* AB: 223; *an* **letheren** *t, rag s* AB: 223; cf.
*LETHER,* **Letheren**, *a litter; pl.* **Letherau** ACB: folio after S 2 verso. GKK suggests that
the plural of this word should be the unattested *\*lytherennow.* The plural is attested,
however, in the form *lytherow: Litera...a letter in a book; a bill or scroll; ones hand writing*
*C* †**Litheren** *plur.* **Litherou** AB: 80b; *ter* **lethero** *kessonyz an deau Davadzheth ma* AB: 223;
*LETHER,* **Letheren**, *a litter; pl.* **Letherau** ACB: folio after S 2 verso; †*LITHEREN, a*
*letter; pl.* **Litherow** ACB: folio after S 2 verso.

**lyverva** [lyverva] 'library': GKK says this word is confined to a single instance in
Lhuyd. This is incorrect: *en* **Levarva** *Cotten en Loundrez* AB: 222; *gerlevran Kernûak*
**Levarva** *Cotten* AB: 223; *ez lebmyn en* **Levarva** *Cotten* AB: 223; *en* **Levarva** *an mer-*
*dheskyz ha'n mer skientek Bednzhivik* AB: 223; *en* **Levarva** *Kollek Iesu en Red Ousk* AB:
223; *levarva, a library* ACB: folio after S 2 verso.

**mayn** [mayn] 'means': GKK says that this word is confined to one example each in PA
and BM. This is incorrect: *mayn yntreze a ve gurys* PA 8c; *meen drethon a veth kefys* BM
1406; *an* **mean** *vs intra du ha den* TH 11; *mean a vova gothvethis* TH 50a.

**melyn** [melen] 'yellow': GKK cites this word as an adjective. It omits to mention that
the word is also used as a noun: **Melyn** *oi* glossing *Vitellus, The yolk of an egg* AB:
175a; **Melyn**-*oi yellow of an egg* Borlase 399; cf. *MELYN-ÔI, the yolk of an egg* ACB: T 2
verso. Nance (1938: 107) has *melen-oy* 'egg yolk'.

**menyster** [menyster] 'minister': GKK says that neither the singular nor the plural is
attested, both being taken from Nance's 1938 dictionary. This is incorrect: *menistror*
glossing *pincerna* ['butler'] OCV; †**Menistror** glossing *Pincerna* AB: 120b; *obedyens res*
*thyn* **minister** TH 42a; *an re na a ve in* **ministers** *in egglos a Crist* TH 41a; *appoyntya the*
*vos pen* **ministers** *war oll y misteris* TH 52a; *the vos* **mynisters** *a'n kythsame sacrament*
*benegas ma* TH 52a. Cf. †*MENISTROR, a butler, buyt as the word come from minister, is*
*may sigifny* [sic] *any other attendant* ACB: T 2.

**menystra** [menystra] 'to administer': GKK says that this word is confined to a single occurrence at BM 523. This is incorrect: *han sacrements vii kefris gòl ha guyth* **menystrys** *wose helma* BM 997-99; *the wull an obereth a* **mynystra** *rag edyfya an corfe a Crist* TH 42.

**meri** [mery] 'merry': GKK says this word is confined to one instance each in OM and BM. This is incorrect: *ny a yl bos fest* **mery** OM 2466; *bethugh* **mery** BM 292; *maga* **fery** *avel hok* BM 1901; *bos pur* **very** CW 601; *bos pur* **verry** CW 692.

**merk** [merk, mark] 'mark': GKK says the plural *\*merkyow* occurs in TH. This is incorrect. The error comes from misreading the second plural imperative of *merkya*, *markya* 'notice' (see next note).

**merkya** [merkya] 'to mark': GKK says this verb is confined to TH, where it is attested 2-3 times. This is incorrect on both counts: *Rag the* **verkye** *me a gura* OM 602; *avel wy* **mark** *attahy* 'like an egg, behold her, look!' BM: 3953; *lemmyn* **merkyow** TH 1a; **markyow** *in ta* TH 6; **merkyow** *an exampill ma* TH 6a; **merkyow** *gyrryow crist* TH 27a; **markyow** *pandr' egy* TH 32; **merkya**, *notya, ha done in keth* TH 34a; *mar menogh* **merkya** TH 38a; *the vos* **merkyys** TH 52a; **merkyow** *pan dra* TH 53; *ow mabe* **merke** *an gyrryow ma* CW 1952; *Mi rygmarkia* AB: 223; *gerrio-ma* **markyz** AB: 223.

**Meryasek** [Meryasek] 'Meriasek': GKK says this name is confined to BM. This is incorrect: *adro an vledhan 388 dadn Kenan* **Meriazhek** AB: 224. In the form *Merrasicks, Merrasickers, Moragicks, Mearagaks, Merry-geeks* and *Mera-jacks* it also survived in Cornish English (see page 13 above). This is not mentioned by GKK.

**methek** [methek] 'ashamed': GKK says that this word is confined to a single occurrence in TH. This in incorrect: *Myterne Davith o* **methek** *rag y pehosow* TH 8a; *nyns o ef* **methek** *the confessia* TH 8a; *na esow ny the vos* **methek** *the confessia an stat* TH 9a; *Ha na esow ny the vos* **methek** *the confessia nag ony* TH 9a; *na esow ny the vos* **methek** *the confessia agan foly* TH 9a; *bos* **methek** *ha kemeras sham* TH 29a.

**Meurth** [Merth] 'Tuesday; March': GKK says this word is confined to a single instance in Lhuyd. This is incorrect: *W. Dydh Maurth, Tuesday; Corn*[ish] *De* **Merh** AB: 14c; *tuesday. C*[ornish] *De* **merh** AB: 54c; **Demer**, *Tuesday* Borlase 383b; *De* **Merh**, *Tuesday* ABC: N verso; **MERH**:...*also, the month of March* ACB: T 2 verso; **Merh**, *March* ACB: folio after T 2; *Flô vye gennes en Miz-***merh** ACB: two folios after F f 2.

**milweyth** [mylweyth] 'a thousand times': GKK says that this word has been taken from Nance (1938), since it is unattested in the texts. This is incorrect: *me re'n cusullyes* **mylwyth** PC 1811; *wolcom* **myl-wyth** *yn ow hel* PC 937; *Theth dewov try* **mylwyth** *fy* BM 915; *thys* **mylwyth** *ha ʒe crist fy* BM 1229; *fy* **mylwyth** *then crustunyon* BM 3510; **mylwyth** *in nos* BM 4452; *Ha* **mylwyth** *purguir in geth* BM 4455; **Miluyth**, *A thousand times* AB: 248c. Cf. **Miluith**, *a thousand times* ACB: folio after T 2.

**mingow** [myngow] 'with lying mouth': GKK says this occurs once in BM. This is incorrect: *an plos* **myngov** BM 2379; *dyso* **myngov** BM 2655.

**mis-Ebryl, mis-Est, mis-Genver, mis-Hwevrer** [mys Ebrel, mys Est, mys Genver, mys Whevrel] 'April, August, January, February': I have already dealt with *mis-Est* [mys Est] above. GKK says that all these month names are unattested anywhere in the texts. This is incorrect. Pryce lists all the months as follows (I omit his English forms and his etymologies): ***Mîs-GENVER; Mîs-HUEVRAL; MIZ-MERH; MIZ-EBRALL; MIZ-M ; MIZ-EPHAN; MIZ-GOREPHAN; MIZ-EAST; MIZ-GUEDN-GALA; MIZ-HEDRA; MIZ-DIU; MIZ-KEVARDHIN*** [leg *KEVARDHIU*] ACB: F f 2 verso. He also cites the names of the month under *Mis* 'month' as follows: *mîs* **Yenver**... **Huevral**... **Merh**... **Ebral**... **Me**... **Ephan**... **Gorephan**... **East**... **Guedngala**... **Hedra**... *Mis diu*...

*Kevardhin* ACB: folio after T 2. Notice also *Miz ebral* glossing *Aprilis* AB: [4]3b and *Miz Ebral Pempas Dydh, sitack canz ha Deg* BF: 46.

**mis-Hedra** [mys Hedra] 'October': GKK says that this is confined to a single instance in Lhuyd. This is incorrect: *an Kensa journa a messe Heddra an Centle* BF: 38; *Hedra, October* ACB: folio after T 2; *MIZ-HEDRA, (October)* ACB: F f 2 verso.

**mis-Metheven** [mys Efen] 'June': GKK says the name is confined to a single instance in Lhuyd. This is incorrect: *Ov gol a veth suer in mes metheven* BM 4302-03; *C[ornish] Efin, Junius* AB: 33a; *Ephan, June* ACB: folio after T 2; *MIZ-EPHAN, (June)* ACB: F f 2 verso. George adds a note: 'Lhuyd actually wrote *miz ephan*, which may mean the month's name was shortened in LateC, as in colloquial Breton *miz even* for *miz mezheven*.' The compiler is clearly unaware of *Efin, Ephan* in Lhuyd and Pryce.

**mita, -tys** [myta, -tys] 'mites': GKK asserts that this word has been taken from Nance (1938), and is unattested in the texts. This is incorrect: *a ruke offrennia ii mittes* SA 64.

**miter** [myter] 'mitre': GKK says that the singular occurs once in BM and the plural once in OM. This is incorrect. Both instances are singular: *kymmer the vytour whare* OM 2615; *settyn muter war y ben* BM 3010.

**moen** [mun] 'ore': GKK says this word is unattested apart from place-names. This is incorrect, since Borlase writes *Mun (Mooun, or Moowyn id. W[elsh])* any fusible Metal 400.

**mokkya** [mockya] 'to mock': GKK says the word is confined to a single instance in TH. This is incorrect: *why ew mockys gonsa* TH 14a; *seducia ha ga mockya* TH 49a.

**molas** [molas] 'molasses': GKK says this word comes from Nance (1938), being unattested in the texts. This is incorrect. Nance got the word from Borlase; see Nance (1938) s.v. *lollas*.

**mollothek** [mollothek] 'accursed': GKK says this word is confined to two examples in PA. This is incorrect. The word occurs once only in PA (i.e. PA 47c). The word does occur in twice in BM, however: *ty map molothek* BM 781; *ty yv thymo molothek* BM 2651.

**morthol** [morthol] 'hammer': GKK says that the singular is confined to a single instance in Lhuyd. This is incorrect: *Morthol* glossing *Malleus, A mallet, a hammer* AB: 84c; *Morthol bian* glossing *Malleolus, A little hammer, a beetle* AB: 84b. Note also *MORTHOL, a hammer, beetle, or maul* ACB: folio after T 2 verso; *Mortholl, a Hammer* Borlase 400.

**morvil** [morvyl] 'whale': GKK recommends the plural *\*morviles* [morvylas] on the grounds that the plural is not attested in the texts. This is incorrect. The plural is attested: *Morvil, s.m. A whale…Pl. morvilow* LCB s.v.; *Ha Dew a wrug an morvilow bras* LCB: 395.

**movya** [muvya] 'to move': GKK says this is confined to 2-3 examples in TH. This is incorrect: *ihesus crist a ve mevijs* PA 4b; *my a vyn kyns es dybarth muvye omma certan tra* BM 259-60; *del ens y moviis* TH 18; *yth yll bos movyes* TH 29a; *ow movya thotha* TH 37a; *thega movya y* TH 44a; *ow movya ve* TH 50.

**Moyses** [Moyses] 'Moses': GKK says this personal name is confined to a single instance in the *Ordinalia*. This is incorrect: *moyses moyses saf ena* OM 1403; *del lauaraf thy's moyses* OM 1433; *lauer moyses* OM 1443; *py tyller yma moyses* OM 1551; *reys yv thy's gorre moyses* OM 1572; *the geusel sur orth moyes* OM 1583; *moyses me a commond thy's* OM 1585; *gallas moyses ha'y pobel* OM 1627; *moyses thy'so lauara* OM 1645; *dev a erghys thy's moyses* OM 1663; *yma moyses pel gyllys* OM 1682; *dev moyses a wruk hemma* 1702; *moyses whek ny a dreha* OM 1715; *moyses del oge den mas* OM 1767; *Ellas moyses ogh tru tru* OM 1777; *moyses mar sos profus lel* OM 1799; *moyses kemer the* *welen* OM 1841; **moyses** *sur my re beghas* OM 1863; *a plansas* **moyses** *hep mar* OM 1931; *a wruk* **moyses** *the planse* OM 1946; *laha* **moyses** *th'm yma* PC 1644; *pur wyr a thalleth* **moyses** RD 1484; *in tyrmyn* **moyses** TH 14; *an la a* **moyses** TH 14; *a la* **moyses** TH 26a; *heno an la* **moyses** TH 27; *in la* **moyses** TH 27a; *the wetha lais* **moyses** TH 27a; *folya an la* **moyses** TH 27a; *in chare* **moyses** TH 34.

**musura** [musura] 'to measure': GKK says this verb is confined to a single unnamed occurrence in Middle Cornish. This is incorrect: *musur y trylles* OM 393; *musurough ef yn len* OM 2506; *my a'n* **musur** OM 2507; *otteve* **musurys** *da* OM 2513; *mar len* **musurys** OM 2550; *may hallo bos* **musurys** OM 2566; *my re wruk y* **vusure** OM 2568; **myserough** *tol th'y thule* PC 2740.

**mynn** [myn] 'young goat, kid': GKK recommends the plural *\*mynnow*, because the plural is not attested. This is incorrect: *Devas ean gever ha* **menas** *Sheep lambs goats and kids* Bilbao MS.

**mysteri** [mystery] 'mystery': GKK suggests that this word is confined to a single instance in CW (i.e. CW 2119). This is incorrect: *y bos an sacrament ma marvelus worthy* **mystery** TH 52-52a; *war oll y* **misteris** TH 52a; *i'n* **mystery** *na* TH 52a; *pan veny oll endewis gans an* **mysteris** *benegas ma* SA 60; *eth esan ny o recevia dan an lell* **mystery** *kigg a'y corf benegas.* SA 61.

**Nadelik** [Nadelek] 'Christmas': GKK implies that this word occurs once in Lhuyd and once in Pryce. This is incorrect: *Corn[ish].* **Nedelik** AB 17a; *C[ornish]* **Nadelik**; *Deu* **nadelik** AB: 97a; *NADELIK, one's birthday; Deu* **nadelik**, *Christmas* ACB: two folios after T 2; *Miz-du ken* **Nadelik** ACB: two folios after F f 2; *Ha Have en Guave terebah* **Nedelack** Ustick MSS. George adds a note: 'Regular development would have given *\*Nadolyk.*' This is also incorrect. The original form was *\*Natâlicia*, where the originally unstressed long *â* would have given *o* in Welsh quite regularly, whence Welsh *Nadolig.* In Cornish and Breton, however, unstressed long *â* would have given *e* via *œ*. Lhuyd's *Nadelik* is exactly what one would expect the Cornish form to be. Compare Breton *Nedeleg.*

**naswydh** [nasweth] 'needle': GKK says this word is confined to 2-3 instances in Middle and Late Cornish together. This is incorrect: *der crov* **nasweth** BM 468; *W. Nodwydh, A Needle; Corn[ish]* **Nadzhedh** AB: 10b; **Nadzhedh** *glossing Acus, A Needle* AB: 41b; *C[ornish]* **Nadzhedh** *glossing ACUS* AB: 290a. Cf. *NADZHEDH, a needle* ACB: two folios after T 2. Lhuyd also writes *nadzha* in his unpublished glossary.

**nawves** [nawves] 'ninth': GKK says this is confined to two instances in Lhuyd. This is incorrect: **Nauhuas** *glossing Nonus, The ninth* AB: 100a; **Nahuaz**, *The ninth* AB: 243b; **nauhuas**, *the ninth* ACB: opposite U; **Nawas**, *the ninth* ACB: F f 2 verso.

**negedhek** [negedhek] 'negative': GKK claims this modern coinage was invented by J[ulyan] G. H[olmes]. This is incorrect: **negedhek**, *adj., negative (W)* (Nance 1938: 117); *negative, n. \*negeth, an nagha, m.; a[dj.]* **negedhek**, *a-nagh* (Nance 1952: 115).

**neyth, -ow** [neyth, -ow] 'nests, nests': GKK tells us that, apart from place-names, the singular is confined to 2-3 examples in Old and Late Cornish. This is incorrect: *neid glossing nidus ['nest']* OCV; **nyth** *heb oy atte omme* BM 3302; *Nidus...C[ornish]* **Neith**, †*nid* AB: 99a; †*NEID, a nest. Hod[ie]* **Nyth** ACB: opposite U; *NYTH.—See NEID* ACB: opposite U 2. GKK also says that the plural is confined to a single instance in Middle Cornish. This is incorrect. I am unable to find an example of the plural in Middle Cornish (although the verb *nyeʒy* 'to nest' does occur at PA 206c). George is apparently unaware, however, that the plural is well attested in Late Cornish: **Neitho**, *Nests* AB: 242c; *Mi 'rig guelaz an Karnou idzha an gullez ha'n idhen mor aral kil y ge* **neitho** AB: 245a; *plural* **Nythow** *(s.v. †NEID)* ACB: opposite U.

**nivera** [nyvera] 'to enumerate': GKK says this verb is confined to one occurrence in PA (i.e. *neuera oll y yscren* PA 183c). This is incorrect: *ny yllons bos **nyfyrys*** OM 1544; *ny yllons bos **nyfyrys*** RD 558; ***Nivera**, Reckon or number; **Nivyryz**, Reckon'd* AB: 248a.

**nomber** [nomber] 'number': GKK's code {M: 3} says this word occurs 4-9 times in Middle Cornish. This is incorrect on both counts: *cans vyl yn **nomber*** OM 1614; ***numbyr** a tremmyl* BM 1516; *heb **numbyr*** BM 3999; ***number** a persons* TH 1a; *mar ver in **number*** TH 8a; *plurel **number*** TH 8a; *an **number** an elect* TH 22a; ***numbyr** bras* TH 31a; ***numbyr** a lyas* TH 44a; *heb **number*** CW 1321; *heb **number*** CW 1990.

**offrynna** [offrynna] 'to offer, to sacrifice': GKK's code {3} means that this word occurs between 4 and 9 times. This is incorrect: *thotho gvetyeugh **offrynne*** OM 441; *ny vynna **offrynne*** OM 500; *hag a **offryn** thy's whare* OM 512; *warnythy my a **offryn*** OM 11183; *bugh **offrynne** my a vyn* OM 1185; *my a **offryn** hep lettye* OM 1194; *goth dek scon my a **offryn*** OM 1195; *my a **offrynn** mallart da* OM 1199; *my a **offryn** scon aral* OM 1205; *y **offrynne** reys yv thy's* OM 1280; *ow map ysak **offrynnys*** OM 1287; *rag **offrynna*** OM 1307; *may fythe gy **offrynnys*** OM 1327; ***offrynnye** an keth mols ma* OM 1384; ***offrynnys** sur me a vyn* BM 3392; ***offrynnyaff** pen margh* BM 3400; *me a **offren*** BM 3407; *me a **offren** lawen cath* BM 3413; *a ruke **offrennia** ii mittes* SA 64; *rag **offryna**, to offer* ABC: opposite U 2.

**osta** [osta] 'thou art': GKK says this form is not attested in Middle Cornish. This is incorrect. It occurs in TH: *benegas **osta** ge* 'blessed art thou' TH 44.

**outray** [outray] 'outrage': GKK says this word is unattested. This is incorrect: *Del yw scrifys prest yma adro ʒynny gans **otry*** PA 21a, rhyming with *pray* and *joy*. The word should perhaps be spelt <otray>.

**oy** [oy] 'egg': GKK says the plural is unattested. This is incorrect: *Mathtath drewgh **eyo** hag amanyn de vi* 'Mayde, brynge me egges and butter' Borde; *OYE, pl. **Oyow**, an egg... **oyow** ethen, bird's eggs* ACB: U 2 verso.

**palas** [palas] 'to dig': GKK says that this verb occurs 2-3 times in Middle and Late Cornish together. This is incorrect: *ty the honyn the **balas*** OM 345; *the thallath **palas*** OM 370; *the **bales** ha the wonys* OM 414; *mos the **balas*** OM 681; *my a vyn **palas*** OM 865; *te tha honyn tha **ballas*** CW 975; *ages tooles tha **ballas*** CW 982; *me a vyn dallath **palas*** CW 1033; ***BALAS**, the balas, the baly, to dig* ACB: opposite L.

**panes** [panes] 'parsnips': GKK says this form in confined to a single instance in Lhuyd. This is incorrect: *S.W. Pannas, Parsnip; Cor[nish] **Panez** AB: 14c; C[ornish] & Ar. **Panez**, S.W. Pannas, Lat. Pastinaca [latifolia]* AB: 33a; *panan [pl. **panez**]* glossing *Pastinaca, A parsnip, a carrot* AB: 114a; *PANAN, a parsnip; pl. **Panez*** ACB: U 2 verso. Notice also that GKK arbitrarily changes the attested singular *panen* to *\*panesen* <panesenn>. Lhuyd is emphatic that the singular is *panen* (see the citations from AB: 114a and ACB above and cf. *panan, A parsnip* AB: 240b). Nance (1938) gives as singular both *\*panesen* and *panen*.

**paper** [paper] 'paper': GKK says the plural is not attested. This is incorrect: *ny vendzha vesga argrafa an **papyrio** hemma* AB: 222.

**parson** 'parson': this word occurs in BM: *ser **parson**, bona dyes* BM 1905. It is also attested in place-names: *Lowerth-Lavender-en-**parson*** (Padel: 154). The word is omitted from GKK. Although the dictionary cites *person*, it does not cite the specialized sense 'parson' in the entry there. Nance (1952) gives *person* as the Cornish for 'parson'.

**paynt** [paynt, pent] 'paint': this borrowing is credited by GKK to G[raham] S[andercock]. This is incorrect. The word spelt <pent> is already in Nance (1952: 123).

**payntya** [payntya, pentya] 'to paint': GKK says that this word is not attested in the texts but has been taken from Nance's 1952 dictionary. This is incorrect: *yma S Paul worth agan **payntia** ny in mes in colors in leas tellar in scriptur* TH 7a.

**pellder** [pellder] 'length of time, distance': GKK says this word is confined to two instances in CW. This is incorrect: *ha pana **peldar** a ruga bewa ena* TH 47a. Cf. ***pelldar**, far off* ACB: folio after U 2.

**Penkast** [Pencast] 'Whitsun, Pentecost': GKK says this word is confined to a single instance in Lhuyd. This is incorrect on both counts: *war du **fencost** myttyn* TH 44a; *Corn[ish] **Pencas**, Whitson-Tide* AB: 20a; ***Penkast** [Corn[ish]] Pentecoste* AB: 32bc; *Pentecoste …The fiftieth day after Easter, Whitsundtide. C[ornish] **Penkast** AB: 116c; **Penkast**, Whitsuntide, Pentecoste* AB: 241a. Cf. ***PENKAST**, Whitsuntide* ACB: folio after U 2 verso.

**perenn** [peren] 'pear': GKK says this is confined to a single instance in Lhuyd. This is incorrect: *Pêr, **peran** glossing Pyrum, A pear* AB: 133a; *Guedhan **peran**, †perbren glossing Pyrus, A pear tree* AB: 133a.

**\*perfumya** 'to perfume': GKK claims that this word is used by Tregear with the meaning 'to perfume'. This is incorrect. The word in TH is a bad spelling for *performya* 'perform': *kepar dell rug eff nena promysya, in della wosa henna eff a rug y **perfumya*** 'as he then promised, thus thereafter did he perform it' TH 51a.

**pervers** [pervers] 'setback': GKK says this word has been taken from Nance (1938), being unattested in the texts. This is incorrect: *ovotte vn **purvers** da lemyn wharfethys* OM 882-83.

**peswardhegves** [peswardhegves] 'fourteenth': GKK says that this word is confined to 2-3 instances in the Tregear manuscript. I am unable to find any of them. The only example of the word known to me is *Paswar **dêgvas**, the fourteenth* ACB: F f 2 verso.

**piba** [pyba] 'to pipe': GKK says that this verb is confined to 2-3 instances in Lhuyd. This is incorrect: *menstrels a ras **pebough** whare* OM 2845-46; *now menstrels **pybygh** bysy* RD 2644; *mynstrels growgh theny **peba*** CW 2546. Cf. ***PEBOUGH**, tune you, pipe you* ACB: folio after U 2.

**pilars** [pyllars] 'pillars': GKK says the plural of *pilar* [pyllar] is confined to a single instance in TH. This is incorrect: *principall **pillers*** TH 35a; *an **pillars** ytowns parys* CW 2192.

**plagya** [plagya] 'to plague, to afflict': GKK's authentication code seems to imply that this verb is confined to a single instance in Late Cornish. This is incorrect: *yma ow leverell fatell rug Du **plagia** cities* TH 53a; *lemyn yth oma **plagys*** CW 1576; *a v[yth] **plagys** creys 3a ve* CW 1616; ***plages** y fetha ragtha* CW 1642.

**plenta** [plenta] 'plenty': GKK says this word is attested three times only, i.e. at OM 2247, 2262 and PC 2229. This is incorrect: *yth esa **plentye** a bup kynde* TH 2; ***plenty** a redemcion* TH 10a; *mar **plenty** dysquethys* TH 11; *ha grace ew **plenty** res* TH 28; *ha'n mowyssye lower **plentye*** CW 1455; ***plenty** lower in pur thefry* CW 1497.

**pliskenn** [plysken] 'shell, husk': GKK says this word is unattested outside Cornish English dialect. This is incorrect. Lhuyd writes: ***Pliskin**, Testa ovi [eggshell]* AB: 163a. Cf ***PLISKIN**, an egg-shell* ACB: opposite X.

**ploumenn** [plumen] 'plum': GKK says this word is confined to a single instance in Lhuyd. This is incorrect: *Mean **plymon** glossing Ossiculum, A little bone; also the stone of a fruit, etc.* AB: 110b; ***Pluman** glossing Prunum, A prune or damson, a plum* AB: 131ab; *Guedhan **pluman**, †plumbren glossing Prunus, A plum-tree* AB: 131b. Cf. ***PLUMAN**, a plumb; guedhan **pluman**, a plumb tree* ACB: opposite X.

"A MODERN AND SCHOLARLY CORNISH-ENGLISH DICTIONARY"

**pokkys** [pockys] 'pox': GKK says that this word is confined to a single instance in Lhuyd. This is incorrect: *Pokkys Frenk* glossing *Lues, The pox* AB: 82a; *Pokkys miniz* glossing *Variolae, Measles* AB: 169. Cf. *POKKYS FRENK, the pox; pokkys miniz, the small pox* ACB: opposite X.

**pojer** 'small bowl': GKK says this word has been taken from Nance (1938), being unattested except in the English dialect of Cornwall. This is incorrect: *PODZHAR, a porringer* ACB: opposite X; *Podzher, a little Dish* Borlase: 403.

**polat** [pollat] 'fellow': GKK says this word is confined to CW. This is incorrect. The word is also attested in 'Jowan Chy an Horth': *an guadn-gyrti genz e follat* 'the adulterous woman with her paramour' BF: 18.

**porposya** [purposya] 'to purpose': GKK says this word has been derived from Nance (1955), since it is not attested in the texts. This is incorrect: *a vynna purposia na predery the wull* TH 29; *Rag yth off purposys dre weras a thu* TH 31; *Ith off ve dre weras a thu purposys* TH 35. Moreover, *porposya* is given s.v. 'purpose' in Nance (1952).

**porthow** [porthow] 'gates': GKK says the plural of *porth* 'gate' is confined to a single instance in PC (i.e. PC 3040). This is incorrect: *hag a dorras an porʒow* PA 212a; *egereugh an porthow* RD 98; *rak an porthow hep dyweth* RD 101; *worto an porthow ny sef* RD 119; *gallas an porthow brewyon* RD 126; *kyn fo porthov neff degeys* BM 1255; †*PORTH, pl. Porthow, a door, a gate* ACB: X; *leb es gyi de porthow* ACB: two folios after E e verso.

**posseshyon** [possessyon] 'possession': GKK says that this word is confined to a single instancee at BM 3486. This is incorrect: *nanelle possessyon an bys* TH 28.

**pottya** [pottya] 'to put': GKK says that this verb is confined to a single instance at BM 3486. This is incorrect: *eff a putt then dore* TH 13.

**poyntys** [poyntys] 'point': GKK says that the plural of *poynt* is confined to two instances in CW. This is incorrect: *An kyth sam poyntys* TH 34; *in pana poyntys speciall* TH 36.

**poyson** [poyson] 'poison': GKK says the word is confined to a single instance in TH. This is incorrect: *an poyson a serpons* TH 7a; *an poyson a heresy* TH 42.

**prays** [prays] 'praise': GKK says that *praysys*, the plural of this noun, occurs once in BM. This is incorrect, since *preysys* at BM 2352 is a verbal adjective: *the larchya preysys fethogh* 'the more you will be praised.' The plural is not attested.

**prederys** [prederys] 'worried': GKK says this word was invented by W[ella] B[rown], being unattested in the texts. This is incorrect. Nance (1938: 134) gives *prederiis, prederys* (C. Voc *priderys*) 'careful, solicitous, anxious.' *Prederys* is in origin the same word as *prederus* (which is a headword in GKK) and bears a similar meaning. Notice also *Pryderys* glossing *Solicitus, Solicitous, crefull, pensive, troubl'd, busie* AB: 151c; *prederez en Kothnanz Tavazow* AB: 222; *prederys, studious, thoughtful* ACB: X. Cf. †*PRIDERYS, pensive, troubled* ACB: X verso.

**prederyans** [prederyans] 'opinion': GKK says that the plural is unattested. This is incorrect: *orth nebez brederyanzo adrô 'n Tavazeth Kernûak* AB: 222.

**present** 'present' adj.: this word is missing from GKK, even though *presens* and *presentya* are both included (and *presens* is out of alphabetical sequence after *presep*). The adj *present* occurs at TH 5, 19a, 26, 34, 37a, 43 and 49. The noun *present* 'present, gift' occurs at BM 3397, 3402 and is in Nance (1938 and 1952). It does not seem to be included in GKK.

**pris** [prys] 'price, value': although the number of occurrences is not given, GKK says that this word is confined to Middle Cornish. This is incorrect. The word is widely attested in Late Cornish: *Price; Corn[ish] Priz* AB: 30b; *Pretium…A price given for a* *thing that is bought, a reward, a hire, a fee, a bribe. C[ornish]* **Priz** AB: 128a; **PRIZ**, *a price; pan a* **priz** *rag hearn? what price for pilchards?* ACB: opposite X 2; *Pana* **priz** *rag hearne? What price for pilchards?* **Priz** *dah. A good price* ACB: opposite F f 2; *nages* **prize** *veeth es moase ragt'angi* Gwavas (LAM: 238); *rag* **prijse** *da eu gwell* Gwavas (LAM: 238).

**proces** 'process': GKK includes the words *procedya* from TH and *processyon* from BM. It does not appear to include *proces* which is attested at TH 43, 46, 49a and 53a x 2.

**profet** [profet] 'prophet': GKK says this word is confined to TH. This is incorrect: *screffez gen an* **prophet** RC 23: 195; *der an* **prophet** RC 23: 199; *Jerman an* **prophet** RC 23: 199.

**provia** [provy·a] 'to provide, to procure': GKK says this verb is confined to 2-3 instances in TH and Lhuyd. This is incorrect: *ware me a* **provy** *moy* BM 1870; *ef a* **provyas** *ragan ny* TH 10a; *praga na ruga* **provia** *rag tra an parna* TH 29; *ha* **provya** *mariag rag y vab* TH 31; *yma peyke thym* **provyes** CW 2290; **Pryvia** glossing *Procuro, To do or solicit another man's business. To Procure* AB: 129b. Cf. **PRYVIA**, *dho* **pryvia**, *to do, or solicit business for another, to procure* ACB: opposite X 2. This is not the same verb as *pro·vya* 'to offer' at BM 485, 1116, 2880.

**provochya** 'to provoke': GKK calls this Late Cornish and correctly cites Lhuyd as the source. It does not mention, however, that the variant *provokya* occurs in TH: *Du a ve* **provokys** *warbyn an bys* TH 7.

**punshya** [punsya] 'to punish': GKK says this verb is confined to 4-9 instances in Middle Cornish. This is incorrect on both counts: **punscie** *y tus mar calas* OM 1482; *ef a wra tyn the* **punssye** OM 1527; *pan os* **punsys** OM 1563; *ty a vyth* **punsys** OM 1600: *correctya ha* **punsya** *vicys* TH 25; **punsya** *ha correctia* TH 25; *the* **punsya** *an drog pobill* TH 25; *the* **punyssya** *ha correctya* TH 38; *the* **punyssya** *oll an rena* TH 38; *agan* **punyssya** TH 40a; *gweffa the vos* **punyshes** CW 587.

**purkat** [purcat] 'pulpit': GKK says this word is confined to a single instance in Lhuyd. This is incorrect: *Rostra…A pulpit, a pleading place. C[ornish]* **Pyrkat** AB; 141c; *Suggestum…A chair, a pulpit. C[ornish]* **Pyrkat** AB: 158a. Cf. **PYRKAT**, *a pulpit, a pleading place* ACB: X 2.

**pychya** [pychya] 'to stab': GKK asserts that this verb is not attested in the texts and is a modern coinage taken from Nance's 1938 dictionary. This is incorrect: *en gew lym ef a* **bechye** *pur ewn yn dan an asow* PA 218cd. GKK wrongly puts the form *pechya* from PA under its own headword. <e> for stressed *y* is common in PA.

**pymthegves** [pymthegves] 'fifteenth': GKK says the word is not attested. This is incorrect: **Pemp dêgvas**, *the fifteenth* ACB: F f 2 verso.

**pyseul** [pysuel] 'how many': GKK says this word is confined to a single instance in TH. This is incorrect on both counts: **pesuell** *one ny kylmys* TH 11; **Pysell** *defferans* TH 27; **paseil** *moy gallus* SA 62a; *Kynifer*, **pezealla** (< *pysuel ha*) glossing *Quot, How many?* AB: 135c. Cf. **PEZEALLA**, *how many, so many as* ACB: two folios after U 2

**pystik** [pystyk] 'hurt': GKK recommends *\*pystigow* as the plural, no plural being attested in the texts. This is incorrect: *oll sortow clevas ha oll* **pesticks** *mesk an boble* RC 23: 192 (Rowe).

**rebuk** [rebuk] 'rebuke': GKK suggests that *rebukys*, the plural of this noun, is confined to a single instance in TH. this is incorrect: *fatell ew kynde an parna an* **rebukys** TH 29a; *ha dre* **rebukys** TH 29a; *han kithsame kense me a* **rebukys** TH 29a.

**rebukya** [rebukya] 'to rebuke': GKK suggests this verb is confined to a number of instances in TH. This is incorrect: *Ragon menough* **rebekis** PA 2c; *ena y an* **rebukyas** PA 112a; *ef a ve veyll* **rebukis** PA 156a.

**remova** [remuvya] 'to remove, to move': GKK says this verb is confined to a single instance in OM. This is incorrect: **remmvys** *the gen tyller* OM 2045; *a fyl aga* **remmvve**

OM 2057; *yn certan mar* **remvfe** RD 396. Cf. **REMUFE**, *to move again* ACB: folio after X 2.

**reperya** [reperya] 'to repair': GKK points out that this word is confined to TH and recommends using *ewnhe* 'repair, mend' instead. This is not very good advice, since the word *reperya* in TH is used only in the sense 'repair to, take refuge with': *the thos ha the* (the) **reperya** *thethy* 'to come and to repair to her' TH 17; *oll an re ew feithfull (po lene a feth) pennagill a vons y, a res assembla po* **reperya** *thethy* 'all those who are faithful (or full of faith), whoever they may be, must assemble or repair unto her' TH 48.

**repreva** [repreva] 'to reprove': GKK says this occurs 2-3 times in Middle Cornish and implies that it is confined to OM and TH. This is incorrect: *pendra wreugh ov* **repryfa** OM 1500; *na* **repreff** *tus vohosek* BM 3120; *why a yll ow* **reprovia** TH 11; *rebukys ha* **reprovys** TH 46a.

**resek** [resek] 'to run': GKK says *resek* means 'to run for pleasure' whereas *ponya* means 'to run in earnest'. This distinction is difficult to maintain: *whath ny rowns y in ta understondia an scryptur lell mas pub ur* **resak** *pelha ha pelha in error* TH 17a; *nena ny russa den vith* **resak** *in heresy* TH 19a; *Alak, tus vas, ha pell ew mer an bobill* **resys** *hethow in jeth theworth an kithsam rulle ma!* TH 37. Tregear even uses the two words together as synonyms: *lyas onyn a rug* **resak** *ha* **ponya** *in stray* TH 30a.

**restorya** 'to restore': GKK cites the noun *restoryta* from BM 2178. It omits the verb *restorya*, however, which is not uncommon: *ha* **restoria** *thymo vy* BM 3594; *thymo* **restoryans** *hy* BM 3778; *drefen nag es* **restorijs** BM 3786; **restorijs** *ov esely* BM 4235; *ov golek thym* **restoryes** BM 4398; *the* **restoria** *mab den* TH 12a.

**reyn** [rayn] 'reign': GKK says the word is taken from Nance's 1955 dictionary, since it is unattested in the texts. This is incorrect: *in dew[e]tha blethan a* **reign** *an cruell Emperour* TH 47; *an xiii-as a* **reign** *Nero* TH 47.

**robya** [robbya] 'to rob, to plunder': GKK says this word is attested 2-3 times in Middle and Late Cornish. This is incorrect: *na vova* **robijs** *in suer* BM 2064; *yth esas ow* **robbya** *sans egglos* TH 14a; *eff a yll* **robbya** *lyas den* TH 25a; *Pan egllossyow a ve* **robbys** TH 40a; *Dho* **robbia** glossing *Depraedor* AB: 54b; **Robbiaz** glossing *Spoliatus, Robb'd* AB: 153c. Cf. **ROBBIA**, *dho* **robbia**, *to rob, spoil*; **robbiaz**, *robbed* ACB: two folios after X 2.

**ronson** [raunson] 'ransom': GKK says this word is confined to 4-9 instances in TH. This is incorrect: *heb* **rawnson** *vetholl na fyne* CW 250. The compiler adds a note: 'The 2nd vowel was nasal in F[rench] and this nasality spread to the 1st vowel in the spelling *raunson* in TH.' I do not understand what he means here. Both vowels were, and indeed are, nasal in French, where the modern spelling is <rançon>. The compiler is perhaps not aware that <raunson> is a common spelling in Middle English.

**rosellen** 'whirl, whorl': GKK includes the verb *\*rosella* 'spin, whirl', a neologism taken from Nance's 1938 dictionary. It omits the noun *rosellen*, however, though it is attested: **Rozellen** glossing *Verticula, A whirl for a spindle* AB: 172b; **ROZELLEN**, *a whirl for a spindle* ACB: second folio after X 2.

**rudh** [rudh] 'red, scarlet': GKK says that apart from place-names this adjective is confined to Old and Middle Cornish where it occurs 4-9 times. This is incorrect: **rud** glossing *ruber* ['red'] OCV 486; *the'n mor* **ruyth** OM 1622; *an mor* **ruyth** OM 1635; *queth* **ruth** PC 2127; *mar* **ruth** *the thylles* RD 2512; **ruth** *the thyllas* RD 2529; **ruth** *y couth thy'mmo bones* RD 2535; *dyllas* **ruth** RD 2547; *pur* **ruth** *age myn* BM 3309; **ruth** *gans e gos* SA 60; **Rydh** glossing *Ruber, Red, ruddy* AB: 141c; *Pedn-***rydh**, *Red-hair'd* AB: 142a; *Risk ha reden* **rydh** [*Bark and red Fern*] AB: 229a; **Rydh** glossing *RUBER* AB: 296b; †**Rud**, *Red, now corrupted to* **Rooz**; *pedn* **rooz**, *a red head*; **Rudh, Ruth, Rydh**, *id.* ACB:

two folios after X 2; *RYDH, red, ruddy; pedn* **ryth,** *a red head, red haired* ACB: opposite Y; **Rydh,** *Red:* **Rydik,** *Reddish* Borlase 405.

**rudhek** [rudhak] 'robin (*Erithacus rubecula*)': GKK recommends the plural \**rudhogyon* devised by K[en] J. G[eorge]. The dictionary is apparently unaware that the plural is already *rudhogas*; see Brian Webb, *Dornlyver Ydhyn* (1984) s.v. Webb's excellent little book is not mentioned in the introduction to GKK and one can only conclude that the compiler was unaware of it. Given that the work was published by Cowethas an Yeth Kernewek, this is a remarkable omission.

**rutya** [ruttya] 'to rub': GKK says this word is confined to a single instance in Lhuyd. This is incorrect: *Dho* **rhittia** glossing *Frico, to rub, chafe or fret* AB: 61b; *Dho* **rhyttia** *'n dha* glossing *Perfrico, To rub all over* AB: 118a. Cf. *RHYTTIA, dho* **rhyttia**'*n dha, to rub all over* ACB: two folios after X 2.

**sabenn** [saben] 'pine': GKK says this word is confined to 2-3 instances in Lhuyd. This is incorrect: *C[ornish]* **Zaban,** *L. Sapinus* AB: 33a; **Zaban** glossing *Abies, A Fir-Tree* AB: 41a; *Aval* **zaban** glossing *Conus, A cone or pine-apple* AB: 51b; *Plankys* **zaban,** *Deal-boards* AB: 242a; **Zaban** glossing *A Fir-tree* AB: 276b; *C[ornish]* **Zaban** glossing *The Pitch tree* AB: 283a. Cf. *plankys* **zaban,** *deal boards* ACB: two folios after U 2; **Zaban,** *a fir tree* ACB: two folios after B b 2.

**Sadorn** [Sadorn] 'Saturn, Saturday': GKK says this is confined to a single instance in Lhuyd: This is incorrect: *W. Sadurn, Saturn; C[ornish]* **Zadarn** AB: 30b; *Saturday: C[ornish] De* **Zadarn** AB: 54c. Cf. *De* **Zadarn,** *Saturday* ACB: N verso; *Dezadarn* Borlase 384a.

**selya** [selya] 'to seal': GKK says this word is taken from Nance's 1938 dictionary since it is not attested in the texts. This is incorrect: *An kigg ew* **selis** *may halla an enaf bos defendis* '[caro] signatur ut anima muniatur' SA 60a. GKK believes *selis* to be for \**sellys* 'salted' but this is unlikely in view of the Latin *signatur* 'is sealed'.

**sens** 'sense': GKK omits this word which is attested in TH: *an letterall* **sens** *a la Moyses* TH 26a; *an lell* **sens** *ha'n understondyng a'n scryptur* TH 36.

**sessya** [cessya] 'to cease': GKK asserts that this is confined to TH. This is incorrect: *ha homma vyth ny* **sestyas** [leg sescyas < cessyas] *aban duthe yn chy thy's pup ur ol amme thu'm treys* PC 523-25. Sandercock's edition of PC reads *ha homma byth ny* **cessyas,** *aban dhutha y'n chy dhys, pup ur-oll amma dhe'm treys.* Cf. *SESTYA, to cease, to give over; ha homma byth ny* **sestyas,** *and she hath never ceased* ACB: Y 2.

**sesya** [sesya] 'to seize': GKK says that this verb is confined to 2-3 instances in Middle Cornish. This is incorrect on both counts: *bethens* **sesijs** BM 972; *praga na ruk y* **sesya** BM 1032; *gene ateve* **sesijs** BM 1886; **sesyogh** *thymmo* BM 3526; *nag onen vyth* **sesijs** BM 3545; *me re ruk sur y* **sesia** BM 3547; *Dho Kymera, dho sindzha, dho* **sesia** glossing *Comprehendo, To take or lay hold on,* etc. AB: 50a.

**seytegves** [seytegves] 'seventeenth': according to GKK this word is confined to a single instance in TH. This is incorrect. The compiler is probably thinnking of *in* **xvii-as** *sermon* TH 46, which is not an example. The only real example is *Seith* **dêgvas,** *the seventeenth* ACB: F f 2, which GKK does not mention.

**seythgweyth** [seythgweyth] 'seven times': GKK says this word is unattested. If GKK accepts *vxii-as* as *seytegves* (see previous), then *vij* **gwythe** *y wra acquyttya* CW 1537 ought to be accepted as an example of *seythgweyth.*

**shakya** [shakya] 'to shake': GKK says this verb is confined to 2-3 occurrences. This is incorrect: *aga fen y a* **sackye** PA 195b; *y a* **shaky** *age barvou* BM 2313; **shackys** *ha tossys* TH 30; *kepar ha flehes ow* **shackya** TH 42; *Gorah an vose tha* **shakiah** *an kala* ACB: opposite F f 2.

**sita** [cyta] 'city': GKK says that the plural is attested once only, i.e. *cytes rych* PC 132. This is incorrect: *fatell rug Du plagia* **cities**, *trevow ha pow* TH 53a. In spite of the Anglicized spelling *cities* in TH is identical with *cytes* in PC.

**sitysan** [cytysan] 'citizen': GKK says that this word was taken from Nance's 1955 dictionary, because it is unattested in the texts. This is incorrect: *mas yth owhy* **citesens** *gansans an syns* TH 33.

**skaldya** [scaldya] 'to scald': GKK tells us that this verb is confined to a single instance in the *Ordinalia*. This is incorrect. It does not occur in the *Ordinalia* but is attested more than once in BM: *ny a veth* **skaldys** BM 2107; *ov golyov luen a plos prest ov* **sclaldya** [leg. *scaldya*] BM 3059.

**skapya** [scappya] 'to escape': GKK says this verb is attested 2-3 times in Middle and Late Cornish together. this is incorrect: *nyns us* **scapya** OM 1656; *ny wren* **scapye** OM 1706; *na* **scapyo** PC 990; *byth na* **scapye** PC 1888; *mar* **scap** RD 378; *pur wyr ny* **scap** RD 383; *ny* **skap** RD 2019; *byth na* **schapye** RD 2270; *y vos* **scappys** BM 1030; *byth ny* **schappyons** BM 2469; *nyg eas* **scappya** CW 1973.

**\*skavel kroenek** [scavel cronek] 'toadstool': GKK omits this neologism although it is in Nance (1938, 1952, 1955) and is used by Caradar: *mos war an bronyon dhe guntell nebes* **scavellow-cronek** (KemK: 39).

**skavel-droes** [scavel dros] 'footstool': GKK says this item is confined to a single instance at CW 21. This is incorrect: *gwregh honora* **scavall e dryes** SA 64a; *pandr' ew an* **scavall e drys** *eff* SA 64a; *an grond ew an* **skavall ow thrys** *ve* SA 64a; *rag honora* **scavall y drys** SA 64a.

**skaw** [scaw] 'elder trees': GKK gives this as the collective plural of *skawenn* [scawen] and says the form is unattested outside place-names. This is incorrect. Polwhele writes: **Scaw** *is still in use for an elder in Cornwall* (quoted in LCB). Cf. **Scao**, *an Elder-tree* Borlase 405.

**skentoleth** [skentoleth] 'wisdom': GKK says this word, which occurs in the *Ordinalia* and BM, is a short form of *\*skiantoleth*. The asterisk implies that the compiler believes the word to be unattested. This is incorrect: *yma an lyver a* **skyantoleth** *ow remembra thyn* TH 6a.

**skiber, -yow** [skyber, -yow] 'barn': GKK says that this word is confined to two instances in PC. It also says that the plural is unattested. The dictionary is doubly incorrect: **Skibor** glossing *Horreum, A barn or corn-house* AB: 66a; *Gorah tees en an* **skeber** *tha drushen* ACB: opposite F f 2; *SKIBOR, pl.* **Skiberio, Skiberiowe**, *a barn* ACB: Y 2 verso.

**sklandra** [sclandra] 'to offend': GKK says that this verb is confined to a single instance in BM. This is incorrect: *na vo den aral* **sclandrys** PC 743; *pur wyr* **sclandrys** PC 891; *kyn fons y ol* **sclandrys** PC 899; *ov* **sclandra** BM 3747; *SCLANDRY, to offend, to slander; why a vyth pur* **sclandrys** *ahannaf, you shall verily be offended at me* ACB: Y.

**skoler** [scoler] 'scholar': GKK says this word is confined to a single instance in Lhuyd. This is incorrect: *Helias asas e mantall in ded gans e* **scholar** SA 60. GKK also says that the plural is not attested. This is also incorrect: *dhyn* **Skolàryo** *ha'n Pednzhivikio* AB: 224; **Skylyrion**, *Scholars* AB: 242c.

**skorjya** [scurjya] 'to scourge': GKK says this word is confined to a single instance in PA, i.e. line 1303a [*recte* 130a]. This is incorrect: **scorgis** *gans an ʒethewon* BM 2602; *kylmys gans lovonow,* **scurgys** TH 15a.

**skourya** [scurya] 'to scour': GKK says this word is taken from Nance's 1938 dictionary, because it is not attested in the texts. This is incorrect: *crist a rug agery an fentan ma*

177

*arta ha's purgias ha's* **scurryas** TH 22. Meanwhile GKK cites Tregear's *scurya* s.v. *skorrya*, but gives no meaning for it.

**skrifer** [screfer] 'scribe, writer': GKK says the singular is not attested. This is incorrect: *Skrepher an gerlevran-na* AB: 223.

**sogh** [sogh] ploughshare': GKK says this word is confined to OCV and Lhuyd. This is incorrect: *Gora an* **soch**, *ha an troher, tha an gove* ACB: F f 2.

**sojet** [sojet] 'subject': GKK mentions that this word at CW 379 is spelt <subject>. The dictionary also claims that the plural is confined to a single instance in PA. This is incorrect. The expression *ol y* **sogete** PA 211d contains a collective, not a plural. GKK is apparently unaware that the plural is attested in TH: *myterneth gwlasow,* **subiectys**, *tus ientyll* TH 6a.

**solempna** [solempna] 'solemn': GKK says this adjective is unattested in the texts. This is incorrect. It is found with the spelling <solem> in TH: *the wull* **solem** *ro in aga begeth* TH 20; *gull* **solem** *promys a vois* TH 51a. The compiler also says he got the word from Nance's 1955 dictionary. The word *solempna*, however, is cited by Nance in both his earlier dictionaries (1938: 153; 1952: 160)

**soveran** [soveran] 'sovereign': GKK says this word is confined to one instance each in OM, BM and TH. This is incorrect: *agan arluth* **sefryn** OM 2189; *agan* **soueran** BM 246; **Souereign** *rewler* TH 2; *po y* **soveran** TH 4a; *blonogath y* **soveran** TH 4a.

**Sows** [Saws] 'Englishman': There are at least four errors in this entry in GKK. First, GKK suggests that the word *Sows* [Saws] is attested once only. This is incorrect: **Zouz** *glossing Anglus, An English-man* AB: 42c and *boz* **Zouz**, *Dan po Norman* AB: 224; cf. **Zouz**, *an English Man* Borlase 413. Secondly, GKK suggests that the plural *Sowson* [Sawson] occurs 4-9 times. This is also incorrect: *car dreeg an* **Sausen** *e thanen* BF: 24; *durt an* **Sausen** BF: 29; *ha whaeh an* **Sousen** BF: 31; *Sousen-Curnow* BF: 31; *Pou an* **Zouzn** *glossing Anglia, England* AB: 42c; *ny aldzha an* **Zouzon** AB: 224; *Mytern ol an* **Zouzon** AB: 224; *mesk an* **Zouzon** AB: 224; *neb Koth-Zouzon* AB: 224; **Zouzon**, *The English* AB: 242c; *Dhan* **Zowzan** *kovaithak* ACB: opposite H h. Thirdly, GKK suggests that Cornish *Sows* [Saws] derives from Latin *Saxo*. This is also incorrect. *Saxo* quite regularly gave \**Seys* in Cornish, a form attested in surnames like *Seys, le Seys* and in toponyms like *Carsize, Tresayes, Trezise, Chyseise* (see Padel: 208). *Saws* is a back-formation from the plural *Sawson < Saxones*. Fourthly, GKK suggests that the Welsh for 'Englishman' is \**Saws*. It is not. The Welsh is *Sais*, pl. *Saeson*.

**Sowsnek** [Sawsnek] 'English': GKK says that this word is confined to 4-9 instances in Late Cornish. This is incorrect: *mouy* **Sousenack** *clappies* BF: 25; *ha clappia* **Sousenack** BF: 25; *an Tavaz* **Sousenack** BF: 25; *tho Ve buz* **Sousenack** BF: 29; *Latten, po an* **Sousenack** BF: 29: *ha an* **Sousenack** *nobla* BF: 29; *gen an* **Sousenack** BF: 31; *meea na vidna cowza* **sawsneck** Carew (Ellis: 73); *W.* **Saisneg**, *English; C[ornish]* **Zasnak** AB: 30b; **Zouznak** *glossing Lingua Anglicana, the English Tongue* AB: 42c; *'ryg traylia an levrouma dhan* **Zouznak** AB: 222; *gerrio* **Zouznak** AB: 223; *dhort an Koth-* **Zouznak** AB: 223; *Kernuak-Zouznak* AB: 223; *skrefyanz an* **Zouznak** AB: 223; *an gerrio* **Zouznak** AB: 223; *en* **Zouznak** *koth* AB: 224; *Ah-skrefo* **Zouznak** AB: 224; *pordha kouz* **Zouznak** AB: 224; *a kouz* **Zouznak** AB: 224; *Kothskreferyon* **Zouznak** AB: 224; **Zawznak**, *the English tongue…* **Sawsnek** ACB: two folios after B b 2 verso; *eden ger* **Sowsnack** Bodinar (LAM: 244).

**Spayn** [Spayn] 'Spain': GKK says that this name is confined to a single instance at RD 2147. This is incorrect: *Dhort henna war Frank ha war* **Span** (LAM: 234).

**spena** [spena] 'to spend': GKK says this verb is confined to BM. This is incorrect: *y* **speynas** *y gyk hay wos* PA 10c.

**spera** [spera] 'spear': GKK says that this word is confined to a single instance at CW 1994. This is incorrect: *gwenys dre an assow the'n golon gans **spera*** TH 15a.

**spikys** [spykys] 'spikes': GKK says that the plural of *spik* 'spike' is confined to a single instance at PC 2140. This is incorrect: ***spykys** bras a horn* TH 15a.

**takkya** [tackya] 'to nail, to fasten': GKK says this is confined to 2-3 instances. This is incorrect: *ha'y yll leff a ve **tackys** PA 179b; En lybell a vue **tackis** PA 189a; **tackis** fast PA 223c; ynny hy bethens **tackys** PC 2164; bethens **tackys** PC 2518; rag **takkye** an fals profus PC 2672; me a **tak** y luef gleth PC 2747; **tackeugh** e a hugh y ben PC 2793; the **tackye** PC 2807; fast **tackyes** PC 2939; **tackys** y'n grous RD 1116; Figo…to fix, to fasten; … C[ornish] Dho kelmy, dho **takkia** AB: 59c. Cf. **TAKKIA**, dho **takkia**, to tack, fasten, to tie* ACB: two folios after Y 2.

**Tamer** [Tamar] 'Tamar': GKK says this river name is confined to a single instance in Middle Cornish. This is incorrect: *an barz ma ze pons **tamar** CF 20; a **tamer** the pen an vlays* BM 2208.

**tavolenn** [tavolen] 'dock plant': GKK asserts that the singular is unattested. This is incorrect: ***tauolen** glossing tilla* ['dock'] OCV; *W. **Tavolen**, A Dock; Corn[ish] **Tavolan** AB: 15b; †**Tavolen** glossing Lapathum, Dock AB: 76b; **Tavolan**, a dock AB: 240c.* Cf. †***TAVOLEN**, dock herb* ACB: opposite Z.

**tavoseth** [tavaseth] 'dialect, idiom': GKK says that this word is confined to a single instance in Lhuyd. This is incorrect: *adrô'n **Tavazeth** Kernûak AB 222; a'n **Tavazeth** Kernûak AB: 222; en **Tavazeth** Kernûak AB: 222; en **Tavadzheth** Guenez AB: 223.* Cf. ***TAVAZETH**, a tongue, or language; **tavazeth** Kernuak, the Cornish tongue* ACB: opposite Z.

**tebel-el** 'devil': Instead of the word *dyawl* Tregear uses *tebel-el*, e.g. at 3, 3a x 3, 5, 10, 13, 15 x 2, 15a x 2, 16, 23a, 25, 28a, 32a. Noteworthy is the expression *an bys, an kyge ha'n tebel-el* 'the world, the flesh and the devil' at TH 9a. Cf. *esel yv then **tebel el** BM 969.* Nance cites *tebel-el* in his 1952 dictionary (s.v. 'devil') and his 1955 dictionary (s.v. *tebel*). *Tebel-el* 'devil' seems to be wanting from GKK.

**tegys** [tegys] 'choked': GKK says this word is unattested. This is incorrect: *Suffocatus…Chok'd or throtl'd. C[ornish] **Tegez** AB: 157c.* Cf. *TAGA, dho taga, to chaoak, to throttle; **teges**, segys, choaked, throttled* ACB: two folios after Y 2.

**tekhe** [tekhe] 'to beautify': GKK says this verb is not attested. This is incorrect: *may fo **tekkeys** eredy* 'that he may be beautified indeed' BM 1601.

**tender** [tender] 'tender': GKK says this is confined to one instance (i.e. at BM 115). This is incorrect: *an **tendyr** kerensa a du an tas* TH 1.

**tewal** [tewal] 'dark gloomy': GKK cites this and the monosyllabic form *tewl* 'dark' as separate headwords. The dictionary also states that *tewal* is unattested. This is incorrect: ***Teual** glossing Obscurus, Obscure, dark,* etc. AB: 103a. Cf. ***TEUAL**, brown, dark, blind* ACB: opposite Z 2.

**tewel** [tewel] 'to be silent': GKK says this verb occurs 2-3 times in Middle and Late Cornish together. This is incorrect: *a **taw** cowyth OM 2749; **taw**, an el a bregewthy OM 229; pan wreta **tewel** PC 1320; **tewel** auel vn bobba PC 2385; nep a **tawo** yn pow-ma PC 2387; **taw** foul a soge gocky PC 2897; **tau** sy cowys renothas RD 405; **tau** harlot out of my sygth RD 619; **teweugh** awos lucyfer RD 669; awos ovn my ny **tauwaf** RD 923; ty a **tew** RD 984; mara colyth ty a **tew** RD 1388; **teweugh** rak meth RD 1495; ny ny **tywyn** ow cane RD 2527; A **taw** na gowse a henna CW 171: **Taw** lucyfer melegas CW 283; **Taw Taw** eva 665; **taw** theth cregye CW 1103; **Tau** glossing Tace* [be silent] AB: 160b; ***Teuel**, To be silent* AB: 245b; ***TEUEL**, **Tewel**, to be silent; **teweugh**, be ye silent* ACB: opposite Z 2. The expression *taw tavas* 'shut up!' survives in English dialect. GKK puts it under the headword *taw* 'silence.' This is also incorrect. *Taw tavas* is the 2nd person imperative followed by the direct object *tavas*. The phrase means literally 'Silence your tongue!'

**ti** [ty] 'to thatch, to roof': GKK says that this verb is confined to two occurrences in OM. This is incorrect on both counts: *tyy py ny agan beth meth* OM 1078; *hag a's ty gans plynkennow* OM 2475; *tyeugh an temple* OM 2485; *ken agesough why ny's ty* OM 2490. Cf.; *TY, …to cover a house either with stones or thatch* ACB: opposite A a 2; also *Tey, to thatch, or cover with straw* Borlase 408.

**titel** [tytel] 'title': GKK glosses this 'legal right' (i.e. legal title) and says it is confined to a single instance in BM. This is incorrect: *oll tytyll ha henow* TH 6; *aga thytyll* TH 6a.

**tobacco** 'tobacco': Lhuyd gives *Tybakko* glossing *Tabacum, Tobacco* AB: 160b. Cf. *TYBAKKO, tobacco; a vulgar modern corruption of Tobacco.—There can be no British word for it* ACB: opposite A a 2. Nance gives *tobacco* as the Cornish for 'tobacco' in both his 1938 and his 1952 dictionary. The word seems to be wanting from GKK.

**toemma** [tomma] 'to heat': GKK says that toemma [tomma] is confined to two instances in Late Cornish. This is incorrect: *tommans onan dour war tan* PC 833; *yma dour tommys* PC 839.

**toemmder** [tomder] 'heat': GKK claims that this word is confined to 2-3 instances in Old and Late Cornish only. This is incorrect on both counts: *tunder* (leg. *tumder*) glossing *calor* OCV 471; *rag tomder ef a wese* PA 58c; *hag y ny russans clowas tomder vith* TH 56a; *tomdar ha yender* CW 1668; *in tomdar tane* CW 1724; *Tomder* glossing *Calor, Heat, warmth* AB: 45c; *Mygilder and tymder, Warmth, heat* AB: 240b. Cf. *\*TOIMDER, heat; Hod[ie] Tumder* ACB: folio after Z 2; *†TUMDER, heat* ACB: A 2

**toes** [tos] 'dough': GKK says this word is not attested. This is incorrect: *Toas, Paste* Borlase 409.

**tollva** [tollva] 'tax office': GKK says this word is derived from Nance's 1938 dictionary, being unattested in the sources. This is incorrect: *Tolva, a Custom House* Borlase 409.

**tollven** [tollven] 'hollow stone': GKK suggests that this word is attested in place-names only. This is not strictly speaking true: *It's common name in Cornwall and Scilly is Tolmen; that is, the Hole of Stone* Borlase 166; *The two Tolmens at Scilly* Borlase 167. Cf. *Tolmen* Borlase 238.

**torment** [torment] 'torment': GKK says the plural is unattested. This is incorrect: *ha paynys intollerabill ha turmontys* TH 15a.

**torr** [tor] 'belly, womb': GKK says that this word is confined to one instance in OCV. This is incorrect: *pan veva genys a dor y vam ʒen bys ma* PA 43d; *a dor ov mam dynythys* OM 1754; *cosk war the tor ha powes* OM 2070; *guregh y cronkye tor ha keyn* PC 2057; *kyns doys a dor ov dama* BM 796; *genis a dore y vam* TH 44a-45; *Tor an daorn* glossing *Palma, The palm of the hand* AB: 111c; *Tor; tor braoz* glossing *Venter, The belly or panch; the stomach, etc.* AB: 171b; *Houl sooth, Tor lean, paravy an gwaynten* Scawen MSS. Cf. *†TOR, the belly* ACB: folio after Z 2 verso. GKK also claims that the plural is unattested. This is likewise incorrect: *may fyth torrow benegas bythqueth na allas e ʒon* PA 169c; *may fenygough an torrow* PC 2646.

**torrva** [torva] 'breach': GKK says that this word is unattested in the texts. This is incorrect: *an violacion ha'n torva a cherite* TH 28; *an keth same torva me a cherite* TH 28-28a.

**traow** [traow] 'things': GKK says this plural of *tra* is unattested. This is incorrect: *ha porskientek en traou erel* AB: 224. Cf. *†TRA, a thing; pl. Traou* ACB: folio after Z 2 verso. *\*Traow* is Lhuyd's invention. Elsewhere it is replaced by *taclow* or *taclennow*.

**trelyans** [treylyans] 'translation': GKK says that the plural of this word is unattested. This is incorrect: *Lenner Brethonek ra medra uar **traillianzo** an gerrio Ladin ma* AB: 222.

**treven** [treven] 'houses': this plural of *tref* with the sense 'houses' is, according to GKK, confined to a single instance in Late Cornish. This is incorrect: *y vab po y virth, chy, **trevyn** po tyrryow* TH 21a; *oagoaze tha e **drevon*** BF: 39; *Tshyi* [*plur **Treven***] glossing *Domus, An house, a lodging* AB: 55c; ***Treven** is also the pl. of Chy* ACB: two folios after Z 2; *Na dale dien gwile **treven** war an treath* ACB: folio after F f 2.

**treveth** [treveth] 'occasion': GKK says this word is confined to a single instance in Nicholas Boson. This is incorrect: *ke weth tresse **treveth** th'y* OM 799; *lyes **trefeth** y'n clewys* PC 1724; *vii **trevath*** TH 8; *rag an **drevath** ma* TH 35; *an tryssa **trevath*** TH 43; ***trevath** arell* TH 53.

**trybedh** [trebeth] 'trivet, tripod': GKK says this word is confined to OCV. This is incorrect: *W. **Trybedh**, A Trivet or Brand-Iron; Cornish **Trebath*** AB: 19a; ***Trebath*** glossing *Tripes* AB: 166c. Cf. ***TREBATH**, a trivet, a three-footed stool; also, a brand iron, a brandice* ACB: two folios after Z 2. Ironically Lhuyd's first citation occurs in a section dealing with the alternation of Welsh <y> with Cornish <e>, a feature of which Kernowek Kemyn is unaware. Nance correctly spelt the Cornish word <trebeth> and UCR follows him.

**tryger** [treger] 'inhabitant': GKK says that the plural *trygoryon* [tregoryon] is unattested in the texts being derived by analogy. This is incorrect: ***Tregoryon** an Enez-ma* AB: 223; *dhort an **Tregoryon** kenza* AB: 223. Cf. *TREGER, pl. **Tregerion**, an inhabitant* ACB: two folios after Z 2.

**turnypenn** [turnypen] 'turnip': GKK says the singular is not attested. This is incorrect: ***Turnupan**, A Turnip* AB: 34a and *Rapum... A rape, a turnip or navew C*[*ornish*] ***tyrnypan*** AB: 136b. Cf. ***TURNUPAN**, a Turnip* ACB: A a; ***TYRNYPAN**, a turnip root* ACB: opposite A a 2; ***Turnupan**, a Turnip* Borlase 410b.

**tykki-Dew** [tycky Dew] 'butterfly' (why the hyphen?): GKK says that this word is confined to a single example in Lhuyd. This is incorrect: *W. **Gloyn Dyu** (i.e. Carbo dei) A Butter-fly; Corn*[*ish*] ***Tikki Deu*** AB: 34a; *C*[*ornish*] ***Tikki deu*** glossing *Papilio* AB 112b. Cf. ***TIKKI-DEN*** [sic], *a butterfly* ACB: folio after Z 2.

**tys ha tas** [tys ha tas] 'tit for tat': GKK says that this phrase is confined to a single instance in PC. This is incorrect: *ha knoukye prest **tys-ha-tas*** PC 2077; *gans ov scorge **tys-ha-tas*** PC 2107; *ha knouk an horn **tys ha tas*** PC 2719. Note also *TYSHATAS, leisurely, by stroke and stroke* ACB: opposite A a 2.

**ugheldir** [uheldyr] 'highlands': GKK suggests that this word is unattested in the texts. This is incorrect: *en **Ehual-dir** an Alban hag en G'laskor Uordhyn* AB: 222.

**usa** [uja, usa] 'to yell, to hoot': GKK says this word is confined to a single instance in CW 1309. This is incorrrect: *yma agys yskar an tebel-ell kepar ha lyon owh **uga*** TH 3a.

**uvelder** [uvelder] 'humility': GKK says this occurs 2-3 times in Middle Cornish. This is incorrect: *der the **vvelder*** BM 2941; *in **vvelder*** BM 4328; *virtu ha **vvelder*** TH 6; *pana **vveldar*** TH 6a; *gans **vvelder*** TH 39.

**veksya** [vexya] 'to vex': GKK says this verb is confined to a single instance at TH 22. This is incorrect, since it occurs also in BM: *me yv **vexijs** anhethek* BM 2630.

**verb** [verb] 'verb': GKK ascribes this neologism to *An Gannas* 1984. This is incorrect, since the word is much older than that. It occurs in Nance and Smith's *Termow Gramasek* of the nineteen-forties. It occurs in CS2 (first published 1955), page 32: *amserow a'n **verb**-ma* and it is not uncommon in ALK: *rag rosa yu parth an **verb** ry* ALK 57 (1957); *Gwerth a yl bos hanow "sale", **verb** "he sells", ha gys gorhemmynek ynweth* ALK 70 (1960); *Tynkyal yu **verb** dyspar* ALK 70 (1960); *deu form dhe nebes*

WRITINGS ON REVIVED CORNISH

*verbow* ALK 72 (1960); *Verbow: - bugelya, devynnes...* ALK 102 (1968); *Verbow ha dhedha –a ha -ya* ALK: 127 (1975).

**walkya** [walkya] 'to walk': GKK says this verb is confined to a single instance in TH. This is incorrect: *Walkyow ha gwandrow* TH 16a; *ef a **walkias** i'n kigg na* SA 64a.

**yaghhe** [yaghhe] 'to heal': GKK says this verb is confined to one instance at RD 1687. This is incorrect: *ow colon yv sur **yaghys*** OM 1381; *ny allaf bos **yagheys*** RD 1591; *bones **yagheys*** RD 1675; *bos **yaghes** thotho yv reys* RD 1708; *te a vyth **yagheys*** RD 1730; *yth of vy **yaghys*** RD 1741; ***yagheys** aban os* RD 1749; *ny yllogh bones **yaghheys*** BM 1500.

**ydhyow** [ydhyow] 'ivy': GKK says this word is confined to a single instance in Lhuyd. This is incorrect: *W. Eidhew, Ivy; Corn[ish] **Idhio*** AB: 15c; ***Idhio** glossing Hedera, The Ivy-tree* AB: 65a. Cf. ***IDHIO**, the ivy tree* ACB: folio after R 2.

**yn** [yn] adverbial particle: under this item GKK gives *yn hwir* 'truly' and says it occurs between 4 and 9 times in Middle and Late Cornish. This is not true, since the form *\*yn whyr* is unattested anywhere in traditional Cornish. 'Truly' in the texts is always *yn gwyr*. This was first pointed out by Caradar (†1950) in his second supplement to CS (published 1955). See now CS2: 31. The expression *an gwyr* 'the truth' is common in the texts. It is likely therefore that *yn gwyr* 'truly' does not contain the adverbial particle *yn* but the preposition *yn* + the definite article *an*. It is for this reason that in the phrase *yn gwyr* the initial *gw* is not mutated. Indeed we should probably write *y'n gwyr* rather than *yn gwyr*. GKK's *\*yn hwir* is wholly spurious. Here are some examples from the texts of *y'n gwyr*: *en gwyr ʒe ʒustynee* PA 210d; *tres aral re got **in guyr*** OM 2549; *lauar **en guyr** thy'm certan* OM 2234; *dew vody tha ough **yn guyr*** OM 2461; *a gevelyn da **yn guyr*** OM 2541. I can find no instances in BM, TH or CW. Notice, however, that Lhuyd writes *En **uir*** 'truly' with lenition (not mixed mutation) glossing *Certe* at AB: 47b and *Quidem* at AB: 134c.

**ynkressya** [encressya] 'to increase': GKK observes that there is also an aphetic form *kressya* [cressya]. The dictionary says that the full form *ynkressya* [encressya] is confined to a single instance in CW. This is incorrect: *encressyens ha bewens pel* OM 48; *encresshys gans charite* TH 49; *theth hays a wra **incressya*** CW 1318; *yth ew **incresshys*** CW 1989.

**yn nes** [yn nes] 'near, by': GKK says that this is confined to a single instance in BM. This is incorrect: *in neys rum caradevder* BM 1309; *saff **in neys*** BM 3470; *in nes in cres paradis* TH 3a; ***in nese** an ii commondment ma* TH 20a.

**ynocent** 'innocent': this adjective is attested in TH: *innocent corffe* TH 15a; *ew da ha **innocent*** TH 25. The plural as a substantive is also attested: *then **ynocens** oma* BM 1708; *gans **Innocentys*** TH 24a. The word appears to be wanting from GKK.

**Ynys** [Enys] 'Shrovetide': GKK says that this is a modern coinage taken from Nance's 1938 dictionary. This is incorrect: *Carnisprivium, ynyd; Shrovetide; C[ornish] **Enez*** AB: 46b. Cf. ***ENEZ**, Shrove tide* ACB: O 2.

**yskar** [yscar] 'canvas, sackcloth': GKK says this word has been taken from Nance's 1955 dictionary, being unattested in the texts. This is incorrect: *a rug usia gwyska **yscar** ha canfas garow, an pith a vetha gwrys syehar anotha* TH 6a; *gans **yskar** ha canfas ha gans dowst ha lusew* TH 6a.

**ys** [ys] 'corn': GKK says this word is confined to two instances in OCV. This is incorrect: *gorre hag **eys** kemyskys* OM 1058; *an dour ha'n **eys** yv posnys* OM 1559; *avel **ys** y[n] nothlennow* PC 881; *bara gwrys a **eys*** TH 57a; *gwrys a kynde vyth a **eys*** TH 57a; *rag rowlya **eys** ha chattell* CW 1064; *an **eys** na'n frutes* CW 1089; *shower a **yees*** CW 1189; *Ise en noare* 'Corn in the ground' Bilbao MS; *Iz bara* glossing *frumentum* AB: 61c; *iz, **iz** saval* glossing *Seges, Standing corn* AB: 147c; *Pedn **iz*** glossing *Spica, The ear of Corn*

AB 153a; *IS, It, Iz, Yd, corn, but chiefly wheat* ACB: folio after R 2; *Whelas megourion tha medge an **isse*** ABC: F f 2; *Whelas colmurian tha kelme an **isse*** ABC: F f 2.

**yssew** [yssew] 'issue': GKK says that this word is confined to CW. This is incorrect: *oll an **ussew** a Adam ha Eva* TH 3.

The errors listed above are neither trivial in nature nor few in number. They do, however, respresent only a fraction of the mistakes in *Gerlyver Kernewek Kemmyn*. Because of lack of time I have not checked the occurrence of words given a frequency code of 4 or higher. Further research would reveal many more errors throughout the work. Certainly, GKK (quite apart from its questionable orthography) compares unfavourably with any of Morton Nance's Cornish dictionaries.

### George, Cornish, and computers

George first described his computational approach to Cornish in a paper "The Use of a Mainframe Computer to Analyse Cornish Orthography" presented to the *Congress of Celtic Studies* in Ottawa in 1986 and published in Maclennan 1988, 89–115. In the published version of the paper George cites a number of etyma and their various spellings in the texts. In figure 11 (page 109) of this article George assures us among other things that the word *ayr(e)* 'air' is unattested in the *Ordinalia*. This is incorrect, for the word is attested in PC: *neb a thue th'agan brugy yn **ayr** deth brus pup huny* PC 1668-69.

Another etymon discussed by George is the Cornish name for *Timothy* which he says is confined to two instances in TH (fig. 12, page 111). He is mistaken, since the name occurs seven times in TH: *in iii chapter the **Tymothe*** TH 17a; *ow scriifa the **timothe*** TH 18a; *O **thimothye*** TH 18a; *in y tressa chapter the **Thimothe*** TH 18a; *Inweth S paule the **Tymothe*** TH 25; *eff a appoyntyas inweth **Thimothe*** TH 33a; *dell rug S paule ordeynya **Tymothe*** TH 33a.

In the same place George asserts that Lhuyd uses the spelling <ithik> for UC *uthek* 'terrible' on one accasion only. I have noticed the following nine examples: ***Ithik*** glossing *Immanis, outrageous, fierce* AB: 68a; ***Ithik**, braz* glossing *Immensus, Unmeasurable, huge* AB: 68a; †*Hail, Leadan,* **ithick**, *braoz* glossing *Largus, Huge, very great; free-hearted, bountiful,* etc. AB: 76c; *Teu, bor. braoz,* ***ithik*** glossing *Obesus* AB: 102a; ***Ithik** tra* glossing *Plurimum, Most of all,* etc. AB: 122b; *Krev,* **ithik** glossing *Strenuus, Valiant, stout, hardy,* etc. AB: 155c; **ithik** *tra* glossing *Valde* AB: 169a; ***ithik** koth* AB: 223 §4 line 8; ***Ithig**, Hugely* AB: 249a.

### Epilogue

George read an early draft of these notes and in a personal communication of the 23 August 1999 explained the errors in GKK as follows:

> My a vynn grassa dhis rag an rol a "fowtow" dannvenys dhymm gans [name]. Rann vrassa anedha yw sevys drefenn: (a) nag esa genev dasskrif kowal a Pryce; (b) ow thowlenn dhe hwilas henwyn-verb hepken; (c) na wrug vri orth ragskrif

Lhuyd in A[rchaeologia] B[ritannica] awos y vos "idiosyncratic and highly Cymricised".

[I want to thank you for the list of "mistakes" sent to me by [name]. The majority of them arose because: (a) I did not have a complete copy of Pryce; (b) my computer program searched for verbal nouns only; (c) I ignored Lhuyd's preface in AB because it was "idiosyncratic and highly Cymricised" (a quotation from the article by me in *Studia Celtica* 32 (1998) 129-154 on pre-occlusion)][1]

A researcher working on a complete computer database of Cornish ought perhaps to have acquired a copy or photocopy of Pryce's important book. If the program used in GKK searched for verbal nouns only, it was clearly unsuited to its task. Besides George's policy with respect to the inclusion of verbal forms in GKK is very inconsistent. GKK includes many idiosyncratic and Cymricized words from Lhuyd. It is not clear why GKK accepts some and repudiates others. The majority of George's omissions from Lhuyd involve the body of *Archæologia Britannica* rather than the few pages (AB: 222-24) of Lhuyd's Cornish preface. In any case it is not apparent why the limitations and qualifications (a), (b) and (c) cited by George were not mentioned in the introduction to GKK.

George's explanation says nothing about the remarkable omissions in GKK from the Middle and Late Cornish texts nor about the other numerous errors of fact. The simplest and most obvious reason for the mistakes in the dictionary is that George's database was inadequate. The database used in compiling GKK, however, had already been used in the construction of Kernowek Kemyn itself. Given that the database was faulty, it is perhaps no wonder that Kernowek Kemyn is so mistaken. A recent attempt by George and P. Dunbar to vindicate Kernowek Kemyn against my criticisms is unconvincing. Indeed Mills (1999) has drawn attention to the shortcomings of Dunbar and George: "To demonstrate individually that each of George's analyses is wrong would take a very long time, simply because there are a lot of analyses and there is very little that could be said to be right about any of them."[2]

And he adds:

Furthermore, when one compares the data reported by Geroge with the primary sources, they do not match. His results and conclusions are, therefore, spurious. George's work thus makes claims about Cornish phonology which are not really justified. Since George's investigation of Cornish phonology is badly flawed, the switch to Kernewek Kemmyn seems to have been an expensive waste of time and energy.[3]

---

1  Now reprinted here, pp. 65–92 above.
2  Mills 1999: 201.
3  Mills 1999: 214.

Mills is critical of all George's work on Cornish phonology and lexicography:

> George's study is, therefore based on conjecture and so, despite his claims, he has not reconstructed the phonology of Cornish. It must be concluded that George's phonology of Cornish is largely invention ... Consensus for an orthography for Revived Cornish will only be reached if that orthography can be demonstrated to be academically sound. It is not for an individual to propose an orthography based on his putative reconstruction of Cornish phonology and then shift the burden of proof by requiring that others demonstrate its shortcomings.[4]

Quite independently of my analysis Mills has arrived at a conclusion identical with mine, namely, that Kernowek Kemyn is a failed experiment in orthographical reform.

---

4    Mills 1999: 200-1.

# PLACE-NAME INCONSISTENCIES IN GEORGE'S *GERLYVER KERNEWEK KEMMYN*

George is very inconsistent about the inclusion of geographical names in GKK. He gives the following names (an asterisk indicates that the name is unattested in the traditional language): *Alban* 'Scotland', *Almayn* 'Germany', *Arabi* 'Arabia', *Bethalem*/*Bethlem* 'Bethlehem', *Dewnens* 'Devonshire', *Ejyp* 'Egypt', *\*Evrek* 'York', *Eynda* 'India', *Frynk* 'France', *Galila* 'Galilee', *\*Gwlas an Hav* 'Somerset', *\*Itali* 'Italy', *Iwerdhon* 'Ireland', *Kembra* 'Wales', *Loundres* 'London', *\*Portyngal* 'Portugal', *Pow Sows* 'England', *Rom* 'Rome', *Spayn* 'Spain' and *Ysrael* 'Israel'. He omits, however, the following attested names:

*Afrika* 'Africa' (**aphrica** TH 32),
*Amerika* 'America' (**America** Gwavas, LAM 238)
*Asia* 'Asia' (**asia** TH 47),
*Beljium* (cf. *Francan-***Belgian** NBoson, LAM 222)
*Bethsaida* 'Bethsaida' (**Bethsaida** TH 47)
*Bithinia* 'Bithynia' (**bithinia** TH 47)
*Bohem* 'Bohemia' (**Bohem** TH 32)
*Ebron* 'Hebron' (*in valy* **ebron** CW 340)
*Galasia* 'Galacia' (**Galacie** TH 47)
*Jermani* 'Germany' (**germany** TH 32, 49a)
*Jerusalem* 'Jerusalem' (**ierusalem** OM 1928, PC 1649; **Jerusalem** TH 27a, 47a, 48; **Jerusalem** Kerew, RC 23: 194 x 2)
*Judi* 'Judea' (**iudi** PC 1594, 1607; **iudy** RD 10)
*Kapadosia* 'Cappadocia' (**cappadocia** TH 47)
*Kreta* 'Crete' (**Creta** TH 33a)
*Lumbardi* 'Lombardy' (**lumbardy** BM 1534)
*Middlesex* 'Middlesex' (*Pow* **Middlesex** Gwavas, LAM 244)
*Nasare* 'Nazareth' (**nazare** PC 1718, 1971, 2197; cf. **Nazareth** Kerew, RC 23: 189)
*Nis* 'Nicea' (*Cucell a* **Nice** SA 65a)
*Pontus* 'Pontus' (**pontus** TH 47)
*Pow an Flemyn* 'Flanders' (**poww an Flemmen** John Tonkin, LAM 226)
*Powys* 'Powys' (*tir* **Powys** Lhuyd, Pryce opposite H h)
*Samaria* 'Samaria' (**Samarya** TH 46a)
*Sesaria* 'Caesarea' (**cesarye** TH 43a)
*Siria* 'Syria' (**Syrya** Kerew RC 23: 192)
*Tir Sans, an* 'the Holy Land' (*the'n* **tyr sans** OM 1879).

# *BEWNANS KE*:
# IMPLICATIONS FOR KERNOWEK KEMYN

In collaboration with Graham Thomas I have recently edited *Bewnans Ke*, a newly discovered Middle Cornish play. Our *editio princeps* of this important work is due to be published later this year (2006) by Exeter University Press. *Bewnans Ke* corroborates most satisfactorily many of the points made in this present work and thus serves to undermine still further the foundations of Kernowek Kemyn. As an epilogue to my various writings on revived Cornish, I should like here to examine some of the ways in which *Bewnans Ke* agrees with the views set out above.

### The date of *Bewnans Ke*
The original text of *Bewnans Ke* was written at some time in the the fifteenth century. Internal evidence seems to sugggest that it was written during the latter part of the reign of Henry VI (1422–61). There are, however, three quite separate scribal strata in the text as we have it. One dating from the period of composition (*c.* 1450), the second probably from the early sixteenth century (*c.* 1500) and the third from the period of the manuscript itself (*c.* 1575-90). This third stratum is particularly interesting inasmuch as it tends to link *Bewnans Ke* in orthography with SA (*c.*? 1570) and CW (1611). Spellings, for example, like *gwyer* 'true' BK 194, 230, 254, 343, 504, *meer* 'great, *mearthysaysys* 'greatly diseased' BK 1227, *thewaw* 'gods' BK 918, *galaraw, gallaraw* 'sorrows' BK 524, 3288, *grasaw* 'graces' BK 536, 1235, *lavaraw* 'utterances' BK 973, 1135, 3089 give the spelling a Late Cornish flavour.

### *Bewnans Ke* and the loss of half-length
George mistakenly believes that Middle Cornish had three separate vocalic lengths, long, half-long and short. Moreover half-long is a variety of long that occurs in disyllables and polysyllables. According to George Middle Cornish *can* 'song' has a long vowel, whereas *canow* 'songs' has a half-long one. Since this latter word has a half-long vowel, we will not find it written with a double <nn>. The spelling *cannow* would not, according to George, occur in Middle Cornish, because that would a) mean that the vowel was short and b) the plural in Late Cornish would perforce be pre-occluded to *\*cadnow*. We do find the plural written with a double <nn> in Late Cornish:

> *Ma **Conna** ve war Hern gen Cock, ha Rûz* 'My songs are of pilchards with boat and net' BF: 46 (Tonkin MS).

George has no problem with this, of course, because he believes that the Prosodic Shift operated *c.* 1625 and the vowel in *canow* 'songs' in Late Cornish is correspondingly short—whereas in Middle Cornish the stressed vowel would, according to George, have been half-long. I, on the other hand, think that half-long was lost in Cornish in the twelfth century and did not exist in Middle Cornish at all. In consequence I should not at all be astonished to see *canow* 'songs' written with a double <nn> in Middle Cornish. The scribe of *Bewnans Ke* agrees with me against George in this matter. He writes:

> *Th'agan palas gwel ew thyn*
> *revertya gans* **cannow** *tek*

> [To our palace it is better for us
> to return with melodious songs] BK 2061-62.

The scribe of *Bewnans Ke* writing *c.* 1575-90 is so sure that the vowel in *canow* 'songs' is short, that he doubles the following <nn> to indicate just that.

### *Thyso* 'to thee' in *Bewnans Ke*
I believe that the spelling <thys>, <ʒys> 'to thee' in Middle Cornish conceals two separate pronunciations. The first is [ði:z] where the vowel is long, and the second is [ðɪs] where the vowel is short. I explain the second of these as deriving from the emphatic form *thyso*, which, I assume, was originally [ði·so]. As a result of the Prosodic Shift the half-long stressed vowel was shortened to give [ðɪsə], which was the basis of the analogical form [ðɪs]. George is emphatic in his denial that the Prosodic Shift had already occurred in Middle Cornish. In his view Cornish did not lose half-length until *c.* 1625. As a result, George claims, *thys* 'to thee' always has a long vowel and in consequence he spells it <dhis> in Kernowek Kemyn. Moreover, according to George, *thyso* always has a half-long stressed vowel and is to be understood as [ði·so]. Unfortunately for George, his putative *thyso* *[ði·so] is not infrequently written with a stressed *e* rather than *y*. This seems to me to be very strong evidence that the word was in fact pronounced with a short (and in consequence lowered) vowel. *Bewnans Ke* spells *thyso* with stressed *e* more frequently than any other Middle Cornish text. I have collected the following examples from the play:

> *Rag trystya* **theso** BK 532
> *ha ry* **theso** *me a ra* BK 627
> *ow ro* **theso** *a vyth clere* BK 640
> *Gramersy* **theso**, *dremas* BK 823
> *ma na relhans* **theso** *bern* BK 859
> **theso** *bys may tewhellyf* BK 1042
> *Syr Teuthar, mer gras* **theso** BK 1081
> *Sau ol* **theso** *me a'n gaf* BK 1097
> *Desympys rys ew* **theso** BK 1112
> **theso** *war ver lavarow* BK 1579
> **theso** *drys an re erall* BK 1989

*Me a wor **theso** mer gras* BK 3073
*neffra **theso** ny falla'* BK 3213.

I assume that in these cases the stressed vowel is short and is /ɪ/, which in open syllables as here, is in free variation with /e/. The spelling of this prepositional pronoun in *Bewnans Ke* would seem to offer very strong evidence indeed that the stressed vowel is short, and thus that the Prosodic Shift was a *fait accompli* in Middle Cornish. In other words, Kernowek Kemyn is based on a mistaken phonology.

### Final stressed -u/-ew in *Bewnans Ke*

George thinks that in Middle Cornish final -u in such words as *du* 'black', *tu* 'side' and *tru* 'pity, alas' was long [y:], i.e. the vowel in French *lune* 'moon'. I cannot follow him here. I agree that *du* was originally [dy:], that is to say a long (trimoric) high front rounded vowel. I believe, however, that as a result of the Prosodic Shift in Middle Cornish [dy:] lost a mora to become dimoric. Schematically we can understand /dy:/ as [dy·y], where the syllable nucleus and the syllabic coda are at the same height. When, as result of the Prosodic Shift, the vowel shortened, the nucleus, because it was shorter, untensed and lowered. It was thus at a different height from the coda, which remained high and rounded. The nucleus, however, unrounded and as a result the whole became [ɪw]. It is for this reason *dew* 'God' is often spelt <du> in the texts. It is also why the in Middle Cornish 'woe, pain' is *gew* and *gu*, 'spear' is *gew* and *gu*, 'sharp' is *glew* and *glu*, 'who' is *pew* and *pu*, 'parish' is *plew* and *plu* and 'side' is *tu* and *tew*.

It is apparent that George has not read the Middle Cornish texts with sufficient care, because he says that we have only one example in Middle Cornish of <ew> to denote /y:/ i.e. *trew* at PC 150, where, he says, it is so written to give an eye-rhyme with *tergwyth hythew* at line 147 (KKC21: 113). He is mistaken: we also have the following examples of historic final -u spelt <ew>:

*trew ny re behas* CW 852 [tru]
*war bub **tewe*** CW 49 [tu]
*yn **tew** ma* CW 56 [tu]
*war bub **tew*** CW 138 [tu]
*neb **tew*** CW 1045 [tu]
*pub **tew*** CW 1256 [tu]
*pub **tew*** CW 1971 [tu]
*war bub **tew*** CW 2142 [tu].

Moreover, since the discovery of *Bewnans Ke*, we have the remarkable line:

*Pandra rama? **Tru, treu, trew**!* 'What shall I do? Alas, alas, alas!' BK 1018.

The scribe spells *tru* (cf. W *tru*) both as *tru* on the one hand and as *treu, trew* on the other. No one could, I think, possibly deny that *tru* and *treu/trew* are the

189

same word and therefore have but one pronunciation, yet they are spelt in two quite separate ways, ie. with either the single vowel <u> or the diphthong <eu>, <ew>. This must surely mean that final -*u* and final -*ew* in this word (and in others like it) are pronounced identically. But they can only be identical in pronunciation, if the Prosodic Shift has operated and final -*u* [y:] has become [ɪw]. This piece of evidence from *Bewnans Ke* seems to me to suggest very clearly that the Prosodic Shift is a *fait accompli* in Middle Cornish and that, in consequence, Kernowek Kemyn is based upon a mistaken phonology.

### *Bewnans Ke* and *bannath* 'blessing'

In my various writings on Cornish, and in particular in my chapter on pre-occlusion above, I have suggested that the pre-occlusion of [n] > [ᵈn] and of [m] > [ᵇm] was a dialect feature, pre-occluded forms being for the most part more westerly than those without pre-occlusion. I have also suggested the more easterly dialects without pre-occlusion lost the distinction between /n:/ and /n/ before pre-occlusion could take place. Moreover, because they had lost this distinction, in compensation they tended to lower [e] to [æ] before original /n/ from earlier /n:/. As a result we find a clear distinction in the Middle Cornish texts between on the one hand westerly dialects exhibiting *benneth* 'blessing' (later *bedneth* BM 198, 224, 225; *bedna* CW 1541) and more easterly ones on the other that show *bannath* and no evidence of pre-occlusion at all.

The text of *Bewnans Ke* as we have it, was written in the last quarter of the sixteenth century, well after the first occurrences of pre-occlusion in BM, in SA and in place-names. *Bewnans Ke* contains over 3,000 lines of Cornish verse and yet there is not a single instance of pre-occlusion anywhere in the text. In addition the word for 'blessing' is invariably spelt with lowered vowel, *bannath, vannath* at BK 651, 1567, 1575, 1583, 2897, 3048, 3055 and 3114. This would seem argue strongly against George's view that pre-occlusion was a function of chronology. If George were right, we would expect to find examples of pre-occlusion somewhere in the play. Indeed the absence of pre-occlusion together with the invariable spelling of *bannath* with a lowered vowel neatly corroborates my view that pre-occlusion was a dialectal feature.

### *Bewnans Ke* and *alenna* 'thence'

Under the word *alena* 'thence' in GKK George adds a note: "N.B. incorrectly spelt *alenna* by Nance; the etymology indicates <n>, and if it had contained /nn/, it would have become *\*aledna* in LateC[ornish]". George is here confusing two quite separate matters. Nance spelt the word *alenna*, because it is so spelt by Kerew: *Ha moaze **alenna**, e a wellaz moy deaw broderath* 'And going thence he saw two more brothers' RC 23: 191. The double <nn> shows that the preceding vowel is short. The spelling <nn> does not necessarily imply pre-occlusion in the later language. Indeed some dialects of later Middle Cornish lacked pre-occlusion completely (cf. the observations above about the dialectal difference between *benneth* and *bannath*).

It is quite customary for the Tudor texts to write both <n> and <nn> in the same word. The geminate spelling merely implies that the preceding vowel is short. It does not mean that the <nn> ought to be pre-occluded. Tregear, for example, writes *cristonnyan* 'Christians' TH 26a, 27, 27a but *cristonyan* TH 28, 28a, 29, 56; *nenna* 'then' TH 16a, but *nena* TH 9a, 17a, 18, 19 and *ynnans, innans* 'in them' TH 6a, 38a but *ynans* TH 14. The same also is true for the scribe of *Bewnans Ke*. He writes *fystynnyn* 'let us hasten' BK 2755 but *fistenyn* BK 1353 and *honnyn* 'self' BK 312 but *honen* BK 466, *honyn* BK 1436, 2750. The scribe of *Bewnans Ke* on occasion writes <nh> as a graph for <nn>, i.e. to indicate that the preceding vowel is short. He writes: *gwenhal* 'swallow' BK 1109, *e gonha* 'his neck' BK 1221 and *the gonha* 'thy neck' BK 2162. He also writes:

*Me a vyn mos, re'n gwerhesow*
*mos thu'm sofran* **alenha**

[I will go, by the holy virgins
to my sovereign thence] (BK: 1308-09).

Here he writes *alenha* for *\*alenna*, to show that the vowel is short. He is not worried that the word will be read with pre-occlusion because his dialect lacks it. The scribe of *Bewnans Ke* also, however, writes *Ow arluth, deugh* **alena** 'My lord, go from thence' BK 1139, with a single <n>. Clearly for him the preceding vowel was short, and he could in consequence write either *alena* or *alenha* (for *alenna*). Although he was writing at the end of the sixteenth century, pre-occlusion is not part of his dialect.

George believes that the vowel in *alena* was half-long. The evidence from *Bewnans Ke* suggests that this was not so. George also believes that pre-occlusion was a function of period, not of dialect. *Bewnans Ke* from the last quarter of the sixteenth century ought, according to George, to show pre-occlusion but it does not. George's view cannot be sustained.

The two spellings *alenha* and *alena* in *Bewnans Ke* are further evidence that Kernowek Kemyn is based upon a mistaken phonology.

### The reflex of Old Cornish -*d*- in *Bewnans Ke*

George appears to believe that Old Cornish -*d*- developed differently in the later language according to whether the segment was after the stressed vowel in a disyllable or a trisyllable. Thus he believes that in disyllables the -*d*- was assibilated early and became either [z] or [dʒ]. Thus we find both *pysy* and *pygy* 'to pray' in Middle Cornish. In trisyllables, however, George claims that -*d*- assibilated to -*dz*- and remained so until *c.* 1675 when it became [dʒ]. This is a remarkable assertion, and one which can easily be shown to be mistaken (see TAC: 15.07). I do not intend here to explain how and why this interpretation of George's is wrong. I should however like to indicate how little *Bewnans Ke* agrees with George on the matter.

George believes that in the Old Cornish personal name *Cadoc* the medial segment would have assibilated before the period of the Middle Cornish texts and would therefore appear in Middle Cornish as either *Casek* or *Cagek* i.e. with either [z] <s> or [dʒ] <g>. Old Cornish *lagadoc* 'large-eyed, observant', on the other hand, would have developed into *lagadzek* at the same time as *Cadoc* > *Casek*, but, according to George, would not have become *lagadgack* until *c.* 1675.

This suggestion of George's is not compelling and I have set out the reasons for my scepticism in TAC. It would appear, moreover, that the scribe of *Bewnans Ke* agrees with me against George on this point. He writes *ny ve the bar re* **Gasak** 'there was not thy like, by St Cadoc' at line BK 722 but *te pen boba* **lagajak** 'you goggle-eyed buffoon' BK 210 and *Gwra indella* **lagajak** 'do so, you goggle-eyed one' BK 367. He also writes *in dryngys dv* **marthojak** 'in God the miraculous Trinity' BK 250. It would seem therefore that *Casek* (without palatalization; cf. *pysy*) is *Casak* to the scribe of *Bewnans Ke* but George's *lagadzek* and *marthodzek* have already palatalized their medial segment to [dʒ] in *Bewnans Ke*, i.e. by *c.* 1575. According to George, however, such palatalization did not occur until *c.* 1675, i.e. a century later.

## *Bewnans Ke* and George's respelling

George is fond of respelling words in the Middle Cornish texts when, as so often, he thinks the writers of traditional Cornish could not spell properly. For example George dislikes *arluth* 'lord', *bewnans* 'life', *bythqueth* 'never (in the past)', *whylas / whelas* 'to seek', *cafus / cafos* 'to get' and *clewes / clowes* 'to hear' and rewrites them *arloedh*, *bywnans*, *bythkweyth*, *hwilas*, *kavoes* and *klywes* respectively. It is not astonishing, therefore, that he decides in GKK to respell the Old Cornish word *pridit* 'poet' as *prysydh* and he adds a note: 'N.B. Up-dated from OldC[ornish].' Here he has not been content merely to adapt the Old Cornish othography to Middle Cornish scribal practice. He has actually assibilated the medial -*d*- without any warrant. Unfortunately for George, the word is now attested in *Bewnans Ke*: *moun senior, an* **prydyth** *mort* BK 2497. I take this to be for *moun senior, re'n prydyth mort* 'my lord, by the dead poet' and to be a reference to Virgil, who was revered in the Middle Ages. Clearly the -*d*- was unassibilated in Middle Cornish, presumably because of the preceding *r*. The -*d*- is also unassibilated in both Unified Cornish and in Unified Cornish Revised. George's "up-dating" is erroneous.

## George's lexical purism and 'lion' in *Bewnans Ke*

George throughout GKK exhibits rather naïve ideas of lexical purism. He not infrequently cites an item, which he takes to be a borrowing from English, and then adds a note advising his readers to use a more native word, in some cases even where the native word does not bear the same sense as the word he is seeking to proscribe. And that is not all. Under *fannya* 'to fan', for example, he advises his readers to use the invented word *gwynsella* in preference, but remarkably does not trouble to include *gwynsella* in his own dictionary.

*Fannya* is indeed borrowed from English but is in origin a Latin word and there are many Latin borrowings that George would not, I think, proscribe, e.g. *eglos* [eglos] 'church', *koska* [cusca] 'to sleep', *dyski* [desky] 'to learn, to teach', *pobel* [pobel] 'people' and *dy' Gwener* [de Gwener] 'Friday' for example.

Under the headword *lion* [lyon] 'lion' George tells his readers to use lew in preference. *Lew* is itself a borrowing from Latin *leo* 'lion', and is attested only in Old Cornish and in Lhuyd, who found it in OCV. The word for 'lion' in Middle Cornish is *lyon* and is attested at PA 21c and TH 3a. It is now also attested in *Bewnans Ke*:

> *Whath **luon** goyth in y ugo thys a ynclyn* 'Moreover a wild lion in his den bows
>    down to you' BK 1777-79.

There is no conceivable reason to use *\*lew*, which is unknown in Middle Cornish, in preference to *lyon*, which is well attested.

### *Procedya* 'to proceed' and *reportya* 'to report' in *Bewnans Ke*

George cites *procedya* from Tregear in GKK s.v. *\*prosedya*. His "authentication code" make it clear that the word is well attested, but George advises his readers to use *mos yn-rag* (why the hyphen?) in preference. It is certainly true that *ke yn rak, dun yn rak*, etc. are not uncommon in the Middle Cornish texts, but *procedya* is not confined to TH, since it also occurs now in *Bewnans Ke*: *mar quver e **procedya*** 'if one is going to proceed with it' BK 1414. Since *procedya* has been in Middle Cornish since the fifteenth century at the latest, George's advice is out of place. There is nothing against using *mos yn rag*, but there is nothing against using *procedya* either.

George cites *reportya* from Tregear in GKK but in a note tells his readers to use *derivas* [deryvas] in preference. This is unnecessary advice, since *reportya* is now to be found three times in *Bewnans Ke*:

> *Du Jovyn ew dyawl pub ur, del ma ef ow **reportya*** 'The God Jovin is a devil, as he
>    always asserts' BK 940-41
> *Ny yl tavas **reportya** i'n tor' ma mur a'th noe* 'Tongue cannot at the moment report
>    much of your nephew' BK 3194a-96a
> *Ny yl tavas **reportya** i'n tur' ma myuns us yna* 'Tongue cannot at this moment
>    report all that is there' BK 3194b-95b.

*Reportya* has clearly been part of the lexicon of Middle Cornish since at least the fifteenth century. Moreover *reportya* 'to report' and *deryvas* 'to relate, tell, state' are not synonyms, although their meanings overlap. Again *Bewnans Ke* undermines George's purism.

### *Lewd, lewdnes* in *Bewnans Ke*

The word *lewd* in English is from Old English *lǽwede* 'lay, ignorant'. By the Middle English period it meant 'base, wicked' and had this sense when it was borrowed into Cornish. Until now we have had one example each of the word *lewd* itself and of the abstract noun *lewdnes* 'wickedness':

> *amendia aga lewde* **bewnans** 'to amend their wicked lives' TH 29a
> *Vn teball person a yll tenna lyas onyn arell the* **lewdnes** 'One evil person can lead many others to wickedness' TH 25a.

With the discovery of *Bewnans Ke*, however, both words are better attested:

> *Ow holan ew crackys quyt drefen why th'y lowenhe der* **lewd** *omthon* 'My heart is quite cracked because you gave him joy by wicked behaviour' BK 2341
> *The* **leud** *desyr a'm cuth por wyer* 'Your wicked desire afflicts me in very truth' BK 2952
> **Leud** *ema owth umbrevy mar goyth pan ra ankevy pryns mar ryall* 'She is proving wicked when she so quickly forgets such a royal prince' BK 3001-03
> *The* **leudnys** *gas rag meth an bys* 'Give over your wickedness for the shame of the world' BK 2209-10.

Neither *lewd* nor *lewdnes* was included by George in his GKK. Thus for reasons of linguistic purism he has omitted from the main dictionary of Kernowek Kemyn two words that have been an essential part of the Cornish lexicon since the fifteenth century at the latest.

### *Spryngya* in *Bewnans Ke*
*Spryngya* 'to spring' occurs five times in TH. George has omitted it from GKK, however, presumably because he did not consider the word to be sufficiently "Cornish." The word is now attested in *Bewnans Ke* and has been in the language at least since the fifteenth century:

> *A Christ, re be benegas! Atomma fyntan* **spryngys!** 'O Christ, be thou blessed! Behold a spring has burst forth! BK: 778-89.

George's omission is regrettable.

### Conclusion
It will be seen from the few pages above that *Bewnans Ke* corroborates in a most satisfactory way some of my many criticisms of Kernowek Kemyn. On the other hand there is no aspect of the orthography or phonology *Bewnans Ke* that gives any comfort to George and his understanding of Middle Cornish. *Bewnans Ke* has severe implications both for Kernowek Kemyn and for George's lexicographical efforts, since the play contradicts George in the following ways:

1) *cannow* 'songs' has a short stressed vowel
2) *thyso* / *theso* 'to thee' has a short stressed vowel, and it is from this that *thys* [ðɪz] 'to thee' is derived by analogy
3) *alenha* 'thence' has a short stressed vowel and the medial consonant is not pre-occluded as is shown from the variant *alena*

4) *benneth* and *bannath* are dialectal variants, and dialects that exhibit *bannath* do no pre-occlude

5) *tru* and *trew* are variant spellings of the same word and they indicate that the vowel sequence in both cases is [ɪw] or [ew] and thus that the Prosodic Shift is already a *fait accompli*

6) *lagajak* and *marthojak* show that George's alleged shift *\*lagadzek > lagagek* "*c.* 1675" is groundless

7) George's respelling of Old Cornish *pridit* as *\*prysydh* is incorrect. The word should be *prydyth* (as is the case in UC and UCR)

8) The word for 'lion' in Middle Cornish is invariably *lyon, luon*; there is no warrant for *\*lew*.

9) *procedya* 'to proceed' and *reportya* 'to report' have been in Cornish at least since the fifteenth century and there is no reason to proscribe either.

10) *lewd* 'wicked', *lewdnes* 'wickedness' and *spryngya* 'to spring' have all formed part of the lexicon of Cornish since the fifteenth century. They should not be omitted from any dictionary of revived Cornish claiming to be "modern and scholarly".

There are also ways in which *Bewnans Ke* corroborates my views against the exposition of Cornish syntax found in Wella Brown's *Grammar of Modern Cornish* of 1993. I have dealt with some of the deficencies in Brown's grammar in my forthcoming book TAC, in which I cite as evidence many examples from *Bewnans Ke*.

Although there is much in *Bewnans Ke* which reinforces my criticisms of Kernowek Kemyn, it contains nothing which might *per contra* support George's system. This is not astonishing. Kernowek Kemyn attempts to recast the entire spelling system of Cornish on the basis of one man's unproven theories. Indeed I, and other commentators, would go so far as to say that Kernowek Kemyn is not Cornish at all, but is rather an artificial language, based more or less on traditional Cornish sources. In this context it is difficult not to agree with the late Peter Pool when he writes:

> Their [i.e. the supporters of Kernowek Kemyn] main success has been the hijacking of the Language Board. Kemyn was first made public in a book published by Kenneth George in 1986; before the end of 1987, a caucus of its supporters had caused the Board to abandon its commitment to Unified and to proclaim that the future lay in Kemyn. They must have been astonished by the ease and rapidity of their initial success; consultation was minimal, and no attempt was made to find out what users of Cornish really wanted. Most supporters of Unified had little idea what was going on until it was too late.... [W]e found that the Language Board, which as followers of Morton Nance we had founded to continue his work for Cornish, based on his Unified system, had fallen into the hands of his detractors and Unified's opponents. The work of sixty years of revival, led by a scholar and prophet of true learning and vision, and then continued by the Language Board, had been cast aside and replaced by the theories of a false prophet.

> (Pool 1995: 7)

# UNIFIED CORNISH REVISED*

Cornish died at the end of the eighteenth century and did not therefore survive long enough to be analysed by modern methods. We cannot in consequence know exactly how it was pronounced at any time in its history—though we can make some informed guesses. All we have are the remains of written Cornish from the twelfth century to the eighteenth. If we want to revive Cornish, these texts must of necessity be our chief source for the language. Place-names are a further source, as are survivals of Cornish words in English dialect.

The texts we have in Cornish date from the Old Cornish period (twelfth century) to the Late Cornish period (eighteenth century). The bulk of our literary survivals, however, are in Middle Cornish. Until the recent discovery of *Bewnans Ke* we had five major texts, namely: *Pascon agan Arluth*, probably composed in the fourteenth century, the three plays of the Ordinalia (*Origo Mundi, Passio Christi, Resurrexio Domini*), dating from the fifteenth century; *Beunans Meriasek* of 1504, John Tregear's homilies of *c.* 1555 and the *Creation of the World*, transcribed in 1611 (though the original is probably early sixteenth century). *Bewnans Ke* was probably composed during the reign of Henry VI (1422–1461) but the manuscript is from about 1575 or 1580 and contains spellings that are suggestive of Late Cornish. Incidentally, the first scholarly edition of *Bewnans Ke*, edited by Graham Thomas and me, will be published by the University of Exeter at the end of next month.

After the *Creation of the World* in 1611, our remains of Cornish are *Nebbaz Gerriau* and *Jowan Chy an Horth*, together with miscellaneous letters, rhymes, poems, translations of scripture, etc. Perhaps the most important lexicographical source for Cornish are those Cornish words listed by the Welsh scholar Edward Lhuyd in his "Comparative Vocabulary" (AB: 41–179).

It is quite clear that Middle Cornish had a traditional orthography. The system varies over time and from text to text, but there is an underlying consistency. The spelling of Middle Cornish is based on the spelling of Old Cornish. This itself was inherited from the early Christian period when the Brythonic peoples, Welsh, Cornish and Bretons, learnt to write from Latin-speaking Christian missionaries. Middle Cornish has adopted features from Norman French and/or Middle English, for example <gh> for [x]. Some commentators deny that Middle Cornish ever had a traditional orthography. They claim that the spelling of Middle Cornish is an *ad hoc* system based for

---

\* A lecture given in Tremough in September 2006, organized by Jenefer Lowe, Cornish Language Development Manager for the Cornish Language Partnership.

the nonce by each scribe on Middle English. This view can be shown to be erroneous for many reasons. Let me list some of them.

1. Middle Cornish spelling and Late Cornish spelling differ greatly. If there was no Cornish orthographical tradition, both Middle Cornish and Late Cornish spelling must alike be based in an *ad hoc* way upon English. In which case we can legitimately ask, why are they so completely different?

2. Middle Cornish orthography with minor variations is the same from the Charter Fragment in the fourteenth century until Tregear's homilies in the second half of the sixteenth century. Thereafter the traditional spelling begins to decay. We can see the orthography deteriorating in *Sacrament an Alter* (?1570) and in the *Creation of the World* (1611). By the later seventeenth century there is no consistency in the way texts are spelt. The same word is written in several different ways by the same author in the same text. It is quite obvious that the dissolution of the monasteries (1538–1541) and the ensuing closure of Glasney (1548) has had a catastrophic effect on the spelling of Cornish. People who learnt to spell in Glasney—John Tregear, for example—continue to spell as they learnt. As a result, the scribal tradition continued for a generation until the last of the writers trained in Glasney died out. A later scribe, William Jordan, when copying the *Creation* is able to preserve much of the old system simply by following his original. By the time of Nicholas Boson, however, there is chaos.

3. One only has to examine the *ad hoc* English-based spelling systems used on occasion to write Irish, to see how inconsistent and indeed misleading such orthographies are. They put one immediately in mind of Late Cornish spelling. The consistent spelling of Middle Cornish is a completely different matter. The Middle Cornish texts suggest to a trained historical linguist that we are dealing with a long tradition, not an *ad hoc* orthography loosely based on another language. I have, incidentally, discussed this question at length in my forthcoming book *Towards Authentic Cornish*, which will be published at the end of November 2006.

4. When we speak of a scribal tradition we mean a consistent spelling system. We find variations within it, since absolute regularity of spelling was not considered necessary until the advent of printing and mass literacy. Nonetheless there was a strong literary tradition in medieval and early Tudor Cornwall. Nobody, I think, would deny this. The plays and *Pascon agan Arluth* are all written in syllabic metres. Lines for the most part contain four or (more commonly)

seven syllables. These metres owe nothing to English. Nor are they based on Breton models, having more in common with Welsh than with anything else. If Cornish had a traditional metrical system, we can be absolutely sure that it had a scribal tradition as well.

5. A final reason for believing that Cornish had a vigorous scribal tradition can be stated negatively. If there was no scribal tradition, no traditional orthography in Cornwall before the Reformation, what was the point of the scriptorium in Glasney? What did it teach its students, if not to read and write literary Cornish?

I therefore take it as given that there was a vigorous scribal tradition in Middle Cornish. In which case it would seem sensible to revive the language using that tradition, that is, using the orthography of Cornish while it was being cultivated by people literate in it. It is unwise, it seems to me, to attempt to revive the unsystematic spelling systems of the Late Cornish period, where the same word is spelt in so many different ways. The chaotic spelling of Late Cornish has a further disadvantage in that it cuts its users off from all other varieties of revived Cornish. They can read Late Cornish but nothing else.

I have just said that we are reviving Cornish, but that is not strictly true. We are not reviving the language but resuscitating it. This is an important point and one which cannot be overemphasized. People sometimes talk about spelling reform in Cornish in the same breath as spelling reforms in other languages. Spelling reform for Cornish, however, is inadmissible. There is nothing wrong with a spelling reform, for example, in German, Breton, or Irish, because all those languages have native speakers. We know exactly how German, Breton, and Irish are pronounced, we know the quality and length of the vowels, the nature of the consonants, the position of the accent, and the intonation. If we want to learn anything about the phonology, all we have to do is listen to native speakers. Indeed the scholars who plan the various spelling reforms are likely themselves to have the language in question as their mother tongue. In Cornish, however, we have no community of native speakers. We know nothing for certain about the phonology, the vowels, consonants, stress or intonation of the language. We are not therefore entitled to respell it. We may spell only as the native speakers spelt. We may regularize spelling for consistency, but we may not invent.

We know very little for certain about the pronunciation of traditional Cornish. But let us say for the sake of argument that we did. That does not then entitle us to rewrite the spelling of the resuscitated language on the basis of our knowledge. We are reviving a language as it was. That means using the spelling that the writers of the traditional language used. If we use any other system, how regular and easy to learn it is—how phonemic even—is irrelevant. Even if the underlying phonology were completely accurate, we would not be reviving Cornish.

Of course, we do not know everything there is to know about the language. Our understanding of the sound system is *ipso facto* inferential, imperfect, hypothetical, and likely to change in the light of further discoveries. If a synthetic orthography contains symbols for "phonemes" that are later shown never to have existed, the offending items will have to be removed at great effort, expense, and indeed embarrassment. We have, therefore only one course open to us: to spell as the scribes of traditional Cornish spelt. If we do otherwise, we lay ourselves open to the charge that the language we are attempting to revive is not really Cornish. It is closer perhaps to fictional and constructed languages than it is to traditional Cornish.

There are no exact parallels for the Cornish revival, although the closest example is probably Manx. The last native speaker of Manx died at the end of 1974 and thus Manx, like Cornish, is a linguistic orphan. The situation in Man is not quite the same as in Cornwall, since we have much more Manx than Cornish. The whole Bible was translated into Manx, and we have two translations of the Book of Common Prayer. We also have dictionaries, secular and religious poetry, hymns and folktales, as well as a huge corpus of speech taken down in phonetic script or on dictaphone from the last generation of speakers (some of this material has recently been transfered to CD). We know therefore exactly how Manx should be pronounced. The spelling of Manx, however, is a nightmare. Manx is unlike its sister languages, Irish and Scottish Gaelic, in not using the common Gaelic orthography. Rather it uses an orthography based on Scottish English of the sixteenth century. Thus, for example, Irish and Scottish Gaelic write *an cuan* 'the harbour, the sea' ([ə kuːən]), whereas Manx writes *y keayn*, which it pronounces with a pre-occluded *n* ([ə kɪᵈn]). Manx orthography is extremely difficult to learn and is full of pitfalls for the unwary. No one, however, has seriously suggested that the revival should respell Manx to make it look like Scottish Gaelic. Scholars and revivalists alike know that to do so would be to relinquish all claims to be reviving Manx. Revived Manx must be written in the spelling of traditional Manx, however awkward this may be. We know exactly how Manx was pronounced, but to recast the spelling in line with the other Gaelic languages, would be to repudiate traditional Manx. The language of revival must be the traditional language. What is true for Manx is as true for Cornish, and indeed more so. We know exactly how Manx was pronounced; we are much less certain with Cornish. We must therefore cling to the traditional spelling, lest we go astray and attempt to revive what was never in the language.

It must be admitted here, however, that there are two small ways in which Unified Cornish Revised (like Unified Cornish) deviates from the Middle Cornish texts. In the first place Unified Cornish Revised uses the graph <dh> to distinguish [ð] from [θ]. If we did not use <dh>, we would have to use <th> for both [ð] and [θ]. This would mean learning in each case, for example, that *netha* 'sew', *cletha* 'sword' and *thetha* 'to them' had [ð] but *gwetha* 'keep', *fetha* 'overcome' and *quetha* 'clothe, cover with cloth' had [θ]. This would greatly increase the difficulty of learning to write the language. It should be pointed out that the use of <dh> for the <th> of the texts is a very well-established practice. The first person to use <dh> when transcribing Middle Cornish was Edward Lhuyd—nearly 300 years ago. He writes for example:

> *Ha hed**h**yu me a d**h**esir dre ow grath dalleth an beys*
> *Y lavaraf nef ha tyr, bed**h**ens formys orth ow brys* (AB: 265)

and

> *Ha Redemsion gran[t]eys*
> *Der vercy a **Dh**ew an Tase*
> *Mynstrells grewgh d**h**eny peba*
> *May hallan warbarth downsia* (ibid.)

and

> *Tays ha mab ha speris sans*
> *Wy a bys a leun golon*
> *Re wronte d**h**eugh gras ha whans*
> ***Dh**e wolsowas y bassyon* (ibid.).

It must be remembered that these quotations from the Ordinalia, the *Creation of the World* and *Pascon agan Arluth* using <dh> were penned when Cornish was still spoken. Lhuyd, therefore, was not introducing anything into an extinct language. It is also worth noting that some writers of Late Cornish, William Gwavas and John Boson, for example, adopted <dh> from Lhuyd when they themselves wrote Cornish.

Like Unified Cornish, Unified Cornish Revised uses <j> to represent the sound [dʒ], where the texts not infrequently write <g>. <j> is a common enough graph for [dʒ] in the Middle Cornish texts in such words as *a'n jeves* 'he has', *an jeth* 'the day', *nynj o* 'was not', *pejadow* 'prayer', *rejoycya* 'rejoice', *an jowl* 'the devil' and *Jowan* 'John'. Unified Cornish Revised (following Unified Cornish) also writes *pejy* 'pray', *mejor* 'reaper' and *ujy* 'is there' although the texts have <g> in these words, not <j>. It should be noted, however, that Lhuyd, writing while Cornish was still alive, spells the [dʒ] in such words as <dzh>. Jenner and Nance considered it legitimate to extend the <j> of the texts to represent the [dʒ] of these items and others like them, which Lhuyd spelt <dzh>. In this matter Unified Cornish Revised follows them. If we spelt exactly as the texts do, we would have to write the [ndʒ] in *changya* 'change' and the [ŋ] in *hangya* 'hang' in exactly the same way; but *chanjya* is more convenient. I should also point out that the recent discovery of *Bewnans Ke* has increased the instances in traditional Cornish of the use of <j> in words where it had previously not been known. We have two examples, for example, of *lagajak* 'sharp-sighted' (UCR *lagajek*) and one of *marthojek* 'miraculous'. If we had more traditional Cornish we would probably find further examples of <j> for [dʒ].

Not everybody is happy with the use of <dh> and <j> in Unified Cornish and thus in Unified Cornish Revised. Indeed were we starting the revival from scratch, I myself would probably recommend using <th> and <g>, exactly as they are attested in our foundation texts. In my book *Clappya Kernowek* I included in Appendix E the entire text of "Jowan Chy an Horth" in a wholly traditional orthography, without <dh>, and with <j> only in those places where it occurs in the texts. It is probable, however, that most Cornish speakers would now consider such a change to be highly inconvenient.

The use of <dh> and <j> in Unified Cornish Revised are small adaptations for the sake of clarity. They do not constitute a system created *de novo* on the basis of this or that unproven hypothesis. For the rest, Unified Cornish Revised attempts to revive Cornish in its traditional spelling. It does so, because no other option is open to revivalists. We must write as the writers of traditional Cornish wrote. We do have a choice, however, as to which era we choose as the foundation period for the Cornish we seek to resuscitate. It seems to me wise to base our revived language on the latest period when Cornish was still widely written in the traditional spelling. Nance based Unified Cornish on the texts of the fifteenth century. Unified Cornish Revised prefers the sixteenth and early seventeenth centuries. *Beunans Meriasek* was written in 1504, Tregear dates from *c*. 1555, *Sacrament an Alter*, the last sermon in the Tregear manuscript dates from *c*. 1575 and the *Creation of the World* was written in 1611, although it is probably a copy of a pre-Reformation original and may have been composed *c*. 1520. *Bewnans Ke* was composed in the mid-fifteenth century but the sole surviving manuscript dates from *c*. 1585. These texts are close in time to one another and form something of a unity. Together they also provide us with by far the largest body of traditional Cornish we have. I calculate that *Beunans Meriasek*, Tregear, *Bewnans Ke* and the *Creation of the World* together give us over 75,000 words of Cornish. This compares with fewer than 60,000 words from *Pascon agan Arluth* and the Ordinalia together.

I believe Tregear is of the greatest possible importance for the Cornish Revival. This is for a number of reasons. In the first place Tregear's text is the only major work we have which is entirely in prose. It is thus entirely without the inversions so common in verse when the writer is anxious to find a rhyme. In the second place, although Tregear's sermons are translations, they deal with practical theology and are aimed at the laity. They are exactly the kind of text that we need, if we wish to develop a simple but idiomatic prose style.

It has been suggested that Tregear was not a native speaker of Cornish—a view which can be summarily dismissed. Tregear's syntax and idiom are perfect in a way that only the speech of a practised native speaker would be perfect. It is true that Tregear uses many English borrowings, but this is likely to reflect the Cornish preaching style of the period rather than anything else, and is reminiscent of *brezonek ar veleien* or 'priests' Breton'. This was a homiletic dialect of Breton which used a great admixture of French words, in part no doubt to impress the listeners with the preacher's erudition.

When in 1995 I first proposed Unified Cornish Revised, I did so because I believed, as I still believe, that there was nothing seriously wrong with Unified. There were a number of errors and infelicities in it that arose, perhaps, because Nance was not a trained linguist. His observations about Cornish phonology are sometimes a little naïve. He says in one place for example that "**gh** is a faintly guttural *h*, tending to become quite silent" (Nance 1949: 2). Linguists these days avoid the term "guttural" as being imprecise and speak rather of a voiceless velar fricative [x] and a voiceless glottal fricative [h]. In the sentence just quoted it is difficult to know exactly what Nance means. Nance also made a number of palpable mistakes. He did not perhaps realise that the vowel in *dues* 'come!' and *an dus* 'the people' was different. Neither did he understand the phonetic alternation of *g/k* in such pairs as *wheg* 'sweet, pleasant' but *anwhek* 'harsh, unpleasant'. He seems wrongly to have believed that *hadre* 'while' was stressed on the first syllable rather than the second, and thus wrongly spells the word *\*hedra*. Overall, however, Nance stayed very close indeed to the language of the texts and thus produced something that was undoubtedly Cornish.

There are, however, two aspects of Unified Cornish that render it less than perfect as a medium for the revival (and I am not talking here about minor errors like those listed above). The first defect, I believe, was that Nance based Unified Cornish on *Pascon agan Arluth* and the Ordinalia. These are fine texts and indeed both have been rightly described as masterpieces. They were, however, in verse and they date from the earliest stages of literary Middle Cornish. The language of both is archaic in form and restricted in scope. It is a pity that Nance did not concentrate more on the looser and more advanced syntax of *Beunans Meriasek* and the less archaic inflection of the *Creation of the World*. Tregear's homilies did not come to light until Nance was an old man and he did not have an opportunity to study them closely until he was in his eighties. One also suspects that Nance instinctively recoiled from Tregear because of the large number of English loanwords which he saw in the homilies.

This brings me to the second unfortunate characteristic of Nancean Unified Cornish. Nance was a great antiquarian and a great patriot. He was, like all really great scholars, simple and modest. If he made a mistake he would willingly admit it. He did, however, have a tendency which in my view was regrettable in the leader of a linguistic revival. He was much too fond of the archaic. When he lived at Nancecledra in Penwith, all water had to be brought into the house from a well. Nance loved this, because he thought that to bring water through metal pipes was a desecration. This same penchant for old-word, pre-industrial quaintness was a significant feature of his Unified Cornish—with unfortunate results. Let me give you a very few examples. Nance thought that feminine *dyw* 'two' and masculine *deu* 'two' ought to be kept apart in Cornish, just as their equivalents were separate in Welsh. He determined, therefore, that the difference be maintained in Unified Cornish, even though the two had fallen together in the earliest texts. He insisted on difficult syntax for indirect speech, though the simpler syntax with *del / fatel* (*Me a welas del wrug ef mos alemma* 'I saw that he went hence') is to be found in the earliest texts. In Middle Cornish 'I shall go abroad tomorrow' is *Me a vyn mos dres mor avorow*, but Nance thought that such the use of *mynnes / mennas* to make the future was insufficiently Celtic and, in consequence, he suppressed it. Nance forbade pre-occlusion completely, believing erroneously that it was function of chronology, rather than of dialect. He says that although

> **m**, **n** in late pronunciation when following a stressed short vowel developed a **b** and a **d** before them, as **pedn**, **tabm**, this is not adopted in unified [*sic*] Cornish (Nance 1949: 1).

Yet pre-occlusion is a distinctive feature of the Cornish written by Lhuyd, upon which Nance relied for the pronunciation of Unified.

Nance was also prone to suppress English borrowings in Cornish, no matter how well established they were in the language. He replaced them with what he considered more Celtic forms, in some cases even inventing a word on the basis of Welsh or Breton. Here is a list of words attested in traditional Cornish but which were suppressed by Nance. I also give the words he promoted in their stead. An asterisk (*) means the item is not attested in any Cornish text; the obelus (†) means that the word is confined to Old Cornish.

*best* 'animal' (*myl* in UC)
*chayr* 'chair' (**cadar* in UC)
*clowd* 'clouds' (**comol* in UC)
*dewfryk* 'nose' (†*tron* in UC)
*fas* 'face' (†*tenep* in UC)
*flowr* 'flower' (†*blejen* in UC)
*frank* 'free' (**ryth* in UC)
*mona* 'money' (*arghans* in UC = 'silver' in the texts)
*nacyon* 'nation' (†*kenethel* in UC)
*opyn* 'open' (**ygor* in UC)
*poyson* 'poison' (†*gwenyn* in UC)
*rom* 'room' (†*stevel* in UC)
*ryver* 'river' (†*avon* in UC)
*tavern* 'tavarn' (**dewotty* in UC).

Unified Cornish Revised differs from Unified in shunning such purism. If a word is well attested in the texts, it should be allowed and certainly preferred over an item that is either attested in Old Cornish only, or has been constructed on the basis of Welsh or Breton. Unified Cornish Revised is emphatic that words from any period may be used in the revived language. This principle I refer to elsewhere as *tota Cornicitas*. The corollary is that, for example, the attested *exylya* 'exile' should be preferred over the unattested reconstruction, *dyvroa* 'exile'.

An important source for the Cornish lexicon is found in survivals of Cornish words in the English dialect of Cornwall. Such survivals include, for example, *pajer paw* 'lizard' (< *pejwar paw* 'four paws') and *kykesow* 'Cornish heath (*Erica vagans*)' (< *\*clegh kesow* 'bells of the turf'). Survivals in Cornish English must, however, be treated with the greatest possible care. Some commentators have assumed that certain words in English dialect were derived from Cornish, when in fact they are of wholly English origin. Many of the items they consider Cornish, are attested in English dialect in other parts of Britain and Ireland. They cannot therefore be considered legitimate parts of the Cornish lexicon and should not be so treated.

Like Unified Cornish, Unified Cornish Revised attempts to stay as close to the foundation texts as is reasonably possible. It allows words, inflection and syntax from any period of Cornish but it does not proscribe anything on purist grounds. There is, incidentally, good reason to countenance the use of diacritical marks in Unified Cornish Revised. There are a number of instances of words which are similarly spelt although their vowels are of differing lengths. In such cases it might be quite sensible to mark the long vowel with a circumflex—a practice familiar to use from Welsh, and used by Lhuyd for Cornish. We would then write *gwyn* 'white' but *gwŷn* 'wine' to disambiguate a minimal pair. Such a convention might be extended to other monosyllables: *splan* 'brilliant' but *glân* 'clean', for example. Similarly one could regularize the use of the graph <ü> to represent the fronted vowel [y] as in *für* 'wise' and *üskys* 'quick', for example.

Let us sum up then. Unified Cornish Revised is not a new system, nor does it add or subtract anything from the corpus of traditional Cornish. It spells as the traditional scribes do, albeit with two very minor modifications (which are already in Unified Cornish). Apart from that, there is nothing in the orthography, phonology, accidence or syntax of Unified Cornish Revised that is not in the traditional language. Unified Cornish Revised is the Cornish language of the sixteenth and early seventeenth centuries. It takes Cornish at its very richest period and spells it in the traditional spelling. It does not use as its foundation texts the impoverished and sometimes inaccurate language of the Late Cornish period. It uses also the traditional orthography, rather than the inconsistent and misleading English-based spelling of Late Cornish. More importantly, Unified Cornish Revised is not the result of unsubstantiated phonological theories—nor is it clothed in an orthography constructed on such a hypothetical basis.

John Tregear translated his sermons during the reign of Mary Tudor (1553–1558), that is, less than ten years after the Prayer Book rebellion of 1549. If, as a result of the rebellion, the Cornish had been granted the Book of Common Prayer in their own language, the translation would have been in a variety of Cornish very similar to that written by John Tregear. The Bible might well have followed and Cornish might have survived much longer than it did. In which case the language we would now be attempting to revive would be the Cornish of John Tregear and his contemporaries.

In conclusion I should like to quote what three different observers have to say about Unified Cornish Revised. I begin with Neil Kennedy. In his review of my English-Cornish dictionary he writes as follows:

> ... UCR seems well placed to contribute to the idea of a united but plural Cornish, a situation that might allow the various standards to inform each other and overlap. In vocabulary, grammar and even pronunciation UCR comes much closer to Late Cornish than UC or KK and seems to occupy a position between all of these alternatives. Williams has been cautious and pragmatic in revising Nance's orthography so is unlikely to lose the support of conservative UC learners. Although I will not endear myself to fellow speakers of Late Cornish by saying so, the plain fact is that the appearance of UCR makes all forms of the language more viable by aiding mutual intelligibility.
>
> (*Cornish Studies: Nine*, 2001, 317).

The second observer is the poet Alan Kent. In his review of my *Testament Noweth* he writes the following:

> The orthography used here is the emended form of revived Cornish known as Unified Cornish Revised, which attempts as far as possible to imitate the Cornish of the sixteenth century, and in particular, John Tregear, the writer of Cornish's longest prose text, 'The Tregear Homilies'. Thankfully, no attempt has been made to purge or purify the language of English borrowings, since Williams believes that the Comish used should reflect the language as it was actually spoken.... Williams has also avoided the more complicated grammatical constructions of the earlier Cornish texts making this a very easy read even for less advanced Cornish speakers.... The Testament Noweth shows the direction anyone interested in the Cornish language should be moving in.
>
> (*An Baner Kernewek/The Cornish Banner* 109, August 2002).

My last commentator is Professor Philip Payton. In his message of 28 November 2005 to the bards of *Gorseth Kernow* he wrote the following:

> Movement towards a Standard Written Form will require a willingness to negotiate and compromise on all sides. This is how democracies work. A Standard Written Form will need to take into account the preferences of those who want to speak medieval Cornish (of which Kemmyn is a hypothetical form) and those who wish to speak the language as it was in more modern times (Modern Cornish). My guess is that a resultant compromise would not be very far away from Unified Cornish Revised. It is interesting that the Gorseth has already adopted Unified (unrevised)—in its ceremonies in Cornwall, Australia and North America—as its *de facto* Standard Written Form, and it would be a short step to adopting UCR. Maybe the Gorseth could show some leadership here.

# RESOURCES IN UCR

Ashworth, Heather. 2006. *Whedhel Gyttern*. Ewny Redreth: Spyrys a Gernow. ISBN: 978-0-9548451-5-5

Litchfield, Jo. 2004. *Everyday Words in Cornish*. Cornish language consultants Ray & Denise Chubb. Portreath: Agan Tavas. ISBN 1-901409-08-2

Palmer, Myghal. 2001. *Rebellyans*. Ewny Redreth: Spyrys a Gernow. ISBN 0-9535975-3-9

Phillips, Andy & Nicholas Williams. 2004. *Lyver Pejadow rag Kenyver Jorna: Cornish Daily Prayer*. Redruth: Spyrys a Gernow. ISBN 0-9535975-8-X

Prohaska, Daniel. 2006. *Kornisch: Wort für Wort*. Bielefeld: Reise Know-how Verlag, Peter Rump GmbH.

Williams, Nicholas. 1997. *Clappya Kernowek: an introduction to Unified Cornish Revised*. Portreath: Agan Tavas. ISBN 1-901409-01-5

Williams, Nicholas, translator. 2002. *Testament Noweth agan Arluth ha Savyour Jesu Cryst*. Ewny Redrteth: Spyrys a Gernow. ISBN 0-9535975-4-7

Williams, Nicholas. 2005. *English-Cornish Dictionary: Gerlyver Sawsnek Kernowek*. Second edition. Redruth: Agan Tavas. ISBN 978-1-901409-09-3. Westport: Evertype. ISBN 978-1-904808-06-0

Williams, Nicholas. 2006. *Cornish Today: An examination of the revived language*. Third edition. Westport: Evertype. ISBN 978-1-904808-07-7

Williams, Nicholas. 2006. *Writings on Revived Cornish*. Westport: Evertype. ISBN 978-1-904808-08-4

Williams, Nicholas. 2006. *Towards Authentic Cornish*. Westport: Evertype. ISBN 978-1-904808-09-1